The Export–Import Bank

An Economic Analysis

This is a volume in
ECONOMIC THEORY, ECONOMETRICS, AND MATHEMATICAL
    ECONOMICS

A Series of Monographs and Textbooks

Consulting Editor: KARL SHELL

A complete list of titles in this series appears at the end of this volume.

The Export–Import Bank
An Economic Analysis

David P. Baron
Graduate School of Business
Stanford University
Stanford, California

1983

ACADEMIC PRESS
A Subsidiary of Harcourt Brace Jovanovich, Publishers
New York   London
Paris   San Diego   San Francisco   São Paulo   Sydney   Tokyo   Toronto

ACADEMIC PRESS, INC.
111 Fifth Avenue, New York, New York 10003

United Kingdom Edition published by
ACADEMIC PRESS, INC. (LONDON) LTD.
24/28 Oval Road, London NW1 7DX

Library of Congress Cataloging in Publication Data

Baron, David P.
    The Export-Import Bank : an economic analysis.

    (Economic theory, econometrics, and mathematical
economics)
    Includes bibliographical references and index.
    1. Export-Import Bank of the United States.
2. Export credit--United States.   I. Title.
II. Series.
HG3754.U5B37   1983   332.1'54   82-24379
ISBN 0-12-079080-7

PRINTED IN THE UNITED STATES OF AMERICA

83 84 85 86   9 8 7 6 5 4 3 2 1

Contents

3. *The Economic Justification for the Programs of the Eximbank*

4. *The Supply and Demand for Government-Supported Export
    Financing*

5. *The Competitiveness of Eximbank Programs*

6. *The Subsidy Provided by Eximbank Financing*

7. The Welfare Consequences of Concessionary Export Financing

8. Additionality and Its Measurement

9. A Test of Additionality

Preface

The Export–Import Bank of the United States is mandated to promote U.S. exports, to provide export financing when international capital markets are unable to do so, and to match officially supported export credits granted by other nations. In recent years, the executive branch and some members of Congress have become increasingly concerned with the cost of Eximbank programs and have begun to question their need. Many nations, however, view international trade and, in particular, export promotion as important components of national economic policy and have used export financing as an instrument of that policy. Government-supported export financing expanded considerably during the 1970s, which led to international rivalry, with one nation matching the export financing of other nations. This export financing has generally been done at below-market interest rates, and the high interest rates of the late 1970s and early 1980s made it extremely costly. The annual subsidy on the outstanding government export credits for 12 major exporting countries in 1979 was $5.5 billion, and estimates developed in this book for Eximbank direct credits indicate subsidies of $550 million on credits authorized in 1979 and more than $1.5 billion for 1981. Using the Eximbank estimates as a basis for extrapolation, the estimated 1981 subsidy for the 12 countries is approximately $15 billion. Although the United States in principle opposes export financing subsidization, the U.S. strategy has been to respond to the concessionary export financing provided by other countries in order to be fair to U.S. exporters and to persuade other countries to cease their subsidized export financing. Some success has been achieved in reducing the cost of financing subsidization and in restricting export financing competition, but the issue of government-assisted export financing remains controversial.

This book provides a critical analysis of the export financing issue and the Eximbank's performance in fulfilling its congressional mandate. The analysis is based on extensive interviews with Eximbank officials and on numerous internal documents in addition to published materials. Considerable documentation and data are presented to provide the reader with a basis for evaluating the analysis and the resulting conclusions. The analysis focuses on the Eximbank's performance from three perspectives. First, an analysis of the need for such financing is presented in conjunction with an assessment of the competitiveness of U.S. programs compared with those provided by other nations. Second, Eximbank performance is evaluated in terms of the cost of its programs, their potential welfare impacts, and the likely impact on U.S. exports. Third, an evaluation is provided of the Eximbank's decision making and its methodology for evaluating the impact of its direct credit program. Recommendations are made concerning U.S. export financing objectives, strategies for achieving those objectives, and Eximbank administrative procedures.

Although the book is written from an economic perspective, considerable attention is given to institutional and administrative issues. The Eximbank's decision making focuses on the additional exports generated by its financing, and a critical evaluation of this additionality standard is presented. The book provides an economic analysis of Eximbank financing and includes a case study of Eximbank decision making in the granting of a $200 million aircraft credit to Ansett Airlines of Australia. The analysis suggests that the Eximbank has granted more generous financing in those cases in which it judged competition from foreign export financing agencies to be greater, indicating that it has allocated its financing with some degree of efficiency. This should not be interpreted, however, as an indication that Eximbank financing is warranted, but only as an indication that if such financing is to be provided, case-by-case decision making is a viable alternative to making government financing an entitlement to U.S. exporters.

This book will be of interest to those concerned with international trade and finance as well as those concerned more broadly with government intervention in markets. Because of the focus on the Eximbank's administrative performance, readers concerned with governmental processes and administrative organizations should also find the book of interest. The book will also be of use to policymakers in assessing the appropriate government role in export financing and in the formulation and implementation of strategies for furthering that role. While the present administration is headed in the general direction that is recommended here, future administrations may see the export financing issue in a different light. The analysis provided should be helpful not only in the development of U.S. export financing policy but also in the congressional and executive branch oversight of Eximbank administrative policies and decision making.

The impetus for this study came from Professor Jordan Jay Hillman of the School of Law at Northwestern University, who was interested in studying government-sponsored enterprises in the United States and who introduced me to the Export–Import Bank and institutional analysis. Although Professor Hillman and I worked together in collecting data and interviewing Eximbank officials, our research took us in somewhat different directions.[1]

The Eximbank was extremely cooperative both in providing data and in allowing us to interview its officials for extended periods. In particular, I would like to thank James Cruse, Warren Glick, and James Hess for the many hours they allotted to us. Without their help it would not have been possible to write this book.

Our work was generously supported by the Alfred P. Sloan Foundation and by the J. L. Kellogg Graduate School of Management at Northwestern University. In particular, I would like to thank Dr. Albert Rees and Arthur Singer of the Sloan Foundation and Dean Donald P. Jacobs of the J. L. Kellogg Graduate School of Management for their encouragement and support.

My efforts in preparing this volume were greatly assisted by Victor Liu, who performed much of the data analysis, and by Dennis Yao, who assisted in the analysis of the 1981 data. A legion of secretaries was involved in typing the manuscript and its revisions, but I would particularly like to thank Donna Finlon and Phyllis Villec for their dedicated work in bringing the manuscript to completion. Theresa Bonk, Jane Castruccio, Arleen Danielson, Renu Garg, Barbara Kantoff, and Rita Terry also spent many hours on the manuscript. Finally, I would like to thank Mary, Douglas, and Matthew, who bore much of the cost of my efforts in writing this book. I hope to repay them in the future.

---

[1] Jordan Jay Hillman, *The Export–Import Bank at Work: Promotional Financing in the Public Sector* (Westport, Conn.: Greenwood Press, 1982).

1

Eximbank: The Controversy, Its Mandate, and Its Programs

I. The Controversy

Once a tranquil institution, the Export–Import Bank of the United States, an independent government agency that finances U.S. exports, now finds itself embroiled in controversy. In his February 18, 1981 economic message to the Congress, President Reagan attacked the subsidization provided by the Eximbank: "We are asking that another major business subsidy, Export–Import Bank loan authority, be reduced by one-third in 1982. We are doing this because the primary beneficiaries of taxpayer funds in this case are the exporting companies themselves—most of them profitable corporations [*Chicago Tribune*, February 19, 1981]." In accord with this view the Reagan administration reduced the Bank's lending authority from $5.5 billion in FY1981 to $4.4 billion in FY1982, with further reductions planned through 1985. In opposing the proposed reductions, Senator John Heinz emphasized in his March 19, 1981 letter to President Reagan the importance of exports and the need to respond to foreign-subsidized export financing [19].

> Mr. President, I sympathize with your desire to cut the budget and to reduce the level of federal borrowing. But, I also believe that exports are simply too important to the U.S. economy to be left exposed to predatory financing ploys by our trade competitors. To reduce Eximbank's credit limit without also taking steps to induce our trade competitors to do likewise would be counterproductive to the long-range goals of employment and balanced growth for our economy which we both share [p. 114].

1

The exporting community also rallied to the defense of the Bank. The arguments advanced by exporters are illustrated by the remarks of T. A. Wilson, chairman and chief executive officer of Boeing, the largest recipient of Eximbank support:

> Wilson argued that major cuts proposed in the loan authority of the Export–Import Bank could become counter-productive in terms of loss of American sales abroad and consequent loss of jobs and revenues at home.
>
> He said the U.S. aircraft industry already is at a competitive disadvantage with Airbus, which has the benefit of multi-government supported "subsidized export financing that U.S. private industry cannot meet without Ex–Im help."
>
> Wilson said each $1 billion in exports accounts for 40,000 U.S. jobs.
>
> "Boeing was the No. 1 exporter in the United States in 1979 and may have been in 1980," he said. "Last year Boeing's export sales of commercial jet transports amounted to about $5 billion. About $3 billion involved Ex–Im financing, which means that our Ex–Im supported sales created 120,000 jobs."
>
> The overseas market accounts for about 60 percent of all Boeing airplane sales.
>
> "Boeing's supplier and subcontract network consists of 1,306 major and 2,247 small and minority business firms in 44 states," Wilson told a House banking subcommittee. "Their sales to Boeing were more than $6 billion in 1979 [*Chicago Tribune*, April 4, 1981]."
>
> With the worsening of the recession in 1982 and the strong Airbus competition in the international market, Boeing President Malcom Stamper stated, "The Export–Import Bank is the only thing we have. Even a big company like ours can't compete against the central banks of three of the major countries in the West [*Newsweek*, May 17, 1982]."[1]

An editorial in *Business Week* went further in arguing for an expanded promotional role for the Bank.

> The Export–Import Bank is probably the most powerful weapon this country can use in the fierce global export rivalry. . . . The Administration should realize that there is an opportunity here to use exports as a means of stimulating the U.S. economy. Other nations have done this with great success. It is time this country tried the same strategy.[2]

In addition to the desire to promote U.S. exports, support for the Bank arises from the belief that even though government-subsidized financing of exports is undesirable, it is a necessary response to the export financing subsidization provided by other countries, a number of which provide considerably more financing support for their exports than does the United States. The Organization for Economic Cooperation and De-

[1] Copyright 1982 by Newsweek Inc. All rights reserved. Reprinted by permission.
[2] Reprinted from the March 2, 1981 issue of *Business Week* by special permission, © 1981 by McGraw-Hill, Inc., New York. All rights reserved.

velopment (OECD), for example, estimated that at year-end 1979, the annual subsidy provided by the concessionary export financing of 12 nations was $5.5 billion, with France accounting for 40% and the United States 6% of the total. With the rise in market interest rates in 1980 and 1981 the total subsidy is likely to have more than doubled from the 1979 estimate. As indicated in Chapter 6, the subsidy provided by Eximbank direct credits increased from $553 million in FY1979 to over $1.5 billion in FY1981. This subsidization is required, advocates argue, in order to give U.S. exporters a fair chance to compete in international markets and to demonstrate to other countries that they can gain no advantage through their subsidized export financing. Proponents of the latter view, including Senator Heinz, introduced "war chest bills" in both the House and the Senate to provide the Bank with a special appropriation to be used to finance U.S. exports that compete with the exports of nations that refuse to reduce their export financing subsidization.

John Moore, chairman of the Bank during the Carter administration, was particularly concerned with responding, as is required by the Bank's legislative mandate, to the concessionary export financing provided by other countries. One of his first actions after assuming the chairmanship in 1977 was to lower the Bank's lending rates to a range of 7.75–8.75% from the previous 8–9% range in order to improve the competitiveness of U.S. export financing. Market interest rates rose dramatically during the next 4 years, but to meet the concessionary interest rates provided by the export financing agencies of countries such as France and the United Kingdom, the Bank maintained that lending rate range until April 1980, when interest rates were increased to 9.25% for commercial jet aircraft exports and 8.75% for all other exports. Since the Bank's lending rates were, even after the increase, 4–5% below the interest rates at which the Bank was borrowing to fund its loans, the profits of the Bank began to erode rapidly. Profits in FY1980 were $110 million, which was down from $159 million in the previous year; and of the $110 million the General Accounting Office (GAO) [12] reported that "93 million . . . was earned but uncollected interest on delinquent loans." A small profit of $12 million was earned in FY1981, and losses of nearly $100 million are expected for FY1982. The GAO concluded that "This situation threatens Eximbank's traditional self-sufficiency and requires that the Congress decide whether it wants Eximbank to give greater attention to remaining self-sufficient or to meeting foreign competition [12]."

Upon taking office the Reagan administration was faced with the conflict between the Bank's tradition of self-sufficiency and its legislative mandates to promote U.S. exports and to meet foreign concessionary export financing. President Reagan appointed William H. Draper III as chairman of the Eximbank, and immediately after his confirmation Draper increased the lending rate to 10.75% and imposed a 2% fee in order to reduce the Bank's projected FY1982 deficit. Later in 1981 the lending rate was increased to 12%, but the Bank's borrowing costs had risen to 15.5% in September 1981, ensuring further deficits.

Whereas the Eximbank has attempted to meet foreign-subsidized export financing, the concern for self-sufficiency has caused the United States to seek an international agreement to eliminate this subsidization. Export financing is currently governed by the OECD-administered "Arrangement on Guidelines for Officially Supported Export Credits [15]" and by certain sectoral understandings that prescribe minimum interest rates and maximum terms on export credits, but the permissible interest rates have been far below market levels. President Carter in his 1981 *Economic Report to the Congress* [1] reported on his administration's efforts to reach a more satisfactory accord:

> The heads of state of the major countries made a specific commitment at the Venice Summit in June of last year to bring export-credit rates more closely into line with market rates. Efforts to negotiate an export-credit agreement based on this commitment failed, but negotiations may resume this year. In some countries—particularly some members of the European Community—it may not be clearly perceived how wasteful and counter-productive export-credit subsidies are [p. 212].

The Reagan administration has also spoken out against export subsidization in an attempt to move the negotiations forward. Deputy Treasury Secretary R. T. McNamar [14] stated

> The Reagan Administration does not intend to live with U.S. or foreign export credit subsidies on a permanent basis. . . . However, if there is to be a credit war, we are certainly prepared to defend U.S. economic interests. And, if we do not see quick signs of progress in the Arrangement talks, our competitors will find that our pockets are far deeper than theirs, our terms of credit much longer, and our resolve even stronger than is true of them. . . . There must be a multilateral agreement to cease export credit subsidies or there indeed will be a war [pp. 8–9].

At the 1981 Ottawa economic summit the Reagan administration pressed for reductions in export financing subsidization, and shortly thereafter an agreement was reached between the United States, France, Germany, and the United Kingdom to increase the interest rate on commercial jet aircraft credits to approximately 12%. In September 1981 the 22 OECD countries agreed to raise the minimum interest rates for nonaircraft loans to a range of 9.5–11.25%, which was still far below market rates. In July 1982 agreement was reached that again increased interest rates, although those rates remained considerably below market rates.

This book is concerned with the need for government-supported export financing programs, the evaluation of the export financing programs of the Eximbank, the Bank's dual roles of financier and promoter of U.S. exports, and the appropriate response to international export financing competition. In order to determine the appropriate governmental role, if any, in export financing, it is necessary to determine not only whether government export financing can potentially provide welfare gains to the United States but also if an organization such as the Eximbank can reasonably be expected to provide export financing in an efficient manner. The conclusion resulting from the following analysis is that whereas there may be a role for self-sustaining government-supported export insurance and guarantee programs, there is no justification for the loan programs of the Eximbank. The loan programs, however, may be warranted in the short run as a component of a strategy intended to convince recalcitrant countries to agree to an international accord eliminating export financing subsidization. If the Bank is to continue in existence either for long-term purposes or only as an instrument to be used to obtain such an international agreement, the efficiency with which the Bank operates is an important determinant of the welfare consequences of these programs for the United States. The emphasis of the analysis is thus both on the economic dimensions of export financing and on the performance of the Bank as an administrative organization. The remainder of this chapter provides a brief overview of the origins and statutory mandate of the Bank, its programs, the international agreements that govern official export financing, and certain policy issues associated with the Bank and export financing.

II. The Origin and Functions of the Eximbank

The first Export–Import Bank was established in 1934 to facilitate trade with the Soviet Union, and a second Export–Import Bank was established shortly thereafter to finance imports of silver from Cuba for domestic coinage. Both Banks had 2-year charters, and the charter of the second Bank was allowed to expire. The charter of the first Bank was extended, and in 1945 it was superseded by the present Export–Import Bank of the United States, which is a statutory agency of the federal government. In the immediate postwar period the Bank assisted in the redevelopment of war-shattered economies by financing the export of capital equipment required for reconstruction [13, p. 3]. By the late 1950s, when the economies of those countries had recovered and developing countries were in the process of establishing export industries, the U.S.

began to incur balance of payments deficits, which became a national concern during the 1960s. Under a fixed exchange rate system, an expansion of exports reduced the balance of payments deficit, strengthened the dollar against other currencies, and increased domestic employment, so the Bank was viewed as an instrument to promote exports in order to achieve employment and balance of payments objectives.

With the floating of exchange rates during the early 1970s, the rationale for promoting exports in order to improve the balance of payments and to increase employment disappeared at least in principle. If the United States were to run a balance of payments deficit, the dollar would fall in value relative to other currencies, which would increase the price of foreign goods to Americans and reduce the price of American goods to foreigners. A balance of payments equilibrium would eventually result, and future exchange rate movements would be determined by the rates of inflation and productivity. Comparative advantage would determine which industries exported and which imported, as well as the levels of those exports and imports.

The pressures for the promotion of exports continued, however, during the early 1970s under the rationale that deficiencies in the international capital markets impeded the financing of exports of long-lived capital equipment, particularly to countries that had poorly developed domestic capital markets. When other countries stepped up their export promotion activities after the 1973–1974 oil embargo and increased their export financing support, the Eximbank found itself in the position of providing financing to neutralize that provided by other major trading countries in order to be fair to U.S. exporters and to avoid the loss of exports. With the dramatic increase in market interest rates during the late 1970s and the early 1980s, the cost of Eximbank programs increased greatly and its self-sufficiency became threatened.

In support of U.S. exports, the Eximbank provides direct credits, discounts loans made by commercial banks, and provides financial guarantees and insurance. Since its creation, the Eximbank has supported over $100 billion in U.S. exports, with a record $18.6 billion supported in FY1981. To finance these exports, the Bank extended loans of approximately $5.4 billion in FY1981 and provided $7.4 billion of insurance and guarantee coverage. At the end of FY1981 the Bank's total exposure was $38.4 billion.

The Bank has $1 billion of equity provided by the Treasury plus approximately $2.2 billion in accumulated reserves, although rescheduled and delinquent loans totaled nearly $1.6 billion at the end of FY1981. The Bank does not accept deposits and funds its loans by borrowing from the Federal Financing Bank (FFB) at the government risk-free interest rate plus a small spread. As of the end of FY1981, the Bank had borrowed over \$12.7 billion from the FFB and \$600 million from other sources that have since been discontinued.[3] The Bank is an "on-budget agency," so its cash flows are included in the federal budget, although the Bank receives no appropriation from Congress. Until FY1982 it had always been self-sufficient in the sense that the interest and fees it received had been sufficient to cover its operating costs and the service on its borrowings. Whereas the Bank earned a small profit in FY1981, for the first time in its history it did not pay a dividend to the Treasury. Because the Bank's lending rates since 1978 have been below the rates at which it borrows from the FFB, the Bank projects continuing deficits for the foreseeable future. The average interest rate on the direct credits authorized by the Bank in FY1981 was 8.74%, and its average FFB borrowing rate was 13.7%. Since market rates averaged over 15% in 1981, the Bank provided a substantial subsidy through its financing. In Chapter 6 that subsidy is estimated to have approximated \$3.1 billion on the direct credits authorized in FY1979, FY1980, and FY1981.

Although the Bank receives no appropriation, the Congress sets an annual authorization limit for the loans, insurance, and guarantees the Bank can extend. The annual authorization hearings provide an opportunity for an expression of congressional intent and for the executive branch, primarily the Office of Management and Budget (OMB) and the Treasury, to influence Bank policies and practices. The Eximbank is a sunset agency whose charter must be renewed every 5 years, and the required renewal provides a regular opportunity to amend the Export–Import Bank Act (referred to hereafter as "the act") as well as a forum for the supporters and opponents of the Bank to express their views. The charter of the Bank was last renewed on November 10, 1978 and extends until September 30, 1983.

The five-member board of directors of the Bank serves at the pleasure of the president with no more than three members from the same political party. Oversight is provided by the Subcommittee on International Finance and Monetary Policy of the Senate Committee on Banking, Housing, and Urban Affairs and by the House Banking, Finance, and Urban Affairs Committee. Direct credits of more than \$100 million require congressional review, and both the preliminary commitments and the final loan authorizations for credits of \$30 million or more are re-

---

[3] The bonds issued by the Eximbank initially were tax-exempt if purchased by Domestic International Sales Corporations (DISCs) but that exemption was later withdrawn. The Bank currently borrows only from the Federal Financing Bank and occasionally sells certificates of beneficial interest under agreements signed during the mid-1970s.

viewed by the National Advisory Council on International Monetary and Financial Policies, which includes representatives of OMB, Treasury, State, the Eximbank, and the Federal Reserve. The members of NAC attend Eximbank board meetings with Treasury and OMB being the most active participants. The Department of State reviews for political and human rights considerations the preliminary commitments and direct credits issued by the Bank.

In providing export financing, the Eximbank works in conjunction with the Private Export Funding Corporation (PEFCO), which was formed in 1970 at the initiative of the Department of the Treasury. PEFCO is a private corporation that participates in export financing with its loans backed by Eximbank financial guarantees. The bonds issued by PEFCO to fund its loans are backed by the full faith and credit of the federal government and thus represent a contingent liability of the United States. PEFCO does not initiate export financing nor does it evaluate credit applications but instead participates in transactions referred to it by the Bank.

The insurance programs of the Bank are operated by the Foreign Credit Insurance Association (FCIA), which was formed in 1961 with the assistance of the Eximbank and which is owned by 51 private insurance companies. Coverage is provided for both commercial and political risks.

III. The Principal Features of the Export–Import Bank Act of 1945

"The objectives and purposes of the bank shall be to aid in financing and to facilitate exports and imports and the exchange of commodities between the United States or any of its Territories or insular possessions and any foreign country or the agencies or nationals thereof [2, p. 1]." Section 2(b)(1)(A) expands on this general purpose in stating,

It is the policy of the United States to foster expansion of exports of manufactured goods, agricultural products, and other goods and services, thereby contributing to the promotion and maintenance of high levels of employment and real income and to the increased development of the productive resources of the United States. To meet this objective, the Export–Import Bank is directed in the exercise of its functions to provide guarantees, insurance, and extensions of credit at rates and on terms and other conditions which are competitive with the government-supported rates and terms and other conditions available for the financing of exports from the principal countries whose exporters compete with United States exporters [2, pp. 3–4].

Although this mandate specifies the objectives of export promotion and the matching of foreign export financing, it does not indicate the extent to which public resources are to be committed in support of these objectives. The matching objective in particular can result in excessive competition among nations to increase exports through government-supported financing. The Congress has judged the present level of competition among export credit agencies to be excessive and has declared that the policy of the United States is to limit export financing competition. Section 2(b)(1)(A) of the act states, "The Bank shall, in cooperation with the export financing instrumentalities of other governments, seek to minimize competition in government-supported export financing, and shall, in cooperation with other appropriate government agencies, seek to reach international agreements to reduce government-subsidized export financing [2, p. 4]." Export financing is currently governed by the OECD "arrangement" (hereafter referred to as "the arrangement" and discussed in more detail in Section VI).

The Export–Import Bank Act Amendments of 1978 [2] are more specific in directing the president of the United States to initiate efforts to limit concessionary export financing and to encourage the Eximbank to retaliate when subsidized credit is granted by other countries in violation of existing agreements. In part this directive resulted from the concessionary export financing provided to Eastern Airlines by the European aircraft manufacturer Airbus Industrie and from an offer by Rolls Royce to subsidize the financing of aircraft engine sales to Pan American [12, p. 15]. Section 1908 of the amendments [2] states:

(a) The President is authorized and requested to begin negotiations at the ministerial level with other major exporting countries to end predatory export financing programs and other forms of export subsidies, including mixed credits, in third country markets as well as within the United States. The President shall report to the Congress prior to January 15, 1979 on progress toward meeting the goals of this Section. (b) The Export–Import Bank of the United States is authorized to provide guarantees, insurance, and extensions of credit at rates and terms and other conditions which are, in the opinion of the Board of Directors of the Bank, competitive with those provided by the government-supported export credit instrumentalities of other nations [p. 22].[4]

The negotiations have not yet resulted in the elimination of subsidized export financing although the arrangement minimums have been increased and an aircraft financing agreement has been achieved as previously mentioned.

---

[4] A mixed credit combines aid and government-supported export financing.

The amendments also direct the secretary of the treasury to request that "non-competitive financing" be withdrawn whenever such financing is offered by a foreign country contrary to international agreements entered into by the United States and other exporting countries. "If the offer is not withdrawn or if there is no immediate response to the withdrawal request, the Secretary of the Treasury shall notify the country offering such financing and all parties to the proposed transaction that the Eximbank may be authorized to provide competing United States sellers with financing to match that available through the foreign official export financing entity [2, p. 22]."

At present the Bank's programs are limited by statute to aggregate exposure of no more than $40 billion with guarantees and insurance counted at 25% of their coverage. Insurance and guarantee exposure is limited to no more than $25 billion. From the point of view of a U.S. exporter or a private lender, a guarantee or insurance eliminates the risk associated with the covered portion of export financing because "All guarantees and insurance issued by the Bank shall be considered contingent obligations backed by the full faith and credit of the United States of America [2, p. 26]."

The only statement in the act that gives legislative guidance for the pricing of Eximbank services is that "loans made by the Bank shall bear interest at rates determined by the Board of Directors of the Bank taking into consideration the average cost of money to the Bank as well as the Bank's mandate to support United States exports at rates and on terms and conditions which are competitive with exports of other countries [2, pp. 4–5]." The act does not require the Bank to be profitable or to pay a dividend to the Treasury, nor does it require the Bank to maintain any specific level of reserves, although it does state: "Net earnings of the Bank after reasonable provision for possible losses shall be used for payment of dividends on capital stock [2, pp. 2–3]." Since the term "average cost of money" is not defined and profitability is not required, the Bank has considerable latitude in setting the rates for its services. Section 1908(b) of the 1978 Amendments further permits the Bank to lend at interest rates that are below its average cost if that is required to support exports facing export competition backed by foreign officially supported financing. During the Carter Administration the Bank emphasized the mandate to meet foreign competition and interpreted the "average cost of money" as the embedded interest cost. This resulted in highly concessionary credits that led to the Bank's current losses.

In its financing of exports the Bank is directed to "supplement and encourage, and not compete with, private capital . . . [2, p. 5]," which requires the Bank to determine which services exporters demand that private financial institutions are unable and unwilling to provide. This has resulted in the Bank's focusing its lending activity on fixed interest rate credits with maturities of 5 to 12 years.

The act also states that loans are to be for "specific purposes" and should "offer reasonable assurance of repayment [2, p. 5]." The "specific purposes" statement has been interpreted to mean that the Bank should generally finance the export of projects and capital goods rather than "off-the-shelf" items and that it should be reluctant to extend general lines of credit. Such lines, however, have been extended occasionally in recent years when judged necessary to meet foreign officially supported export credit competition.

The "reasonable assurance of repayment" standard has been interpreted as requiring the Bank to be a "hard loan agency." This has been institutionalized in two ways. First, the Bank rejects credit applications if it judges that the project for which credit has been requested is technically infeasible or is unlikely to be commercially successful. To assess the commercial viability of a project or of a capital asset export, the Bank maintains economics and engineering divisions that provide assessments of the likely success of individual projects. Second, the Bank in most cases requires a guarantor of the credits it extends. Guarantors include foreign governments and their ministries, government-owned and private foreign banks, branches of U.S. banks, and foreign and U.S. corporations. For example, in FY1979, both General Dynamics and Continental Telephone Corporation guaranteed loans, as did the North Carolina National Bank and subsidiaries of the Bank of America and Chase Manhattan Bank. Typically, no guarantor is required for loans made directly to governments or to government banks.

In order to encourage the Bank to take greater risks in its lending than those consistent with the reasonable assurance of repayment standard, the Congress enacted Public Law 90-390 (90th Congress, July 7, 1968) [2] which authorizes the Bank to use a less restrictive standard for a portion of its activities "in order to actively foster the foreign trade and long-term commercial interest of the United States [p. 25]." PL 90-390 allows the Bank, under the Export Expansion Facility (EEF) authorization, to extend credits (plus 25% of the contractual liabilities of guarantees and insurance) up to $500 million with a weaker "sufficient likelihood of repayment" standard. The authorization does not provide any additional funds to the Bank, although the Treasury does bear any losses above $100 million on EEF financing. The Bank has been reluctant to use this authorization and has extended only approximately $300 million of credits under the EEF program primarily in cases of interest to the Department of State.

The Bank is also required to "take into account any serious adverse effect of such loan or guarantee on the competitive position of United States industry, the availability of materials which are in short supply in the United States, and employment in the United States [2, pp. 5–6]." Two areas in which this has been of concern are turnkey plants and commercial aircraft. The Bank has been particularly concerned about the export of plants intended to produce goods for import into the United States. As a result of the concern over the concessionary financing of aircraft exports, Senator Jacob Javits in 1974 initiated an inquiry into whether Eximbank financing of U.S. aircraft exports gave foreign airlines an advantage in competing with TWA and Pan American, which were in financial difficulty at the time. In response to both its legislative mandate and to such Congressional concerns, the Bank provides an annual assessment [3] of the "adverse impact" of its financing.

The Bank is required to make its export financing decisions based on financial and commercial standards except when the president determines that the denial of support would advance United States policy regarding "international terrorism, nuclear proliferation, environmental protection, and human rights [2, p. 6]."[5] The Bank, upon notification by the secretary of state, is required to deny export support to signatory countries that have violated the International Atomic Energy Agency nuclear safeguards unless otherwise directed by the president. The Bank is also prohibited from financing exports to Communist countries, but "The President of the United States determined . . . that it was in the national interest for the Bank to do business with Yugoslavia, Romania, the U.S.S.R., Poland, and Hungary, respectively. However, the Bank ceased to do business with the U.S.S.R. on January 3, 1975 as a result of the passage of the Trade Act of 1974, Public Law 93-618, 93rd Cong. (88 Stat. 1978), January 3, 1975 [2, p. 34]."

IV. Eximbank Programs

The Eximbank, in association with PEFCO and FCIA, provides officially supported credits, guarantees and insurance for U.S. exports. The Eximbank extends short- and medium-term supplier credits with terms to 5 years and buyer credits for terms up to 12 years and in some cases to 20

---

[5] The Bank is also restricted in supporting the export of military supplies and equipment unless otherwise directed by the president and is prohibited from supporting exports to the Republic of South Africa.

years. The bulk of the credits issued by the Eximbank are long-term buyer credits with over 90% of the $5.4 billion of loans authorized by the Bank in FY1981 associated with its long-term direct credit program. In accord with the arrangement, the Bank requires a minimum cash payment of 15% on any export subject to arrangement provisions and has provided financing for 30 to 85% of the export value of the item with an average of 61% in FY1981. The Bank lends only at fixed interest rates and frequently participates with PEFCO or a commercial bank. In such cases the private lender generally takes the shorter maturity, with the Eximbank taking the longer maturity. The Bank does not take risk into account in determining the interest rate on a direct credit, although from October 1977 to April 1980 it did charge higher interest rates the longer the loan term.[6]

Eximbank policy has been to provide support through its long-term direct credit programs for projects and capital goods. To limit the demand for its credits, the Bank adopted a $5 million minimum export value for eligibility for its direct credit program. Smaller exports were eligible for the medium-term discount financing program. In late 1981 the Bank introduced a program to finance exports of $5 million or less by small firms at more favorable terms than available for higher valued exports.

In providing a direct credit, the Eximbank initially issues either a letter of interest or a preliminary commitment, and when the export has been won by the U.S. exporter a final loan authorization is made. Letters of interest state that the Bank is prepared to consider financing the export in question, but the terms of the possible financial support are not specified in the letter. At the time at which the U.S. exporter makes a formal offer for a foreign contract or has begun negotiations with an importer, the Bank issues a preliminary commitment that states the amount, terms, and conditions of financial assistance that it will provide. When the exporter wins the sale, a final loan or guarantee application is required before the Bank authorizes the credit or guarantee specified in the preliminary commitment.

In considering whether to issue a preliminary commitment or to authorize a credit, the Bank assigns to each application a team consisting of a loan officer for the geographic region in which the importer is located, an economist who specializes in economic and political analysis of the importing country, an engineer who makes a technical review of the export, and a lawyer who provides legal services required to process the

---

[6] "For loans with a term of 6 years or less from date of authorization, the rate was $7\frac{3}{4}\%$. For each additional year, the rate increased $\frac{1}{8}$ of 1% up to a maximum of 0.75% for loans repayable in more than 1 year from date of commitment. Deviations could be made to meet foreign officially supported competition [8, p. 2]."

application. This group makes a recommendation to the board of directors which must approve all preliminary commitments and loan authorizations.

In addition to its direct credit program the Bank offers a discount loan program which [5]

> supports U.S. commercial banks in extending fixed-rate medium-term export credits that they would otherwise be unable to undertake. The program is available only for fixed rate financing and banks must certify that they are not prepared to extend the financing on the proposed terms without the use of the discount program [pp. 21–22].

These requirements are intended to make the Bank a lender of last resort for medium-term credits. The long-term buyer credit program has no such requirement, but information is requested regarding attempts made to finance the export in private capital markets. The major difference, however, is that in the long-term direct credit program the financing has been concessionary and hence no commercial bank would be prepared to extend credit at the Eximbank lending rate. In the discount loan program, however, the Bank lends at an interest rate that is pegged to the Federal Reserve discount rate, so the amount of the concession is smaller. In July 1981 the Bank lowered its discount interest from 16 to 14%, and in October 1981 reduced it to 10.75% for the exports of small manufacturers. In FY1981 credits of $352 million were extended under the discount loan program.

A third credit program operated by the Bank is the Cooperative Financing Facility (CFF) which provides medium-term credits primarily for exports to developing countries. Under the CFF program the Bank authorizes foreign commercial banks to arrange lines of credit for importers in their countries for use in the purchase of U.S. exports [5].

> Exim extends a direct loan to the foreign financial institution covering 50 percent of the financed portion of each sale, with the cooperating bank covering the other half from its own resources. In each case the foreign buyer is required to make a minimum 15% cash payment. If the foreign bank borrows its half of the funds from an American bank, Eximbank may guarantee repayment to the U.S. institution on a case by case basis [p. 23].

The CFF program has not been heavily used and the Bank has decided to discontinue it.

In addition to its credit programs the Bank provides guarantees for medium- and long-term credits extended by U.S. banks. The medium-term commercial bank guarantee program "offers protection against commercial and political risks, on debt obligations acquired by banks from U.S. exporters [5, p. 20]." Coverage is generally provided for up to 90% of the obligation. "Eximbank does not specify the rate of interest on the export credit; but in the guarantee program, in the event of default, cover is limited to 6 percent, or less if the underlying credit carries a lower rate. In the event of default, Exim will pay interest accrued to the date of payment of the claim [5, pp. 20–21]." Bank guarantees amounted to $571 million in FY1981. Medium-term guarantees are also available for bank-to-bank transactions in which lines of credit in developing countries are established by a U.S. bank with a foreign bank for the purpose of importing U.S. products.

The Bank also provides financial guarantees for long-term credits issued by U.S. banks. These financial guarantees are often used in conjunction with participation by private lenders in Eximbank direct credits. Financial guarantees of approximately $890 million were issued in FY1981, and in FY1980 the Bank authorized $1.9 billion in financial guarantees, nearly $1.1 billion of which was issued in September 1980 to PEFCO for credits it extended in conjunction with the Bank's FY1980 supplemental authorization.[7] For financial guarantees the Bank recently adopted a "standard charge of 0.50 percent" to replace "the former fee structure (in force since 1978) which ranged from 0.5 to 1.0 percent depending upon the degree of sovereign risk involved [4, p. 5]."

The insurance programs of the Bank are operated in conjunction with FCIA and cover both commercial and political risks. The political risks are borne entirely by the Eximbank with FCIA insuring the commercial risk backed by Eximbank reinsurance for any excess commercial risk. "Political risks covered include, but are not limited to war, revolution, insurrection, expropriation and currency inconvertibility, while commercial risks include the buyer's insolvency or protracted default [5, p. 13]." Both short-term coverage for transactions with repayment terms up to 180 days and medium-term coverage for transactions with repayment terms up to 5 years are provided. Comprehensive insurance can be purchased for short-term coverage of 90% of the commercial risks and 95% of the political risk, and a political-risk-only policy with coverage up to 90% of the insured value is also available. U.S. exporters can also obtain a master policy that allows them to "determine the amount of insured credit extended to individual buyers in a discretionary limit assigned to the policy [5, p. 15]." Exports of agricultural commodities can also be insured with coverage up to 98% for both commercial and political risks. Insurance is also provided for services associated with "such activities as overseas oil drilling, data-processing, consulting, and telecommunications design, as well as for engineering, architectural and management consulting [5, p. 16]."

---

[7] The arrangement with PEFCO will be considered further in Chapters 2 and 6.

Short-term comprehensive policies are available with blanket coverage under which an exporter insures all or most of its short-term sales with FCIA. A major purpose of the short-term insurance programs is to allow U.S. exporters to obtain financing for their export receivables.

Medium-term insurance offered by FCIA is written on a case-by-case, seller-to-buyer basis and requires the foreign buyer to make a cash payment of 15% of the contract price at the time of delivery and requires the exporter to retain the risk on at least 10% of the difference between the export value and the cash payment. Insurance is also available for medium-term lines of credit extended by U.S. banks to foreign banks.

In FY1981 the Bank provided short-term insurance coverage of approximately $3.8 billion and medium-term insurance coverage of approximately $340 million. Combination and master policies were issued for coverage of nearly $1.8 billion.

V. Related Organizations

A. Private Export Funding Corporation (PEFCO)

A 1980 report [6] on PEFCO prepared by the policy analysis staff of the Eximbank provides both a summary of the performance of PEFCO and recommendations for its continued operation. This section briefly summarizes selected aspects of that report.

The impetus for the creation of PEFCO was a 1968 decision by the Bankers Association for Foreign Trade to commission a study of financing for commercial jet aircraft exports. Other banks that were not involved with aircraft financing also saw a need for an organization to help support U.S. exports, to meet volume demands, and to cover maturity gaps in private markets. As a response to these needs PEFCO was incorporated in April 1970 and began operations in May 1971. Ownership in PEFCO is currently held by 54 commercial banks, 7 industrial corporations and 1 investment banking house, although ownership is available to all eligible commercial banks, non-bank financial institutions and U.S. exporters. The investment banking house, Dillon, Reed and Co., Inc. acts as the lead underwriter for the sale of PEFCO notes and bonds. The industrial companies with ownership in PEFCO are Boeing, Cessna Aircraft, McDonnell–Douglas, United Technologies, Combustion Engineering, GATX Corp., and General Electric. The extent of the exports of each of these companies financed by the Eximbank and PEFCO is not reported.

Because the owners invested only $14 million in capital in PEFCO, it was necessary to borrow in order to finance loans of any magnitude.

Although PEFCO may not borrow from the Federal Financing Bank as the Eximbank can, the Eximbank provides a guarantee on the obligations issued by PEFCO. In exchange for this guarantee PEFCO pays a fee of approximately $133,000 annually. The Eximbank also provides PEFCO with a $50 million revolving line of credit.

In addition to the Bank's guarantee on PEFCO borrowings, PEFCO has an advantage in raising funds in the capital markets because its obligations are eligible purchases for Domestic International Sales Corporations (DISCs). For example, on May 15, 1980 PEFCO sold $100 million of 8-year notes at 10.25% which was only 0.3% higher than the interest rate on Treasury securities of similar maturity. PEFCO thus benefits in raising funds both from its eligibility for purchase by DISCs and because of the guarantee provided by the Eximbank. Because of tight money and uncertainty about DISC legislation in 1981, PEFCO was able to raise only $33 million in medium-term funds at favorable rates, and its two long-term note issues carried interest rates of over 16%.

Eximbank also provides PEFCO with protection against interest rate movements. On March 11, 1971 PEFCO and Exim entered into the following agreement: "If PEFCO's cost of money (including an allowance for expenses and return on investment) is higher than its committed lending rate on a fixed rate loan, PEFCO can request and Exim will increase its participation as necessary to allow PEFCO's portion of the loan package to bear interest at its 'cost of money' rate, with the overall blended rate to the foreign borrower to remain unchanged [6, p. 4]." This protection was waived by PEFCO from December 1976 through September 30, 1982, although the agreement remains in effect.

As a result of a Justice Department review, PEFCO was initially restricted to financing the later maturities of loan packages, but in recent years PEFCO has frequently taken the early maturities of exports financed jointly with the Eximbank. Loan discussions are initiated either by the Eximbank, a U.S. exporter, or a commercial bank, and as stated in its 1980 prospectus: "Since all loans made by PEFCO are guaranteed as to the due and punctual payment of principal by Eximbank, PEFCO relies upon the guarantee of Eximbank and is not involved in evaluation of credit risks, appraisal of economic conditions in foreign countries, or review of other factors affecting collectability of its loans [17, p. 3]."

The Eximbank provides PEFCO with a guarantee for the "punctual payment of principal and the *full* amount of interest on the PEFCO loan, [6, p. 3]" which is more generous coverage than the usual financial guarantees issued by the Bank to other private lenders. The interest rate on a PEFCO loan is based on the "agency yield curve" rate in Salomon Brothers *Bond Market Round-Up*. In addition to that rate a margin of 0.15% is added to reflect the cost of issuing bonds and 0.25% is added to reflect the "approximate premium that PEFCO estimated it had to pay in excess of the agency yield curve rate [6, p. 9]." A margin of 0.25% is also added to cover PEFCO's administrative expense, risk and profit, and funding risk. In May 1978 PEFCO reduced its margins, but in March 1980 it returned to the previous fee schedule. During 1980 PEFCO's lending rates ranged between 10.375% and 13%, which compared quite favorably with the best available private market interests rates. In 1981 lending rates were as high as 16.7%.

PEFCO's loan portfolio as of December 31, 1981 was $1.55 billion and undispersed loan commitments totalled $1.5 billion. Approximately 70% of the $1.5 billion of undispersed loan commitments was deferred fixed-rate financing committed in conjunction with the supplemental authority provided by Congress to the Eximbank in August 1980. Under deferred pricing the interest rate on loans is not determined until the time at which the funds are actually disbursed. This policy change was intended to reduce the funding risk on PEFCO's commitments.

B. Foreign Credit Insurance Association (FCIA)

FCIA is an unincorporated joint underwriting association that acts as the agent of the Eximbank and provides coverage for commercial risks associated with export transactions.[8] FCIA does not provide coverage for political risks which are covered by the Bank, and the Bank reinsures FCIA for excess commercial losses. As of 1979 the stop loss retention was $14.9 million per company and $7.3 million per country, so the members of FCIA are well protected against large losses.

During FY1981 FCIA issued insurance coverage of nearly $6 billion which was distributed regionally as shown in Table 1.1. During 1981 FCIA paid $4.6 million and $15.0 million, respectively, in claims for political and commercial risk coverage. Since FCIA is an association, it does not publish data on its profits.

C. Overseas Private Investment Corporation (OPIC)

Eximbank's insurance, guarantee, and financing programs provide support for U.S. exports but not for U.S. direct investment abroad. Official insurance and financing for U.S. direct investments abroad is provided by the Overseas Private Investment Corporation (OPIC), which is not affiliated with the Eximbank. OPIC is an independent, self-supporting

---

[8] FCIA programs are described in [9].

TABLE 1.1

Insurance Coverage Issued by the FCIA, FY1981[a]

Region	Amount ($ million)	Percentage of total
Canada	255	4.4
Latin America	2956	51.5
Europe	1171	20.4
Africa	214	3.7
Middle East	477	8.3
East/South Asia and Australasia	663	11.6
Total	5736	100.0

[a] From [10].

U.S. government corporation that supports "eligible U.S. private investment in friendly developing countries in areas around the World [16, p. 1]." Unlike the mandate of the Eximbank, OPIC has been charged with aiding developing countries by encouraging private U.S. investment in those countries. Legislation adopted in 1978 "directed that OPIC undertake special efforts to channel support for projects to the neediest countries and that it limit such support in those nations with annual per capita GNP's in excess of $1000 [16, p. 2]."

OPIC insurance provides coverage against "the political risks of inconvertibility of currency, loss of investment due to expropriation by the host government, and loss due to war, revolution, or insurrection [16, p. 7]." "Insurance coverage is generally available for up to twenty years at a combined annual premium rate of $1\frac{1}{2}$ percent of insured investment per annum for the three political risks named above, subject to modification on the basis of individual project risk assessment [16, p. 8]." At the end of 1981 $8.5 billion of OPIC insurance was in force.

OPIC also provides direct financing for projects through loans and guarantees. Loans are normally in the range of $100,000 to $4 million primarily for projects of smaller companies which are given preferential treatment by OPIC's enabling legislation. Guarantees in the range of $3 million to $50 million are also provided for loans extended by U.S. financial institutions. OPIC financing is priced at $1\frac{3}{4}$ to $2\frac{1}{2}$ percentage points above the rate on U.S. Treasury securities of similar maturity. Furthermore, loan guarantees carry an average fee of about 2% per year, while the Eximbank's guarantee programs have a fee of less than 1% on average. Project financing of $101 million was provided in 1981, and outstanding loans and guarantees total $346 million. In 1981 OPIC earned a net income of approximately $76 million and had capital and reserves of $726 million. In contrast to the Eximbank, OPIC's net income in 1981 was 15% greater than in 1980, although income from U.S. government securities accounted for $57 million of its $76 million net income.

VI. International Agreements Pertaining to Export Credits

In an attempt to reduce export financing competition and the resulting subsidization, the United States and other exporting countries entered into the Arrangement on Guidelines for Officially Supported Export Credits [15], which is administered by the OECD Secretariat. This agreement resulted from negotiations described as follows by former Assistant Treasury Secretary C. Fred Bergsten [18]

> At the Rambouillet Summit in 1975, the general principles of a Consensus on Export Credits were laid down. That Consensus provided for the beginning of discipline in the export credit area by establishing minimum interest rates and maximum maturity terms. This first step was followed by a second at the London Summit of 1977. The London Summit provided the impetus for an International Arrangement on Guidelines for Officially Supported Export Credits, a more formal understanding, which came into force in April 1978 [p. 148].

The participants in the arrangement are Australia, Canada, the members of the European Economic Community, Finland, Japan, Norway, Portugal, Sweden, Switzerland, and the United States.

The arrangement is a gentlemen's agreement that includes no legal or financial sanctions but provides means of detecting and disciplining countries that derogate its terms. The arrangement requires the exchange of information in any case in which an exporting country provides credit that violates the terms of the arrangement and allows participants to request information from other participants regarding their responses to preliminary commitments for official export financing. The arrangement encourages other countries to match directly any financing that violates its conditions, which fosters compliance. Nearly all financing done by the signatory countries for export sectors covered by the arrangement has conformed to the conditions of the arrangement, but in 1982 the United States began derogating on the loan term in order to respond to the lower interest rates offered by other countries.

The conditions of the arrangement may be summarized as follows:

1. Cash payments of at least 15% are required, and no official support for those payments is permitted except for insurance or guarantees against the "usual pre-credit risks."

TABLE 1.2

Minimum Interest Rates Specified by the Arrangement on Guidelines for Officially Supported Export Credits (%), 1979[a]

Classification of country	Number of years in maximum repayment term		
	2 to 5	Over 5 to 8.5	Over 8.5 to 10
Relatively rich[b]	7.75	8.00	Not applicable
Intermediate[c]	7.25	7.75	Not applicable
Relatively poor[d]	7.25	7.50	7.50

[a] From [15].
[b] Annual per capita income above $3000.
[c] Annual per capita income between $1000 and $3000.
[d] Annual per capita income below $1000.

2. The arrangement "matrix" specifies minimum interest rates by loan term and country classification. The original matrix is shown in Table 1.2. In May 1980 the signatories agreed to raise the minimum interest rates in the matrix by 0.25% for relatively poor countries and 0.75% for countries in the intermediate and rich categories. In September 1981 the minimum interest rates were increased from 2 to 2.5%. Further increases were made in July 1982, as will be discussed in Chapter 11.
3. Principal payments are to be made no less frequently than at 6-month intervals, with the first payment beginning within 6 months of the conclusion of the credit arrangement. Interest "shall not normally be capitalized."
4. The arrangement does not allow support for local costs incurred in the importing country in excess of the cash payment, and the conditions for supporting local costs cannot be more favorable than the terms on the credits themselves. For relatively rich countries only insurance and guarantees can be provided in support of local costs.
5. Credit mixed with foreign aid is permitted only if the aid is less than 25% of the total.
6. The arrangement also states that (a) the limits on export credits are not expected to become norms, (b) terms less generous than the minimum specified in the arrangement should become customary, and (c) the erosion of those customary terms should be avoided.
7. There are certain exceptions to these conditions:
   a. The term on credits financing conventional power plants can extend to 12 years.

b. The term on credits to finance ground satellite communications stations cannot exceed 8 years.
c. The conditions of the arrangement apply to the financing of ships only if those ships are not covered by the OECD Understanding.[9]
d. Certain items are not covered by the arrangement, including military equipment, agricultural commodities, aircraft, nuclear power plants, and ships covered by the OECD Understanding.

Aircraft financing is covered by a "standstill agreement" which limits financing to no more than 90% of the export value. The agreement imposes no restrictions on interest rates, however. In August 1981 an agreement was reached by the United States, France, Germany, and the United Kingdom to increase interest rates on aircraft credits to approximately 12%.

In addition to specifying limits on the terms of export credits, the arrangement requires notification of participants when credit with terms from 5 to 8.5 years is extended to relatively rich countries or if a credit is not in conformity with the arrangement. In the latter case, a participant must notify the other participants 10 days prior to making any commitment, and any participant can request a discussion with the initiating participant which will result in another 10-day delay. Usually these discussions take place by Telex, but a participant can request a face-to-face meeting. If there are any changes in the terms of the financing commitment that result because of the discussion, other participants must be notified of those changes. The information exchange also applies to credits mixed with aid. The arrangement specifies that if a participant notifies other participants of the terms of the credit it intends to extend and requests data on what the others will do, the initiating participant will assume that the most generous credit terms allowed will be granted if no response is received within 7 days.

The arrangement provides for periodic reviews and for modifications when deemed appropriate. As a result of the Export–Import Bank Act Amendments of 1978 the United States attempted to obtain changes in the arrangement that would (1) increase the minimum interest rates, (2) end official support for local costs, (3) put additional limits on the use of mixed credits, and (4) include agriculture, aircraft, nuclear power plants, and ship exports under the conditions of the arrangement (see [18, p. 102]).

---

[9] "Ships are almost always financed in accordance with the OECD Ship Agreement, the terms of which included a maximum of 17 semi-annual repayments, a minimum interest rate of eight percent, and a minimum cash payment of 20 percent [4, p. 14]."

Modifications, however, require unanimous agreement of the participants, and the initial negotiations were unsuccessful. In March, 1979
President Carter decided to abandon the negotiations and to take an aggressive policy of matching the export subsidization provided by other
countries. In his March 16, 1979 letter to Congress, President Carter
stated

> Accordingly, this Administration has sought to make the Bank's financing
> more competitive with the official export financing provided by other govern-
> ments and, at the same time, to improve the International Arrangement on
> Export Credits so as to avoid costly and self-defeating export credit competition
> between sovereign governments.
>
> Although the substance of our proposals appeared to constitute a basis for
> negotiations, the required unanimity for the changes we sought in the Arrange-
> ment were lacking. As a result, no agreement regarding modifications in the
> Arrangement acceptable to the U.S. government could be reached.
>
> I have therefore reluctantly concluded that further negotiations would not be
> productive at this time. If the countries which have opposed the improvements
> we have suggested evidence their willingness to be more forthcoming, I would be
> prepared to resume negotiations at any time.
>
> For example, Eximbank will continue its recently adopted policy of match-
> ing mixed credits on a selective basis, a policy which proved effective recently
> when an American exporter was awarded a contract based on an Eximbank
> financing package that matched the mixed credit offer of a foreign government.
> (Reproduced as Appendix II of [18, pp. 103–4]).

President Carter subsequently requested increased authorizations for the
Eximbank for fiscal years 1980 and 1981. Negotiations resumed in March
1980 and focused on the Wallen Report [18, pp. 16–65] which proposed
two systems that would increase interest rates to the level of government
bond rates, but no agreement on either system was realized primarily
because of French opposition. Increases in the matrix minimum interest
rates were agreed to, however, as previously indicated.

In addition to the arrangement the United States participates through
the Eximbank in the Berne Union of export insurers [13].

> Founded in 1934 this association of private and government guarantors seeks to
> "ensure that the practice of export credit insurance develops in a rational pat-
> tern." This is achieved through regular meetings, exchanges among members on
> credit transactions (for credits with repayment terms of 5 years or less), and the
> circulation of information about program changes of member agencies, default-
> ing buyers, and claims experience [p. 42].

For example, a December 9, 1979 Eximbank memorandum [7] reported
on Berne Union exchanges of information on OECD agreements and
understandings regarding processed and unprocessed wools and man-
made fibers, buses and bus chassis, breeding cattle, containers and semi-

trailers, fertilizers and insecticides, on-highway trucks and truck chassis, and paper and pulp. The conditions of the agreements and understandings specify required cash payments, installment payment periods and terms, and indicate which participants have agreed to the conditions and which have not.

The issue of subsidized export financing has also been addressed in the Multilateral Trade Negotiations, which contain an agreement on subsidies and countervailing measures. Former U.S. Trade Representative Reubin O'D. Askew described the agreements as follows [18]:

> The MTN Agreement on Subsidies and Countervailing Measures clearly states: 'Signatories shall not grant export subsidies on products other than certain primary products.' This Agreement, more commonly known as the Subsidies Code, goes on to list those primary products explicitly and to provide a list of practices illustrative of export subsidies. One of the practices specifically cited as a prohibited export subsidy is: "The grant by governments (or special institutions controlled by and/or acting under the authority of governments) of export credits at rates below those which they actually have to pay for the funds so employed (or would have to pay if they borrowed on international capital markets in order to obtain funds of the same maturity and denominated in the same currency as the export credit), or the payment by them of all or part of the costs incurred by exporters or financial institutions in obtaining credits, insofar as they are used to secure a material advantage in the field of export credit terms." However, the Subsidies Code provides an important exception—export credits, even if at rates substantially below the cost of funds, are not a prohibited export subsidy if they are consistent with the OECD Arrangement on Export Credits, or a successor agreement [p. 135].

VII. Policy Issues Associated with the Eximbank

The principal policy issue pertaining to the Eximbank is whether the United States should provide government supported export financing programs. Resolution of this issue depends on the efficiency of the international capital markets and on the actions of other nations. If significant market imperfections are present, the appropriate government intervention, if any, must be determined by assessing the likely benefits and the opportunity cost of the resources committed to that intervention. As will be indicated in Chapter 3, political risks and information problems may provide an economic rationale for government intervention in the form of the financial guarantee and insurance programs of the Bank, but the justification for the Bank's loan programs is much weaker. As argued in that chapter, the principal imperfection to which the Eximbank responds is not an inherent feature of the international capital market but instead results from the concessionary export financing of other countries. Even if the Eximbank's loan programs are not warranted based on long-run considerations, they may be warranted in the short run as a component of a strategy to persuade foreign governments to eliminate their concessionary export financing.

The objective of eliminating the subsidy in export financing seems noncontroversial, but how such an agreement can be achieved remains a problem, given the desire of certain countries such as France to use concessionary export financing as a component of commercial, industrial, and foreign policy. One alternative for the United States is to take the lead by increasing the Eximbank's interest rate to the level of private market rates or at least to the Treasury borrowing rate with the hope that other countries will then agree to eliminate their concessionary export financing. Whereas this strategy has the advantages of reducing the cost of the Bank's programs and possibly inducing some other countries to follow, it may have little influence on countries that view concessionary export financing as an important instrument of national economic policy. What might be achievable through a policy of unilaterally reducing the concession provided by Eximbank financing is an equilibrium level of export financing competition that involves less subsidization than at present. If this strategy is adopted, bilateral negotiations may be required to encourage other countries to increase their interest rates.

A second alternative is to deny other countries any possible benefit from their concessionary export financing by matching the terms of their financing, while at the same time attempting through bilateral and multilateral negotiations to achieve an enforceable agreement to eliminate concessionary financing. The United States has been working to reach such an agreement within the context of the arrangement, but only limited success has been realized. Because the arrangement is only a gentlemen's agreement covering the OECD industrialized countries, an agreement included in the General Agreement on Trade and Tariffs (GATT) may be preferable.

If the Eximbank is to be used as an instrument to deny advantage to other countries in order to encourage meaningful negotiations, the appropriate level of resources to be committed to this purpose must be determined. The increased authorization for the Bank during the Carter administration apparently did not convince other nations that their concessionary export financing would not benefit them, and the present reductions in the Bank's authorization may not give the United States adequate bargaining strength. The "war chest bill" passed by the House and Senate in 1981 would provide a $1 billion appropriation for interest subsidies to meet foreign concessionary financing, but even that measure may be insufficient.

Before an agreement can be reached to eliminate concessionary export financing, the issue of what constitutes concessionary financing will have to be resolved. Many nations are likely to define as nonconcessionary any interest rate that exceeds the interest rate at which their government can borrow in the domestic or international capital markets. Any lending rate that is below the interest rate at which an importer could borrow in the domestic or international capital markets, however, provides a concession to the borrower and imposes a cost on the economy of the lending nation. The United States is likely to have difficulty reaching agreement on this market definition of concessionary financing, since it is tantamount to eliminating the demand for government loans. The United States thus may be forced to settle for the former definition. Since the differences between the rate at which a foreign importer can borrow and the rate at which the U.S. Treasury can borrow may be several percent, the United States will in such an event have to decide whether to provide export credits at the government borrowing rate or to provide credits only at private market rates.

Proponents of the continuation of the Eximbank's direct credit program may argue that there are imperfections in the international capital markets that warrant the governmental extension of export credits. In particular, many developing countries have difficulty borrowing in international capital markets at acceptable rates and terms, and that difficulty has been used to justify direct loans in support of exports to those countries. Whether capital market imperfections justify such a program in the presence of an agreement to eliminate concessionary financing remains to be determined.

Even though the elimination of government export financing may be an objective consistent with U.S. economic policy, political support for the Bank may be sufficient for it to continue in its present role. If that is the case, the appropriate balance must be struck among the mandates to promote exports, to meet foreign officially supported export credits, and to respond to capital market imperfections. If priority is given to the mandate of promoting exports, Eximbank financing could become viewed as an entitlement to exporters. With concessionary interest rates, all exporters, other than those whose exports are supported by the programs of other agencies, would be expected to seek Bank support which would result in an unacceptable burden on U.S. taxpayers. If priority is given to the mandate to meet foreign officially supported export credits by restricting credits to those cases in which concessionary financing is offered by a foreign country, a similar problem may arise unless the burden of proof regarding the foreign credit offer is placed on the foreign importer and

U.S. exporter. Otherwise, the assumption that concessionary financing is available from a foreign country would effectively make the direct credit program an entitlement to eligible exports. If priority is given to the mandate to "supplement and encourage, and not compete with, private capital [2, p. 5]," the Bank's programs could be restricted, for example, to long-term credits to countries that have difficulty raising funds in the international capital markets. Such a policy, however, must rest on the conclusion that the Bank should accept risks that private lenders are unwilling to accept or should provide a subsidy that the exporter is unwilling to provide through a reduced export price. Unless there is a clear statement of priorities by the Congress, the Bank will continue to interpret its mandate in a manner consistent with needs as it or the executive branch sees them.

If a policy of responding to foreign concessionary export financing is adopted, the appropriate standard for implementing that policy must be determined. One alternative is to be "fair" to U.S. exporters by neutralizing foreign concessionary financing so that U.S. and foreign exporters compete from the same relative position they would have in the absence of that financing. Such a policy would not result in a misallocation of resources between U.S. and foreign exporters, but more resources would be provided to those industries receiving the concessionary financing than would be economically efficient. Furthermore, the allocation of domestic resources between supported export sectors and other sectors of the U.S. economy would in part be dictated by the decisions foreign countries make about the allocation of their export credits. Since concessionary financing transfers wealth from the export subsidizing country to the importing country, a second alternative would be to reduce the subsidization by providing only the minimum level of support required to gain the export in those cases in which full neutralizing is not required. A central issue is then whether the Bank can reasonably be expected to have the information required to implement this policy, since it requires judgments about the extent of product advantages or disadvantages in order to determine the minimum level of support.

The amount of funds to commit to the Bank for the purposes of responding to foreign concessionary export financing and to market imperfections depends in part on the opportunity cost of those funds. When the Bank borrows from the Federal Financing Bank, U.S. interest rates are increased and some borrowers are crowded out of the capital market. Thus, the minimum opportunity cost of the Bank's programs is the government borrowing rate but more appropriately should be viewed as the interest rate at which private parties must borrow. The benefits from the allocation of resources to the Bank should at least exceed this opportunity cost. Thus, if concessionary financing is provided, the cost of that financing should be measured relative to the private market interest rate.

One possibility for controlling the cost of the Bank's programs is to require the Bank to be self-supporting. Such a requirement, however, would prevent the Bank from meeting foreign concessionary export financing. As the GAO indicates [12], if the United States is to match foreign export financing competition, the Congress must determine if there should be limitations on the profitability of the Bank and if the Bank should receive a budget appropriation. One possibility would be to separate the credits extended by the Bank in response to capital market imperfections from those credits authorized in response to foreign concessionary export financing. The former could be extended at market rates, while the latter could be funded by an appropriation such as that called for in the war chest bills.

Whatever level of resources is provided to the Bank, the efficiency with which those resources are allocated will be an important test of the Bank's performance. A minimum standard for judging how efficiently resources are utilized is whether the supported exports are "additional" or whether those exports would have been made in the absence of Bank financing. An additional export may result from the Bank's response to foreign officially supported export credits or to an importer's inability to obtain financing in domestic or international capital markets.

In imperfectly competitive industries exporters would generally be expected to increase their export prices in anticipation of concessionary export financing and hence to capture a portion of the subsidy in the form of higher profits. The extent to which the Bank can detect such behavior will affect the efficiency with which it utilizes the resources it is allocated.

The Bank's lending activities primarily involve long-term credits, but foreign export financing agencies provide substantial medium-term credits in addition to their long-term credits. France, for example, promotes its exports by refinancing or discounting at concessionary interest rates short-term and medium-term commercial bank loans made to French exporters. The Eximbank also discounts loans on a smaller scale at interest rates pegged to the Federal Reserve Bank discount rate, but this provides a much smaller subsidy than provided by France. If U.S. policy is to match foreign officially supported export financing in order to further negotiations to limit export financing subsidization, the likelihood of success of that policy is diminished if matching only pertains to long-term credits. The United States must determine if expanding the Bank's medium-term loan program would provide increased leverage in the negotiations.

If the Eximbank is to meet foreign concessionary export financing so that U.S. exporters are not disadvantaged in their competition for foreign sales, the United States must determine if it is only to respond to the export financing subsidization provided by foreign countries or if it is also to attempt to offset the effects of other forms of export support. For example, France and certain other countries have been active in providing mixed credits that combine foreign aid and export financing. Until recently the United States has refrained from such mixed financing, but in FY1979 "Exim approved a $100 million line of credit to the Government of Tunisia to match the terms of mixed credit financing available from the Governments of France, West Germany and Japan. Exim's line of credit to Tunisia bears an overall interest rate of 5.5 percent [9, p. 9].'' Whether the U.S. should be more active in granting mixed credits as a means of meeting the export financing subsidization of other countries must be determined in the context of the U.S. strategy for resolving the export financing problem.

Another policy issue pertains to the support of local costs incurred by foreign importers in conjunction with the importation of American goods. For example, if the United States exports a grassroots factory, the physical capital may be supplied directly by a U.S. exporter and the project may be managed by a U.S. engineering firm, but local labor and materials will be used in the on-site construction and may constitute a substantial portion of the total project cost. If the objective is to promote such exports, there is a natural incentive to provide export financing for the locally incurred costs. The U.S. has attempted to limit the financing of local costs through the OECD Arrangement, but the extent to which the Bank should finance local costs to maintain the competitiveness of U.S. exports remains an important issue.

While the Eximbank provides guarantees and insurance coverage for political risks and certain commercial risks, the export financing agencies of some foreign countries provide additional forms of insurance support for their exports. For example, the French export insurance agency Compagnie Française d'Assurance pour le Commerce Extérieur (COFACE) provides insurance against both exchange rate risk and inflation risk.[10] While the Eximbank has not provided such coverage, its statutory mandate does not appear to prohibit it from doing so. If the Bank is to meet foreign competition, policymakers must determine if such insurance should be provided, how it would be priced if it is provided, and whether a budget appropriation should be made to support the program.

---

[10] Inflation risk refers to the risk associated with the difference between the final delivered price of the export and the original price quotation.

These and other issues will be addressed in the following chapters. Chapter 2 provides a review of the activities of the Bank, and Chapter 3 presents an evaluation of the economic justifications that have been given for the Bank's programs. Chapter 4 addresses the political support for the Bank's activities, while Chapter 5 provides an analysis of the competitive position of the Eximbank relative to the export financing agencies of other major trading countries. Chapter 6 is concerned with the measurement of the subsidy provided by the Bank's programs, and Chapter 7 provides an analysis of the welfare consequences of the Bank's direct credit program given the level of concessionary financing provided by other countries.

An important aspect of the performance of the Bank is whether the exports it finances are additional or whether they would have taken place in the absence of Eximbank financing. The additionality studies conducted by the Bank and by the Treasury are evaluated in Chapter 8, and in Chapter 9 an econometric analysis of the aircraft credits authorized by the Bank from FY1979 to FY1981 is presented. As an example of the Bank's decision making, Chapter 10 presents a case study of the $200 million Eximbank credit extended to Ansett Airlines of Australia. The final chapter addresses the appropriate objectives for the United States with respect to government-supported export financing and provides recommendations for how those objectives might be achieved. Recommendations are also provided for the administration of the Eximbank if it is to continue in its present role.

References

1. Council of Economic Advisors. *Economic Report of the President,* Washington, D.C., January 1981.
2. Export–Import Bank, "Export–Import Bank Act of 1945 as Amended through November 10, 1978," Washington, D.C., 1979.
3. Export–Import Bank, "Adverse Impact Annual Review," unpublished paper, Washington, D.C., 1980.
4. Export–Import Bank, "Report to the U.S. Congress on Export Credit Competition and the Export–Import Bank of the United States," Washington, D.C., 1980.
5. Export–Import Bank, "The Export–Import Bank: Financing for American Exports— Support for American Jobs," Washington, D.C., 1979.
6. Export–Import Bank, "PEFCO: Past Performance and Options for the Future," unpublished paper, Washington, D.C., 1980.
7. Export–Import Bank, "Berne Union, OECD Sector Agreements and General Understandings," by Jane Bungard, unpublished paper, Washington, D.C., 1979.
8. Export–Import Bank, "Lending Rates," unpublished paper, Washington, D.C., 1980.
9. Export–Import Bank, *1979 Annual Report,* Washington, D.C., 1980.
10. Foreign Credit Insurance Association (FCIA), "Export Credit Insurance: the Competi-

tive Edge. For the 1980's . . . You'll Need All the Help You Can Get." New York, January 1980.

11. Foreign Credit Insurance Association (FCIA), "FCIA, The Key to Export Profits," New York, 1982.

12. General Accounting Office [GAO], "To Be Self-Sufficient or Competitive? Eximbank Needs Congressional Guidance," Washington, D.C., 1981.

13. Glick, W. W. and Duff, J. M., Jr., "Export–Import Bank of the United States," unpublished paper, Washington, D.C., 1979.

14. McNamar, R. T., "Free Trade or the 'New Protectionism': The Choice of the 1980's," *Department of the Treasury News,* Washington, D.C., 1981.

15. Organization for Economic Cooperation and Development (OECD), "Arrangement on Guidelines for Officially Supported Export Credits," Paris, February 27, 1978.

16. Overseas Private Investment Corporation (OPIC), "Private Investment: Helping People to Help Themselves," Washington, D.C., 1979.

17. Private Export Funding Corporation (PEFCO), "Prospectus," New York, 1980.

18. U.S. Senate, Subcommittee on International Finance, "Hearing on Competitive Export Financing," Washington, D.C., 1980.

19. U.S. Senate, Subcommittee on International Finance and Monetary Policy, "Hearings on International Affairs Functions of the Treasury and the Export Administration Act," Washington, D.C., 1981.

2

A Review of the Bank's Activities: 1970–1981

I. Introduction

An historical perspective on the Eximbank since its inception has been provided by Jordan Jay Hillman [17], so this chapter presents only a brief review of the Bank's activities since 1970. During that period the Bank has had five chairmen. Henry Kearns served as chairman through 1973, when he was succeeded by William Casey who served 2 years until President Ford appointed Steven DuBrul, Jr. John Moore was appointed by President Carter in May 1977 and served until 1981. William H. Draper III was confirmed by the Senate in July 1981 and currently serves as chairman.

As Hillman indicates, the chairman of the Bank has had an important impact on its operations. Kearns emphasized the promotional role of the Bank and was criticized for maintaining the Bank's lending rate at 6% when long-term interest rates moved above that level in the early 1970s. Casey continued the promotional role of the Bank but increased interest rates significantly. A dramatic change in the operation of the Bank occurred during the DuBrul chairmanship when a very conservative role was adopted. DuBrul raised the Bank's lending rate above the long-term market interest rate, but more important, he significantly reduced the scale of the Bank's lending.

Moore reversed DuBrul's policies by emphasizing the promotional role of the Bank and the need to meet foreign concessionary export financing competition. Moore both lowered the Bank's lending rates and, with congressional backing, increased the credits extended to historically high levels. In part this increased support reflected the belief that U.S. exports faced increased product competition often supported by foreign concessionary financing and, hence, that the United States should assist its exporters in competing for export sales. Because of increasing market rates, by 1980 the Bank was lending at interest rates 5–8% below market rates. Immediately after taking office, Draper increased interest rates by 2% for nonaircraft direct credits and imposed a 2%, one-time fee, in order to reduce the projected operating losses of the Bank. Draper also focused the Bank's direct credit program on cases facing foreign product and concessionary export financing competition and acted to make the discount loan program more attractive by reducing the interest rate from 14 to 12%. Later in 1981 interest rates for long-term direct credits were increased to 12%, and with the 1982 revision in the arrangement, a variable lending rate policy was adopted with interest rates between 11 and 12.4%.

The following sections provide a more detailed review of the Bank's performance.

II. Eximbank Performance

A. Loans and Interest Rates

As indicated in Table 2.1, the Bank expanded its total support for U.S. exports from approximately $4 billion in FY1970 to nearly $13 billion in FY1981 with the direct credits extended by the Bank more than doubling over that period. Under the Kearns administration direct credits increased to a level of approximately $3.8 billion in 1974 before falling under the Casey and DeBrul administrations to less than $1 billion for the 15-month period including FY1977 and the transition quarter. The Moore administration greatly expanded the direct credit program so that in FY1981 nearly $5 billion in direct credits were authorized. Beginning in FY1977 the discount loan program was contracted and since then has operated at about half the FY1972–1976 average.

Table 2.2 presents market interest rates and the Eximbank's direct credit lending rate and indicates that concessionary interest rates were provided by the Bank in 1969 when market rates increased and Kearns maintained the Bank's 6% lending rate. Upon assuming the chairmanship,

TABLE 2.1A

Eximbank Authorizations: 1978–1981[a]

Program	FY1978 Amount authorized	FY1978 Export value	FY1979 Amount authorized	FY1979 Export value	FY1980 Amount authorized	FY1980 Export value	FY1981 Amount authorized	FY1981 Export value
Loans								
Direct credits	2.872	4.552	3.725	6.199	4.045	7.736	5.046	8.304
CFF and relending	0.055	0.106	0.100	0.211	0.042	0.083	0.034	0.081
Discount	0.497	0.359	0.650	0.435	0.491	0.297	0.352	0.190
Total	3.425	5.017	4.475	6.844	4.578	8.116	5.428	8.575
Guarantees[b]								
Financial	0.242	0.273	0.506	0.333	1.905	1.056	0.904	1.026
Bank	0.347	0.473	0.399	0.546	0.473	0.554	0.557	0.650
Other	—	—	0.003	0.020	0.132	0.264	0.052	0.127
Total	0.589	0.746	0.908	0.899	2.510	1.874	1.513	1.803
Insurance								
Short-term	1.962	1.962	2.453	2.453	3.018	3.018	3.770	3.770
Medium-term	0.324	0.429	0.348	0.478	0.530	0.693	0.343	0.394
Combined short–medium term	0.203	0.207	0.201	0.211	0.196	0.192	0.171	0.171
Master policies	0.874	2.281	1.107	2.726	1.777	4.215	1.626	3.886
Total	3.362	4.879	4.108	5.867	5.522	8.118	5.910	8.221
Grand total	7.376	10.642	9.491	13.610	12.609	18.108	12.854	18.598

[a] $ Billion.
[b] When financial guarantees are combined with loans, the export value is reported under the loan category.

TABLE 2.1B

Eximbank Authorizations: 1974–1977[a]

Program	FY1977 and transition quarter		FY1976		FY1975		FY1974	
	Amount authorized	Export value	Amount authorized	Export value	Amount authorized	Export value	Amount authorized	Export value
Loans								
Direct credits	0.967	2.041	2.141	4.896	2.534	6.643	3.769	7.979
CFF and relending	0.062	0.115	0.144	0.277	0.167	0.329	0.213	0.383
Discount	0.640	0.295	1.204	0.678	1.112	0.390	0.924	0.433
Total	1.669	2.451	3.489	5.851	3.813	7.362	4.905	8.795
Guarantees[b]								
Financial	0.646	1.107	1.082	0.154	1.144	0.054	1.191	0.004
Bank	0.647	0.931	0.564	0.759	0.423	0.550	0.324	0.417
Other	—	—	0.015	0.018	0.007	0.008	0.079	0.009
Total	1.293	2.038	1.661	0.930	1.574	0.613	1.594	0.431
Insurance								
Short-term	2.421	2.421	2.186	2.186	1.832	1.832	1.612	1.613
Medium-term	0.413	0.201	0.483	0.628	0.268	0.343	0.251	0.320
Combined short–medium term	0.136	0.550	0.224	0.232	0.204	0.209	0.209	0.215
Master policies	1.119	2.852	0.577	2.168	0.625	2.142	0.529	1.385
Total	4.089	6.023	3.470	5.214	2.929	4.526	2.601	3.532
Grand total	7.051	10.513	8.620	11.996	8.315	12.500	9.100	12.759

[a] $ Billion.
[b] When financial guarantees are combined with loans, the export value is reported under the loan category.

TABLE 2.1C

Eximbank Authorizations: 1970–1973[a]

Program	FY1970 Amount authorized	FY1970 Export value	FY1971 Amount authorized	FY1971 Export value	FY1972 Amount authorized	FY1972 Export value	FY1973 Amount authorized	FY1973 Export value
Loans								
Direct credits	1.634	NA[c]	1.817	3.946	2.226	4.581	2.322	5.155
CFF and relending	0.091	NA	0.022	0.040	0.070	0.132	0.092	0.186
Discount	0.584	NA	0.522	0.380	0.989	0.704	1.640	1.217
Total	2.209	NA	2.362	4.365	3.285	5.417	4.054	6.558
Guarantees[b]								
Financial	0.335	NA	1.077	0.056	1.220	0.004	1.530	0.005
Bank	0.265	NA	0.303	0.385	0.493	0.617	0.360	0.463
Other	0.013	NA	0.040	0.048	0.030	0.039	0.098	0.057
Total	0.613	NA	1.420	0.489	1.743	0.660	1.988	0.524
Insurance								
Short-term	0.771	NA	0.888	0.888	0.962	0.962	1.405	1.405
Medium-term	0.288	NA	0.310	0.413	0.394	0.504	0.418	0.541
Combined short–medium term	0.057	NA	0.102	0.108	0.178	0.184	0.126	0.133
Master policies	0.030	NA	0.314	0.610	0.669	1.773	0.523	1.385
Total	1.147	NA	1.615	2.019	2.202	3.423	2.473	3.464
Grand total	3.968	5.455	5.397	6.873	7.230	9.500	8.514	10.546

[a] $ Billion.
[b] When financial guarantees are combined with loans, the export value is reported under the loan category.
[c] NA = not available.

TABLE 2.2

Eximbank and Market Interest Rates[a]

	10-year gov'ts	Aaa corporate bonds	Five-year eurodollar rate	Eximbank average lending rate on new direct loans	Eximbank lending rate
1960	4.12	4.41	NA[b]	NA	5.75
1961	3.88	4.35	NA	NA	5.75
1962	3.95	4.33	NA	NA	5.75
1963	4.00	4.26	NA	NA	5.75
1964	4.19	4.40	NA	NA	4.75–5.50
1965	4.28	4.49	NA	NA	5.50; 6.00[c]
1966	4.92	5.13	NA	NA	6.00
1967	5.07	5.51	NA	NA	6.00
1968	5.65	6.18	NA	NA	6.00
1969	6.67	7.03	NA	NA	6.00
1970	7.35	8.04	NA	NA	6.00
1971	6.16	7.39	NA	6.00	6.00
1972	6.21	7.21	NA	6.00	6.00
1973	6.84	7.44	NA	6.00	6.00
1974	7.56	8.57	NA	6.38	7.00; 7.00–8.50[c]
1975	7.99	8.83	9.55	7.90	7.00–9.00; 8.25–9.50[c]
1976	7.61	8.43	8.68	8.42	8.25–9.50
1977	7.42	8.02	7.92	8.50	8.00–9.00; 7.75–8.75[c]
1978	8.41	8.73	9.19	8.38	7.75–8.75
1979	9.44	9.63	10.60	8.28	7.75–8.75
1980	11.46	11.94	12.80	8.44	8.75 and 9.25
1981	13.91	14.17	15.70	8.74	10.75; 12[c]

[a] Sources: Council of Economic Advisors. *Economic Report of the President 1981*, Washington, D.C., 1981, p. 308. Congressional Budget Office, "The Benefits and Costs of the Export–Import Bank Loan Subsidy Program," Washington, D.C., 1981.

[b] NA = not available.

[c] Rates were changed during the year.

Casey took steps to eliminate the interest rate problem as he indicated in his chairman's letter in the *1974 Annual Report* [4]:

1. We changed the interest rate on credits from 6% to a band ranging from 7% to 8.5%.
2. We moved the interest rate on Cooperative Financing Facility lines from 7% to 8%.
3. Instead of routinely authorizing loans equal to 45% of the contract price, we are reducing that participation on a case-by-case basis to as low as 30%. [p. 7]

TABLE 2.3

Indices of Eximbank Performance

	FY1981	FY1980	FY1979	FY1978
Net income ($ million)	12.1	109.7	158.7	139.1
As a % of equity and reserves	0.38	3.44	7.64	7.12
Dividends ($ million)	0.0	35.0	35.0	35.0
As a % of equity and reserves	0.0	1.1	1.68	1.79
Direct credit/export value (%)	60.8	66.5[a]	60.1	63.1
Direct credit and financial guarantee/export value (%)	66.0	67.7	66.4	66.3
Average lending rate (new loans) (%)	8.74	8.44	8.28	8.38
Interest rate on 10-year gov't bonds (%)	13.91	11.46	9.44	8.41
Average FFB borrowing rate (%)	13.86	11.196	9.393	8.25
Equity and reserves ($ millions)	3,199.5	3,187.4	3,077.7	2,954.0
Total exposure ($ millions)	38,406.2	33,161.6	28,699.1	26,300.0
Equity and reserves/total exposure (%)	8.3	9.6	10.7	11.2

DuBrul went further by increasing the lending rates above the Aaa corporate bond yield and also adopted an interest rate schedule that increased with the term of the credit beginning with an 8.25% rate for a 6-year credit plus a 0.25% increase for each two years of additional term. In addition to reducing the loan authorizations, DuBrul also reduced the percentage of the export value financed by direct credits as indicated in Table 2.3. By increasing the use of financial guarantees, however, he maintained approximately the same proportion of the export value financed by direct credits plus financial guarantees as in previous years.

When John Moore became chairman in May 1977, concern about foreign concessionary export financing was increasing as were complaints by U.S. exporters about the contraction in the Bank's lending activity. Moore set out to reverse the policies of the Casey and DuBrul administrations by aggressively responding to foreign export financing. As Moore stated in the *1978 Annual Report,* "We also trimmed our interest rates to the minimum we could justify, while still preserving the financial security

TABLE 2.3 (*continued*)

FY1977 and transition quarter	FY1976	FY1975	FY1974	FY1973	FY1972	FY1971	FY1970
137.4	115.4	80.5	110.3	139.7	147.9	119.5	110.7
7.43	6.71	4.96	7.06	9.29	10.5	9.09	8.88
35.0	20.0	20.0	50.0	50.0	50.0	50.0	50.0
1.89	1.16	1.23	3.20	3.33	3.54	3.80	4.01
47.4	43.7	38.1	47.2	45.0	48.6	46.0	NA
61.2	64.6	54.7	62.2	74.8	75.3	74.4	NA
8.50	8.42	7.90	6.38	6.00	6.00	6.00	NA
7.42	7.61	7.99	7.56	6.84	6.21	6.16	7.35
7.33	8.00	—	—	—	—	—	—
2,850.0	2,719.0	2,624.0	2,563.0	2,503.0	2,413.0	2,315.0	2,246.0
NA[b]	28,100.0	25,700.0	NA	NA	NA	NA	NA
NA	9.7	10.2	NA	NA	NA	NA	NA

[a] Includes the PEFCO loans authorized in conjunction with the FY1980 supplemental authority.

[b] NA = not available.

of the Bank as a self-sustaining institution. Although the prime rate rose dramatically last year the average cost of our loans decreased from 8.53% in the fiscal year 1979 to 8.25% [5, p. 3].'' This decrease in the lending rates by the Bank occurred at the time when interest rates on government borrowing were beginning a climb from 7.5 to over 15% in 1981. In spite of increasing borrowing costs the Bank maintained its interest rate schedule until April 1980 when, forced to borrow at an interest rate of over 13% from the Federal Financing Bank, it increased its lending rates to 8.75% for nonaircraft credits and 9.25% for aircraft credits.

Moore also dramatically increased authorization for direct credits and increased the cover provided by direct credits and guarantees to above 60%, as indicated in Table 2.3. The loan programs of the Bank also shifted from a relatively heavy use of the discount loan program in 1975–1976 to a greater use of the long-term direct credit program. For example, in 1976 the discount loan program represented more than a third of the Bank's lending, while in FY1981 discount loans represented only 7%. In addition to reducing interest rates and expanding authorizations, Moore also sought to respond to the export financing programs of other countries by broadening the programs of the Bank. The Bank began to offer lines of credit, provided credits in conjunction with foreign aid, and expanded the Bank's financing of local costs. Table 2.4 lists the lines of credit and the local cost financing authorized in FY1980 and FY1981 and, although the amounts are modest, these loans do reflect the Bank's resolve during the Moore chairmanship to respond to foreign concessionary export financing.

In addition to increasing interest rates for direct credits to 12% and imposing a 2% fee, Draper ceased authorizing lines of credit, reduced lending to high-income countries, and discontinued direct credit support for older generation commercial jet aircraft. The percentage of the export value financed with direct credits was reduced from 85 to 65% for large export firms, although 85% financing for exports of small firms was provided at an interest rate of 10.75%. In part the reduction in the percentage of exports financed was necessitated by the reduction in the Bank's direct credit authorization and further reductions are anticipated in the near future. To increase the support provided by its limited authorization, the Bank intends to increase its use of guarantees.

The Eximbank's interest rate for direct credits plus the 2% fee made the cost of U.S. financing significantly higher than that offered by France and the United Kingdom, in particular, which lend at the arrangement minimums. To remain competitive, the Eximbank in FY1982 began to extend the terms of its credits beyond the 10-year maximum allowed in the arrangement. Fifteen credits for $1.8 billion have been authorized with terms as long as 22 years (*Business Week,* May 17, 1982.) When the arrangement was revised in 1982, the Bank adopted a policy of lending to most countries at the minimum allowed interest rates, which equated the nominal cost of Eximbank credits with that of most other OECD countries.

B. Exports Supported

As indicated in Table 2.5, in spite of the increase in direct credit authorizations since 1970, the Bank supported a far smaller percentage of U.S. capital goods exports in 1980 than in the early 1970s. For example, in 1971 the Eximbank supported approximately $3.9 billion of exports which represented 25.7% of U.S. capital goods exports. By 1981 the Bank's direct credits supported $8.3 billion of exports, which represented 10.1% of U.S. capital goods exports. In addition to the decline in the support

TABLE 2.4A

Lines of Credit (FY1980 and FY1981)

FY1981		FY1980	
Country	Credit ($ million)	Country	Credit ($ million)
India	21.250	Israel	6.375
Morocco	35.000	Israel	5.000
Philippines	42.500	Poland	25.000
		Romania	18.594
Total	98.750		54.969

TABLE 2.4B

Local Cost Credits (FY1980 and FY1981)

FY1981		FY1980	
Country	Credit ($ million)	Country	Credit ($ million)
Mexico	26.700	Argentina	5.165
Argentina	5.400	Israel	0.825
		Israel	30.000
		Israel	10.125
		Mexico	7.500
		Venezuela	6.900
Total	32.100		60.515

provided by the Bank relative to exports, the number of direct credits authorized by the Bank declined significantly until recent years, so fewer exports received greater support.

The reduction in the share of capital goods exports supported by the Bank was a result of an approximately fivefold increase in capital goods exports. Inflation accounted for less than half of this increase with the producer price index for capital equipment increasing from 112.0 in 1970 to 264.3 in 1981. The cause of this relative decrease in support by the Eximbank is unclear. It could have been the result of a reduced need for government financing because of the development of more efficient international financial markets and a growing expertise of U.S. banks financing international trade. It also could have been due to congressional unwill-

TABLE 2.5

U.S. Exports and Eximbank Support ($ Billion)[a]

Year	Total	Nonagricultural			Agricultural	Exports supported by Exim direct credits	Percentage of capital goods exports supported by Exim[b]	Exports supported by credits and guarantees	As a percentage of capital goods exports
		Total	Capital goods	Other goods					
1970	42.469	35.095	14.659	20.436	7.374	NA	NA	NA	NA
1971	43.319	35.488	15.372	20.116	7.831	3.946	25.7	4.854	31.6
1972	49.381	39.868	16.914	22.954	9.513	4.581	27.1	6.077	35.9
1973	71.410	53.432	21.999	31.433	17.978	5.155	23.4	7.082	32.2
1974	98.306	75.895	30.878	45.016	22.412	7.979	25.8	9.226	29.9
1975	107.088	84.846	36.639	48.207	22.242	6.643	18.1	7.975	21.8
1976	114.745	91.364	39.112	52.252	23.381	4.896	12.5	6.781	17.3
1977	120.816	96.485	39.767	56.718	24.331	2.041	5.1	4.489	11.3
1978	142.054	112.152	46.470	65.682	29.902	4.552	9.8	5.763	12.4
1979	184.473	148.879	58.842	90.037	35.594	6.199	10.7	7.743	13.3
1980	223.966	181.734	74.077	107.657	42.232	7.736	10.6	9.990	13.7
1981[b]	179.622	143.762	61.947	83.815	33.850	8.304	10.1[c]	10.378	12.6[c]

[a] Sources: Council of Economic Advisors, *Economic Report of President*, Washington, D.C., 1982, Table B-102, p. 348. Export-Import Bank, *Annual Report*, 1971–1981.

[b] First three quarters.

[c] Capital goods exports extrapolated to full year for 1981.

TABLE 2.6

Eximbank Credits and Exposure by OECD Group[a]

OECD Group[b]	FY1979 direct credits ($ million)	Percentage of total	Total exposure ($ million)[c]	Percentage of total
Industrial countries	414	10.8	3,963	15.1
Higher income	307	8.0	3,856	14.7
Upper middle income	1,673	43.7	11,206	42.7
Lower middle income	1,054	27.6	5,379	20.5
Low income	376	9.8	1,811	6.9
Total	3,825	99.9	26,215	99.9

[a] Source: Export–Import Bank, *Annual Report 1979*. Washington, D.C., 1980.

[b] Excludes credits and exposure for five Eximbank-designated groups for which individual countries cannot be identified: West Indies–British, West Indies–French, West Indies–Netherlands, Various European Countries and Various Countries–Unallocable. No direct credits were recorded for these groups in FY1979 and total exposure was approximately $250 million.

[c] Includes loans, insurance, and financial guarantees.

ingness to increase the authorization limit for the Bank's programs at a rate commensurate with the rate of increase in exports.

During the 1970s the nature of the Bank's export lending changed somewhat from its traditional support of exports to LDCs toward increased lending to industrial countries. This may have been a natural result of the pace of commercial activity or it may have been a result of the changing emphasis of Bank policy from a focus on capital market deficiencies to a focus on meeting foreign concessionary export financing. Cruse and Whitsitt state "During the past ten years, the level of "core" exports (i.e., primarily non-nuclear, non-air capital goods to LDC's) which Eximbank has been able to support has fallen dramatically from roughly 30 percent during FY 70–75 to 12 percent during FY 76–80 [3, p. 8]." Table 2.6 presents data on FY1979 direct credit authorizations and total loan, insurance, and guarantee exposure at the end of FY1979 grouped by OECD country income categories. Approximately 19% of the direct credits and nearly 30% of the total exposure were associated with the OECD "industrial" and "higher income" countries, whereas approximately 43% of the credits and exposure were associated with upper-middle-income countries. Seventy-nine percent of the exposure for the upper-middle-income countries was accounted for by Algeria, Brazil, Taiwan, Mexico, and Yugoslavia, while 27.6% of the direct credits and

TABLE 2.7

Supported Aircraft Exports and Eximbank Credits (FY1979–1981)

	Aircraft exports		Aircraft credits	
	Value ($ million)	Percentage	Amount ($ million)	Percentage
Canada	2,335.4	20.7	1,601.7	27.6
Europe	3,703.2	33.1	1,709.5	29.7
Africa	502.7	4.6	254.8	4.5
Asia	3,498.7	31.1	1,826.1	31.7
Latin America	1,166.6	10.4	371.3	6.5
Total	11,206.6	100.0	5,763.4	100.0

20.5% of the exposure was associated with lower-middle-income countries of which Korea and the Philippines account for 64%. In recent years Eximbank credits thus tend to be associated with the level of commercial activity of the recipient countries, and the bulk of the financing is concentrated on a relatively small number of countries.

Aircraft exports supported by the Bank are even more concentrated among high-income countries than is total exposure. Table 2.7 indicates that approximately half of the aircraft exports and credits authorized during fiscal years 1979, 1980, and 1981 went to Canada and Europe, with Asia accounting for slightly more than 30%. As indicated in Table 2.8, the OECD higher income and industrial countries received over 60% of the aircraft credits.

TABLE 2.8

Aircraft Exports and Credits by OECD Group (FY1979–1980)

	Aircraft exports		Aircraft credits	
OECD Group	Value ($ million)	Percentage	Amount ($ million)	Percentage
Industrial countries	3,251.1	47.9	1,666.1	50.4
Higher income	942.7	13.9	333.2	10.1
Upper middle income	1,777.5	17.3	590.7	15.4
Lower middle income	709.5	10.4	492.6	14.9
Low income	709.3	10.4	305.1	9.2
Total	6,790.1	100.0	3,306.7	100.0

The data on the distribution of supported exports by industrial sector presented in Table 2.9 indicate that the transportation, construction, electric power, and mining and refining sectors receive the bulk of Eximbank support. While aircraft exports have constituted approximately 20% of supported exports from 1971 through 1980, this figure does not reflect the true degree of support since aircraft exports receive a much greater share of the direct credits which carry most of the subsidy provided by the Bank. For example, in FY1979–1980 aircraft exports received approximately 40% of the direct credits authorized by the Bank. Electric power exports received 26% of the direct credits during the 2-year period. The distribution of direct credits by sector for FY1980 and FY1981 including the PEFCO credits authorized in conjunction with the FY1980 supplemental authorization, is presented in Table 2.10 and indicates that half the FY1981 direct credits supported aircraft exports.

Although complete information is not available on the distribution of direct credits by exporter, *Forbes* (June 22, 1981, p. 82) reported that "Last year, two-thirds of its $4 billion in direct loans financed sales by seven companies: Boeing, McDonnell–Douglas, Lockheed, General Electric, Westinghouse, Western Electric and Combustion Engineering." During fiscal years 1979, 1980, and 1981, Boeing exports were supported by $4.536 billion of credit which was 35% of the total direct credits authorized. The largest direct credits issued by the Bank were $936.3 million to the Korea Electric Company for two Westinghouse nuclear power plants and $1057.8 million to Air Canada for the purchase of 24 Boeing 767 aircraft.[1]

Eximbank may deny applications for direct credits if a transaction does not meet the reasonable assurance of repayment standard, and Table 2.11 presents data on authorizations approved and denied for fiscal years 1978 through 1981. Relatively few applications are denied and those tend to have smaller credit requests than the approved applications. The Bank also discourages some potential applicants from applying, so the data in Table 2.11 do not fully reflect the set of potential requests for funding.

C. Financial Performance

In 1976 borrowing by independent U.S. agencies was consolidated by the creation of the Federal Financing Bank, and subsequent Eximbank

---

[1] In June 1982 Air Canada announced that it would seek to delay delivery of 12 of the 767s if it could arrange satisfactory refinancing with the Eximbank.

TABLE 2.9

Distribution of Eximbank-Supported Exports by Sector (Percentage)[a]

Sector	FY1981[b]	FY1980[b]	FY1979[b]	FY1978	FY1977 and TQ	FY1976	FY1975	FY1974	FY1973	FY1972	FY1971
Transportation	31	29	36	18	21	19	16	25	24	21	28
Communications	6	6	2	3	4	5	9	5	9	7	9
Construction	16	15	18	15	20	15	27	11	12	12	7
Electric power	7	16	12	15	10	20	3	14	9	18	15
Manufacturing	17	4	6	6	7	9	22	13	12	10	7
Mining and refining	9	4	9	23	7	8	4	13	14	10	15
Agriculture	4	4	3	6	8	6	10	8	10	6	9
Other	10	22	14	15	24	18	9	11	10	17	12

[a] Source: Export–Import Bank, *Annual Report 1971–1981*, Washington, D.C.
[b] Estimated from pie charts and graphs.

TABLE 2.10

FY1980 and FY1981 Direct Credits by Sector[a]

Sector	FY1981 Credits ($ million)	FY1981 Percentage of total	FY1980 Credits ($ million)	FY1980 Percentage of total
Agriculture/construction	5.1	0.1	14.2	0.2
Communications	336.9	6.7	420.6	8.8
Manufacturing	428.9	8.5	319.4	6.7
Mining/refining	873.8	17.3	400.8	8.4
Power	739.1	14.7	1,469.9	30.7
Transportation				
Aircraft	2,457.1	48.8	1,966.6	40.9
Other	60.9	1.2	96.7	2.0
Miscellaneous	137.3	2.7	109.2	2.3
Total	5,039.1	100.0	4,787.4	100.0

[a] Source: Export–Import Bank, "Additionality of Eximbank's FY1980 Credits," Washington, D.C., 1981, and Export–Import Bank, "FY1981 Additionality Study: Results," Washington, D.C., 1982.

borrowings from the FFB are summarized in Table 2.12. The borrowing rate increased from 7.325% in FY1977 to nearly 14% in FY1981. While the borrowing rate nearly doubled, the average lending rate of the Bank increased very little and was lower in FY1980 than in FY1977. Total borrowing by the Bank exceeded $13 billion in 1981, as indicated in Table 2.13.

TABLE 2.11

Eximbank Direct Credit Applications Approved and Denied[a]

Applications	FY1981	FY1980	FY1979	FY1978
Approved				
Number of credits	127	138	99	66
Loan amounts ($ million)	5,039.1	5,144.3[b]	3,724.7	2,872.4
Denied				
Number of credits	11	18	4	20
Loan amounts ($ million)	138.3	205.9	24.9	228.8

[a] Sources: Export–Import Bank, *Annual Reports,* 1978–1981, Washington, D.C. Export–Import Bank, "Denial Listing by Date-Denied as of 12/31/81," Washington, D.C., 1982.

[b] Includes PEFCO credits authorized under the Eximbank supplement authority.

TABLE 2.12

Eximbank FFB Borrowings, Interest Rates, and Lending Rates[a]

Fiscal year	Amount borrowed ($ million)	Average borrowing rate (%)[b]	Average lending rate (%)
1976	0.218	7.997	8.42[c]
1977 and TQ	3.918	7.325	8.53[d]
1978	0.517	8.252	8.25[d]
1979	2.533	9.393	8.34[d]
1980	3.704	11.196	8.44[c]
1981	3.953	13.862	NA
1982 (1st quarter)	0.778	12.878	NA

[a] Source: Export–Import Bank, "Borrowings from Federal Financing Bank," Washington, D.C., 1982.

[b] Weighted average.

[c] As reported by the Congressional Budget Office "The Benefits and Costs of the Export–Import Bank Loan Subsidy Program," Washington, D.C., 1981.

[d] As reported in the Chairman's letters in annual reports.

TABLE 2.13

Eximbank Outstanding Borrowings (1973–1981)[a]

Calendar year	Outstanding borrowing ($ billion)	
	Total	FFB
1981	13.339	12.741
1980	11.250	10.654
1979	9.191	8.353
1978	8.711	6.898
1977	8.671	5.834
1976	8.574	5.208
1975	7.188	4.595
1974	2.893	—
1973	2.625	—

[a] Source: Table, A35, Federal Reserve System, Board of Governors, "Federal Reserve Bulletin," Washington, D.C., 1982.

As indicated in Table 2.3, the net income of the Bank, which had risen to nearly $150 million in FY1972, declined to $80.5 million in FY1975 largely as a result of the Kearns administration's policy of lending at rates below the Bank's borrowing rates. The actions taken during the Casey and DuBrul years resulted in higher lending rates and increased profits in subsequent years with profits rising to nearly $160 million in FY1979. Whereas profits rose to a record level in FY1979, profit as a percentage of equity and reserves was only 7.64% compared to the levels of 9 to 10% in fiscal years 1972 and 1973. As a consequence of the lending policies of the Bank under the Moore administration, profit decreased to approximately $12 million in FY1981. Even with the increase in the lending rates in 1981, the Bank may lose $100 million in FY1982, and deficits of this magnitude are expected for the next several years. After having increased the Bank's annual dividend paid to the Treasury from $20 million during the DuBrul administration to $35 million during fiscal years 1977–1980, the Bank omitted its dividend in FY1981.

The level of profitability of the Bank suggested by these figures is misleading because the Bank includes earned, but uncollected, interest on delinquent loans as income. In FY1979 this uncollected interest represented $25 million of the $159 million net income, whereas in FY1980 it represented $93 million of the $110 million net income. In FY1981 uncollected interest was $89 million, and net income was $12 million.

The deteriorating profit performance of the Bank in fiscal years 1980 and 1981 has been accompanied by a deteriorating financial position due to an increase in delinquent loans and purchases of Eximbank guaranteed loans and insurance. The Bank tends not to write off delinquent loans and still carries $63 million of loans to China and Cuba on its books. A GAO report stated that "No loans were written off in fiscal years 1979 and 1980, and only $8 million in loans has been charged off against income since 1934 [16, p. 14]." Furthermore, when a government defaults on a loan guaranteed by the Bank, the Bank typically purchases the loan and carries it as an asset.[2] Rescheduled loans increased by $81 million in FY1981, delinquent loans increased by $152 million and loans purchased increased by $52 million. At the end of FY1981 rescheduled loans of $715 million, delinquent loans of $888 million, and purchased loans of $245 million were carried on the Bank's books as assets.

---

[2] "Claim payments under Eximbank's medium- and short-term guarantee and insurance programs are treated as purchases of assets and recorded as loans receivable when, in the opinion of the Board, the prospects of repayment and other factors, including materiality and country-wide debt consolidation considerations, justifies such treatment [8, p. 17]."

Although no single measure can provide a complete picture of the Bank's financial position, one conservative measure of the net assets of the Bank is its capital and reserves less the rescheduled, delinquent, and purchased loans and delinquent interest. Using this measure, the net assets of the Bank decreased by $519 million from FY1977 to FY1981 as indicated in Table 2.14 even though the Bank earned profits of over $400 million in those 4 years. This indicates that the quality of the Bank's loan and guarantee portfolio has declined significantly in recent years.

The insurance and guarantee programs of the Bank are not accounted for separately in the Bank's annual report, but the Bank stated that "present Eximbank accounting standards show the FGP (financial guarantee program) running a cumulative net income of some $78 million; however, the treatment of over $90 million in net claims as asset purchases is the single most important determinant of the program's present accounting profitability [6, p. 1]." If the $90 million had been written off, the Bank would have incurred a small cumulative loss in the financial guarantee program. Table 2.15 reproduces the Bank's financial guarantee experience for 1970 through 1979, and Table 2.16 provides a summary of the income from that program. The Bank argues that there is little risk associated with the financial guarantee program since 83% of the exposure is guaranteed by the full faith and credit of foreign governments. Furthermore, the Bank has concluded that the program is likely to be self-sufficient in the future [6].

> The present portfolio and its associated risk and fee structure can be expected to generate adequate fee income over the next 10 years to create a 2.5% reserve after payment of "normal" net claims and administrative expenses; this outcome reflects the very low net claims expected for the type of debt which dominates the FGP (i.e., some 90% government or industrial country aircraft).

A review of the commercial bank guarantee and insurance programs of the Bank is not available, but in its budget estimates for FY1982 the Bank stated [8]

> net claims paid under guarantee and insurance programs have also been small. Since inception, the Bank has paid 132.5 million dollars in claims but has recovered 56.8 million dollars leaving a net of 75.7 million dollars which has been charged to net income in the years incurred. Claims paid in FY1980 totaled $24.2 million and recoveries $8.1 million leaving a net of $16.1 million charged to net income during the year [p. h]."

The substantial increase in rescheduled and delinquent loans, purchased loans and net write-offs of guarantees and insurance in FY1980 and FY1981 reflects in part the worsening global economic conditions but

TABLE 2.14

Financial Position of the Eximbank ($ Million)[a]

	FY1981	FY1980	FY1979	FY1978	TQ and FY1977	FY1976	FY1975	FY1974
Cash and securities	0.7	0.2	0.1	7.7	12.9	10.1	20.8	21.0
Loans								
Current	13,923.7	12,203.2	10,540.3	10,414.4	10,568.0	9,880.2	8,501.4	6,901.2
Rescheduled	715.4	634.7	592.9	617.6	624.7	669.1	794.6	928.5
Delinquent	887.7	735.9	620.2	468.4	327.6	281.1	112.9	72.0
Loans purchased	275.6	191.3	105.6	49.8	18.1	—	—	—
Accrued interest and fees								
Current	313.1	263.9	223.1	213.6	198.9	172.5	143.0	110.7
Delinquent interest	89.3	59.9	52.4	31.7	28.7	29.3	16.6	13.9
Other assets	3.7	1.7	2.1	3.9	3.7	4.2	6.0	9.3
Total assets	16,209.2	14,090.1	12,136.7	11,807.1	11,782.6	11,046.5	9,595.3	8,056.6
Reserves and capital	3,199.5	13,187.4	3,077.7	2,954.0	2,849.9	2,718.9	2,623.5	2,563.0
Reserves and capital less rescheduled, delinquent, and purchased loans and less delinquent interest	1,231.5	1,565.6	1,706.6	1,786.5	1,850.8	1,739.4	1,699.4	1,548.6

[a] Source: Export–Import Bank, *Annual Reports*, 1974–1981, Washington, D.C.

TABLE 2.17

PEFCO Loans October 1, 1979–September 30, 1980[a]

Authori-zation date	Country	Product	Regular loans	
			Export value ($ million)	Financial guarantee ($ million)
12-6	Honduras	Cement plant	5.0	1.0
1-23	Italy	747 (9) 727-200 (6)	669.7	100.0
1-23	Belgium	DC-10-30 (2)	103.8	31.1
1-29	U.K.	DC-10-30 (5)	228.0	74.4
1-31	Philippines	Drilling rigs	7.0	3.0
2-14	Brazil	DC-10-30 (1)	51.2	18.9
2-28	Spain	Gas turbine generators (2)	5.0	1.7
3-31	PEFCO[c]	Line of credit	—	6.9
4-22	Spain	747 (2)	192.7	50.7
5-12	PEFCO[c]	Guaranteed interest	—	5.1
6-3	Argentina[b]	747-200 (2)	159.0	47.7
6-19	France	747 (2)	122.8	24.6
6-24	Brazil[b]	Telecommunications system	26.5	11.3
6-24	Guinea	737-200 (1)	19.8	2.5
7-8	U.K.	DC-10-30 (4)	192.9	38.6
7-29	Nigeria	Telephone cable plant	13.5	3.4
9-17	Ecuador[b]	727-200 (1)	20.0	8.5
9-30	U.K.	Gulfstream aircraft	10.5	6.3
Total			1827.4	435.7

In recent years PEFCO has been quite profitable with after-tax net income representing 16% of net worth in 1976, 17% in 1977, 24.1% in 1978, 27.3% in 1979, 21.8% in 1980 and 22.3% in 1981. One reason for these high returns has been the interest earned on short-term investments resulting from temporary surplus funds. In 1980 these short-term investments, which average $345 million, yielded approximately $42 million of interest income which exceeds the total before-tax income of $25.7 million. In 1981 short-term investments averaged $46.5 million and yielded before-tax income of $73 million, whereas total before-tax income was only $31.4 million. These data indicate that in recent years PEFCO has incurred losses on its outstanding loans.

The policy analysis staff of the Eximbank had projected that PEFCO would have a lower net income in 1981 than in 1980 and would incur losses in 1982 and 1983 before its profits begin to rise slowly through 1989.

TABLE 2.17 (*continued*)

Authori- zation date	Country	Product	Loans approved under Eximbank supplemental authority	
			Export value ($ million)	PEFCO credit ($ million)
9-23	Thailand	Gas pipeline	88.2	58.1
9-23	Korea	Telecommunications	144.0	94.8
9-23	Brazil	Platform jacket	76.0	50.1
9-23	Brazil	Gas pipeline	47.8	24.1
9-23	Israel	Power station	300.0	232.5
9-23	Egypt	Power equipment	56.4	32.8
9-23	Canada	767 (4)	180.7	114.5
9-23	Canada	DC-10 (2), 737 (6)	179.6	83.5
9-23	Spain	Power plant	34.9	22.9
9-23	Spain	Power plant	31.7	20.9
9-23	Spain	Power plant	47.3	31.2
9-23	Spain	Power plant	60.9	40.1
9-23	Norway	767 (2)	101.9	57.2
9-23	Yugoslavia	727-200 (2)	38.8	12.8
9-30	U.K.[b]	767 (5)	263.0	223.5
Total			1651.2	1099.0

[a] Source: Export–Import Bank, "Regular Loans Approved FY1980 through 9-30-80," Washington, D.C., 1981.

[b] Eximbank provided direct credits for all but these four transactions.

[c] No country listed.

TABLE 2.18

PEFCO Loans October 1, 1980–September 30, 1981[a]

Authorization date	Country	Product	Export value ($ million)	PEFCO credit ($ million)
3-17	Zambia[b]	Mining equipment	41.0	20.5
4-29	Sri Lanka[b]	L-1011-500	83.0	35.2
5-6	France	747 (2)	171.6	27.7
7-14	Israel	737-200 (2)	38.0	13.3
8-26	Malta	737 (3) and 757 (2)	166.6	9.6
9-23	Ecuador[b]	737-200	17.0	7.2
9-29	Philippines	Various	93.1	39.6
Total			610.3	153.1

[a] Source: Export–Import Bank, "Regular Loans Approved FY1981 through 9-30-81," Washington, D.C., 1982.

[b] Eximbank provided direct credits for all cases except these.

TABLE 2.19

**PEFCO Loans by Sector, October 1,
1979–September 30, 1981**[a]

Sector	Credits ($ million)	Percentage
Aircraft	987.8	58.5
Communications	106.1	6.3
Mining and refining	155.8	9.2
Manufacturing	4.4	0.3
Power	382.1	22.6
Other	51.6	3.1
Total	1,687.8	100.0

[a] Sources: (1) Export–Import Bank, "Regular Loans Approved FY1980 through 9-30-80," Washington, D.C., 1981. (2) Export–Import Bank, "Regular Loans Approved FY1981 through 9-30-81," Washington, D.C., 1982.

The Bank estimates that in 1989 PEFCO will be earning only about 12% of its net worth. The basis for these projections of deteriorating earnings is the assumption that PEFCO will borrow at 12% to fund all commitments that were unfunded as of March 31, 1980. Those unfunded commitments are estimated to carry an interest rate of 9.4%. Furthermore, PEFCO is estimated to lend on new commitments with only a 0.5% spread between its lending and its borrowing rates. The earnings on short-term investments have covered the losses on long-term loans in recent years, but since PEFCO had to borrow at over 16% in 1981, the Eximbank's projection for 1982 and beyond may be more accurate than for 1981. One cause of PEFCO's deteriorating earnings is the policy of committing a lending rate at the time the loan is authorized but not fully funding the loan until disbursement. During a period of rising interest rates, this policy results in losses, and as indicated in the previous chapter, in 1980 PEFCO adopted a policy of deferred pricing of its loans.

Through 1977 PEFCO retained all of its earnings, but beginning in 1978 dividends have been paid at the rate of between 2 and 3% on net worth. The retained earnings and dividend policy of PEFCO are limited by an agreement with the Eximbank as indicated in PEFCO's 1980 prospectus [18]:

> Retained earnings—under an agreement with Eximbank—PEFCO will not without prior approval declare or pay any dividend if (i) after giving effect to such dividend payment the retained earnings of PEFCO are less than paid in capital or

(ii) all such dividends would at the time of declaration exceed 50% of cumulative net income of PEFCO from May 26, 1971, the date PEFCO commenced operations. At its December meeting, the Board of Directors declared a $90 per share dividend payable on January 15, 1980. After giving effect to this dividend $15,876,000 of retained earnings is free of restriction [p. A-5].

IV. Conclusions

The export financing provided by the Eximbank and PEFCO expanded greatly under the Carter administration although the percentage of capital equipment exports supported was below the levels of the early 1970s. The high market interest rates during the late 1970s and the early 1980s and the Bank's emphasis on export promotion and meeting the highly concessionary export financing provided by other countries have resulted in operating losses and a weakened financial condition. Even with the increases in Eximbank lending rates in 1981, the financial condition of the Bank will worsen in the next several years. If market interest rates remain high, the Bank's authorizations will continue to carry a substantial subsidy.

The subsidy provided by the Bank's programs will be analyzed in Chapter 6, whereas Chapters 3 and 4 are concerned with the economic justification for the Bank's programs and the political support they receive.

References

1. Congressional Budget Office (CBO), "The Benefits and Costs of the Export–Import Bank Loan Subsidy Program," Washington, D.C., 1981.
2. Council of Economics Advisors, *Economic Report of the President,* Washington, D.C., 1981.
3. Cruse, James and Whitsitt, Susan, "Eximbank in the 1980's," Washington, D.C., 1981.
4. Export–Import Bank. *Annual Report,* Washington, D.C., 1981.
5. Export–Import Bank. *Annual Report,* Washington, D.C., 1979.
6. Export–Import Bank, "Financial Guarantee Report," unpublished paper, Washington, D.C., 1980.
7. Export–Import Bank, "PEFCO: Past Performance and Options for the Future," unpublished paper, Washington, D.C., 1980.
8. Export–Import Bank, "Report to the Congress on Bank's Budget Estimates for Fiscal Year Ending September 30, 1982 (Based on the March 10, 1981 Revision)," Washington, D.C., 1981.
9. Export–Import Bank, "Additionality of Eximbank's FY1980 Credits," unpublished paper, Washington, D.C., 1981.

10. Export–Import Bank, "FY1981 Additionality Study: Results," unpublished paper, Washington, D.C., 1982.
11. Export–Import Bank, "Denial Listing by Date-Denied as of 12-31-81," Washington, D.C., 1982.
12. Export–Import Bank, "Borrowings from Federal Financing Bank," Washington, D.C., 1982.
13. Export–Import Bank, "Regular Loans Approved FY1980 through 9-30-80," Washington, D.C., 1981.
14. Export–Import Bank, "Regular Loans Approved FY1981 through 9-30-81," Washington, D.C., 1982.
15. Federal Reserve System, Board of Governors, "Federal Reserve Bulletin," Washington, D.C., 1982.
16. General Accounting Office (GAO), "To Be Self-Sufficient or Competitive? Eximbank Needs Congressional Guidance," Washington, D.C., 1981.
17. Hillman, Jordan Jay. *The Export–Import Bank at Work: Promotional Financing in the Public Sector,* Greenwood Press, Westport, Conn., 1982.
18. Private Export Funding Corporation (PEFCO), "Prospectus," New York, 1980.

3

The Economic Justification for
the Programs of the Eximbank

I. Introduction

Although Congress had mandated that the Eximbank promote U.S. exports, meet foreign officially supported export financing, and supplement private export financing, the need for the Bank's credit, guarantee, and insurance programs remains a controversial issue. This chapter provides an assessment of the economic justification for these programs, and the following chapter deals with the political support for the Bank's programs.

Six principal economic rationales have been advanced in support of the Eximbank's programs. First, Bank programs have been justified as a means of responding to capital market imperfections that impede foreign trade. Second, Bank programs have been justified as a response to capital market deficiencies that are perceived to bias the market-dictated allocation of resources against the export of large-scale projects and long-lived capital assets such as nuclear power plants and commercial jet aircraft. Third, Bank programs have been justified as direct measures to improve the balance of payments and to increase employment. Economic policy objectives, such as maintaining United States product dominance in certain industries, are a fourth justification that has been offered for Eximbank programs. A fifth rationale advanced by some countries for such programs is that officially supported export financing acts as a form of aid to developing countries. A sixth rationale for the Bank's programs is that foreign officially supported export financing necessitates a U.S. response in order both to maintain the competitiveness of U.S. exports and to convince other nations to cease their concessionary financing.

The analysis of these rationales leads to the conclusion that while capital market imperfections may justify insurance and/or guarantee programs, the first five rationales provide no justification for the Bank's loan programs. The loan programs of the Bank, however, may be warranted as a component of a U.S. strategy to persuade other countries to eliminate their concessionary export financing programs. The ultimate objective of such a strategy should be the privatization of export financing with the government providing, only where necessary, insurance and guarantees at prices reflecting the costs of funds and the associated risks.

II. Capital Market Imperfections

The term "capital market imperfection" will be used to refer to a specific failure in the capital markets that prevents the attainment of an efficient allocation of resources. The term "capital market deficiency" will be used to refer to a market-dictated allocation that is judged to be undesirable according to criteria supported by some significant constituency. To illustrate the difference between these two, consider the Bank's description of its long-term loan program in its FY1982 report to Congress [8]

> The purpose of this program is to supplement and encourage private sources of financing when the private sector is unwilling or unable to:
> 1. provide U.S. exporters with terms and conditions which are competitive with those offered by foreign government-supported competition.
> 2. extend their normal repayment terms to those necessary and appropriate for the financing of capital equipment, and
> 3. make the entire loan because of commercial and political risks or other reasons [p. c].

The first of these three purposes will be addressed in Section VI in the context of a U.S. strategy to achieve an agreement to eliminate concessionary export financing. The second is a capital market deficiency since it refers to a market-dictated outcome that is believed to reduce the level of trade below the appropriate level as will be considered in Section III. The third purpose pertains in part to a capital market imperfection since the risk that political forces will interfere with the repayment of a loan is a structural characteristic of international markets. Four market imperfections will be considered in this section: political risks, certain commercial risks, incomplete information, and poorly developed capital markets.

A. Political Risks

Lending to foreign borrowers may involve political risks not associated with domestic lending. For example, after a change in government or political or economic system, a country may find it advantageous to default on previously contracted debts. This has been the case in the Soviet Union, China, Cuba, and Iran, for example. In a less extreme form governments may not take repayment schedules seriously when they understand that debts will be rescheduled if there is default. Not only does the Eximbank reschedule loans, but so do the World Bank and the International Monetary Fund (IMF), although they often impose restrictions in exchange for loan extensions. Even if countries take repayment schedules seriously, they may at the time at which they borrow have overly optimistic expectations of their ability to meet the repayment schedule.

Another form of political risk is associated with restrictions on the ability of a lender to repatriate loan principal or interest. Governments, even stable governments of developed countries, have at times instituted exchange controls or otherwise impeded the convertibility of their currency. In such cases a lender faces at a minimum the risk of a delay in payment.

The response of the international capital markets to these risks was addressed in the Treasury's 1980 study of the additionality of Eximbank-supported exports: "With respect to country risk, foreign borrowing must reflect the possibility of political upheavals, or of imprudent foreign financial policies that could lead to the imposition of credit controls, defaults, or debt rescheduling. To compensate for these added risks, lenders will normally charge foreign borrowers premium interest rates, with the result that market funds for financing exports may appear to be inadequate [13, p. 3]." Even though these risks are real, they do not represent a capital market imperfection unless the borrower or borrowing country has an incentive to default or to become delinquent in the payments. Otherwise, the market pricing of credits would be expected to be commensurate with the magnitude of the risks.[1] A sufficient number of countries have de-

---

[1] The data used in Chapters 6 and 9 on the spreads on international borrowings by the countries to which the Bank has extended credits reflect in part the political risk associated with those countries. Those spreads range from less than 0.5 to over 2.1%. Fees for OPIC insurance for direct foreign investments are steeply graduated as a function of risk. OPIC fees are reported to range "from 0.3% to 12% of their insured values per year" for "relatively safe countries . . . and for projects involving higher risk, premiums may reach 18% or more [*Wall Street Journal*, July 28, 1980. Reprinted by permission of *The Wall Street Journal*, © Dow Jones & Company, Inc. (1980). All Rights Reserved.]." The insurance and guarantees provided by Eximbank and FCIA, however, are priced at standard fees that are the same for all borrowers and for all countries.

faulted or imposed exchange controls, however, to indicate that political risks are of sufficient importance that the capital market may not allocate export financing efficiently.

If private insurance markets could be relied on to provide guarantees and insurance against specific political risks, government programs to deal with those risks would not be needed. Private insurance markets, however, might not supply coverage for political risks associated with export financing, since some foreign governments would be more willing to default on creditors from whom they may wish to borrow in the future if they knew that the losses would be covered by insurance. Consequently, a market for the insurance of political risks might not exist, and competitive guides for setting interest rates for loans subject to political risks would not be available. Whereas some insurance against political risks is provided by Lloyd's, that market cannot be considered to be sufficient for dealing with the level of political risks associated with international trade. The reluctance of private insurers to accept political risks is perhaps evidenced by the Eximbank's arrangement with FCIA in which the Bank provides political risk coverage while FCIA provides coverage for commercial risks.

Government intervention in response to uninsurable political risks should be similar to the way in which an efficiently functioning market would deal with such risks if such a market existed. In an efficient market, political risks would be dealt with through insurance issued to suppliers and guarantees issued to financial institutions with fees set so that the programs would be self-supporting. Since appropriately priced insurance and loan guarantees should be sufficient to deal with political risks, this market imperfection does not justify a government-supported loan program.

B. Commercial Risks

In addition to political risks, export financing is subject to a commercial risk that may not be present in domestic lending. An institution that finances a long-lived asset purchased by a U.S. firm will frequently require that the asset be pledged as collateral, as with loans for the purchase of commercial aircraft, for example, so that in the event of default on the loan the lender has recourse to the asset. Collateral can also be pledged for an export loan, but in the case of default the lender may have difficulty taking possession of the asset and subsequently disposing of it. For example, differences between the legal system in the importing country and that in the exporting country may make it relatively more difficult and more costly to gain recourse to the asset. In response to such commercial risks, the capital markets would increase the interest rate. Alternatively, the borrowing country could guarantee the repayment of the credit, but a political risk may also be present if the asset is sufficiently important that the foreign government might override normal legal procedures for dealing with a default. Commercial risks of this nature that are intertwined with political risks would be expected to be difficult to insure in private markets and, hence, government-supported insurance or guarantee programs may be appropriate.

C. Incomplete Information

A market imperfection could also arise because of information problems. For example, because the lender is farther removed from a foreign importer, a U.S. lender may have more difficulty assessing the risk associated with extending credit to an importer than it has assessing the risk associated with a domestic credit. As the Treasury stated in its 1980 additionality study: "Since information about foreign borrowers is likely to be less precise than information about domestic borrowers, the commercial risk involved in lending to foreign borrowers is naturally greater [13, p. 3]." Greater but identifiable risk does not constitute a capital market imperfection, however, since that risk can be priced accordingly in the capital markets.

A U.S. lender that is unable to distinguish effectively between good and bad foreign risks, however, is forced to set interest rates based on the average risk for a class of borrowers whose risk characteristics are otherwise indistinguishable. Low-risk borrowers in that class may be unwilling to borrow at the interest rate established for that class and thus may decide to forego the import. The borrowers remaining in that class then would be those of higher risk on average, so the lender would be forced to increase the interest rate charged to those remaining. Again the lower risk borrowers among those remaining might be unwilling to borrow at the new interest rate established for the class. As lower risk borrowers drop out of the market, lenders would have to charge higher and higher interest rates to the remaining importers, and it is possible as in Ackerlof's [1] model that no equilibrium interest rate would exist at which the lender would be willing to lend to the remaining borrowers. An equilibrium could exist in such a situation, but the possibility that it might not constitutes a capital market imperfection.

Although the information problems involved in assessing the commercial risks associated with an export credit can reasonably be expected to be more severe than with a domestic loan, lenders do have means of obtaining information and of reducing the remaining risks. For example, most commercial banks that finance international trade have foreign branches that can provide information on foreign borrowers and on the commercial viability of the projects for which financing is requested. Even if a bank does not have an office in the country of the borrower, the bank may be able to obtain information through a working relationship with a local bank or with an international bank with an office in that country. Since international lending by commercial banks often involves a syndicate, the potential sources of information may be numerous.[2]

If efforts to obtain information do not resolve the incomplete information problem, the lender may be able to reduce the remaining risks. For example, a private lender to a foreign government-owned corporation may be able to obtain a guarantee from the foreign government that would eliminate the commercial risk associated with the loan. Similarly, the borrower may be able to pledge collateral or the lender may be able to form a syndicate as a means of sharing the risk. Even though information problems may be more severe in international than in domestic lending, lenders do have means of obtaining information and reducing or sharing the remaining risks. Consequently, whereas information problems resulting from an inability to distinguish among commercial risks and from less precise information about foreign borrowers than about domestic borrowers may impede international trade, government intervention in the form of guarantee and insurance programs, but not a direct credit program, should be a sufficient response.

D. Poorly Developed Capital Markets

If lenders in an exporting country are unwilling to extend credit to foreign importers at acceptable interest rates, importers would likely be expected to borrow in their domestic capital market. Since domestic lenders would be better informed about the commercial risks than would a lender in the exporting country, domestic credit may be more accessible to importers than is foreign credit. The ability of foreign importers to borrow in their home country may be limited, however, by the state of development of their domestic capital markets.

An importer in a country with a poorly developed capital market

---

[2] The information problem, in addition to risk sharing, may explain the formation of loan syndicates.

may find it difficult, if not impossible, to obtain financing domestically at rates sufficiently attractive to warrant the import. This may be accentuated if the returns from the imported good are generated over an extended horizon. While there are certainly many countries that have poorly developed domestic capital markets, an importer in principle has access to international capital markets and hence may be able to obtain capital internationally when capital cannot be raised domestically. Although a borrower may find the interest rate higher, or the term shorter, than desired and may as a consequence decide not to purchase the asset, this may simply be a consequence of the efficient functioning of the capital markets. Lenders can be expected to respond to greater risks by increasing interest rates, reducing the term of the loan, requiring larger cash payments, and requiring collateral or a guarantee. These requirements may force some borrowers out of the market, but they are likely to reflect the natural functioning of the capital markets rather than an imperfection.[3]

Even if an importer is able to borrow domestically or internationally at the market interest rate, some importers, and hence some exporters, may feel that the capital markets allocate capital inequitably to importers in high-risk countries or discriminate against them through high interest rates. The activities of the World Bank, the IMF, regional development banks, and the foreign aid programs of developed countries are appropriate responses to these concerns, and whether government-supported export financing is also needed is a political rather than an economic issue. The inability of importers to borrow on terms acceptable to them for reasons other than those considered in the previous three subsections is not evidence of a capital market imperfection and will be addressed in more detail in the next section in the context of perceived capital market deficiencies.

[3] The data on Eximbank lending may appear to support the poorly developed domestic capital market argument since, as indicated in Table 2.6, 81% of the Bank's direct credits and 70% of its total exposure at the end of FY1979 were associated with countries in the OECD upper middle, low middle and low income groups. While these data suggest that a disproportionate amount of financing is being extended to countries that may not be able to finance imports domestically, the data may reflect a high commercial demand for capital goods in countries that do not have domestic capital goods industries but have vigorous economies and access to international capital. This latter interpretation of the credit and exposure data seems the more plausible, since 64% of the exposure associated with countries in the low middle income group is accounted for by Korea and the Philippines and 79% of the exposure for upper middle income countries is accounted for by Algeria, Brazil, Taiwan, Mexico, and Yugoslavia.

III. Capital Market Deficiencies

A. Deficiencies and the Demand
   for Eximbank Financing

The direct credit programs of the Eximbank are justified more often by what have been referred to above as capital market deficiencies than by the capital market imperfections considered in the previous section. The deficiencies most frequently cited in support of Eximbank programs are the difficulty in obtaining long-term export financing, the unwillingness of commercial banks to lend to importers at fixed U.S. dollar interest rates, and the difficulty of financing large-scale projects in the private capital markets.

The demand for Eximbank credits has been cited as evidence of the need for a government response to these capital market deficiencies. The demand for the Bank's programs may, however, be a reflection of product demand cycles, the subsidy provided by Eximbank financing, the inflated value of traded goods, and the increased volume of international trade. As an example of the product cycle effects, the increased demand for aircraft export financing is due in part to the demand for quieter and more fuel-efficient aircraft and is stimulated by the competition between the new generation U.S. aircraft and the Airbus.

The demand for export financing is also affected by the timing of purchases by importers. For example, the decision to purchase new aircraft is based both on commercial needs and on the total cost of the purchases. Since the Eximbank's rates and lending policy are publicly known, the importer and the exporter can predict with some degree of accuracy the extent of the concessionary financing likely to be provided by the Bank. As the differences between the Bank's lending rate and the market interest rate increases, the real cost to importers decreases, thus increasing demand. Furthermore, if the exporter and importer recognize that the Eximbank would be forced at some point to increase its lending rate because of profitability considerations, importers would have an incentive to advance their purchases. This incentive would be accentuated by the risk to importers and exporters that the major exporting countries might reach an agreement to finance exports at market rates. Consequently, the demand for export financing may increase both because the subsidy provided by Eximbank financing has increased and because the subsidy might be decreased in the future. By the end of 1981 when the Bank increased its interest rates to 12%, its outstanding preliminary commitments were approximately equal to the Bank's total loan authorization for the next 2 years, which may in part be due to the timing of the demand for Eximbank financing.

As indicated in Chapter 2, U.S. exports expanded rapidly during the past decade because of both inflation and increased volume. What is somewhat surprising is that the demand for the Bank's financing has not increased more than it has. One explanation may be the tighter federal budget which has reduced the Bank's authorization and made an application for financing less likely to be approved for the requested amount. Another explanation, however, may be that the international capital markets have become increasingly efficient and that capital market deficiencies are not a major impediment to international trade.

B. Long-Lived Assets and Corresponding Loan Terms

Since capital assets generate returns over extended periods of time, importers naturally prefer long-term financing in order to match the cash flows from the asset with the payments required to amortize the financing. Foreign importers and U.S. exporters have claimed to the Eximbank that U.S. exports are impeded because international capital markets do not provide financing with sufficiently long terms. Airlines and aircraft manufacturers support this argument by citing evidence that domestic loans to U.S. airlines for new aircraft have 15–20-year terms, while loans to foreign airlines may carry terms of only half that length. Cruse and Wigg [5, p. 56], for example, argue that it is appropriate for the Bank to provide long-term financing because investment banks and insurance companies are reluctant to extend credits to foreign importers and because commercial banks do not make long-term loans even in the United States. This, however, may simply indicate that the greater risks associated with foreign lending cause lenders to insist on shorter terms. Another possible explanation for the demand for long-term financing is that when export financing is provided at concessionary interest rates, the subsidy associated with that financing is greater the longer is the term. If concessionary interest rates were to be discontinued, however, the assertion that the capital markets do not provide financing with sufficiently long terms would in all likelihood continue to be advanced as a justification for the Eximbank's direct credit program. Consequently, the financing alternatives available to importers must be examined to determine if there is a capital market deficiency that warrants an Eximbank loan program.

An importer has five basic alternatives for financing long-term capital

assets. First, an importer may finance the asset through internally generated funds. Second, an importer may arrange for financing from the exporting country either from financial institutions or from the exporter who
would then arrange its own local financing. Third, the importer may borrow internationally in the Eurocurrency markets. Fourth, the importer
may borrow in its domestic capital market. The international integration
of the capital markets of developed countries through the Eurocurrency
market, however, means that foreign borrowing by importers in those
countries should be priced efficiently relative to domestic borrowing.
Fifth, importers can finance the assets through short- or medium-term
loans and then roll-over the loans at maturity.

   In the absence of the market imperfections discussed in the previous
section, importers have a variety of alternatives for financing commercially viable projects at market rates even if cash flows are generated over
an extended horizon. Because of political and commercial risks, however,
longer terms imply greater risks to the lender than do shorter terms, and
in such cases the capital market would price longer term credits at higher
interest rates. Some lenders, such as commercial banks that must fund
their loans with short-term deposits, may thus decide not to participate in
that segment of the market. While banks have in recent years extended
the terms of their credits, they still prefer shorter maturities primarily
because of the funding risk resulting from the volatility of short-term
interest rates. As a result, banks are not a principal source of long-term
financing for U.S. firms and should not be expected to be for exports of
long-lived assets. Although aircraft financing in the United States is primarily done through insurance companies and banks on a secured, or
sometimes an unsecured, basis, these lenders may be unwilling to finance
aircraft exports on the same terms because of the difficulties in making
collateral arrangements or because of political risks. These difficulties,
however, do not justify the Bank's direct credit program since loan guarantees should be sufficient to induce commercial banks to lend at longer
terms for export financing.

C. Interest Rate Illusion

   Foreign importers have often told the Eximbank that in comparing
competing financing offers they are concerned with the nominal interest
rates charged and not with the currency in which the loan is denominated.
The arrangement matrix discussed in Chapter 1 may be viewed as a reflection of this focus on nominal interest rates, since the interest rate minimums are the same for all currencies. In commenting on a draft of a GAO

report that also reflected this view, former Assistant Secretary of the Treasury C. Fred Bergsten stated [9]

> The report appears to accept the notion that numerous foreign buyers suffer from an interest rate illusion. Buyers suffering from this illusion are said to be concerned only with the nominal interest rate on a loan and not with the currency in which a loan is denominated. The rationale for the illusion is that future exchange rates are unpredictable, and hence currency expectations will be disregarded by foreign borrowers.
>
> No one can predict with confidence what relative exchange rates will be in the future, but the existence of this illusion is supported neither by experience nor by theory. Buyers ordinarily do have some exchange rate expectations in mind when considering competing export credit offers. Indeed, expected exchange rate movements are generally reflected in interest rate differentials. Some buyers may suffer from interest rate illusion, but it is unlikely that all buyers are ignorant of the difference between dollar finance and Swiss franc finance. It makes little sense to recommend that the U.S. Government should answer an illusion of this type by offering, say, the Swiss franc interest rate for a U.S. dollar credit [p. 35].

Although the Bank attaches importance to the argument that importers are concerned only with nominal interest rates, it does recognize the importance of real interest rates. In response to a question from former Senator Adlai Stevenson, the Bank stated [14]

> Answer: Not all transactions require an interest rate from Eximbank which is exactly equivalent to that offered by other official credit agencies. Depending on the borrower's perception of nominal interest rates vs. currency strength or weakness (e.g., it is less expensive overall to borrow at a higher nominal rate in a weaker currency), the strength of U.S. manufacturers in certain product sectors, and established trade patterns between U.S. suppliers and foreign purchasers, it may be possible to increase the interest rate offered on certain transactions above the present standard Exim rates and still assist the U.S. exporter in winning the sale. While Exim would continue to offer a lower rate in cases where a truly competitive rate was necessary, the average rate on Exim credits as a whole could increase somewhat [p. 132].

To indicate the magnitude of the interest rate differences, Table 3.1 presents Eurocurrency deposit rates and prime rates for six major currencies. Major differences between the lower inflation rate countries—Germany, Switzerland, and Japan—and the higher inflation rate countries— the United States, France, and the United Kingdom—have persisted in recent years. With interest rate differences of these magnitudes and the likelihood that these differences will be reflected in exchange rate movements, it is implausible that importers would suffer from interest rate illusion. Importers cannot be expected to be indifferent to the differences between a 10% U.S. dollar interest rate, a 10% French franc interest rate, and a 10% Deutschemark interest rate. If importers have interest rate illu-

TABLE 3.1

Comparative Interest Rates[a]

	Twelve month Euro-currency deposit rates				Commercial bank lending rates to prime borrowers			
Currency	Dec. 1978	Dec. 1979	Dec. 1980	Dec. 1981	Dec. 1978	Dec. 1979	Dec. 1980	Dec. 1981
U.S. dollar	12.00	12.87	14.87	14.75	11.75	15.25	21.50	15.75
German mark	3.81	8.12	8.93	10.25	5.50	9.75	11.50	13.00
Swiss franc	0.62	5.56	5.50	8.50	5.00	5.00	5.75	8.00
British pound	13.00	15.25	14.00	15.37	13.50	18.00	15.00	14.50
French franc	10.25	13.75	12.87	18.25	9.80	12.50	12.25	14.00
Japanese yen	2.19	7.94	9.37	6.87	4.50	6.51	8.16	7.00

[a] From [11a].

sion, the U.S. response should be to lend to those importers at fixed interest rates in a currency that might be expected to appreciate in value against the U.S. dollar over the term of the loan.

The magnitude of the potential interest rate illusion problem is illustrated by the data in Table 3.2 provided by Acting Assistant Secretary for the Treasury for International Affairs Thomas Leddy, who reported the secondary market yields and officially supported export credit rates of the five principal exporting countries. These data indicate that French officially supported export financing carries the greatest subsidy and hence that an importer should prefer an 8.35% French franc interest rate to a 7.85% yen rate.

While the differences in the interest rates across currencies are quite substantial, Cruse and Whitsitt [4] argue that interest rate illusion is not a very serious issue.

> There is little "interest rate illusion" (i.e., comparing rates in different currencies) involved in these rate comparisons because only the French and Germans (representing less than 30 percent of long-term export credit extended by the major competitors) deal basically in their domestic currency, and frequently buyers insist on a fixed stream of debt payment expressed in U.S. dollars [p. 6].

The Wallen report [20, p. 10] indicates that France and Germany accounted for nearly 45% (or approximately $76 billion) of the outstanding officially supported export credits at the end of 1979, so the potential effect may be substantial. It seems unlikely, however, that foreign importers would be indifferent to the differences between a French franc loan, a Deutschemark loan, and a U.S. dollar loan each with the same nominal interest rate.

TABLE 3.2

**Secondary Market Yields and Export Credit Rates of
Leading Exporting Countries[a]**

Currency	Export credit rate most frequently charged (%)	Long-term government bond yield (%)[b]
U.S. dollar	8.60	12.23
German mark	8.90	9.80
British pound	8.10	13.84
French franc	8.35	15.05
Japanese yen	7.85	8.79

[a] From [18, p. 18].
[b] February 1981.

D. Fixed Dollar Borrowing Rates

Many foreign importers have indicated to the Eximbank that they prefer to borrow at fixed interest rates, rather than at floating rates as is customary in international lending, since fixed rates give them assurance of the total amount they will be required to repay. For example, in supporting the Eximbank during Congressional testimony, David Copley, Treasurer of the Fluor Corporation, referred to "The kinds of credits that are mandatory for capital-intensive major projects . . . that is, long-term, fixed rate credits where the economies of the project can be understood and analyzed at the outset [14, p. 156]." In response to these preferences and because private banks do not make fixed rate loans, all Eximbank loans are made at fixed rates, although the Bank is not prevented from offering floating rate loans. In commenting on the demand for fixed interest rate loans the Bank stated [6]:

> The principal objective of the Discount Loan program is to improve the conditions under which medium-term export financing is provided by enabling commercial banks to offer fixed-rate financing. However, there is some question how necessary fixed rates really are, particularly given the greater variability in foreign exchange rates and prices. Nevertheless, many foreign buyers, particularly small- and medium-size buyers, and some public buyers prefer (and even insist on) fixed rates, and they are offered by other export credit agencies [p. II.D.].

The argument that foreign importers prefer fixed interest rate, U.S. dollar loans because that fixes the amounts to be repaid is unpersuasive because a foreign exporter that borrows in U.S. dollars must make principal and interest payments in dollars and therefore will be subject to changes in the value of the dollar relative to its home currency. In some cases, fixed rate dollar financing may be preferred by a borrower that, for example, conducts its affairs in U.S. dollars. The International Air Transport Association, for example, sets international air fares in U.S. dollars, and hence, foreign airlines find it natural, it is argued, to borrow dollars at fixed interest rates to finance their aircraft purchases. Also, a country that conducts its international trade largely in U.S. dollars may find it appropriate to borrow dollars at a fixed interest rate. Such cases cannot be considered pervasive, however. The more typical case is that of an importer that earns revenues denominated in its domestic currency from the imported asset. A fixed dollar rate loan thus implies fluctuating domestic currency requirements to meet the loan payments.

Even though their revenues may not be in dollars, some foreign borrowers may prefer fixed rate U.S. dollar financing if they anticipate that their currency will rise in value relative to the dollar. Borrowers with a currency that is anticipated to fall relative to the dollar, however, might prefer a floating interest rate that would adjust based on market conditions and provide the possibility of offsetting some of the exchange rate risk associated with the financing. An example was provided in Mr. Moore's response to a question by Senator Stevenson [15]:

> I can give you one example where China Airlines from Taiwan had an offer of a financial guarantee and a financing package at 9¾ percent fixed rate of interest about a year ago and they came in and politely declined us saying that they preferred to take floating dollars in private markets because their estimate was that that would cost them 8.4 percent over the next 10 years. They're shrewd, and I guess they're right [pp. 30–31].

That Eximbank borrowers are accustomed to floating rates is indicated by the fact that 20% of the private financing that is combined with Eximbank financing of a U.S. export carries floating interest rates [7, p. 14].

If competitive forward exchange markets existed for all currencies and extended to long maturities, borrowers would be indifferent to the differences between borrowing at fixed or floating interests rates because the borrower could purchase forward contracts to generate his preferred risk profile. Forward markets are incomplete, however, and equivalent long-term hedging instruments may not be available. This incompleteness may be due to a demand that is insufficient to warrant the set-up costs required to develop a market or it may be a reflection of political risks that preclude a competitive market from being established. Because of the incompleteness of these markets, foreign borrowers may not be able to obtain the risk profile of repayments they prefer. Furthermore, because commercial banks tend to have short-term deposits, they prefer to lend with floating rates and leave borrowers to do their best to hedge their risks. Given the widespread acceptance of floating rate loans in international finance, however, a preference on the part of some borrowers for fixed interest rate loans is not a sufficient justification for a government-supported, fixed-rate export credit program.

E. Financing Large Projects

Another capital market deficiency is claimed to result from the difficulty in raising sufficient private capital to finance high-valued projects of the types supported by the Bank. Examples such as the private financing of the Alaskan pipeline and of domestic nuclear power plants, however, indicate that large amounts of capital can be raised even given the limitations on the exposure that a commercial bank can have with an individual borrower or a country. In its 1978 study the Treasury used these limitations as a factor indicating the additionality of Eximbank supported exports, but in its 1980 additionality study, the Treasury concluded: "Treasury's previous study had been influenced by Federal and state banking laws that prohibit a single bank from lending sizable amounts to a single borrower. Since then, it has become clear that U.S. banks routinely form consortia of banks to finance larger U.S. export sales [12, p. 7]." The largest credits extended by the Bank were $936.3 million to the Korea Electric Company to finance the purchase of two nuclear power plants and $1.057 billion to Canada for the purchase of 24 Boeing 767s. Although these are considerable sums, private capital markets should have little difficulty in providing such amounts if the projects are commercially viable and the level of risk acceptable.

IV. Promotion of Exports, the Balance of Payments, and Employment

In addition to justifications based on capital market imperfections and deficiencies, the programs of the Eximbank have been supported as means to promote exports in order to reduce the U.S. balance of payments deficit and to stimulate employment. For example, in its February 22, 1980 testimony, the Chamber of Commerce stated [14]:

> Further improvements are needed, however, to bring Eximbank financing to the level necessary to ensure sufficient export expansion to correct the U.S. trade deficit. One such improvement would be an increase in Eximbank's authorization, beginning with the budget for fiscal year 1980 . . .

> To redress its intolerable trade imbalance, the United States must rapidly expand its export trade. Export financing is an integral part of U.S. trade performance and carries with it an "additionality" that contributes significantly to GNP, tax revenues, and jobs. . . .
>
> U.S. industry appears to have begun to reverse the downward trend in its share of the world's export trade. It would be most unfortunate if this turnaround were frustrated by an inadequate authorization which has proven to be cost-effective and to place no burden on the U.S. taxpayers. An adequate authorization is also needed if Eximbank is to meet the Congressional mandate to be competitive with the rates and terms provided by the government-supported export credit agencies of other nations. It is, therefore, recommended that the Eximbank direct loan authorization for FY1980 be increased to $7 billion and the proposed level for FY1981 to $8 billion [pp. 169–170].

Concessionary export financing may not, however, improve the U.S. balance of payments. At one extreme, if a supported export is completely additional, the balance of payments is improved by the value of the export less the portion of the financing subsidy captured by the importer. At the other extreme, if a supported export is not additional and would have been made in the absence of Eximbank concessionary financing, the balance of payments is worsened to the extent that the importer captures a share of the subsidy. As the Congressional Budget Office (CBO) stated [2]

> Where the interest rate subsidy is small and the subsidized loan produces a large increase in the total value of exports, an export credit subsidy program may produce dollar exchange rate appreciation. But where the interest rate subsidy is large and the loan does not produce a much larger increase in exports, the subsidy will at first increase the trade balance and produce dollar appreciation. But after the merchandise shipments are complete, the U.S. receipt of interest payment on the subsidized loan will fall short of U.S. payments on foreign loans made by U.S. citizens who were originally crowded out of the U.S. capital market. The net drain on interest payments will reduce the current account; once the merchandise shipments are complete, therefore, the subsidized loan may produce a current account deficit and exchange rate depreciation [p. 14].

In a system of floating exchange rates government export financing that increases exports will increase employment in the supported industries and result in an equilibrium in the balance of payments with a higher exchange rate than in the absence of that financing. The higher exchange rate, however, will increase imports and decrease employment in import-competing industries. In the long run, the principal effect of government-supported export financing is to direct resources toward those export sectors receiving the support and away from domestic industries that compete with imports.

The initial effect on the balance of payments depends on the elasticity of demand of the supported exports given the level of foreign officially supported export credits. The greater is the elasticity of demand (or the greater the degree of additionality) the more likely it is that the balance of payments will be improved. To the extent that the Eximbank is able effectively to focus its support on those exports most likely to be additional, the elasticity of supported export demand would be expected to be high. Some limited evidence on the effect of Eximbank direct credits on net exports is presented in Chapter 7, and the issue of additionality is considered in Chapters 8 and 9. The conclusion resulting from this evidence, unfortunately, is that little is known about the additionality of Eximbank supported exports.

If the United States as a matter of public policy adopts the objective of attempting to improve the balance of payments and to stimulate employment by promoting exports, it does not necessarily follow that government, and in particular concessionary, export financing is the most effective means of achieving this objective. At the macroeconomic level the CBO has argued that monetary and fiscal policy should be preferred to subsidized export financing [2].

> When there is general unemployment, subsidizing export credit could increase total employment. But the subsidy will increase some exports relative to both other exports and to other economic activities, while monetary and fiscal policies would have more neutral expansionary effects [p. vii].

The tax system can also be used to promote exports through tax deferrals such as those available to DISCs. At the microeconomic level the Department of Commerce has a variety of programs intended to promote exports in the absence of subsidies. Structural approaches are also available. For example, an alternative to existing export promotion programs is the formation of Japanese-style trading companies that would facilitate industry cooperation for the purpose of exportation as well as providing marketing and financing support for companies that have found it prohibitively costly to develop their own export capabilities. For example, in March 1982 General Electric announced that it would start a trading company to assist small- and medium-sized companies to export. The Webb–Pomerene Act allows some industries to cooperate for export purpose, but since its antitrust exemption has been narrowly interpreted (see [11]), the Congress enacted the Export Trading Company Act of 1981 [17] to facilitate the formation of export trading companies. Most of these measures have advantages over the Eximbank direct credit programs in that they involve less government direction of resources to specific industries and firms.

The political support for export promotion is often articulated in terms of its effect on unemployment. For example, in a letter to President Reagan supporting increases in the Eximbank authorization to enable the Bank to respond to foreign concessionary export financing, Senator Heinz stated [18]

> In order to take advantage of foreign export credit support, U.S. companies are likely to adopt one or more of the following strategies: (1) a shift to foreign procurement for major components of large capital goods; (2) long-term, off-shore subcontractor relationships, particularly in the case of airframe and air-craft engine manufacturers, and, (3) a shift to off-shore facilities for entire proj-ects, which many multinational manufacturing and construction companies already have and more are likely to acquire.
>
> What these likely corporate strategies add up to is a significant loss of U.S. jobs and tax revenues. Ironically, although large corporations are recipients of the majority of Eximbank support, it is the smaller U.S. subcontractors who are likely to be hurt the most. Boeing, for example, placed nearly $6 billion in subcontracts for parts and equipment to 3500 subcontractors and suppliers in 44 states during 1979. Approximately $3 billion of those purchases were for foreign aircraft sales.
>
> The Congressional Budget Office has estimated that every $1 billion in ex-port sales generates 40,000 to 50,000 jobs. The complement to that calculation is that every 50,000 unemployed Americans costs the Treasury $1 billion in lost revenue and transfer payments [p. 113].

Such arguments have considerable public appeal, and while they focus only on the direct effects of exports, public support for export promotion can be expected to persist.

One argument against the use of the Eximbank as a means of reducing U.S. unemployment is that the industries supported by Eximbank credits primarily produce high-technology capital assets. Employees in these industries tend to be higher skilled than the average for the United States, so greater exports by those industries will disproportionately increase the demand for highly skilled labor and have a much smaller effect on structural unemployment. Cruse and Wigg report, for example, that "In FY1974, over 80 percent of Eximbank's direct credits went to the industrial power and transportation sectors—all areas of substantial high-level labor skills [5, p. 65]." According to Boeing "The airplane manufacturing industry requires considerable skill of its workers, in the factories, as well as in the laboratories and offices. Commercial jetliners are not mass produced—they are custom built. Consequently, average airplane wages are consistently 20% to 25% higher than manufacturing wages generally. This higher wage rate reflects the greater amount of experience, training, and productive ability possessed by airplane workers [19, p. 522]." Boeing reported the following distribution of aircraft industry workers:

Category	Percentage
Unskilled	5
Semiskilled	17
Skilled	26
Factory foreman	4
Professional and management	13
Engineering, technical and scientific	27
Office/clerical	8

To the extent that Eximbank credits primarily raise the wages of engineers and highly skilled hourly workers, progress in reducing unemployment by expanding Eximbank export financing is less than might be expected.

Although Eximbank financing increases employment in the supported sectors to the extent that additional exports result, the net effect on employment is unclear. Furthermore, if specific government programs are to be adopted to alleviate unemployment, support of more labor intensive industries such as housing would likely be preferred. Employment objectives thus do not provide a sufficient justification for Eximbank programs.

V. Maintaining U.S. Product Dominance

Eximbank financing has also been supported as a means of maintaining U.S. product dominance in high technology industries, such as commercial jet aircraft, nuclear power, and telecommunications. For the United States to remain a leader in the development of new technologies, it will be necessary to have sufficient volume to make research and development expenditures remunerative. Although U.S. industries allocate resources to research and development on the basis of anticipated profitability, many foreign firms receive direct government subsidies to support their research and development activities. France, for example, has a policy of supporting its capital goods industries, both by subsidizing research and development and by subsidizing the financing of exports in order to increase total sales and contribute to the recovery of research and development expenditures. Export financing may be a relatively inexpensive means of increasing sales volume in high technology industries when foreign demand is more price elastic than is domestic demand, but if the objective is to promote research and development, direct means of support may be more efficient.

If the Bank has been following a policy of supporting certain high technology industries, the chosen industries can be identified by its financing activities. In FY1980 the sectors receiving the most support from the Bank's direct credit program were aircraft and electric power which received 41 and 31%, respectively, of the dollars authorized. In FY1981 nearly half the direct credits supported aircraft exports and 15% supported exports of power equipment. These two sectors have traditionally been the largest recipients of Eximbank support, although there is no evidence of explicit Bank policy of support for these industries.

If the United States adopts an explicit policy of supporting certain high technology industries, one alternative for their selection is for the government to make the choices based on criteria provided by Congress. Such a procedure might involve the submission of applications for support with review and selection by a government agency with the Eximbank playing a role in the financing of the exports from those industries. Whereas there is considerable disagreement about whether the government should play a role in revitalizing declining industries, in supporting high technology industries, or in directing resources for other purposes, economic theory does not recommend such a role for government unless there are market imperfections that inhibit the efficient allocation of resources. In a free enterprise economy the burden of proof should rest on those who favor government intervention to demonstrate that it would be beneficial and, in the absence of an explicit policy enacted by Congress, pressure to support high technology industries does not provide a justification for the programs of the Eximbank.

An alternative to direct government intervention in support of high technology industries would be to rely on market forces to determine which industries are to be supported given sector-neutral incentives provided by the government. This might be implemented by providing a subsidy or tax credit for research and development, for the export of new products, or for increases in the volume of exports of existing products. If such policies were adopted, any role for the Eximbank would have to be neutral across industries. For example, the Bank could provide guarantees and insurance for political and certain commercial risks, perhaps restricted to exports to developing countries.

One potential benefit from government export financing is that U.S. consumers could benefit to the extent that additional export sales result in lower costs that are passed on in the form of lower domestic prices. Aircraft manufacturers for example, have argued that the price of aircraft to domestic airlines would be substantially higher if the export volume were not available to enable manufacturers to realize economies of scale and to spread the fixed costs associated with the development of an aircraft model over a greater volume. Although this argument has some validity, it does not necessarily justify concessionary export financing. An obvious alternative would be to subsidize domestic sales in order to obtain the same cost economies while keeping the subsidy within the United States. The ability to achieve the same cost economies through domestic subsidization, however, may be limited by the elasticity of domestic demand. If foreign demand is more elastic than U.S. demand, export subsidization may provide greater cost decreases for the same subsidy. This issue will be explored in more detail in Chapter 7. It should be recalled, however, that the United States typically does not provide subsidies to decreasing cost industries in order to obtain lower costs and prices.

VI.   Concessionary Export Financing as Aid

Since concessionary export financing provides a subsidy to the importing country, some exporting countries have justified their financing as a means of providing aid. However, Deputy Treasury Secretary R. T. McNamar, speaking for the Treasury, characterized this argument as follows: "many industrialized countries are promoting their own mercantilist trade policies under the banner of aid to LDC's to mask the intent to support inefficient industries [12, p. 3]." Mr. Moore offered a different interpretation based on the political problems faced by developed countries in providing aid [15].

> As to developing countries, while the United States does not share this position, there is a position held by a number of countries that they cannot in their legislatures get sufficient bilateral aid programs adopted and that they want, therefore, to extend favorable and somewhat concessional credits to developing countries. The U.S. position is to support strongly doing this on a multilateral basis rather than through export credits [pp. 86–87].

Aid is in principle to be allocated on the basis of need and is intended for structural purposes, whereas export credits are primarily allocated on the basis of commercial demand and hence flow disproportionately to the industrialized and the higher income developing countries. For example, as the data on Eximbank direct credits and exposure by OECD income categories presented in Table 2.6 indicate, only 9.8% of the direct credits and 6.9% of the exposure are accounted for by the lowest income countries. Although 20.5% of the exposure is associated with lower-middle-income countries, 64% of that amount is represented by two countries,

Korea and the Philippines. In FY1981, 23% of the direct credits went to Canada with another 16% to Australia, the United Kingdom and Japan. Mexico, Nigeria, Korea, Israel, and Brazil accounted for another 33%. Table 3.3 is reproduced from the CBO report on the Eximbank, and as the report states [2]

> Eximbank loans are more concentrated in Europe than is foreign aid, and do not bear much relation to the pattern of foreign aid disbursements in areas outside Europe. Eximbank loans are not distributed in the way that the Congress and the Administration have jointly agreed to distribute the existing block of foreign assistance [p. 20].

The issue of concessionary export financing as a component of aid also arises in the context of the U.S. response to foreign mixed credits that combine aid and officially supported export financing. Former Assistant Treasury Secretary C. Fred Bergsten has argued against combining Eximbank export financing with foreign aid [16]:

> First, an export credit program should be viewed as a commercial program designed to facilitate exports through assumption, by the government, of various credit risks private creditors are unwilling to take. Export credit programs should not be seen as a substitute for genuine aid. If countries wish to increase the aid they give LDCs, they should do it through programs that directly benefit the LDCs rather than their own exporters.
>
> Second, the main beneficiaries of official export credits are the richer LDCs, such as Korea and Mexico, and the intermediate category countries such as the nations of Eastern Europe. These nations do not require aid nearly as much as countries that have low per capita incomes, if they need it at all.
>
> Third, the sectors that benefit from official export credits are not necessarily the ones that most benefit the poorest segments of an LDC economy. The exports tend to be capital-intensive manufactured goods, while the truly poor people need help in more basic areas such as agriculture.
>
> Finally, the World Bank, the regional development banks, the International Monetary Fund and bilateral assistance agencies are far more efficient and effective in addressing development and balance of payment problems than are official export credit agencies. The purposes of the two sets of agencies should not be confused [pp. 152–153].

If aid is to be given, the most efficient means of providing that aid is to extend direct grants to the recipient country perhaps tied to the purchase of U.S. goods. This efficiency argument may be politically naive because of the difficulty in obtaining legislative approval for aid budgets, but back-door aid in the form of concessionary export financing is both transparent and inappropriate. Although the Eximbank authorization is not viewed as a component of the aid budget, in the budgetary process that authorization is considered in conjunction with the foreign assistance budget. This grouping tends to confuse the quite separate purposes of

TABLE 3.3

Distribution of U.S. Economic Assistance and Eximbank Loans, by Region, Fiscal Years 1962–1979 (Percentage of Annual Totals)[a]

	1962–1976		1977		1978		1979	
	Economic assistance	Eximbank loans	Economic assistance	Eximbank loans	Economic assistance	Eximbank loans	Economic assistance	Eximbank loans
Near East and South Asia	38.2	11.4	63.5	2.8	59.5	2.3	63.8	8.9
Latin America	19.4	22.0	9.3	21.1	8.9	32.9	11.1	15.0
East Asia	28.7	20.6	9.0	33.2	8.7	38.8	8.7	40.1
Africa	10.3	5.6	11.1	19.8	13.9	19.1	14.8	16.2
Europe	2.1	32.6	4.1	21.5	9.0	5.9	1.5	18.7
Canada	0.0	1.8	0.0	0.1	0.0	0.8	0.0	0.3
Oceania	1.3	6.0	3.0	1.4	0.1	0.3	0.2	0.8
Total[b]	100.0	100.0	100.0	100.0	100.0	100.0	100.0	100.0

[a] Source: Agency for International Development, *U.S. Overseas Loans and Grants and Assitance from International Organizations, Obligations and Loan Authorizations, July 1, 1945–September 30, 1979.* Reproduced from [2].

[b] Detail may not add to totals due to rounding.

export financing and aid and embroils the Bank unnecessarily in the politics of foreign aid. For example, the 1980 authorization for the Bank was delayed in the Congress for almost the entire 1980 fiscal year because of the political debate over foreign aid. As a result, the Chamber of Commerce of the United States [3] has argued that the Bank's authorization should be separated from the foreign assistance budget. Whatever the budgetary treatment, Eximbank programs cannot be justified as a form of aid.

VII. Meeting Foreign-Subsidized Export Financing

As foreign official export financing has expanded and the concessions have increased, the Bank's programs increasingly have been rationalized as a necessary response to foreign concessionary export financing. This foreign financing is viewed as a capital market imperfection, and the Eximbank direct credit program is thus justified, it is argued, as a response to that imperfection. In contrast to the capital market imperfections considered in Section II, however, this imperfection is not a structural characteristic of the international capital markets but instead is a result of strategies chosen by other trading countries. Matching foreign concessionary export financing thus has been justified on three grounds: (1) fairness to U.S. exporters, (2) avoiding temporary dislocations in U.S. industries, and (3) as a component of a strategy to convince other nations to cease their export financing subsidization.

If the United States does not respond to concessionary export financing provided by foreign countries, foreign firms in the supported sectors will gain market share relative to U.S. firms. If the United States were to match that financing, however, U.S. firms would be able to maintain the same share that they would otherwise have had in the absence of the foreign credits. Supporters of the Bank's direct credit program thus argue that matching is fair to U.S. exporters and should be continued on those grounds. Furthermore, the failure to match would allow foreign governments to dictate the scale of competing U.S. export industries, which is contrary to U.S. principles.[4] For example, in cases in which exporters in

---

[4] David Copley, Treasurer of Fluor Corporation, described a case in which, even though Fluor was the successful bidder, the work was sourced abroad because of officially supported export financing [14].

In 1976, Fluor applied for support for a petrochemical project in Korea. Eximbank was very restrictive regarding Korea at that time. Even though both Fluor

the United States compete for a sale in a third country against a foreign competitor backed by concessionary export financing, matching by the United States would result in a subsidy to the importer and a cost to U.S. taxpayers. Not responding, however, would result in a loss in exports and a reduction in employment in the United States in the short run. Even if exchange rates were to adjust quickly to offset this effect, the subsidization offered by other countries, unless matched, would distort the allocation of resources within the United States, resulting in underinvestment in export industries that compete against subsidized exports from other countries. Avoiding such distortions by matching foreign concessionary export financing has been a principal rationale for Eximbank programs.

When foreigners are willing to subsidize imports to the United States, the United States benefits, just as when the United States subsidizes exports through concessionary financing the United States bestows a gift on the citizens of the importing country and imposes costs on U.S. taxpayers. If the subsidies provided were permanent, the United States would be able to reallocate resources from competing with foreign subsidized exports to other industries where those resources could more valuably be employed. Similarly, if permanent export subsidies were offered in support of sales to third countries, the United States would be better off by reallocating resources away from competing industries than matching the subsidies. The danger in this policy is that the foreign country may cease the subsidization once the U.S. has withdrawn resources from its industries that compete with the foreign subsidized exports.[5] In this case, the U.S. would be forced to reallocate resources to those industries at some cost. As the CBO report states, ''Whether the United States benefits from matching a temporary subsidy depends on whether the costs of subsidized competing in the short run are outweighed by the benefits of avoiding the costs of shifting U.S. production factors first out and then back into the export market [2, p. 8].'' Uncertainty about whether foreign

---

and our prospective client wanted to place the work in one of our U.S. Engineering Offices, with U.S. Equipment Procurement, the job was shifted to the United Kingdom where ECGD (the U.K. export financing agency) was able to offer financing support. Even though Fluor was still able to win the job by doing the engineering, procurement and project management work in our London Engineering Office, the U.S. lost almost $200 million in equipment procurement and other services [p. 161].

[5] Laffer [10] goes even further in arguing that if a foreign country wishes to subsidize exports to the United States, the United States should purchase the subsidized good, hold it, and resell it once the subsidizing country has decided to cease transferring its wealth to foreigners.

concessionary financing is permanent or temporary makes this determination complicated and has caused U.S. policymakers to prefer matching foreign concessionary export financing.

Given the substantial cost of matching the export subsidization provided by foreign governments through concessionary export financing and the cost of reallocating resources within the United States, an appropriate U.S. strategy would be to match their financing in order to deny an advantage to foreign exporters and to persuade them to agree to an enforceable international arrangement to eliminate concessionary financing. Whereas this strategy may be the best U.S. response to foreign concessionary export financing, it would be naive to expect foreign countries not to subsidize their exports through other means if they believe that that serves their interests. Matching has in recent years been the cornerstone of the U.S. strategy to reach an agreement to eliminate export financing subsidization, and this and other U.S. strategies to deal with foreign concessionary export financing will be evaluated in the final chapter.

VIII. Conclusions

From an economic efficiency viewpoint government intervention to deal with a market imperfection may be justified if that intervention results in efficiency gains that exceed its cost. There is no necessary economic justification, however, for intervening in international capital markets solely to overcome market deficiencies. The unwillingness of private lenders to extend credits to foreign importers does not justify the government assumption of risks that private lenders reject. Even if the government were, because of its risk-spreading ability, able to bear risks more efficiently than could private markets, it does not follow that foreign risks should be assumed before domestic risks. Capital market deficiencies thus do not provide a justification for the direct credit programs of the Bank. Since, however, political risks are associated with export financing that are not associated with domestic credits, government intervention in the form of insurance and guarantee programs may be warranted.

Arguments that attempt to justify the Bank's credit programs as a means of improving the balance of payments and stimulating employment, as a form of aid, or as a means to support high technology industries are not persuasive since export credit programs are not as appropriate as other alternatives to achieve such objectives. Unemployment, for example, could be stimulated more effectively by allocating resources to industries that are more labor intensive than those supported by the Eximbank.

Also, the allocation of export financing does not correspond to an appropriate allocation of aid, and concessionary export financing is only one means, and perhaps not the most efficient means, of supporting high-technology industries. With a system of floating exchange rates, support of exports can improve the balance of payments at the margin, but in the long run productivity, inflation rates, and relative prices will determine exchange rates and the terms of trade.

The preceding analysis leads to the conclusion that while there may be an economic justification for the guarantee and insurance programs of the Eximbank, no such justification for the Bank's direct credit program is evident. A strategic rationale for that program, however, can be found as an element of a strategy of matching foreign concessionary export financing in order to persuade other countries to agree to eliminate their concessionary financing. Support for the Eximbank manifests itself ultimately through the political process, and an analysis of the demand for and the supply of the Bank's programs may provide a better explanation for those programs than does an analysis of market imperfections and economic objectives. The next chapter provides such an analysis.

References

1. Ackerlof, George. "The market for 'lemons': qualitative uncertainty and the market mechanism," *Quarterly Journal of Economics* **84,** (August 1970), 488–500.
2. Congressional Budget Office (CBO), "The Benefits and Costs of the Export–Import Bank Loan Subsidy Program," Washington, D.C., 1981.
3. Chamber of Commerce of the United States, "Recommendations for Alternative Budgetary Treatment for the U.S. Export–Import Bank," 1980.
4. Cruse, James and Whitsitt, Susan "Eximbank in the 1980's," unpublished paper, Washington, D.C., 1981.
5. Cruse, James C. and Wigg, David G. "The Role of the Eximbank in U.S. Export and East–West Trade." In *U.S. Financing of East–West Trade* (P. Marer, ed.) Indiana University, Bloomington, Indiana, 1975, pp. 49–74.
6. Export–Import Bank, "Review of Policies and Programs," unpublished paper, Washington, D.C., 1980.
7. Export–Import Bank, "Report to the U.S. Congress on Export Credit Competition and the Export–Import Bank of the United States," Washington, D.C., 1980.
8. Export–Import Bank, "Report to the Congress on Bank's Budget Estimates for Fiscal Year Ending September 30, 1982 (Based on the March 10, 1981 Revisions)," Washington, D.C., 1981.
9. General Accounting Office (GAO), "Financial and Other Constraints Prevent Eximbank From Consistently Offering Competitive Financing For U.S. Exports," ID-80-16, Washington, D.C., 1980.
10. Laffer, Arthur B., "Statement of Arthur B. Laffer," Hearings, Subcommittee on International Finance, U.S. Senate, Part 4, Washington, D.C., 1978, pp. 441–446.

11. Larson, David A. "An economic analysis of the Webb–Pomerene Act," *Journal of Law and Economics,* **13,** (October 1970), 461–500.
11a. Morgan Guarantee Bank, "World Financial Markets," New York, 1982.
12. McNamar, R. T., "Free Trade or the 'New Protectionism': The Choice of the 1980's," *Department of the Treasury News,* Washington, D.C., 1981.
13. U.S. Department of the Treasury, "Report on the Additionality of U.S. Export–Import Bank Programs in Fiscal Year 1978," Washington, D.C., 1980.
14. U.S. Senate, Subcommittee on International Finance, Committee on Banking, Housing, and Urban Affairs, "Hearing on Export–Import Bank Program and Budget," U.S. Government Printing Office, Washington, D.C., 1980.
15. U.S. Senate, Committee on Banking, Housing and Urban Affairs, "Hearings on Ansett Loan and Export–Import Aircraft Financing Policies," U.S. Government Printing Office, Washington, D.C., 1980.
16. U.S. Senate, Subcommittee on International Finance, Committee on Banking, Housing, and Urban Affairs, "Hearing on Competitive Export Financing," U.S. Government Printing Office, Washington, D.C., 1980.
17. U.S. Senate, Committee on Banking, Housing, and Urban Affairs, "Hearings on Export Trading Company Act of 1981," Washington, D.C., 1981.
18. U.S. Senate, Subcommittee on International Finance and Monetary Policy, Committee on Banking, Housing, and Urban Affairs, "Hearings on International Affairs Functions of the Treasury and the Export Administration Act," Washington, D.C., 1981.
19. U.S. Senate, Subcommittee on International Finance, Committee on Banking, Housing, and Urban Affairs, "Hearings on Export Policy," Washington, D.C., 1978.
20. Wallen, Axel. "Annex I: Interest Rates and Weighting Systems for Determining Average Interest Rates," OECD, Paris, 1980. Reproduced in [16, pp. 45–52].

4

The Supply and Demand
for Government-Supported
Export Financing

I. Introduction

In the previous chapter a number of economic rationales for Eximbank export financing programs were examined, but in the absence of
foreign officially supported export financing those economic rationales do
not provide a justification for, and hence an explanation of, the continuation of the loan programs of the Bank. Such an explanation is more likely
to be found in an analysis of the demand for and the supply of government-supported financing of international trade. The potential benefits
from such financing would be expected to generate a demand for the
continuation of the Bank's programs, and the ability of the beneficiaries to
supply political support for those programs may provide a better explanation of the durability of Eximbank programs than do the economic rationales. An analysis of the demand and supply of government financing for
international trade may also explain why only exports and not imports are
supported and why nearly all of the Bank's lending is provided in the form
of long-term direct credits.

Whereas both U.S. importers and U.S. exporters would be expected
to have a demand for concessionary financing and while the Export–
Import Bank Act states that the Bank is to "facilitate exports and im-

ports," the programs of the Bank have only supported exports.[1] As Chairman Draper stated, "The perception is [that the Bank] has something to do with exports and imports, but actually, we have nothing to do with imports. We don't encourage imports. We are trying to facilitate exports [*San Francisco Chronicle*, August 16, 1981]." This asymmetric support cannot be explained in terms of the demand of the potential beneficiaries, since importers and their customers could have as much to gain from concessionary financing as would exporters. Consequently, the explanation for the restriction of the Bank's support to exports must be found in the relative abilities of export and import industries to achieve the supply of concessionary financing through the political process.

The Bank's principal financing program is the long-term direct-credit program which primarily supports the exports of long-lived capital assets. One possible explanation for this focus is that the Congress and the Eximbank have chosen which exports to support based on capital market imperfections and deficiencies or on the presence of foreign concessionary export financing. Because capital market imperfections and deficiencies can be dealt with through the use of guarantees and insurance, these rationales do not explain the focus on the long-term direct-credit program. Although the presence of foreign concessionary export financing may explain that program either in terms of equity to U.S. exporters or as a component of a strategy to achieve an agreement to prohibit concessionary financing, it does not explain why more U.S. concessionary financing is not provided for medium-term transactions that face foreign concessionary financing. This chapter is intended to broaden the analysis of the determinants of the Eximbank's financing programs using the economic theory of regulation introduced by Stigler [10] and extended by Peltzman [6], Posner [7], and Stigler [11] as a framework for analyzing the demand and supply for government intervention in the financing of international trade.

II. The Demand for and Supply of Government Financing of International Trade

A. Export Support versus Import Support

When the United States was running a balance of payments deficit under a system of fixed exchange rates, export industries had a greater

---

[1] Japan has used government assistance for the import of raw materials, such as ores and metals, for input to their steel and metal refining industries, much of whose output is exported.

ability than import industries to supply political support for the Bank because increases in exports would reduce the deficit, strengthen the dollar, and increase employment, whereas increased imports would have the opposite effects. Consequently, export industries, both firms and labor, were able to demonstrate directly that government financial support promoted national objectives. Even with a system of floating exchange rates, the support for exports can be given the same justification even if that justification pertains primarily to the short-run, direct effects of increased exports and less so to the long-run effects. For example, during a period of high unemployment and balance of payments deficits, even under a system of freely fluctuating exchange rates, exporters would have an important political advantage over importers whose imports might compete with U.S. produced goods and exacerbate the unemployment and balance of payment problems.

Importers could also argue that government financing of imports benefits the United States, since such financing would make goods available to U.S. consumers at prices lower than would otherwise prevail in the absence of that support. Furthermore, with government-supported import financing Americans would be expected to capture the major portion of the subsidy provided, whereas concessionary export financing would transfer a major portion of the subsidy to foreigners. Consequently, both importers and exporters would be expected to have a demand for government financing, and both could attempt to justify that support by the benefits it produces.

Although both importers and exporters could in principle advance arguments about the benefits to the United States from government financing, importers may be more reluctant than exporters to do so. If U.S. importers were to request concessionary import financing, that financing would likely be viewed as a direct subsidy and, given the reluctance of the Congress to subsidize business directly, would undoubtedly be granted only with restrictions. For example, importers might be required to pass the subsidy on to consumers in the form of lower prices in exchange for financing support, which would remove the incentive for importers to seek that financing. Although consumers might be expected to have a demand for concessionary import financing that resulted in lower prices, the difficulty in organizing their efforts to supply political support for that financing would in all likelihood outweigh their potential gains.

Concessionary export financing does not constitute a direct subsidy to exporters but instead benefits exporters indirectly through the opportunity provided to charge a more favorable export price and through the effect on the scale of their operations. Since the benefits accrue indirectly to exporters, export financing would be expected to face fewer restrictions than would import financing.

In addition to the possibility that government import financing might carry restrictions that would deny benefits to importers, importers are not able to buttress their demands with the economic rationales examined in the previous chapter. For example, exporters can argue that political and commercial risks and term problems impede the financing of U.S. exports, but those factors do not pertain to imports. Without the ability to rely on economic justifications for support, importers are in a weak position to generate political support for government import financing. Consequently, government financing support for international trade is likely to continue to be denied to imports.

B. The Demand for Export Financing

To assess the demand for government-provided concessionary export financing, the value of that financing and its distribution must be determined. The value to U.S. exporters is a function of the magnitude of the subsidy provided, the share of the subsidy exporters capture, and any indirect effects of that financing. An expression for the subsidy resulting from concessionary financing has been presented by Horvath [3, 4] and is used in Chapter 6 to estimate the subsidy provided by the Bank's direct credit programs for fiscal years 1979, 1980, and 1981. The subsidy is, of course, greater the lower is the Eximbank interest rate and the higher are market interest rates. When the Eximbank interest rate is concessionary, the subsidy is also greater as the term of the credit or the moratorium or grace period on repayment increase. Since the interest rate and the cover provided by the Eximbank are not, by policy, functions of the value of the export, the subsidy is directly proportional to the amount of the financing provided. Consequently, exporters of long-lived, high-valued assets would be expected to have a greater demand for government-supported financing than would other exporters and hence would have the strongest incentive to support the Bank politically.

The greatest demand for government-supported concessionary financing would thus be found in industries with products with high values and long economic lives. Since the locus of this demand corresponds to two perceived capital market deficiencies, large-project and long-term financing, discussed in the preceding chapter, those with the most to gain from concessionary export financing would be able to establish the credibility of their claims for Eximbank support by reference to alleged failures in the international capital markets. To the extent, however, that those failures are due to political risks and to certain commercial risks not associated with domestic loans, the opponents of the Bank's direct credit program can argue that insurance and guarantee programs would be sufficient government responses.

The cost structure of the industry also affects the benefit from Eximbank export financing. Industries characterized by decreasing average costs due to economies of scale or learning curve effects, even if only in the short run, would be expected to gain more, other things equal, from government-supported export financing than would industries characterized by constant or increasing average costs. Increasing-cost industries would also experience increased profits from the government stimulation of their exports, although those profits could be dissipated by entry into the industry or captured by factor inputs with inelastic supply. Consequently, decreasing-cost export industries and increasing-cost industries that have substantial barriers to entry and elastic factor supplies would be expected to have the greatest demand for Eximbank financing.

Although the potential benefits to exporters of concessionary export financing are evident, there are costs associated with seeking that support. The information required for an application for an Eximbank preliminary commitment is substantial and may discourage applications from exporters who would receive only a small subsidy from that financing. In particular, exporters of low-valued goods and/or goods requiring relatively short-term financing might not receive a subsidy sufficient to cover the cost associated with applying. These costs thus may screen some exports from Eximbank financing and concentrate export financing in support of high-valued, long-lived assets. Of course, as the difference between the market rate of interest and the Eximbank rate increases, a broader range of exports would potentially benefit from Eximbank financing.

The number of foreign customers also affects the cost of seeking concessionary export financing. If there are few customers so that sales tend to involve negotiations and the tailoring of offers to the customer's particular needs, the U.S. exporter would have relatively low costs for having its customers apply to the Bank for financing.[2] Furthermore, export product offers and financing would be easier to arrange, and trade-offs between price, financing, and performance features would provide more opportunities for the exporter to gain from the availability of the financing. If customers are numerous so that sales tend to involve more standard configurations of equipment and list prices, the opportunities for trade-offs and negotiations are more limited. Furthermore, the U.S. exporter would have higher costs of assisting its customers in applying to

---

[2] U.S. exporters often assist foreign importers with the applications for Eximbank financing, so they bear a part of the cost.

the Bank. Of course, the greater the value of the export, the lower are those costs relative to the potential benefits.

The demand for concessionary export financing also depends on how the subsidy is shared between exporters and foreign importers. On the one hand, if the exporter were able to increase the export price by an amount equivalent to the subsidy, the exporter would capture the entire subsidy. On the other hand, if the market for the export good were perfectly competitive, additional exports would result and the foreign importer would capture all of the subsidy. In the former case, the concessionary export financing would have no effect on the quantity of the good exported, on employment, or on U.S. export earnings. Consequently, whereas the exporter would have a demand for such financing, he would not likely be able to raise broad support from labor or those concerned with the balance of payments.

When the supported exports are additional, the output of the exporter would increase as would employment and U.S. export earnings. Although the exporter might realize greater profit from the higher output, those gains could soon be dissipated by the forces of competition or shared with the factors of employment. Even though the exporter would gain only marginally in such cases, broad support for Eximbank export financing would be expected from labor and those concerned with the balance of payments. The exporter's incentive to seek Eximbank financing thus tends to be negatively correlated with the support that can be expected from labor and from the proponents of government efforts to improve the balance of payments.

Neither of these two extremes is likely to be characteristic of the export sectors supported by the Bank, however, and the position of an export industry between these two extremes depends on the elasticities of demand and supply for the product. The effect of an export financing subsidy on the export price is analyzed in Chapter 7, and for a competitive industry the elasticity of the export price with respect to the subsidy is shown to be an increasing function of the elasticity of demand when the supply function is upward-sloping. Export financing subsidization reduces the effective price of the product, which increases demand, and in an industry with an increasing supply function the export price must increase in order to induce the industry to satisfy the additional demand. The greater the elasticity of demand the greater is the additional demand generated by an export financing subsidy and hence the greater is the price increase and the resulting increase in profits of the exporter. The less elastic is the supply function the greater is the price increase required to induce the industry to satisfy the additional demand and hence the greater is industry profit. Consequently, competitive industries that face elastic demands and have inelastic supply functions would be expected to have a greater demand for concessionary export financing than would competitive industries with less elastic demand and more elastic supply.

Industries with decreasing average costs would also be expected to have a demand for concessionary export financing because the increase in output would reduce costs. These industries would also be expected to be concentrated because of the incentive for firms in the industry to attempt to cartelize the industry through mergers, parallel policies, or other collusive strategies, so individual producers would be expected to capture a substantial share of the subsidy provided by concessionary export financing.

If the Bank, however, is successful in restricting its credits to those cases in which the export would be lost to foreign competitors in the absence of Bank financing, the elasticity of demand for those supported exports would be expected to be relatively high and the importer would be expected to capture a large share of the subsidy.[3] If the U.S. industries facing highly elastic demand are concentrated, coordination of their political efforts would be relatively easy. Since they would also have the backing of labor and those concerned with the balance of payments, political support for government export financing would be expected to be most effective in concentrated industries that face an elastic export demand.

United States exporters facing competitors supported by foreign concessionary export financing also argue for Eximbank financing on equity grounds. Claims of unfair competition and predatory financing appeal to traditional concerns in the United States with unfair practices and hence meet with sympathy from Congress and the Executive branch. The equity claims appear to be both a prime factor in generating demand for export financing and an important rationale for the supply of that financing.

Similarly, U.S. firms that compete in the U.S. market with imports supported by foreign concessionary financing would be expected to demand matching financing in order to be able to compete on an equal footing with the foreign supplier. For example, Stephen Sohn, representing

---

[3] In preparation for a study of the importance of credit for the export of high technology products, SRI International [9] asked foreign airlines if they would agree to be interviewed about the basis for their choices among aircraft models. Of the 55 foreign carriers contacted by SRI, 40 responded and 20 of them agreed to provide information on the factors affecting their choices. (Two other carriers were uncertain about whether they would participate and 7 had not made a purchase during the period covered.) This willingness to participate may simply have been a reflection of a desire to contribute to such a study or it may have been a reflection of their gains from government export financing.

the United States Chamber of Commerce, stated in congressional testimony [15]:

> A U.S. manufacturer recently decided to purchase approximately $2 million worth of capital equipment. Potential suppliers existed in Europe and in the United States. We are told that the decision to purchase European equipment was made on the basis of financing.
>
> The cost to the U.S. importer was $8\frac{3}{4}$ percent per annum. A U.S. supplier competing for the sale could have arranged financing commercially, but at a rate of at least 15 percent per annum.
>
> Our primary point of this example is not that a U.S. supplier lost a domestic sale, but that a foreign supplier gained an export sale because of financing at lower than commercial rates of interest. Had the buyer been in a third country, our domestic supplier would presumably still have lost the sale, because 15 percent financing under the (Eximbank) discount loan program does not compare favorably with $8\frac{3}{4}$ percent financing [p. 165].

If an objective of the Eximbank is either to increase U.S. employment and improve the U.S. balance of payments or to be equitable to U.S. firms, providing financing to meet the foreign concessionary financing offered to a U.S. customer is as effective as providing matching financing for the hypothetical sale to the third country referred to by Sohn. As indicated in Section II,A, the direct subsidy to the U.S. customer resulting from subsidized financing in all likelihood explains why the Congress has not mandated that the Eximbank match concessionary financing offered to U.S. purchasers.

Except in the case of a perfectly competitive industry with constant returns to scale, concessionary export financing would be expected to affect the prices domestic consumers pay for the goods produced by the supported sectors. If long-run average costs are increasing or U-shaped and entry into the industry is not free or if factor supplies are inelastic, increased exports would result in increases in the domestic price of the export goods. If long-run average costs are decreasing because of economies of scale or learning curve effects, as they might be for the aircraft industry which has high fixed costs associated with the design and engineering of new aircraft models, an additional export would reduce costs and could reduce the domestic price.[4] Decreasing cost industries thus would be able to argue that support for their exports would benefit domestic consumers, whereas industries with increasing costs would have no basis for such an argument. Boeing, for example, has argued that its costs are 30–40% lower because of its exports. The customers of decreasing-cost industries would thus be expected to demand government export

---

[4] The effect on domestic prices is considered in Chapter 7.

financing for those industries unless the foreign importers were able to use the product to compete against the domestic users of that product. For example, concessionary financing of aircraft exports would give foreign airlines a cost advantage relative to U.S. airlines on international routes, so U.S. airlines might be expected to oppose that financing.

Commercial banks might also be expected to have a demand for government-supported export financing, particularly if there were capital market imperfections that impede the financing of international trade or that allow banks to participate with reduced risk. Testimony offered at congressional hearings, however, shows little direct evidence of such demand. This absence of direct support by commercial banks may reflect the extent of competition in international banking that denies them the opportunity to benefit from participation with the Eximbank in export financing, or it may indicate that Eximbank programs compete with commercial bank financing. While the latter would explain why commercial banks do not support the Eximbank before the Congress, it does not explain why commercial banks do not oppose it. The most plausible conclusion is that the Eximbank's programs do not compete directly with the programs of commercial banks and that the international capital markets are sufficiently competitive that banks are denied any significant excess return to their participation in financing Eximbank-supported exports.

C. The Supply of Government-Supported Export Financing

The ability to generate political support for the Eximbank depends on the stakes involved and the costs associated with organizing that support. The stakes may be sufficiently great for Boeing, for example, to participate regularly in the political process in support of the Bank. For most exporters, however, coordinated efforts may be more efficient. In general, the potential support would be a function of the number who benefit from the programs as well as the magnitude of the benefits. The effective support, however, would depend on the ability of the beneficiaries to coordinate their activities. This section is concerned with the factors that influence both the potential and effective support, and the next section addresses the opposition to that support.

A principal basis for the political support for export financing is the direct stimulation provided to U.S. employment and the hardship that would result from the withdrawal of that financing. Employment in export industries is identifiable, and individuals who could lose their jobs if that financing were discontinued can appeal to their elected representatives for continuation of that support. For example, during the 1978 hearings on the renewal of the Eximbank's charter, Boeing argued that "On the average over the past 2 years, therefore, about 100,000 U.S. employees owed their jobs directly to the export of commercial jets—or to the major spares, maintenance materials, and airplane modification services that resulted because of prior jetliner exports [12, p. 521]." By 1980 Boeing estimated that nearly 200,000 jobs resulted from aircraft exports [14, p. 178]. Furthermore, recognizing the Congressional concern for small business, Boeing stated that [12]:

> The DC-10 program, for example, is supported by more than 4,000 suppliers and subcontractors. And last year close to half of the DC-10 subcontract and supplier business (in dollar terms) was handled by minority and small businesses. About 85% of the firms supplying parts for the Lockheed L-1011 are small businesses (some 1,275 firms to be precise), and Boeing placed orders with 2,195 small businesses in 46 states during the 1975–76 time period in support of its jetliner programs [p. 518].

In its testimony Boeing included a 49-page list of its suppliers and their locations. McDonnell–Douglas adopted a similar approach by presenting projections of the employment associated with DC-9 and DC-10 aircraft exports for the 1977–1982 period [12, p. 898].

The concern with U.S. employment objectives suggests that industries that produce exclusively in the United States would have a greater ability to muster political support than would industries and firms that produce both in the United States and in foreign countries. Similarly, firms and industries that have a high percentage of value added in the United States would be expected to be able to generate more political support for assistance of their exports than would exports with a lower percentage of value added in the United States.

The ability to supply government export financing through the political process also depends on the cost of generating political support for the Bank.[5] Concentrated industries would have lower costs of coordinating their political activities than would unconcentrated industries and thus would be more likely to be successful in achieving the supply of government export financing. In particular, industries with decreasing long-run average costs or with substantial barriers to entry would be expected to be

---

[5] One means by which U.S. exporters express their support for and need for Eximbank financing is through the surveys conducted by the Bank as required by the act. The survey results are presented in the Bank's "Competitiveness Reports" made to the Congress and are analyzed in the next chapter. The most recent survey [2], for example, indicates that U.S. exporters not only support the Bank's programs but also argue strongly for increased financing by the Bank. Such surveys provide a low cost means of supplying political support for the Bank, but to the extent that they are viewed as self-serving, survey results would be expected to have only a limited impact.

more concentrated than other industries and would also have the most to gain from expanded exports.

The ability of an industry to coordinate its efforts to supply government export financing is also related to the commonality of interests of the firms in the industry. The more divergent the interests and positions of the firms the more difficult it would be for them to coordinate their activities in the political arena. Because the market shares and strengths of the three U.S. commercial jet aircraft manufacturers differ dramatically, those three firms might be expected to have dissimilar interests in supporting government export financing.[6] Eximbank support, however, is identical for all three U.S. manufacturers in cases in which they compete for foreign sales. Each can be viewed as competing with the Airbus, so the positions of the three are similar with respect to that financing. Because the potential gains from Eximbank financing of aircraft exports are substantial and their interests are parallel, although not identical, strong support from the aircraft industry would be expected in spite of the asymmetry of positions of the firms in the industry. The stakes of the three manufacturers, of course, differ according to the volume of their potential export sales.

A small company would in most cases not have an incentive to act on its own to supply support for the Eximbank because its size implies that its potential gain is small relative to the cost of supplying that support. Also, export industries with low concentration would be expected to have coordination difficulties that would impede their ability to obtain the supply of subsidized financing for their exports, but if they could organize, their numbers and geographic dispersion could give them considerable political influence. In such cases, means of reducing those costs would be sought through, for example, trade associations or other organizations that could serve a variety of purposes in addition to supporting the Eximbank. The National Association of Manufacturers and the United States Chamber of Commerce to some extent represent the interests of small companies and industries with low concentration and have offered testimony in congressional hearings pertaining to the Bank. However, because the Eximbank's direct credits have primarily supported the exports of long-lived capital assets which tend to be produced in concentrated industries, this potential strength has not been fully realized.

Low concentration industries have, however, sought other means to facilitate their exports. For example, unconcentrated industries, as well as concentrated industries, benefit from the tax deferrals available

---

[6] Lockheed announced in December 1981 that it would cease production of the L-1011, leaving the United States with only two commercial jet aircraft manufacturers.

through DISCs, and political support for that program has been strong and well organized. As a result of petitions by European governments, DISCs have been declared contrary to the GATT, but because of political pressure the Congress has not repealed the act granting the tax deferral. "Complicating the issue is the strong support that DISC has found in the American business community, as well as in Congress where earlier Carter Administration efforts to repeal it were defeated by heavy majorities. The Special Committee for United States Exports, a lobbyist group organized to preserve the DISC, has a membership of 1,800 companies and 80 trade associations (*New York Times,* December 25, 1980)."

As another example, the Webb–Pomerene Act [see 5] provides a limited antitrust exemption that permits industries to coordinate their activities for export purposes. The Export Trading Company Act of 1982 [6] passed by the Congress is intended to broaden the permissible activities of export trading companies and to allow commercial bank participation. Such legislative initiatives are most likely to be supported by industries with low concentration because of the difficulty those industries have in coordinating their political efforts to obtain direct government financial support. For example, both the Chamber of Commerce and the National Machine Tool Builders' Association testified in favor of the Export Trading Company Act.

Prior to October 1981, Bank policy restricted direct credits to exports of at least $5 million, which, in conjunction with its term policy, tended to focus support on long-lived, high valued assets. The $5 million limit may have been a response to the perceived need to finance large exports, but the more likely explanation is that it served to hold the demand for the Bank's financing, and its authorization requests to Congress, to a politically acceptable level. In addition, the congressional mandate to supplement and not compete with private capital focuses the Bank's direct credit programs on long-term financing, which commercial banks are less willing to provide. One explanation of the limited use of Eximbank programs by small business may simply be that those firms tend not to produce long-lived capital assets whose value and economic life would naturally fall under the limits for the Bank's direct credit program. The exports of small businesses tend to be eligible for the Bank's short-term and medium-term insurance, bank guarantee, and discount loan programs that carry small subsidies, if any. Since there is little subsidization, the demand for those programs would not be expected to be substantial, particularly in the case of exports to countries with low political risk. If a greater subsidy were provided on the Bank's medium-term financing program, the demand for financing under that program would increase, and small businesses would have a greater incentive to bear the organizational costs to mount a campaign to support the Bank's programs. This line of reasoning, however, does not explain why small businesses have not invested in organizing their political support to obtain concessionary Eximbank financing for medium-term transactions. Given that France and other countries provide substantial amounts of medium-term concessionary financing, an opportunity has existed to attempt to expand the Eximbank's program of meeting foreign concessionary financing.[7]

---

[7] This is particularly striking given the Bank's mandate to support small business as required by Section 2(b)(1)(B) of the Export–Import Bank Act [1]:

> the Bank shall give due recognition to the policy stated in section 2(a) of the Small Business Act that "the Government should aid, counsel, assist, and protect, insofar as is possible, the interests of small business concerns in order to preserve free competitive enterprise" and that in furtherance of this policy the Board of Directors shall designate an officer of the Bank who shall be responsible to the President of the Bank for all matters concerning or affecting small business concerns and who, among other duties, shall be responsible for advising small businessmen of the opportunities for small business concerns in the functions of the Bank and for maintaining liaison with the Small Business Administration and other departments and agencies in matters affecting small business concerns [p. 5].

The Bank has attempted to fulfill this mandate in a variety of ways other than by providing generous export financing as indicated by the comments of board member Margaret W. Kahliff [13]:

> Mr. Moore always says I'm a liaison to the small business community because I ran two small businesses and I'm one of the founders of the largest small business organization in the country which is called COSI of Cleveland. We have 3,000 members; we started with 50. So we really have a big meet.
>
> I have been involved in trying to help small business from Eximbank now for $3\frac{1}{2}$ years. I've participated in at least 30 small business conferences all over the country. We put in a hotline. We've advertised that widely, all over the country.
>
> If small business persons or even large business persons call on the hotline, we practically lead them by the hand, find out what it is they want to know, what it is we can do for them. Maybe they don't need financing; they just need to know about exporting. We take them to the Commerce Department. We take them to SBA. We take them to OPIC.
>
> We have had, I believe, about 10,000 calls on the hotline. And it has been in effect a little over 1 year. This is one of the things we have done.
>
> We did start the small business export policy in conjunction with FCIA. We have at this point more than 100 of those policies in effect. Now, they cannot use this policy if they had done business before with Eximbank or if they had exported more than $350,000 a year. So these are small exporters . . .
>
> We are doing something else at Eximbank. We're going to conduct our first trade mission with just small businessmen, and it will be next fall [pp. 92–93].

In recent years political pressure for expanded export financing for small firms has increased. The Chamber of Commerce has focused on the discount loan program which it views as "available to support smaller transactions, many of which are, or would be, undertaken by small- and medium-sized firms" [14, p. 165]:

> The cost of 5-year discount loans, when all fees are included, is something in excess of 15 percent per annum, as compared to a 5-year direct loan, which costs $7\frac{3}{4}$ percent per annum. . . .
>
> Eximbank must have the authorization and be directed to fully support discount loans. It is our belief that the United States should consistently tailor its export credit programs to meet foreign export finance competition. The goal is not to subsidize U.S. exporters, big or small, but simply to minimize the adverse effects of foreign governmental support programs which cost the United States export sales and to eventually return the world of export finance to commercial terms [14, pp. 165–166].

The National Association of Manufacturers has also supported an expansion of the Bank's discount loan program [15]:

> A careful look at a new system for rediscounting export paper (or an equivalent technique) offers promise as a broad institutional change of the type the U.S. economy could successfully use. It would be designed mainly to assist the export sector to cope with prolonged periods of inflation and credit stringency. . . .
>
> We would suggest that the subcommittee on International Finance request both the Eximbank and the Federal Reserve to file separate reports on the existing discount facilities of our foreign competition and invite them to make recommendations for improving the U.S. export financing systems, particularly by means of a broadly based discount or rediscount facility operated by the Federal Reserve System separately or in conjunction with the Eximbank [pp. 207–208].

These arguments may have been persuasive to Chairman Draper, whose experience as a venture capitalist may have predisposed him to be sympathetic to the concerns of small businesses. In October 1981 the Bank reduced its interest rate on discount loans from 14 to 12% and broadened its direct credit program to finance exports of $5 million or less on a preferential basis. Compared to the standard policy of a 12% interest rate and a maximum of 65% financing for exports of $5 million or more, the lower valued exports will receive a 10.75% interest rate and 85% financing. While these initiatives should increase the demand for Eximbank financing on the part of small- and medium-sized exporters, the reductions in the Bank's authorization will limit the availability of that financing. These initiatives should, however, strengthen the opposition to further reductions in the authorization.

III. The Response to Challenges to the Eximbank

Because of its concessionary interest rates, the expansion of its authorization through fiscal year 1981, and its promotional activities, the Bank has come under severe criticism from a variety of sources including Senator William Proxmire, OMB Director David Stockman, and former Chairman Stephen DuBrul (see [13, p. 72–73]). Reich [8] and Wilson [17] predict that when the benefits of government intervention are concentrated and the costs of that intervention are widely dispersed, the recipients of the benefits would act through the political system to preserve those benefits. This "client politics" would arise because the magnitude of the benefits are sufficient to provide the needed incentive, and the concentration of those benefits allows the beneficiaries to organize and coordinate their efforts with relative ease. The wide dispersion of the costs not only would make opposition difficult to organize and coordinate, but the per capita costs would be sufficiently small that the incentive to organize would be weak.

The direct cost of the Bank's concessionary financing is borne by U.S. taxpayers who are poorly organized and cannot be expected to oppose effectively the Bank in the political arena. As a result of federal budgetary concerns, taxpayer interests have been represented by the Reagan administration, which has opposed the subsidy provided in the Bank's financing. United States exporters, however, were prepared for this opposition, and key members of the Congress were generally committed to an expansion of the Bank's programs to meet foreign concessionary export financing. Their combined activities were successful in not only avoiding the FY1981 reductions in the Bank's authorization requested by the Reagan administration but in increasing the authorization by $500 million above that requested. Congress did, however, agree to the Reagan administration's authorization reduction for the Bank for FY1982 as a part of the overall reduction in federal expenditures.[8] Additional reductions for FY1983 are expected.

---

[8] Opposition to the reduction in the Eximbank authorization has been strong both in the Congress and in the business community. For example, an editorial in *Business Week* stated

The Reagan Administration's deep new cut in the Export–Import Bank's lending authority for fiscal 1983 is seriously short-sighted. One result will be that many thousands of jobs will be lost in this country, perhaps for good. Beyond that, this budget cut risks hobbling key high-technology industries whose health and growth are vital to the growth and prosperity, and even the security, of the U.S. in an increasingly competitive world [Reprinted from the January 25, 1982 issue of *Business Week* by special permission, © 1982 by McGraw-Hill, Inc., New York, N.Y. 10020. All rights reserved].

The indirect cost of Eximbank financing is borne by firms crowded out of the capital markets by the Bank's borrowing, and to the extent that the Bank's support of exports strengthens the dollar, costs are also borne by domestic industries that compete with imports to the United States and export industries that do not receive Eximbank support. Since the incidence of the indirect effects of crowding out, of import competition, and of exchange rate appreciation is determined by market forces, identification of those who bear the cost is difficult, and measuring their burden is even harder. For example, predicting the loss in employment in the U.S. textile or steel industries as a result of an appreciation in the value of the dollar caused by Eximbank programs is not an easy matter. Furthermore, many of the workers who have lost jobs in those industries because of that appreciation already have found jobs in other industries and hence would have little incentive to supply political opposition to export financing programs.

Critics of the Bank's programs could argue that the direct and indirect costs outweigh the benefits to the supported export industries and that exchange rate adjustments would act to offset the effects of curtailed Eximbank support, resulting in a more efficient allocation of U.S. resources. The acceptance of such reasoning requires considerable faith in economic theory and a willingness to count the gains to unidentifiable, and hence unrepresented, beneficiaries as equal to the losses to identifiable victims of that curtailed support. Furthermore, those critics would likely find few members of the Congress who believed that the appropriate policy for the United States is to lose exports to foreign suppliers supported by subsidized export financing and to rely on the depreciation of the dollar to offset those losses.

Opposition to the Bank arises at another level because of concern about whether the Bank's programs actually achieve their intended purposes. Advocates of the efficient allocation of Bank resources can be expected to apply economic criteria to the evaluation of Eximbank programs and to oppose those programs that do not meet the criteria. One criterion is the additionality of the supported exports, since if exports supported by the Bank would have been made in the absence of Bank financing, the resources committed to the support of those exports could have been returned to taxpayers or allocated where they would have a greater likelihood of increasing the level of economic activity.

The Bank has tended to give the benefit of the doubt to exporters who claim that they would lose exports in the absence of Eximbank financing, primarily because the evaluation of these claims is limited by the lack of information on the decision-making behavior of foreign importers. One program, however, for which the additionality of the supported exports was judged to be insufficient to warrant its continuation, was the Cooperative Financing Facility (CFF) program. The Treasury argued that the CFF program was equivalent to a line of credit that would be used to finance exports that would have been made in the absence of that financing, since foreign importers would simply request CFF financing for their customary imports. Pressure from the Treasury was sufficient to result in the elimination of the CFF program at the end of FY1981. Similar criticism has been directed to lines of credit, and the Bank has also discontinued their use.

Opponents of the Eximbank's program can also be expected to use economic analysis to identify the cost to U.S. taxpayers and to demand that the supporters of those programs demonstrate that the benefits received exceed that cost. However, to challenge effectively the Bank's concessionary financing using economic criteria, the cost of that financing to taxpayers and the likely impact of that financing on resource allocation in the U.S. economy must be determined. These issues will be considered in Chapters 6 and 7.

IV. Conclusions

The preceding analysis results in the following predictions:

1. The value of concessionary export financing would be greatest for high-valued exports with long economic lives produced in industries with barriers to entry and elastic factor supplies or in industries with decreasing average costs. The demand for that financing would be stronger in concentrated rather than unconcentrated industries and where there are relatively few customers.

2. The ability to obtain the supply of concessionary export financing would be greatest for concentrated industries, industries with decreasing average costs, industries that produce solely in the United States or have a high U.S. value added, and industries whose exports have a highly elastic demand so that additional exports would have a significant impact on employment. Industries facing competitors backed by foreign concessionary export financing would be able to generate political support for matching Eximbank financing by using equity arguments.

3. In cases in which concessionary export financing is currently provided, the recipient exporters would be expected to utilize the political

process to preserve the level of that financing when faced with attempts to reduce it or the concession provided.

These predictions are not sufficiently precise to allow the identification of industries that would be expected to receive Eximbank support, so no empirical test will be conducted. The disposition of the Bank's direct credits do, however, appear to be consistent with the first two predictions, and there is considerable evidence of participation of the aircraft and nuclear power industries in support of the Eximbank.

Perhaps the principal message of this chapter is that there is a demand for government-supported export financing for reasons other than the conventional public policy rationales analyzed in the previous chapter. Furthermore, the supply of this financing is not solely determined by a rational response to capital market imperfections and deficiencies or even to foreign concessionary financing. Instead that supply is likely to be influenced by the ability of U.S. exporters to coordinate their efforts to exert political support for government export financing and by the value of that financing to exporters and their employees relative to the costs of coordination.

References

1. Export–Import Bank, "The Export–Import Bank Act of 1945," Washington, D.C., 1979.
2. Export–Import Bank, "Report to the U.S. Congress on Export Credit Competition and the Export–Import Bank of the United States for the Period July 1, 1980, through December 31, 1980," Washington, D.C., 1981.
3. Horvath, Janos. "Are Eximbank Credits Subsidized: Toward an Empirical Analysis." In *U.S. Financing of East–West Trade*, (P. Marer, ed.). International Development Research Center, Bloomington, Indiana, 1975, pp. 105–137.
4. Horvath, Janos. "The Scope of the International Grants Economy: The Case of the Eximbank." In *Frontiers in Social Thought*, (M. Pfaff, ed.). North-Holland, Amsterdam, 1976, pp. 121–142.
5. Larson, David A. "An economic analysis of the Webb–Pomerene Act," *Journal of Law and Economics*, **13**, (October 1970), 461–500.
6. Peltzman, S. "Toward a more general theory of regulation," *Journal of Law and Economics*, **19**, (August 1976), 211–240.
7. Posner, R. A. "Theories of economic regulation," *Bell Journal of Economics*, **5** (Autumn 1974), 335–358.
8. Reich, R. B. "Warring critiques of regulation," **3**, *Regulation*, (January/February 1979), 37–42.
9. SRI International, "Assessment of U.S. Government Export Financing of High-Technology Products, Phase 1 Research Approach," Menlo Park, California, 1981.
10. Stigler, G. "The theory of economic regulation," *Bell Journal of Economics*, **2** (Spring 1971), 3–21.

11. Stigler, G. "Free riders and collective action," *Bell Journal of Economics,* 5 (Autumn 1974), 359–365.
12. U.S. Senate, Subcommittee on International Finance Committee on Banking, Housing, and Urban Affairs, "Hearings, Part 4: Export–Import Bank Authorization and Related Issues," Washington, D.C., 1978.
13. U.S. Senate, Committee on Banking, Housing, and Urban Affairs, "Hearings on Ansett Loan and Export–Import Aircraft Financing Policies," Washington, D.C., 1980.
14. U.S. Senate, Subcommittee on International Finance, Committee on Banking, Housing, and Urban Affairs, "Hearing on Export–Import Bank Programs and Budget," Washington, D.C., 1980.
15. U.S. Senate, Subcommittee on International Finance, Committee on Banking, Housing, and Urban Affairs, "Hearing on Competitive Export Financing," Washington, D.C., 1980.
16. U.S. Senate, Subcommittee on International Finance and Monetary Policy, Committee on Banking, Housing, and Urban Affairs, "Hearings: Export Trading Company Act of 1981," Washington, D.C., 1981.
17. Wilson, J. Q. (ed.). *The Politics of Regulation,* Basic Books, New York, 1980.

5

The Competitiveness
of Eximbank Programs

I. Introduction

In conjunction with its mandate to provide financing competitive with that provided by other countries, the Export–Import Bank Act requires the Bank to report regularly to the Congress on the competitiveness of its programs relative to those of other principal exporting countries. The Bank's assessment of its competitiveness is based on three factors: (1) the breadth of its programs relative to the programs offered by other countries, (2) the amount of support provided relative to that of competing countries, and (3) the win–loss record for the preliminary commitments it issues. For example, the Bank's October 1981 "Competitiveness Report" concluded "that in 1980, Eximbank was fully competitive in the short-term programs where repayment terms are 180 days or less, relatively competitive in the long-term program of over five years, and generally less competitive in the medium-term program of 181 days to five years [4, p. 1]." Because neither the United States nor other nations offers concessionary short-term export financing, the Eximbank insurance programs tend to be competitive except that the Eximbank does not provide inflation risk and exchange rate risk programs as do some countries. The medium-term financing provided by the Bank is not highly concessionary, unlike the medium-term financing of some other countries, so the United States is uncompetitive in this segment of export financing. The United

States provides concessionary long-term loans to meet those provided by other countries, so the Eximbank's long-term programs tend to be relatively competitive. "In order to sustain a relatively competitive position in its long-term program, however, the Bank was forced to offer more highly subsidized rates than ever before, with the amount of the subsidy increasing almost by three from 1979 to 1980 [4, p. 1]." The Bank's 1981 increase in its interest rate on direct credits was intended to reduce the subsidy but may also have lessened the competitiveness of that program.

The purpose of this chapter is to assess in more detail the competitiveness of the Bank's programs. The next section summarizes the programs offered by six major competitors of the United States, with a more detailed description presented in Appendix A. Section III provides an analysis of the level of support provided by those countries, and Section IV provides an analysis of the disposition of the preliminary commitments issued by the Bank. Surveys of exporters are analyzed in Section V, and conclusions are offered in the final section.

II. Official Export Financing Programs of Six Major Trading Countries

This section summarizes the scope of the export financing programs of Canada, France, Germany, Italy, Japan, and the United Kingdom, based on the program reviews presented in the Eximbank's 1980 and 1981 competitiveness reports [3, 4].[1]

A. Canada

The Export Development Corporation (EDC) of Canada provides long-term loans at fixed rates for exports with at least 80% Canadian content. EDC typically finances between 60 and 70% of the export value with commercial banks providing the remainder at times with an EDC guarantee [3].

> EDC's self-sustaining status, which requires it to maintain a lending spread sufficient to meet operating expenses and net claims, often raises the interest rate charged to unattractive levels. In the case of large export transactions considered to be in the national interest, EDC can extend credits at lower interest rates and charge the transactions to the Canadian government's account [p. 53].

---

[1] An earlier review of the programs of 21 OECD countries is presented in [10].

Because of the self-sustaining requirement, EDC tends not to be competitive in long-term financing with either the Eximbank or with the programs of a number of other countries.

EDC does not provide medium-term or short-term export credits but does offer insurance and guarantees to support exports with short- and medium-term repayment schedules. Both commercial and political risk coverage is provided at levels that appear to be similar to those of the Eximbank and FCIA. EDC also offers additional programs, including performance and bid bonds, foreign currency insurance, local cost support, parallel financing, and lines of credit. "As of the end of 1980, EDC had 15 lines of credit in place with a total of $4.9 billion available for allocation [4, p. 36]."

For 1979, EDC is authorized to have outstanding up to C$12.5 billion in export credits and C$13.5 billion of insurance and guarantee coverage. The insurance and guarantee programs provided by EDC are accounted for separately from the export loan programs and earned approximately C$3.4 million in 1979, indicating that these programs tend to be priced on a self-sustaining basis. In 1980 EDC earned a total of C$17.7 on its loan, insurance, and guarantee programs, which was down from C$34.7 million in 1979.

B. France

Long-term credits are extended by the Bank of France and the Banque Française du Commerce Exterior (BFCE) either through direct loans to buyers or by discounting commercial bank loans to French exporters. "BFCE supports its long-term preferential financing facility by issuing bonds; the Treasury covers the difference between the preferential rate (*taux de sortie*) and the bond interest rate [3, p. 60]." The preferential rates at which direct credits are extended tend to be the minimums provided in the OECD arrangement, so the French long-term credit programs provide an extremely large subsidy. In addition, the French utilize mixed credits, generally in accord with the conditions of the arrangement. "The most typical interest rate on the aid portion of the mixed credits extended in 1980 was 3.5 percent with a 20-year repayment. Mixed credits accounted for approximately 10 percent of all official export credit extended by France during 1980 [4, p. 43]."

The biggest difference between the export financing programs of France and those of the United States is that France provides highly concessionary financing for exports with repayment terms from 18 months to 7 years. This financing is viewed as an entitlement to French exporters, and both supplier and buyer credits are provided at fixed interest rates in accord with the terms of the arrangement. Medium-term credits are provided by commercial banks which have the right to rediscount the credits at BFCE at an interest rate of 4.5%. The proportion of each loan that can be discounted at this rate, however, varies in order to achieve the arrangement minimum interest rates. Commercial risk coverage from Compagnie Française d'Assurance pour le Commerce Extérieur (COFACE) is required for all supported transactions with a term beyond 3 years. "During 1980, COFACE insured medium-term (6 months to 5 years) insurance amounting to $12.2 billion, an increase of 17 percent from the amount of business insured from 1979 [4, p. 40]."

Financing for exports with repayment terms up to 18 months is not provided by the government, but COFACE does offer insurance and guarantees for both exporters and commercial banks. In 1979 COFACE provided short-term insurance coverage of $14.6 billion.

France also provides financing for foreign content, performance and bid bond guarantees, local cost support, and exchange risk insurance, and COFACE provides inflation insurance that "allows a French exporter to insure against production cost increases that exceed 6.5% annually [3, p. 64]." "In 1976, cost-escalation schemes cost France FFr2.2 billion ($460m)—equal to 15% of the value which benefited from them. By 1978, the bill had climbed to nearly FFr2.8 billion ($620m). The government then intervened and set a FFr2 billion limit ($440m) (*The Economist*, February 14, 1981)." The Eximbank estimates that "the total French expenditures [by BFCE and COFACE] in 1980 could range anywhere between $2.0 and $2.5 billion [4, p. 44]." In 1980 the cost of the COFACE programs was estimated to be $108 million, the BFCE subsidy was $540 million, and the inflation risk insurance net loss was $475 million. The French programs continue to be considerably broader and more generous than those provided by the United States.

C. Germany

Long-term financing for German exports is provided by the Ausfuhrkredit Gesellschaft (AKA), a syndicate of 58 commercial banks, and the Kreditanstalt fuer Wiederaufbau (KfW), a government development bank. The long-term credit programs offered by KfW are limited by a 1980 ceiling of $436 million with interest rates ranging between 8.5 and 9.5%. This financing was extended in accord with the conditions of the arrangement, and since German interest rates tended to be lower than the arrangement minimums prior to 1980, concessions were not provided. With the higher German interest rates in 1980 and 1981 a concession has resulted, however.

AKA provides financing from its A, B, and C funds. The B fund is primarily used to finance medium-term credits, and the A and C funds are operated like PEFCO for financing long-term transactions. The A fund is provided by commercial banks and used for supplier credits with a DM10 billion limit with credits extended at fixed interest rates between 8.75 and 10.0% in 1980. The C fund is also provided by AKA member banks and is used for buyer credits with payment terms ranging between 2 and 10 years. During 1980 this fund was limited to DM8.5 billion, and interest rates ranged between 9 and 11%. For credits with repayment terms beyond 5 years the interest rate range was 8.5 to 10.0%.

The AKA B fund provides supplier credits for transactions with developing countries with repayment terms between 1 and 4 years. In 1980 DM3 billion were available from this fund. "Credits funded can be rediscounted by the Bundesbank at a preferential rate of 1.5 percent above its discount rate (which ranged from 4.5 to 6.0 percent during 1979) [4, p. 48]." The effective interest rates on B fund credits are in accord with the conditions of the arrangement.

Germany also provides financing for local costs, performance and bid bond insurance, exchange rate risk insurance, and mixed credits. "During 1979, ten projects were financed under the mixed credit scheme and totaled DM619 million ($337.7 million). The export credit portion of these projects totaled DM254 [million] ($138.6 million) [3, p. 71]."

Insurance and guarantees are provided by Hermes, a private company. "Hermes cover for medium-term exports increased during 1980 to DM3.7 billion ($2.04 billion), from DM1.6 billion ($888 million) in 1979 [4, p. 50]." Short-term insurance coverage was DM18.3 billion ($10.0 billion) during 1979. Hermes earned a profit of $87 million during 1980, indicating that its insurance and guarantees were priced on a self-sustaining basis.

D. Italy

Italy provides highly concessionary export financing, but that financing is more limited than French financing. "During 1980, exports with a total contract value of 4,766 billion lira ($5.56 billion) received official financing support. [4, p. 55]." Concessionary export financing involving an interest rate subsidy is provided by Mediocredito, and in 1980 that subsidy ranged between 7.50 and 8.25%, depending on the maturity of the credit. Banks are also able to rediscount their export credits, although the concession provided is smaller than on the direct credits. "During 1980 Mediocredito paid some $338.4 million in export credit interest rate subsidies and had a year-end liability to pay some $3.56 billion in interest rate subsidy over the next 10 to 15 years [4, p. 60]."

SACE, a state-owned insurance group, provides insurance and guarantees for short-, medium-, and long-term export transactions. Although information on medium- and long-term insurance and guarantee coverage is not available, SACE provided approximately $2.2 billion of coverage for short-term transactions in 1979. In 1980 SACE had a net deficit of $19.8 million.

In addition to these financing and insurance programs, Italy provides foreign content financing, performance and bid bonds, political risk insurance for overseas investments, and some local cost support in accord with the arrangement. Italy also has provided tied aid credits and exchange rate risk insurance for credits denominated in U.S. dollars.

E. Japan

The Export–Import Bank of Japan provides both supplier credit and buyer credit programs for transactions with repayment terms in excess of 5 years. "For buyer credits, Eximbank normally funds 60 percent of the typical 85 percent financed portion at a fixed rate of interest; the balance is funded by commercial banks. The resulting blended interest rate conforms to Arrangement guidelines [3, p. 82]." "Almost all Japanese medium and long-term export credits benefit from preferential fixed-rate financing by Eximbank. Most of Eximbank's activity has been on a supplier credit basis, but the amount of buyer credit activity is increasing. Supplier credits are used exclusively to support medium-term export transactions [3, p. 82]." Exports with repayment schedules of less than 1 year are rediscounted at the Bank of Japan at the official discount rate. Because Japanese interest rates have tended to be near the arrangement minimums, this financing has not been highly concessionary. The extent of any subsidy provided by the Japanese Eximbank is unclear, but the Eximbank does report a profit and receives no appropriation of funds. The Eximbank's loan limit was $4.7 billion in 1980.

Insurance for political and commercial risks associated with long-term transactions is provided by the Ministry for International Trade and Industry (MITI). MITI provides insurance guarantees for medium- and short-term transactions, and in 1980 $4.9 billion in medium-term and $48.4 billion in short-term insurance were provided.

Japan also offers performance bond guarantees, refund bond guarantees, construction work guarantees, local cost support, and exchange risk insurance.

F. United Kingdom

The United Kingdom offers one of the most comprehensive official export credit and insurance systems of all the major competitors. This reflects the post-World War II involvement in all facets of the economy. Although such involvement is not in keeping with the present Conservative Government's point of view, no major changes are anticipated in the near future. Export promotion continues to be considered of paramount importance in promoting jobs, income, and balance of payments stability [3, p. 86].

The United Kingdom's Export Credits Guarantee Department (ECGD) provides long-term export financing programs that conform to the arrangement minimums, so substantial subsidies are thus provided. Approximately 74% of the 1980 credits are extended in foreign currencies. Exports with medium-term repayment schedules are virtually all financed by ECGD which issues both guarantees and provides an interest rate subsidy to participating banks. ECGD, however, does not provide interest rate subsidies for short-term transactions. "The net cost to public funds of ECGD's interest rate support scheme for fixed-rate sterling and foreign currency export financing during the fiscal year ending March 1981 amounted to 500 million pounds ($1,182.0 million) [4, p. 82]." ECGD also finances rather liberally the foreign content of UK exports. ECGD participates in mixed credits, but during 1980 only two projects were financed in this manner.

ECGD provides insurance and guarantee programs for long-term, medium-term, and short-term transactions, and provides some local cost support, exchange risk insurance, inflation insurance, and contractor guarantees. The insurance and guarantee programs offered by the ECGD, with the exception of the cost escalation program, are intended to operate without the provision of public funds, but in 1980 ECGD had a loss of $221 million on its insurance operations.

G. Summary

This survey indicates that the export financing programs of France, Italy, and the United Kingdom are the most generous. As indicated in Table 5.1, France, Germany, Italy, Japan, and the United Kingdom offer a much broader range of extraordinary programs than does the United

TABLE 5.1

Evaluation of Extraordinary Export Support Programs: Frequency of Use[a,b]

Type of support	France		Germany		Japan		U.K.		U.S.	
	1979	1980	1979	1980	1979	1980	1979	1980	1979	1980
Inflation insurance	3	3	0	0	0	0	2	2	0	0
Exchange rate insurance	3	3	2	2	2	2	2	2	0	0
Mixed credits/tied-aid	3	3	2	2	2	2	2	2	1	1[c]
Local cost support	2	2	3	3	3	3	2	2	2	1[c]

[a] Reproduced from [4, p. 5].

[b] Ranking: 0 = Not available; 1 = Used only in special circumstances to match competing offers; 2 = Available, but infrequently used, program; 3 = Extensively used program.

[c] Facilities available, but not used during FY1980 for new commitments.

States, although beginning in 1979 the United States expanded its offerings to include mixed credits, lines of credit, and local cost support. These programs were curtailed in 1981, however. The United States also offers support for a somewhat more restrictive class of exports than do the other countries as indicated in Table 5.2. While the breadth of programs offered by the United States is more limited than that of these other countries, the amount of the support provided is more important to the impact on exports.

III. The Level of Official Export Financing

The determination of the amount of export support provided by the United States and other major trading countries is complicated by the quite different roles of insurance, guarantees, and loans. In a letter to former Senator Adlai Stevenson, former Assistant Treasury Secretary C. Fred Bergsten stated that approximately 8.5% of U.S. exports received some official financing support by the Export–Import Bank, the Foreign Military Sales program, and the Commodity Credit Corporation, with approximately 70% of that amount provided by the Eximbank [12, p. 136]. In its 1980 report [9] on the Eximbank, the General Accounting Office reported that the percentages of total exports officially supported by either insurance, guarantees, or direct credits during 1978 were Japan 35, the United Kingdom 35, France 29, Germany 12, and the United States 6. In a statement prepared for the Senate Subcommittee for International Finance, Bergsten, however, indicated that the United States supports

TABLE 5.2

Exports of Services That May Be Officially Supported[a]

Category	Canada	France	Germany	Italy	Japan	United Kingdom	United States
Lease contracts	Yes	Yes	Yes	Yes	Yes	Yes	Yes
Exports of services and contract work abroad	Yes	Yes	Yes	Yes	Yes	Yes	Yes
Holding of construction equipment abroad	Yes	Yes	Yes	Yes	Yes	Yes	Yes
Exhibit at trade fairs overseas	Yes	Yes	Yes	No	No	Yes	Yes
Preshipment coverage	Yes	Yes	Yes	Yes	Yes	Yes	Yes
Bid bonds	Yes	Yes	Yes	Yes	Yes	Yes	[b]
Performance bonds	Yes	Yes	Yes	Yes	Yes	Yes	[b]
Retention payment bonds	Yes	Yes	Yes	Yes	No	Yes	[b]
Royalties	Yes	Yes	Yes	No	Yes	Yes	No
Overseas investments	Yes	Yes	Yes	Yes	Yes	Yes	[b]
Export promotion	No	[c]	No	No	[d]	No	No

[a] Reproduced from: [3, p. 102].

[b] Not by Eximbank, but by Overseas Private Investment Corporation for work in less-developed countries.

[c] For market entry: research, mission salaries, overseas cost of running sales office, demonstrations, publicity.

[d] Overseas advertisements.

approximately the same percentage of exports with long-term direct credits as do its major export competitors. He reported the following ratios of long-term direct credits to total exports: Japan 2.2%, the United Kingdom 1.6%, France 3.9%, West Germany 1.8%, and the United States 2.7% [12, p. 82].

Data on official export support are presented in Table 5.3 for 1975 and 1976, and indicate that U.S. support was less than that provided by France, Japan, and the United Kingdom on both a total dollar basis and as a percentage of manufactured and total exports. The United States, Canada, Germany and Italy supported about the same percentage of 1976 manufactured and total exports with insurance, guarantees, and loans. In terms of government loans, the United States provided a greater volume than any of the other six countries except France, and as a percentage of manufactured exports the U.S. support was comparable to that of the other countries with the exception of France.

Data for 1978 and 1979 are summarized in Table 5.4 and are consistent with those for 1975 and 1976, although the United Kingdom increased the percentage of its total exports supported whereas the percentage supported by Japan decreased. When attention is restricted to capital goods exports, however, the data in Table 5.5 indicate that the long-term credit programs of the Bank provide a level of support that is comparable to that of the United Kingdom, is greater than that provided by Germany and Japan, and is less than that provided by France and Italy. If medium-term credits are included, however, the ratio of capital goods exports supported by official financing increases to 37% for France, 31% for Italy, and 29% for the United Kingdom.

The significance of these differences in the level of support is difficult to determine. A draft of a GAO report included the statement that guarantee and insurance programs are "usually of minor importance in international competition for export sales [9, p. 34]." In response to criticism by Bergsten of the GAO's grouping of guarantee and insurance with direct credits, the GAO dropped this statement but did report the grouped data. If the GAO's initial statement is correct that guarantees and insurance are of only minor importance, the magnitude of U.S. long-term financing of exports appears to be about average for those countries surveyed, but the Bank's medium-term credit support is substantially less than that provided by a number of countries.

Table 5.6 presents Eximbank data on medium-term interest rates and subsidies per billion dollars of financing for France, Germany, Japan, the United Kingdom, and the United States. The Eximbank's medium-term lending rate is pegged to the Federal Reserve discount rate and is consid-

TABLE 5.3

Official Export Support by Seven Major Trading Countries, 1975 and 1976 ($ Million)[a]

Country	Year	Insurance and guarantee authorizations ($)	Direct and discount loan authorizations ($)	Direct and discount loan authorizations as a percentage of		Total official support ($)	Total official support as a percentage of	
				Manufactured exports	Total exports		Manufactured exports	Total exports
Canada	1975	911	1,137	7.0	3.6	2,048	12.6	6.4
	1976	1,339	718	3.6	1.9	2,057	10.3	5.5
France	1975	19,626	7,326	18.2	14.2	19,626	48.9	38.0
	1976	21,920	7,595	17.6	13.6	21,920	50.7	39.4
Germany	1975	7,950	1,252	1.5	1.4	7,950	9.8	8.8
	1976	10,387	1,544	1.7	1.5	10,387	11.2	10.2
Italy	1975	4,596	2,859	9.7	8.2	4,596	15.7	13.2
	1976	3,306	1,451	4.6	3.9	3,306	11.6	9.8
Japan	1975	25,968	2,377	4.4	4.3	25,968	48.1	46.5
	1976	32,034	3,266	5.0	4.9	32,034	49.0	47.6
United Kingdom	1975	9,645	1,402	3.7	3.2	9,645	25.6	22.0
	1976	10,519	1,152	2.9	2.5	10,519	26.5	22.7
United States	1975	3,744	3,813	5.1	3.6	7,557	10.2	7.1
	1976	4,800	3,489	4.4	3.1	8,289	10.4	7.3

[a] "For the European countries and Japan, overall volume figures are the same as insurance and guarantee volume statistics because official as well as private portions of direct official credits are insured in these countries [1, p. 170]." Reprinted by permission of the publisher, from *The International Economic Policy of the United States: Selected Papers of C. Fred Bergsten,* by C. Fred Bergsten, pp. 170–172 (Lexington, Mass.: D. C. Heath and Company, Lexington Books, Copyright 1980, D. C. Heath and Company).

TABLE 5.4

Exports and Official Export Support ($ Billion)[a]

Country	1978			1979		
	Exports	Official support[b]	Percent supported	Exports	Official support[b]	Percent supported
Canada	46.3	4.030	8.7	55.8	3.535	6.3
France	79.2	30.660	38.7	100.6	32.155	32.0
Germany	141.9	14.960	10.5	171.7	14.505	8.4
Italy	55.9	8.705	15.6	72.2	8.020	11.1
Japan	97.5	31.810	32.6	103.0	39.355	38.2
United Kingdom	67.3	35.115	52.2	86.3	33.430	38.7
United States	143.6	7.375	5.1	181.6	9.490	5.2

[a] Source: [3].

[b] "The figures for the European countries and Japan represent only insurance and guarantee authorizations, since the official agencies in these countries require cover for all transactions receiving financing support. The data for Canada and the United States do not impose this requirement, thus the data reflect both financing support and insurance/guarantee cover [3, p. 4]."

erably higher than the nominal interest rates of the other four countries. The subsidy rates measured relative to government borrowing costs are greatest for France and the United Kingdom, and are also significant for Germany and Japan. No subsidy is reported for the United States because

TABLE 5.5

Exports Supported With Long-Term, Official Credits (1978 and 1979)[a]

Country	1978		1979	
	Exports supported with long-term credits ($ billion)	Percentage of exports supported to capital goods exports	Exports supported with long-term credits ($ billion)	Percentage of exports supported to capital goods exports
France	2.940	19.5	3.975	20.6
Germany	2.475	6.0	2.845	6.0
Italy	2.585	21.1	3.925	27.0
Japan	2.520	3.9	2.195	7.3
United Kingdom	1.690	9.5	3.015	14.4
United States	3.855	10.4	6.665	14.8

[a] Source: [3, Table 3].

TABLE 5.6

Medium-Term Credit Program[a]

Country	Effective fixed export credit interest rates (percentage)[b]			Subsidy per billion dollars of medium-term financing ($ million)[c]		
	1978	1979	1980[d]	1978	1979	1980
France	8.00	8.00	8.00/8.25	103	109	179
Germany	7.80	8.30	8.30/9.80	None	23	49
Japan[e]	7.85	7.85	7.85/8.10	24	50	85
United Kingdom[f]	7.85	7.85	7.85/8.10	98	120	153
United States[g]	9.58	11.33	13.13	None	None	None

[a] Reproduced, including footnotes, from [4, pp. 11, 13].

[b] Includes the average insurance premium for a medium-term sale to public buyer in upper-tier countries such as Brazil.

[c] Total interest expense over a 5-year repayment of each $1.0 billion of authorizations. Expense calculated by subtracting the face rates shown above from the average government bond rate for the period and, whenever a negative results, taking that figure times $2.5 billion (one-half the volume = average annual outstanding times 5 years).

[d] The rate shown in front of the slash is the old rate charged before arrangement rates changed in July 1980; the other rates are after the change.

[e] Assuming roughly one-half of transactions are on-lent by Japanese supplier in dollars.

[f] Assuming roughly one-third of transactions in U.S. dollars and two-thirds in sterling.

[g] Average Eximbank discount rate, plus 1.0%, plus front-end fee.

the Eximbank interest rate was greater than the government borrowing rate. As will be indicated in Chapter 6, the subsidy should, however, be measured relative to interest rates available to private borrowers. Since the borrowing cost for private borrowers is greater than that for the government, the Eximbank's medium-term financing program does provide a subsidy. That subsidy, however, is likely to be less than that provided by the other four countries.

Table 5.7 presents Eximbank estimates of the subsidy provided by the long-term financing programs of the five countries. As with medium-term credits, France and the United Kingdom provide the most generous financing, with the United States providing slightly more generous financing than Japan and considerably more generous financing than Germany. These estimates, however, do not conclusively measure the relative competitiveness of the programs of the five countries because neither the percentage of individual transactions financed nor the total amount of financing provided is known. The data in Tables 5.6 and 5.7 do suggest,

TABLE 5.7

Subsidy per Billion Dollars of Long-Term Export Financing ($ Million)[a,b]

Country	1978	1979	1980
France	197	210	342
Germany	None	None	43
Japan[c]	14	40	130
United Kingdom[d]	146	195	249
United States[e]	9	55	145

[a] Reproduced, including footnotes, from [4, p. 6].

[b] Total interest expense over a 10-year repayment of each $1.0 billion of authorizations. Expense calculated by subtracting the face lending rates shown in Table 1 of [4] from the average government bond rate for the period and, whenever a negative results, taking that figure times $5.0 billion (one-half the volume = average annual outstanding, times 10 years).

[c] Assuming roughly one-half of transactions are on-lent by Japanese supplier in dollars.

[d] Assuming roughly two-thirds of transactions in U.S. dollars and one-third in sterling.

[e] For the United States, the export credit rate used is the average rate on credits authorized in that period, not the lending rate shown in Table 1 of [4].

however, that France and the United Kingdom provide much greater export financing subsidization than do Germany, Japan, and the United States.

Data on the amount of officially supported export credit outstanding at the end of 1979 were presented in the OECD Wallen report [14, pp. 16–65] and are summarized in Table 5.8. The 12 principal exporting countries included in the study had credits outstanding of $166 billion which yielded an annual subsidy of approximately $5.5 billion based on the difference in interest received on the outstanding credits and the interest that would have been received had the credits been refinanced at the government long-term borrowing rates. Compared to the arrangement minimum, the average interest rate subsidy for the 12 countries was 3.45%, ranging from zero for Switzerland to 9.95% for Denmark. Because of the volume of the credits outstanding, 40% of the $5.5 billion subsidy is accounted for by

TABLE 5.8

Official Export Financing and Its Cost[a]

Country	Credits outstanding end-1979 ($ billion)	Average subsidy rate (%)	Annual cost[b] ($ billion)
Belgium	3.914	4.01	0.157
Canada	3.106	4.40	0.137
Denmark	1.059	9.95	0.105
France	43.861	5.34	2.342
Germany	32.060	0.67	0.215
Italy	5.954	7.14	0.425
Japan	37.712	1.50	0.566
Netherlands	2.373	2.25	0.053
Sweden	3.570	3.66	0.131
Switzerland	6.080	—	—
United Kingdom	15.491	6.97	1.000
United States	11.052	2.85	0.315
	116.332	3.45	5.526

[a] Source: [14, p. 54].

[b] Using year-end 1979 government long-term interest rates.

France, approximately 20% by the United Kingdom, and less than 6% by the United States. The subsidies may be overstated, however, since the calculations were based on the assumption that "all credits outstanding have been extended at the minimum rates foreseen in the present (Arrangement) matrix . . . [14, p. 55]." Even if the figures are overstated because some official credits were granted at interest rates above the arrangement minimums, these estimates confirm the preceding analysis that France and the United Kingdom provide more generous export financing than does the United States, while Germany and Japan provide less generous financing.

One major difference between the long-term financing provided by the Eximbank and that provided by France and the United Kingdom is that those countries tend to lend at the arrangement matrix minimums, while even if the Eximbank interest rate is at the matrix minimum, it often blends its credits with private credits. The resulting blended interest rate can be much higher than that offered by France or the United Kingdom. For FY1980 the Bank authorized $4.783 billion in long-term credits to finance $7.736 billion in exports, which, if importers were to make a cash payment of 15% of the export value, implies that the Eximbank financed

72.7% of the remaining value.[2] Since private market interest rates were 4 to 5% higher than the Bank's lending rate, the blended interest rate on Eximbank-financed exports would be significantly greater than that for exports financed with 85% cover by France or the United Kingdom. While the importance of the difference in cover and real interest rates for the selection of a supplier by an importer is difficult to determine, an analysis of the disposition of the preliminary commitments issued by the Bank can shed some light on the Bank's competitiveness.

IV. Analysis of the Disposition of Preliminary Commitments

Table 5.9 presents data on preliminary commitments disposed of from October 1, 1978 to March 31, 1981 and indicates that 43% of the PCs were won by U.S. exporters and converted to direct credits while the other 57% were cancelled.[3] When a preliminary commitment is cancelled, the U.S. exporter is required to indicate the cause of the cancellation, and although the responses may not be without bias, they do provide some insight into the competitiveness of Eximbank financing. Twenty-nine percent of the PCs were lost to foreign suppliers, while most of the other cancellations resulted from the deferral or cancellation of the project. A few PCs were cancelled even though a U.S. exporter won the sale because other financing, generally provided by the importer's government or a development bank, was used.

Of the 131 exports in Table 5.9 lost as a result of competition, approximately 40% were lost because of a more favorable price offered by a foreign supplier, while 49% were lost because of other considerations, of which technical factors such as quality and delivery schedules were the most common. Other factors such as political pressure and side deals were also of importance in some cases. Only 15 exports were lost because of financing and, as indicated in Table 5.10, all but 4 of those were lost because of export credits mixed with aid. This assessment clearly indicates that the financing of those exports supported by the Bank has been quite competitive with the export financing offered by other countries and

[2] The $4.783 billion direct credit figure includes the PEFCO credits authorized in conjunction with the Bank's FY1980 supplemental authorization.

[3] These disposition data cover Preliminary Commitments issued both before and after the change in the Bank's direct credit policy in April, 1980. A comparison between the PCs issued before and those issued after the change will be presented later in this section.

TABLE 5.9

Disposition of Preliminary Commitments: October 1, 1978 to March 31, 1981[a]

Period	Total PCs	Direct credits authorized		Cancellations		Reasons for cancellation				
		Number	Export value ($ million)	Number	Export value ($ million)	Lost due to competition on			Project deferred	U.S. won but Eximbank not needed
						Price	Financing	Other		
10-1-80 to 3-31-81	111	49	2087	62	3298	13	6	12	26	5
4-1-80 to 9-30-30	111	59	2899	52	1669	12	0	9	26	5
10-1-79 to 3-31-80	87	37	3221	50	2786	12	1	16	17	4
4-1-79 to 9-30-79	79	31	2931	48	3760	5	6	13	22	2
10-1-78 to 3-31-79	68	22	990	46	2662	10	2	14	16	4
Total	456	198	12128	258	14175	52	15	64	107	20

[a] Source: Export–Import Bank, "Disposition of Preliminary Commitments," Washington, D.C., 1980–1981.

TABLE 5.10

Cause of Preliminary Commitments Lost Due to Competition: FY1979 and FY1980 (Number of Cases)[a]

| Period | Price | Financing | | Other | | Total |
		Normal	Aid/Mixed	Technical	Other	
10-1-80 to 3-31-81	13	3	3	12[b]		21
4-1-80 to 9-30-80	12	0	0	9[b]		31
10-1-79 to 3-31-80	12	0	1	4	12	29
4-1-79 to 9-30-79	5	1	5	4	9	24
10-1-78 to 3-31-79	10	0	2	5	9	26

[a] Source: Export–Import Bank, "Disposition of Preliminary Commitments," Washington, D.C., 1980, 1981.

[b] No breakdown was given for these two 6-month periods.

suggests the possibility that Eximbank financing may be more generous than required to gain the export sale.[4]

A survey of 22 foreign importers conducted by the Bank explored the reasons for the importers' purchase decisions. While power cases were overrepresented among the 22 cases and over ⅔ of the cases were authorized by the DuBrul board, the study provides the only available direct information on importers' decisions. In assessing the cause of an importer's decision, the policy analysis and direct credit staffs of the Bank interviewed both the U.S. exporters and the foreign buyers. The conclusions, however, were primarily based on the response of the buyer. The study concluded [2]

> Product price is the most frequent determinant of which potential supplier wins an export sale. There is a significant minority of cases where technology, availability, or compatibility with existing plant and equipment favor certain suppliers to such an extent that competitors have difficulty gaining consideration. Seldom is financing alone the prime factor in the buyer's decision. Moreover, it appears that, unless the competitor prices are close (within 5 to 10 percent), a significantly (perhaps extraordinarily) better financing offer must be made and maintained to keep the competitive changes equal [p. 5].

[4] This conclusion does not pertain to the issue of whether the Bank provides support for a sufficiently broad class of exports.

In its analysis of preliminary commitment dispositions for the October 1980 to March 1981 period, the policy analysis staff, however, identified a possible trend that may indicate that Eximbank financing has become less competitive [7]:

> During the past six months, a potential trend has surfaced which, if it were to continue over the longer term, could be indicative of declining competitiveness in Exim financing offers. Losses due to financing, while relatively small when compared to other losses during the six-month period, accounted for about 40% of all financing losses since this study began two and one-half years ago. Further, a greater percentage (50% vs. 10% historically) of these financing losses occurred as a result of "normal" (as opposed to "concessional") finance competition.
>
> The policy changes resulting from the implementation of the "walking paper" in April 1980 could be partially responsible for the above change: 60% of the cases won or lost during this six-month period were initially approved as PCs under the new guidelines, as were almost 70% of the cases lost due to financing. Although it is still too early to make any judgments as to the walking paper guidelines' impact on Exim's "real world" competitive situation, future PC follow-up reports will track this issue more closely by categorizing final PC resolutions according to the period during which PCs are initially authorized (i.e., pre- and post-walking paper periods) as opposed to the period in which PCs are resolved [p. 1].

The "walking paper" referred to in this quotation is the April 1980 change in Bank policy from an interest rate range of 7.75 to 8.75% to a fixed interest rate of 9.25% for aircraft and 8.75% for other exports. A standard 65% cover for all exports except older generation aircraft was also adopted which was less than the typical 85% cover previously provided.

A more recent study [5] of the disposition of preliminary commitments compared those issued from October 1978 through March 1980, prior to the walking paper, with those issued during the April 1980 through June 1981 period.[5] Tables 5.11a, 5.11b, and 5.11c summarize the data for the aircraft, power, and all other sectors, respectively. All aircraft cases were authorized and disposed after the policy changes were won, which suggests no decrease in Eximbank competitiveness. Of the six PCs authorized during the first period that were lost, none was lost because of financing. In part this performance is due to the U.S. product advantages in aircraft, but since the United States has little if any advantage in the power sector, the data for that sector may be more indicative of U.S. competitiveness.

---

[5] A few PCs authorized during the first period had not been disposed at the time of the study. Twenty-one PCs authorized during the second period had not yet been disposed. Whether these differ from those already disposed is unclear.

TABLE 5.11a

Disposition of Preliminary Commitments: Aircraft[a]

	Date preliminary commitment authorized			
	10/78 to 3/80		4/80 to 6/81	
	Number	Export value ($ billion)	Number	Export value ($ billion)
Resolution				
Won	43	6.599	12	1.068
Lost	6	1.865	0	0
Deferred	3	0.094	1	0.360
Total	52	8.558	13	1.428
Reasons for losses				
Price	2	1.069		
Export credit	0	0	(No Losses)	
Aid financing	0	0		
Other	4	0.796		

[a] Source: [5, Table 1].

TABLE 5.11b

Disposition of Preliminary Commitments: Power Sector[a]

	Date preliminary commitment authorized			
	10/78 to 3/80		4/80 to 6/81	
	Number	Export value ($ billion)	Number	Export value ($ billion)
Resolution				
Won	24	1.521	16	0.692
Lost	27	2.217	13	0.430
Deferred	9	0.298	4	0.048
Total	60	4.036	33	1.170
Reasons for losses				
Price	15	1.260	7	0.199
Export credit	0	0	0	0
Aid financing	2	0.030	0	0
Other	10	0.927	6	0.231

[a] Source: [5, Table 2].

TABLE 5.11c

Disposition of Preliminary Commitments: Nonaircraft/Nonpower Sectors[a]

| | Date preliminary commitment authorized | | | |
| | 10/78 to 3/80 | | 4/80 to 6/81 | |
	Number	Export value ($ billion)	Number	Export value ($ billion)
Resolution				
Won	72	2.863	65	1.873
Lost	45	0.998	17	0.620
Deferred	56	2.977	16	0.858
Total	173	6.838	98	3.351
Reasons for losses				
Price	11	0.172	7	0.206
Export credit	1	0.008	3	0.245
Aid financing	4	0.042	2	0.038
Other	29	0.776	5	0.131

[a] Source: [5, Table 3].

Nearly half the power cases were lost, although only two were lost due to financing and both were prior to the change in the Bank's financing policy. The success rate after the policy change was also better than before the change, suggesting that the Bank's financing was not less competitive after the walking paper. For nonaircraft, nonpower cases the success ratio was also better after the change in financing policy, although a higher percentage of the cases were lost because of financing. The Bank's report concluded that "An Eximbank rate roughly 100 basis points above the typical rate offered by foreign official export credit agencies does *not* appear to noticeably change the competitiveness of U.S. capital goods exporters [5, p. 2]." While this statement focuses on the Eximbank interest rate increases, the accompanying reduction in the cover probably was more important to the cost of financing to a foreign importer, since more market rate financing by private lenders was required.[6]

The preceding analysis pertains to cases for which preliminary commitments were authorized, but some applications for financing are denied, others are referred to the Bank's supplier credit programs, and others

[6] The Bank intends to conduct a similar study on the effect of the changes in financing policies adopted when Mr. Draper assumed the Chairmanship.

receive only financial guarantees. The budget stringencies during FY1981 caused by the large number of PCs authorized in the preceeding years forced the Bank to use these alternatives more frequently than in the recent past. Analysis of these cases led the policy analysis staff of the Bank to conclude that the success rate of those cases referred to the supplier credit program was considerably below that for cases authorized under the direct credit program, particularly for public buyers, but outcomes of the cases for which no financing was provided or for which a financial guarantee was provided were as favorable as for those cases for which direct credits were offered. The policy analysis staff concluded that [6]:

> The assumption that certain case characteristics can be used to identify transactions not as likely to require direct loan resources was generally supported by this follow-up. The no-credit gamble seems to have been particularly worth taking with energy-related projects, especially in developed countries. However, providing no credit to non-energy cases not possessing a unique selling characteristic appears to be a highly risky undertaking. That is, the likelihood of financing being directly linked to a lost sale here is relatively high [p. 2].

This study suggests that the Bank can maintain its competitiveness in conjunction with a policy that denies financing in cases that are likely to be won when private financing is used.

Of the exports lost because of competition from October 1, 1978 to March 31, 1981, Japan, France, and Germany accounted for more than half, as indicated in Table 5.12. Of the cases lost to Japan most were lost because of price considerations, whereas those cases lost to France were

TABLE 5.12

Cause of Preliminary Commitments Lost Due to Competition, by Competitor Country October 1, 1978 to March 31, 1981, (Number of Cases)[a]

Competitor country	Price	Financing		Other	Total
		Normal	Aid/Mixed		
France	5	0	2	15	22
Germany	9	1	2	8	20
Japan	17	1	0	8	26
United Kingdom	2	1	3	2	8
Other	19	1	4	31	55
Total	52	4	11	64	131

[a] Source: Export–Import Bank, "Disposition of Preliminary Commitments," Washington, D.C., 1980, 1981.

TABLE 5.13

Cause of Preliminary Commitments Lost Due to Competition, by Sector
October 1, 1978 to March 31, 1980 (Number of Cases)[a]

Sector	Price	Financing		Other		Total
		Normal	Aid/Mixed	Technical	Other	
Agriculture/construction	1	0	0	0	3	4
Communication	7	0	1	3	5	16
Manufacturing	0	1	1	1	1	4
Mining and refining	2	0	0	0	4	6
Power	16	0	4	5	5	30
Transportation	0	0	2	3	11	16
(Commercial jet aircraft)	(0)	(0)	(0)	(2)	(2)	(4)
Other	1	0	0	1	1	3
Total	27	1	8	13	30	79

[a] Source: Export–Import Bank, "Disposition of Preliminary Commitments," Washington, D.C., 1980, 1981.

largely the result of technical and other factors. Germany, France, and the United Kingdom won sales as a result of mixed credits. Of the 79 sales lost due to competition during the October 1, 1978 to March 31, 1980 period, 30 were lost in the power sector and 16 in communications in most part because of price considerations as indicated in Table 5.13.[7] Four sales in the power sector were lost because of mixed financing. The policy analysis staff concluded [8]

> It appears that the low success rates in these sectors reflect the existence of a "special" problem in each sector: price uncompetitiveness seems to plague the power sector, while the communications sector appears especially prone to the use of extra incentives (e.g., AID financing, government-to-government deals) by foreign exporters [p. 1].

Sixteen sales were lost in the transportation sector of which only four were commercial jet aircraft cases. Of those four, none was judged to have been lost because of either price or financing considerations.

Table 5.14 indicates that although 50 of 86 power cases were lost between October 1, 1978 and March 31, 1981, only 4 were lost because of financing, and all 4 were due to mixed credits. Of the 57 aircraft cases only 6 were lost, none as a result of financing. The financing offered for the aircraft and power sectors thus appears to be quite competitive with that

---

[7] After March 1980 the Bank reported preliminary commitment disposition data by sector only for aircraft and power.

TABLE 5.14

Disposition of Aircraft and Power Preliminary Commitments
October 1, 1978 to March 31, 1981[a]

| | | | | | Reason for loss | | |
| | | | | | Financing | | |
Sector	Number	Won	Lost	Price	Normal	Aid	Other
Aircraft	57	51	6	2	0	0	4
Power	86	36	50	29	0	4	17

[a] Source: Export–Import Bank, "Disposition of Preliminary Commitments," Washington, D.C., 1980, 1981.

offered by other countries, and the difference between the percentages of the cases won in the two sectors is apparently due to product competition and to price considerations.

Table 5.15 presents data on the PCs won and lost from October 1, 1978 to March 31, 1980, separated into "at scale" and "below scale" categories. The below scale cases involve a lower interest rate and a greater Eximbank cover, and hence a greater concession, than the at scale cases. The cases lost, however, carried approximately the same interest rate as the cases won and had a higher Eximbank cover, which suggests that the Bank may have offered greater concessions in those cases in which it perceived greater competition, but those concessions were not sufficient to win the export. It is possible, however, that the differences are due largely to differences between commercial jet aircraft and power cases. The former receive a lower Eximbank cover than do other credits, whereas power cases tend to receive a greater than average cover. Almost all aircraft cases are won, whereas the majority of power cases are lost, as indicated in Tables 5.13 and 5.14. Thus, aircraft cases are overrepresented among the cases won, while power cases are overrepresented among the cases lost. The over- or underrepresentation of these cases in the two categories in Table 5.15 may explain the greater cover for the cases lost. Since power cases tend to be lost because of price and nonfinancing factors, the observation that more generous financing is provided for credits lost than won thus may be due to sector policies of the Bank rather than to the competitiveness of Eximbank financing.

The possible interpretations of these PC disposition data are indicated by the quite different conclusions drawn by the GAO and by Bergsten. In its 1980 report the GAO reviewed the Eximbank Preliminary

TABLE 5.15

Eximbank Financing: Preliminary Commitments Disposed in FY1979 and FY1980[a]

Period	Cases won			Cases lost to foreign competition		
	At scale	Below scale	All	At scale	Below scale	All
10-1-79 to 3-31-80						
Average export value ($ million)	59.2	152.0	87.1	40.0	70.0	51.4
Average Eximbank cover (%)	54.7	70.0	62.7	65.2	81.8	73.7
Average interest rate (%)[b]	8.291	7.873	8.167	8.193	8.068	8.146
Average reduction from scale (%)		0.69			0.53	
4-1-79 to 9-30-79						
Average export value ($ million)	82.2	120.3	94.5	14.0	94.5	54.2
Average Eximbank cover (%)	50.5	84.1	64.3	70.5	75.5	74.8
Average interest rate (%)[b]	8.190	8.088	8.157	8.240	8.104	8.172
Average reduction from scale (%)		0.54			0.48	
10-1-78 to 3-31-79						
Average export value ($ million)	38.9	54.4	44.5	61.3	26.0	45.2
Average Eximbank cover (%)	49.2	69.5	58.2	66.4	81.5	70.4
Average interest rate (%)[b]	8.32	8.00	8.21	8.31	8.06	8.20
Average reduction from scale (%)		NA			NA	

[a] Source: Export–Import Bank, "Disposition of Preliminary Commitments," Washington, D.C., 1980, 1981.

[b] The simple average of the interest rates.

Commitment disposition data for the period April 1, 1978 to March 31, 1979 and chose to emphasize the lost sales. The report concluded [9]

> A recent Eximbank analysis shows that 7 of 55 sales lost to foreign competitors (about 13%) were lost primarily because of uncompetitive financing. Responses to a GAO questionnaire showed that U.S. firms lost some exports when other countries offered better financing than Eximbank. The questionnaire responses also showed that U.S. firms lost sales when they did not apply for Eximbank financing because the expected financing terms were known to be unsuitable [p. ii].

In commenting on a draft of that report, Bergsten drew the opposite conclusion in stating [9]

> Of fifty-five lost sales, which had been supported by Eximbank, only seven were lost because the buyer had a more attractive foreign official export financing offer. And of the seven, four were lost because of foreign aid financing, not foreign official export credits. Thus only three—less than 6%—were lost because of foreign official export credit competition. If U.S. Eximbank rates are as uncompetitive as the draft would have us believe, why weren't more than three

sales lost because of uncompetitive Eximbank financing? Clearly other factors—
such as price, quality and service—are important to foreign buyers [pp. 35–36].

In testimony before the Senate Subcommittee on International Finance, Bergsten commented further [11]:

> Charges are often made that Eximbank has been less competitive than its foreign
> counterparts in supporting U.S. exporters. This is simply not true. Of 143 Exim-
> bank supported credit transactions in FY1979, Eximbank studies show that only
> *one* was lost because Eximbank offered less competitive financing than other
> official export credit agencies. Seven other sales were lost because foreign gov-
> ernments provided aid type financing, which Eximbank can meet only on a
> selective basis.
>
> Uncompetitive pricing by the U.S. seller accounted for 35% of 47 losses to
> foreign competition, while poor quality and inability to meet delivery schedules
> were significant additional reasons for loss of sales. These factors, of course,
> cannot be influenced by Eximbank. We firmly believe that Eximbank has stood
> solidly behind the U.S. exporter in providing competitive official financial assis-
> tance and that the facts demonstrate it [p. 83].

Bergsten's conclusion is supported by the more recent data and by the
analysis of the effect of the change in the Bank's financing policy in April
1980. If anything, the Bank's support appears to have been overly generous. The increases in interest rates and reductions in cover adopted by the
Bank in 1981 may have altered this situation, but data on the disposition
of preliminary commitments authorized thereafter is required before any
conclusion can be drawn.

V. Surveys of Exporters

As a part of its study, the GAO conducted a questionnaire survey of
U.S. exporters pertaining to 1978 exports supported by Eximbank long-
term credits [9].

> The 86 responses identified 10 sales, valued at $434 million, that were lost to
> foreign competitors primarily because of uncompetitive financing. . . . The 10
> lost sales include only those for which exporters applied for and received Exim-
> bank preliminary commitments for long-term financing. We also asked exporters
> for potential 1978 sales for which they did not formally request Eximbank financ-
> ing. Eight firms responded that one reason they did not apply was that the
> expected financing terms were known to be unsuitable. These firms indicated
> that 44 potential sales valued at about $½ billion, were lost because they were
> unable to arrange for competitive financing [pp. 10–11].

The GAO appears to have considerable confidence that the responses
to its questionnaire were accurate and not self-serving, but the reliability

of exporter responses to surveys must be questioned. Even Mr. J. Kenneth Fasick, who supervised the preparation of the GAO report, had been skeptical of such claims in the past. In the 1973 Senate hearings, Mr. Fasick, then the director of the international division of the GAO, stated: "In the past, Eximbank has relied mainly on endorsements of the people it services to demonstrate its effectiveness. But, since the importer and the exporter stand to gain by Eximbank financing, these views may not be completely objective [13, p. 68]." The GAO survey provides an opportunity for exporters to "demonstrate" the need for expanded Eximbank programs, and it seems quite possible that the responses were self-serving. This may also have been a problem in the Eximbank's analysis of PC dispositions, but the Bank has a better chance of obtaining truthful responses because of its continuing relationships with exporters. Moreover, if exporters had falsely claimed in their responses that cases were lost because of uncompetitive financing in order to demonstrate a need for more generous financing, the conclusion to be drawn from the data is that Eximbank long-term financing is even more generous than indicated above.

The Bank also conducts surveys of U.S. exporters and commercial banks as a part of its assessment of the competitiveness of its programs. For its October 1981 competitiveness report, the Bank conducted a questionnaire survey of representative exporters and banks that asked them to rate the "cost, repayment term, cover, and extraordinary support such as local cost financing . . . in terms of their importance to the effectiveness of Eximbank [4, p. 17]." The survey results indicated that [4]

> The exporters and banks surveyed ranked Eximbank programs overall as less competitive than any of the other five major trading nations included in the survey by a fairly wide margin. . . . The cost of Eximbank financing under the long-term programs was considered as the most important element of competitiveness and this element was reported to have deteriorated over the previous year both as to Eximbank's interest rates on direct loans and in the blended rate (including private market interest rate) which is largely determined by the percentage of contract value supported by Eximbank direct loans [p. 17].

These survey results appear to be in direct conflict with the conclusions drawn from the analysis of the data on the disposition of preliminary commitments, which suggests that the survey responses may be self-serving. This possibility is supported by the respondents' suggestions about improving the Bank's performance [4].

> Not surprisingly, suggestions to improve the competitiveness of the long-term programs centered overwhelmingly on the perceived need to offer lower cost financing packages to meet official foreign competition. Additional direct loan funding for Eximbank was suggested repeatedly (as it was the previous year) to permit a higher percentage direct loan coverage at present or lower interest rates,

thus reducing the blended interest cost to the borrower. Present Eximbank direct loan support of 42.5 to 65.0 percent of export value was stated as inadequate to match the usual foreign support of 85 percent. Only one suggestion was made to improve the international arrangement to eliminate subsidies in export finance, and this was thought to be a dubious prospect [p. 19].

The emphasis of the respondents on increasing the generosity of the Bank's financing undoubtedly reflects their concern about exports lost because of foreign export financing subsidization, but the paucity of suggestions to eliminate that subsidization suggests that the subsidization serves their purposes. Even if the Eximbank only matches foreign concessionary export financing, exporters in the supported sectors would have higher exports than they would have had if all concessionary financing were prohibited by an international agreement. Consequently, exporters would be expected to call for more generous Eximbank financing in their survey responses.

VI. Conclusions

The United States offers a more limited set of export support programs through the Eximbank than do most of the other major trading countries, and the total authorized support is substantially less, as a percentage of total exports, than that provided by France, Germany, Italy, Japan, and the United Kingdom. Except in the cases of France and Italy, however, this higher percentage is due largely to insurance and guarantees which generally do not contain a substantial level of subsidization. Except for France and the United Kingdom, subsidization is provided primarily through loan programs, and although the United States provides substantially less medium-term financing than do other countries, the long-term financing provided by the United States for capital goods exports in 1979 was about the average for the six countries studied. France and Italy support a substantially greater percentage of their capital goods exports with long-term financing than does the United States, but Germany and Japan support. a smaller percentage. Furthermore, the long-term, direct credit program of the Eximbank provides a smaller subsidy than provided by France and the United Kingdom, but the subsidy is greater than that provided by Germany and Japan. The medium-term credit programs of France and the United Kingdom are also considerably more generous than those provided by the Eximbank. The Eximbank's programs thus are least competitive for medium-term transactions and considerably less generous than those provided by France and the United Kingdom.

Analysis of the disposition of preliminary commitments issued by the Bank indicates that the Bank's long-term, direct credit program, however, has been quite competitive with that of other countries and that few export sales are lost due to financing. Whereas the direct credit program appears to have met the congressional mandate to provide financing competitive with that provided by other countries, the program has a substantial cost to the United States. Estimates of that cost are considered in the next chapter.

Appendix 5.A. The Export Financing Programs of Six Other Countries

This appendix describes the principal export support programs of six major countries, Canada, France, Germany, Japan, Italy, and the United Kingdom, whose exporters compete with U.S. exporters. The descriptions are taken from the Bank's October 1980, "Competitiveness Report" [3].

A. Canada

The Government of Canada offers limited and relatively cost-uncompetitive support for Canadian exports. The limited aspect is basically due to the fact that a significant portion of Canadian exports is composed of agricultural commodities and mineral resources and that the bulk of Canadian exports are destined for the United States. Official support is not considered to be critical for such exports. Deterioration of Canada's international trade position, coupled with a declining world market share during the 1970's, however, has begun to highlight the importance of export promotion and the comparative lack of official support for exports by the Canadian Government.

An Export Promotion Review Committee was formed in December 1978 by the Ministry of Industry, Trade and Commerce. The Committee examined existing government export promotion programs and made recommendations on how they could be improved. The final report of the Committee, entitled "Strengthening Canada Abroad," was published November 30, 1979. The main thrust of the Committee's recommendations is to encourage the growth of exports through an improvement of the competitiveness of export services, a more liberal policy toward direct investment in Canada, increased tax incentives as a means to stimulate innovation and growth in the Canadian industrial sector, and improved coordination between CIDA (the Canadian International Development Agency) and EDC (the Export Development Corporation). . . .

Export credits, insurance, and guarantees are provided by the Export Development Corporation, a Crown holding company established in 1969 to succeed the

Export Credit Insurance Corporation. EDC is an autonomous, unsubsidized government corporation with authority to commit total export support of up to C$26 billion (U.S.$22.2 billion). It is accountable to the Canadian Parliament through the Minister of Industry, Trade and Commerce. . . .

Enabling legislation for EDC sets out separate loan and contingent liability limits for a Corporate Account and a Canada Account. Transactions which, in the opinion of the Board of Directors, carry risks due to size or term that are beyond those normally undertaken by EDC, may be authorized by the Governor in Council for the Canada Account. These transactions must be judged to be in the national interest by the Minister of Industry, Trade and Commerce and are administered by EDC. Funds required for such transactions are paid to EDC out of the national government's Consolidated Revenue Fund.

EDC programs are not designed to subsidize Canadian exports, but rather to assist exporters whose products are competitive in terms of price, quality, delivery, and after-sales service. To the greatest extent possible, and consistent with its corporate purpose of providing and encouraging financial assistance in support of Canada's export trade, EDC conducts its operations on a financially self-sustaining basis in accordance with commercial principles.

EDC Offers: fixed and floating rate long-term export financing, including lines of credit; insurance for political and commercial credit risks; political risk insurance for Canadian investments abroad; and performance-related insurance and guarantees.

B. France

The French Government administers one of the most comprehensive, aggressive, and competitive export credit systems in the world. A high degree of government involvement in the export sector, as in virtually all sectors of the French economy, can be traced back to the post-World War II reconstruction period. Increased emphasis, however, has been placed on official support of exports as a result of the 1974 balance-of-payments crisis.

The French export credit system is unique in that it is centralized, yet appears to be flexibly managed, and is capable of providing exporters with financing terms and conditions suited to individual transactions. The French system can be described as an "entitlement system"; it is open-ended in terms of budgetary costs. The exporting sector is a priority sector in France and, in the view of the government, deserves unlimited government assistance.

The French Government considers its extensive official export support to be a necessary and positive feature. Such support helps compensate for what the French regard as weaknesses in the domestic economy which put the exporting community at a competitive disadvantage. The French capital market and commercial banking system are not as well developed as those in several other major trading nations. The commercial banking sector is at the heart of the export system, and government intervention is deemed necessary to keep the banks active by making their business both profitable and risk-free. Domestic interest rates are relatively high, and official intervention is considered necessary to keep them in line with rates in other industrialized countries. Therefore, the government, by providing fixed-rate export financing at reduced rates and subsidizing a comprehensive insurance and guarantee program, administers what is perhaps the most costly export credit system among the industrialized nations.

OFFICIAL EXPORT CREDIT INSTITUTIONS The Directorate Relations Economique Exterieur (DREE), an agency of the French Ministry of the Economy, is the policy-making agency regarding official export credit support. The three institutions—the Bank of France, the Banque Française du Commerce Extérieur (BFCE), and Compagnie Française d'Assurance pour le Commerce Extérieur (COFACE)—which actually provide official support for French exports, operate under the direction of DREE. The Bank of France provides official discounting for export credits with medium repayment terms, from 18 months to seven years. For longer term export credits, BFCE finances the later maturities either through direct loans or by discounting credits extended by banks to French exporters. COFACE provides credit insurance and guarantees for commercial and political risks. COFACE cover is mandatory for all transactions benefiting from preferential financing and having a repayment term exceeding three years. During 1979, the percentage of French exports receiving official credit support was 30 percent of total exports.

Programs and forms of support offered under the French export credit system are as follows: export credits for medium- and long-term transactions in line with International Arrangement minimum interest rates; mixed credits; export credit insurance and guarantees; inflation insurance; exchange risk insurance; and contractor guarantees and performance and bid bonds.

C. Germany

Germany's successful export performance is not directly attributable to government subsidies in the financing of exports; government assistance in this area has been minimal. To a large extent, it can be attributed to national government guidance and planned cooperation between the government, commercial banks, and the business sector. The government, through various grants and tax-relief programs, also assures that an adequate amount of capital will be allocated for research and development purposes. This is part of a broader government policy aimed at developing competitiveness in the capital-intensive and more technologically sophisticated sectors of the economy. German firms, as a result, are able to market a high-quality, price competitive product for which financing terms become a relatively minor issue.

It can be argued that, given the special role commercial banks play in the German economy, direct official support is not necessary. The banks provide short-, medium-, and long-term credits at floating rates of interest. Long-term, fixed-rate financing for exports is made available through the Ausfuhrkredit Gesellschaft (AKA), a syndicate of 58 commercial banks. Market interest rates have until recently been competitive, on a nominal basis, with most foreign officially-supported rates. As a result, AKA's B fund, the only one of its three funds that is governmentally supported, was seldom used during 1978 and 1979. . . .

OFFICIAL EXPORT CREDIT INSTITUTIONS   Financing support for German exports is provided by two institutions: Ausfuhrkredit Gesellschaft (AKA), and Kreditanstalt fuer Wiederaufbau (KfW). AKA offers as one of its services a limited quantity of preferential-rate refinancing for medium-term supplier credits. KfW, a government development bank that provides domestic investment financing and financial and technical assistance to developing countries, extends preferential, fixed-rate export loans for projects with long repayment terms.

Export credit insurance is provided by Deutsche Revisions and Treuhand AG (Treuarbeit), a public agency, and Hermes Kreditversicherung AG, a private company. In almost every case, Hermes insurance is a precondition to obtaining medium- and long-term export financing.

The programs offered by the official German export credit system include: direct credit support for medium- and long-term transactions; commercial and political risk guarantees for short-, medium-, and long-term financing; local cost insurance; exchange risk insurance; and performance and bid bond insurance.

D. Italy

The Italian Government, realizing the crucial impact of foreign trade on the Italian economy, feels compelled to assist the private sector in the export of goods and services. At the same time, it appears to be sensitive to the drain on the Italian Treasury of export subsidization and would undoubtedly favor measures to reduce the level of subsidies provided by OECD member countries. It can be argued, however, that the pendulum is swinging toward increased government assistance to, and promotion of, Italian exports.

An Export Financing Regulation (Law No. 227), passed in May 1977, introduced flexible and innovative approaches for assisting exports over a broad spectrum. It established two agencies within the Interministerial Committee for Economic Planning: CIPES (Interministerial Committee for Foreign Economic Policy), which coordinates governmental export assistance and development aid policies; and SACE (Special Section on Export Credit Insurance), an independent government agency that administers Italy's official export credit insurance and guarantee programs. . . .

OFFICIAL EXPORT CREDIT INSTITUTIONS   Official support for exports is provided by Mediocredito Centrale (Instituto Centrale per il Credito a Medio Termine) and SACE (Special Section on Export Credit Insurance). Mediocredito works with Italy's special medium- and long-term credit institutions and commercial banks, both foreign and domestic, and provides competitive financing by granting interest rate subsidies and by refinancing credits extended by these institutions. The percentage of Italian exports covered by SACE was approximately 13 percent in 1978 and 11 percent in 1979. Mediocredito offered interest rate support for approximately seven percent of Italian exports in 1979, up from six percent in 1978.

Although it has no budgetary ceilings, authorizations by Mediocredito Centrale are limited by Treasury allocations. Mediocredito is permitted to borrow from the Treasury and private capital markets, both domestic and international.

SACE, established in 1977 to provide insurance coverage for exports, is legally a part of INA (Instituto Nazionale delle Assicurazioni), the state-owned insurance group. SACE issues authorizations for export credits with maturities of up to seven years. Authorizations for credits with maturities beyond seven years are issued by the Ministry of Foreign Trade. SACE's insurance cover is itself guaranteed by the Italian Treasury. Annual budgetary ceilings for medium and long-term coverage are set by the Treasury. For 1979, the ceiling was 3,500 billion lire ($4.2 billion). For short-term transactions (under two years) the ceiling was 5,000 lire ($6 billion).

The basic programs offered through Italian export credit agencies include: preferential fixed-rate financing for transactions over two years; insurances for short-, medium-, and long-term commercial and political risks; local cost financing; and performance bonds.

E. Japan

Government involvement in the exporting sectors is far-reaching and diverse. In the area of export credits and guarantees, the Eximbank of Japan, the Japan Development Bank, and the Bank of Japan have been active in providing financing assistance for long- and medium-term export transactions and major projects. The Japanese Government has been one of the most aggressive of all industrialized-country governments providing export financing. Officially-supported financing consistently adheres to the guidelines of the International Arrangement regarding interest rates and repayment terms.

The Japanese Government has also devised a rather extensive aid program. Major projects in developing countries are often financed through a mixture of aid funds and official export credit support. Use of this form of mixed credit support appears to be increasing as Japan's export promotion policy puts more and more emphasis on sales to developing countries. While much of Japan's aid is untied, it is believed that a substantial percentage of untied aid results in Japanese procurement.

Other forms of official support for exports included tax incentives, coverage of R&D expenditures, and guaranteed loans for working capital. Following World War II, these forms of assistance were made available to promote development in the basic industries. Today, such assistance is directed toward the development of new industries and sectors that will eventually play a significant role in the Japanese economy. Government-guaranteed loans for working-capital expenses are offered at or near the official discount rate to enable companies to reduce prices and thereby maintain their market share. The decisive factors in Japanese industry appear to be maintaining full employment and market share, rather than increasing profits. Japanese companies appear quite willing to operate at a loss over the short-run in order to maintain or increase market share. . . .

OFFICIAL EXPORT CREDIT INSTITUTIONS Primary responsibility for Japanese export credit and insurance support is vested in the Ministry for International Trade and Industry (MITI), Export Insurance Division. MITI provides export credit insurance and guarantees covering commercial and political risks to exporters, commercial banks, and the Export–Import Bank of Japan.

The Export–Import Bank of Japan was established in 1950 as an independent governmental financial institution to provide a wide range of financial facilities aimed at supplementing and encouraging financing by commercial banks. The Bank's activities include both supplier and buyer credits and guarantees for various financial obligations. In addition, Eximbank Japan provides overseas investment credits to Japanese investors for their enterprises abroad and for their participation in joint ventures. Overseas investment funds are also provided to foreign governments as capital contributions to joint-venture projects with Japanese firms. The Bank's total assets as of December 31, 1979, were 4,955 billion yen ($20.7 billion). Major sources of funds include capital subscribed by the Japanese Government, borrowings from the government's postal savings Trust Fund Bureau and Foreign Exchange Funds Special Account, and revenues generated by the Bank's various activities.

Aid to developing countries is provided by the Japanese Overseas Economic Cooperation Fund (OECF) and by the Export–Import Bank. The OECF extends soft loans to the governments of developing nations carrying interest rates as low as 1.75 percent per annum and maturities of up to 30 years. Hard loans extended by OECF typically have an interest rate of five percent and a maturity of 20 years with a five-year grace period. OECF also extends commercial loans to Japanese corporations with interest rates ranging from 3.5 to 7.25 percent per annum with ten-year repayment terms. Occasionally, the OECF and Eximbank combine their funds to provide mixed credit financing. Interest rates on these loans range from four to 6.75 percent per annum and carry maturities up to 25 years. Mixed credit financing is most frequently used to support natural resource development projects.

The programs of the export financing agencies include: preferential fixed-rate financing for credits over two years; project lines of credit extended by the government and private firms at preferential, fixed interest rates; credit insurance for commercial and political risks; local cost financing; aid financing in particular situations; exchange risk insurance; and performance bond guarantees.

F. United Kingdom

Export finance and credit insurance is provided by the Export Credits Guarantee Department (ECGD), an executive agency of the British Government established in 1919. ECGD provides a vast array of services to exporters, commercial banks, and foreign buyers. ECGD's comprehensive insurance policies enable exporters to aggressively pursue sales by providing them cover against the risk of nonpayment. Its unconditional guarantees of 100 percent repayment and interest rate subsidies for commercial banks enable them to finance exports at competitive interest rates.

ECGD is a separate department of the British Government, but it is accountable to the same ministers as is the Department of Trade. For a large portion of its export insurance, it follows the recommendations of an Advisory Council, the members of which are appointed by the Secretary of State for Trade. . . .

The operations of ECGD are divided into trading and non-trading operations. The trading operation covers all insurance programs except the inflation risk scheme and all bank guarantee programs. Programs under the trading operation are designed to operate without using public funds. Non-trading operations include the fixed-rate export finance scheme, inflation risk insurance, and an economic assistance program. These programs are financed with public funds.

ECGD derives its authority from the Export Guarantees and Overseas Investment Act of 1978. Under Section 1 of the Act (the commercial account), ECGD insures on a purely commercial basis. This involves about 90 percent of its business. The remainder of the department's credit insurance business is done under Section 2 of the Act (the national interest account). This involves business which cannot be commercially justified, but is covered as a public service. Both of these accounts are intended to be self-supporting.

ECGD's budget is voted annually by Parliament; any surplus or loss from operations becomes a part of the national budget. The Export Guarantees and Overseas Investment Act of 1978 sets limits on the maximum outstanding liabilities which ECGD may incur. There is a limit of 25 billion pounds ($53 billion) for cumulative outstanding liabilities incurred in sterling; it may be increased to 40 billion pounds ($84.9 billion) by affirmative resolutions in the House of Commons. There is a limit of SDR10 billion (U.S.$13 billion) for cumulative outstanding liabilities incurred in foreign currencies; this may be increased to SDR25 billion (U.S.$32.6 billion) by affirmative resolutions. The only operations not covered by these statutory limits are fixed-rate sterling loans and the foreign currency export finance scheme. Both of these programs use public funds.

ECGD offers: insurance—comprehensive and specific policies for both exports and overseas investment risks for short-, medium-, and long-term transactions; bank guarantees for short-, medium-, and long-term transactions; cost escalation insurance; performance and tender bond insurance; inflation risk insurance; and interest rate subsidies for medium- and long-term transactions.

References

1. Bergsten, C. Fred. *The International Economic Policy of the United States: Selected Papers of C. Fred Bergsten, 1977–1979,* Lexington Books, Lexington, Massachusetts, 1980.

2. Export–Import Bank, Policy Analysis Staff, "Primary Factors in Buyers' Decisions: 'The Causation Study,'" unpublished paper, Washington, D.C., 1979.
3. Export–Import Bank, "Report to the Congress on Export Credit Competition and the Export–Import Bank of the United States for the Period July 1, 1979 through June 30, 1980," Washington, D.C., 1980.
4. Export–Import Bank, "Report to the Congress on Export Credit Competition and the Export–Import Bank of the United States for the Period July 1, 1980 through December 31, 1980," Washington, D.C., 1981.
5. Export–Import Bank, Policy Analysis Staff. "Follow-Up Studies," unpublished paper, Washington, D.C., 1981.
6. Export–Import Bank, Policy Analysis Staff. "Follow-Up on Cases Denied Direct Loan Support," unpublished paper, Washington, D.C., 1981.
7. Export–Import Bank, "Disposition of Preliminary Commitments," unpublished paper, Washington, D.C., 1981.
8. Export–Import Bank, "Disposition of Preliminary Commitments," unpublished paper, Washington, D.C., 1980.
9. General Accounting Office (GAO), "Financial and Other Constraints Prevent Eximbank from Consistently Offering Competitive Financing for U.S. Exports," Washington, D.C., 1980.
10. Organization for Economic Cooperation and Development (OECD). *The Export Credit Financing Systems in OECD Member Countries,* Paris, 1976.
11. U.S. Senate, Subcommittee on International Finance, Committee on Banking, Housing, and Urban Affairs, "Hearing on Competitive Export Financing," Washington, D.C., 1980.
12. U.S. Senate, Subcommittee on International Finance, Committee on Banking, Housing, and Urban Affairs, "Hearing on Export–Import Bank Programs and Budget," Washington, D.C., 1980.
13. U.S. Senate, Subcommittee on International Finance, Committee on Banking, Housing, and Urban Affairs, "Hearings," Washington, D.C., 1973.
14. Wallen, Axel. "Implications for the Arrangement of Operational Alternatives to the Present Matrix," Organization for Economic Cooperation and Development, Paris, 1980; reproduced in [11, pp. 16–65].

6

The Subsidy Provided
by Eximbank Financing

I. Introduction

Export financing at concessionary interest rates not only provides a subsidy to foreign importers and/or to domestic exporters but also affects the allocation of resources among countries and among sectors within a country. The subsidy thus differs from the welfare effects of that financing to the extent that the output of the supported goods is affected and resources are directed to the supported sectors. Concessionary export financing may also affect the domestic and export prices of supported goods as well as the profits in the supported sectors. The estimates of the subsidy presented in this chapter do not take into account the effects of Eximbank financing on prices or profits, so the estimates are not measures of the welfare consequences for foreign importers or for the United States. The welfare consequences of concessionary export financing are identified in the following chapter, although only very limited estimates can be developed given the available data.

In order to calculate the subsidy provided by Eximbank financing, the opportunity cost of the funds the Bank lends must be determined. A lower bound on that opportunity cost is the Federal Financing Bank (FFB) rate at which the Bank borrows to fund its loans. When the Eximbank borrows from the FFB, however, the Treasury is required to borrow in the U.S. capital markets, which increases the demand for funds and crowds some borrowers out of the market. The projects that are crowded out by the Treasury borrowing have marginal returns approximately equal to the market rate of interest or else they would have been financed at the higher interest rate. Consequently, the relevant opportunity cost to the U.S. economy of Eximbank financing is the market rate of interest.

When crowded out of the U.S. capital market, some borrowers will obtain funds in the international capital markets usually in the form of Eurodollar borrowings. This suggests that the Eurodollar interest rate would be the relevant opportunity cost of Eximbank financing, but the credits extended by the Bank are likely to be riskier than U.S. projects financed in the Eurodollar market. Risk is priced by the spread above the Eurodollar deposit rate, so the opportunity cost will be taken to be the Eurodollar deposit rate plus the spread on the borrowings of the country to which the Eximbank extended the credit. This interest rate is equivalent to the rate at which the foreign importers of U.S. goods would have had to borrow had Eximbank financing not been available. The subsidy estimated using this opportunity cost thus reflects the gain to the foreign importer as well as the cost to the U.S. economy.

Several recent estimates of the subsidy provided by Eximbank financing are reviewed in the next section, but since most of those estimates do not take into account certain important characteristics of Eximbank loans, they tend to understate the actual subsidy. Section III presents an expression for the subsidy provided on an individual Eximbank credit, and Section IV reports estimates of this subsidy for the direct credits authorized by the Bank in FY1979, FY1980, and FY1981. Section V provides a statistical analysis of the Bank's direct credits, and conclusions are offered in the final section.

II. Estimates of the Subsidy

An estimate of the savings from increasing the interest rates on government-supported export loans to the level of government long-term borrowing rates was presented in the OECD's Wallen report [20], as discussed in Chapter 5 (see Table 5.8). The estimate was based on the difference between the interest received on the official export credits outstanding at year-end 1979 and the interest that would have been received had the credits been refinanced at the May 1980 government long-term bond rate, which at the time was 10.375% for the United States. Because the OECD did not have data on the actual interest rates on the outstanding export credits, all credits were assumed to have been made at the "average minimum interest rate" specified in the arrangement matrix.

The average interest rate difference for the Eximbank was 2.85%, and with $11.052 billion in outstanding credits the estimated annual interest savings was $315 million. If the Bank ceased making loans at fiscal year-end 1979 and the average term of the outstanding credits was 5 years, the present value of the subsidy discounted at the government long-term borrowing rate of 10.375% would have been $1.229 billion.[1]

The savings reported in the Wallen report is an underestimate of the subsidy provided by Eximbank financing because it takes the government long-term borrowing rate as the opportunity cost of Eximbank funds. At year-end 1979, the 5-year Eurodollar deposit rate was 11.88% and, if the average spread on Eurodollar loans was 0.75%, the opportunity cost was 12.63%, or 2.355% above the interest rate used by the OECD in its estimates. The average interest rate on all outstanding Eximbank credits was 7.00% at the end of December 1979, which was approximately 5.63% below the opportunity cost. This implies an annual subsidy of $622 million, which, when discounted at 12.63% for 5 years, is $2.426 billion. Although the average interest rate on outstanding Eximbank credits has been increasing over time as the 6% loans issued during the Kearns administration are repaid and new credits are issued at higher interest rates, the 5-year Eurodollar rate as of September 1981 was approximately 17%, so the interest rate differential was even greater than at the end of 1979.

A second estimate of the subsidy provided by Eximbank financing was prepared by the Treasury Department for the December 3, 1980 "USTR [United States Trade Representative]– Treasury Meeting on Export Financing." The Treasury calculated the subsidy provided by the credits issued during the previous three fiscal years rather than the subsidy on the Bank's loan portfolio. The estimated subsidies are [19]

Fiscal year	Present value of the subsidy ($ million)
1980	456
1979	132
1978	9

"These subsidies are calculated by setting up theoretical 10 year repayment streams for the annual Eximbank budget from foreign importers to Eximbank and from Eximbank to the Treasury Department. The difference between the repayment streams is then discounted at the prevailing

---

[1] The present values for average terms of 3 and 7 years are $0.812 billion and $1.567 billion, respectively.

TABLE 6.1

CBO Estimates of the Eximbank Loan Subsidies[a,b]

Fiscal year	Weighted average interest rate on direct loans (%)	Direct loan authorizations ($ billion)	Aaa Corporate bond yield (%)	Estimated subsidy ($ million)
1971	6.0	2.3	7.39	32.0
1972	6.0	2.2	7.21	26.6
1973	6.0	2.9	7.44	41.8
1974	6.38	4.3	8.57	94.2
1975	7.9	2.3	8.83	21.4
1976	8.42	2.1	8.43	0.2
1977	8.5	0.8	8.02	−3.8
1978	8.38	2.9	8.73	10.2
1979	8.28	4.3	9.63	58.1
1980	8.44	3.6	11.94	126.0
		27.7		406.5

[a] Reproduced from [2].

[b] Weighted average interest rate on direct loans and direct loan authorizations were supplied by Eximbank staff. The Aaa corporate bond yield was taken from Federal Reserve Board, *Annual Statistical Digest* and *Federal Reserve Bulletin,* various issues.

U.S. Treasury bond yield [19, p. 1].'' This approach provides an estimate of the burden on U.S. taxpayers of Eximbank loans but understates the subsidy relative to the market rate of interest.

A third estimate of the subsidy on Eximbank credits was provided by the Congressional Budget Office [2]. The CBO calculated the annual interest rate subsidy for direct loans issued in each year from 1971 through 1980 using the Aaa corporate bond yield as the opportunity cost. The results are presented in Table 6.1 and indicate an annual subsidy of $406.5 million on the credits issued over the 10-year period. Assuming that half of those credits are still outstanding, the CBO estimated an annual cost of approximately $200 million. For credits authorized in 1980, the annual subsidy was $126 million.[2] Discounting the 1980 subsidy at the Aaa bond yield of 11.94% assuming an average term of 10 years yields a present value of the subsidy of $735 million. This estimate exceeds that of the

[2] This estimate is based on direct loan authorizations of $3.6 billion in FY1980, but actual authorizations, including the PEFCO loans receiving an Eximbank interest rate subsidy, were close to $4.8 billion.

Treasury because the Aaa corporate bond yield was above the Eximbank's FFB borrowing rate, which averaged 11.196% in FY1980.

The CBO also estimated the subsidy on the assumption that the relevant market interest rate was the Eurodollar rate which was taken to be 14% for 1980. The interest rate differential on the Bank's portfolio of $13.8 billion, which carried an average interest rate of 7.31%, was 6.69% for an annual cost of $923 million. The present value of the FY1980 subsidy of $200 million is $1.076 billion using a discount rate of 14%.

James Cruse and Susan Whitsitt of the policy analysis staff of the Bank also provided an estimate of the subsidy based on the difference between a lending rate of 9.5% and various FFB borrowing rates.[3] For each $1.0 billion of 10-year loans, their estimates of the present value of the subsidy are [3, p. 12]

	Subsidy per $1 billion in loans FFB borrowing rate (%)		
	10	12	14
Subsidy ($ million)	15	115	195

At an FFB borrowing rate of 14%, a $4 billion authorization has a present value cost of $780 million. This is a conservative estimate for two reasons. First, the average Eximbank lending rate was substantially below 9.5% until the mid-1981 increase to 10.75%. Second, the opportunity cost has been taken as the FFB rate rather than the market rate, although the subsidies can be reinterpreted as pertaining to market rates equal to the stated FFB rates.

These four studies imply that the annual subsidy on Eximbank loans was between $200 and $900 million in 1980.[4] As indicated in the next section, however, these estimates are likely to understate significantly the subsidy even when they are based on market rates of interest because of the nature of the repayment schedule on Eximbank loans. A fifth estimate of the present value of the subsidy has been presented by Dwight Phaup

[3] Cruse and Whitsitt also estimate that if the Bank over the past 10 years had loaned at interest rates that allowed it to break even on current loans, the Bank's reserves would have been $480 million greater by the end of 1980. It is not clear if this estimate is based on breaking even, including a cost for equity and reserves, or if equity and reserves were assumed to be costless.

[4] None of these studies includes the subsidy on PEFCO loans.

[16] whose estimates take into account the effect of the repayment schedule using equation (1) below. Taking as the opportunity cost the 15.16% "average rate on long-term commercial loans for FY1980 [p. 6]," Phaup estimates the subsidy for FY1980 direct credits as $861 million, assuming that repayment of all loans to the Bank commences 6 months after the loan authorization. Since the moratorium or grace period on Eximbank loans was not known, he also calculated the subsidy as $1.241 billion, with the moratorium defined as the time from the authorization the credit to time of the first repayment. Phaup's estimates are closer to those to be presented here than are the other four estimates. The estimates differ, however, because of different measures of the market interest rate and the moratorium, and because Phaup did not include the subsidy on the PEFCO credits authorized in conjunction with the Bank's FY1980 supplemental authorization.

III. The Subsidy Provided by an Eximbank Credit

Many of the exports supported by Eximbank financing involve the participation of a private lender, and in these transactions the private lender typically takes the short maturity with the Eximbank taking the long maturity. For example, in a 10-year loan in which a private lender and the Bank each take equal shares, the principal would be repaid in 20 equal semiannual installments, with the first 10 payments made to the private lender and the last 10 payments made to the Eximbank. Interest is paid to the Eximbank on the outstanding balance during the first 5 years, but on such a loan the Eximbank credit is outstanding for an average period of 7.5 years. If private lending had not been involved and the Bank had provided the entire credit, the loan would have been outstanding for an average of 5.0 years. The subsidy provided per dollar of financing is greater the greater is the average term, so an expression for the subsidy that takes into account the repayment schedule is required.

The subsidy provided by an Eximbank credit is a function of the Eximbank lending rate r, the market interest rate i, the term T of the loan, and the moratorium M on the repayment of principal to the Bank, which usually corresponds to the time, if any, during which payments are made to the private lender. The subsidy S can be expressed as the subsidy rate s per dollar of the loan multiplied by the loan principal L, and with the assumption that the discount rate is equal to the market interest rate i, the subsidy rate, using continuous compounding, is given by

$$s = (1 - r/i) [1 - (e^{-iM} - e^{-iT})/(i(T - M))]. \tag{1}$$

This expression has been used by Horvath [13] [14] and Phaup [16] and is derived in Appendix 5.A. As would be expected, the subsidy rate on a concessionary interest rate loan is greater the greater is either the moratorium M or the loan term T.[5]

The subsidy on an Eximbank credit equals the subsidy rate multiplied by the amount of the credit, but that subsidy does not measure the effect of Eximbank financing on the cost of the export to the purchaser. That effect may be measured by the proportion of export value paid by the importer. For example, if a subsidy S is provided by an Eximbank credit authorized to finance an export of value V, the importer actually pays ($V - S$) for the export or a proportion $(1 - \rho)$ of the export value given by

$$1 - \rho = (V - S)/V,$$

where ρ denotes the discount from the export price provided by the subsidy. The measure $1 - \rho$ will be referred to as the effective price paid.

The blended cost of financing on an Eximbank-supported export is a blend of the Eximbank interest rate and the cost of the private capital, both cash payments and borrowings from private lenders. The blended cost h is defined here as the interest rate on a hypothetical loan of the same term as that actually extended which equates the present value of the principal and interest payments on the hypothetical loan to the present value of the principal and interest payments on the combined Eximbank and private credit. With the assumption that the discount rate equals the market interest rate i, the blended interest rate h is given by

$$h = L(V - S)/V - (1 - e^{-iT})/(1 - (1 - e^{-iT})/(iT)), \qquad (2)$$

where V is the value of the export and S is the subsidy computed as above. This expression is derived in Appendix 6.A.

---

[5] To show that the subsidy rate is increasing in T, differentiate equation (1) to obtain

$$\frac{\partial s}{\partial T} = \frac{(1 - r/i)}{i(T - M)^2} [e^{-iM} - e^{-iT}(1 + i(T - M))].$$

Since $r < i$, the subsidy rate is increasing if the term in brackets is positive or equivalently if

$$e^{i(T-M)} > 1 + i(T + M)$$

or if

$$i(T - M) > \ln(1 + i(T - M)).$$

Letting $a = i(T - M)$, it is straightforward to show that for $a > 0$, the left side increases at a rate of 1 while the right side increases at a rate of $1/(1 + a)$. Since at $a = 0$, the two sides are equal, for all $i(T - M) > 0$, $\partial s/\partial T > 0$.

TABLE 6.2

**Example of the Subsidy Effect of Eximbank Taking the
Long Maturity in Blended Financing**[a]

Blended interest rate (%)	Subsidy ($ million)[b]		
	Boeing calculation	Uniform repayment[c]	Delayed repayment[d]
10	0.000	0.000	0.000
9	3.769	3.679	5.226
8	7.538	7.358	10.452
7	11.307	11.037	15.679
6	15.076	14.715	20.904
5	18.844	18.395	26.130

[a] The Boeing calculation is presented on page 182 of
the February 22, 1980 Senate hearings [15].

[b] Calculations assume a $100,000,000 loan with a 10
year term, a 10% discount rate, 50% financing at 10% in
the private market, and 50% Eximbank financing at the
interest rate required to yield the blended interest rate.

[c] Assumes that 50% of each principal payment goes
to the private lender and to Eximbank.

[d] Assumes that the principal repayments for the first
5 years are made to the private lender and for the last 5
years are made to the Eximbank.

The subsidy provided by concessionary Eximbank financing can be
thought of as resulting directly from an interest rate r that is below the
market interest rate i and indirectly from the repayment schedule. To
illustrate the effect of the repayment schedule on the magnitude of the
subsidy, an example [15] given by J. B. L. Pierce, treasurer on the Boeing
Company, will be used.

Pierce's purpose was not to measure the subsidy provided by an
Eximbank credit but to show the difference in cost to an aircraft purchaser when the blended interest rate on an Eximbank–commercial bank
credit exceeds the interest rate on a financing package offered by Airbus
Industrie. If the interest rate differential is reinterpreted, however, as the
difference between the market rate of interest i and the blended interest
rate h in equation (2), the subsidy provided by the Eximbank credit is
obtained. The subsidy calculations provided by Pierce were computed as
a function of the interest rate difference $(i - h)$ for a $100 million credit,
half of which is financed by the Eximbank and repaid uniformly over 10
years. Columns 2 and 3 of Table 6.2 present, respectively, his calculation

and the subsidy computed from equation (1) for blended interest rates between 5 and 10%, using the Boeing assumption of a 10% discount rate. The differences between the estimates is apparently due to the continuous discounting used here and the discrete discounting used by Boeing.

The subsidy estimates in columns 2 and 3 of Table 6.2 are appropriate for Eximbank financing when the Bank provides all the credit but are inappropriate for blended credits in which the Bank does not receive principal repayments uniformly over the term of the credit. When the Bank takes the long maturity on a credit involving private participation so that principal repayments do not commence until the private loan has been repaid, the subsidy provided by an Eximbank concessionary interest rate loan is substantially greater than that reported in columns 2 and 3. For example, if the Bank receives the principal payments in years 6 through 10 instead of uniformly over the 10 years, the subsidy is 42% greater, as reported in column 4. The subsidy provided by Eximbank concessionary financing in a blended credit in which the Bank takes the later maturity is thus due directly to the concessionary interest rate and indirectly to the repayment schedule. For the example presented in Table 6.2, the latter effect is 42% of the former and is thus substantial enough that it must be taken into account in any analysis of the subsidy provided by Eximbank financing. The effect of the repayment schedule was not taken into account in any of the estimates reviewed in Section II except Phaup's.

As another example of the effect of the repayment schedule on the subsidy, the change in lending policy adopted shortly after Draper assumed the chairmanship of the Bank will be considered. At that time the interest rate on nonaircraft direct credits was increased from 8.75 to 10.75% and the percentage of the export value financed was reduced.[6] While these changes permit more exports to be supported with the same authorization and increase the net income of the Bank, the actual subsidy provided, or equivalently the cost borne by the United States, could increase. Consider, for example, a $100 million credit at 8.75% with a 10-year term and no moratorium that finances 85% of the value of an export. This credit provides a subsidy of $20.09 million when the market interest rate is 15%. An increase in the lending rate to 10.75% would reduce the subsidy to $13.66 million (a 32% reduction) on a credit of the same term and moratorium. If instead, however, the Bank were to reduce its cover from 85 to 42.5%, with private lenders receiving the payments during the

---

[6] When the Bank increased its lending rates, it also imposed a 2% fee which reduces the subsidy and acts to offset partially the effect of any increase in the average period over which the credit is outstanding. The 2% fee was applied to six credits authorized in FY1981, resulting in income of $3.4 million.

first 5 years and the Bank receiving the payments during the last 5 years, the subsidy provided on two such $50 million Eximbank credits with 10.75% interest rates would be $18.92 million, a reduction of less than 6%. If the cover were reduced to 25% with the Bank taking the repayments during the last 2.5 years of a 10-year credit blended with private financing, the subsidy would be $20.66 million, an increase of nearly 3%. Consequently, while an increase in the Eximbank lending rate reduces the subsidy if credits are authorized with the same term and moratorium as before, an increase in the moratorium, and hence in the average term of the loan, could increase the cost to the United States.[7]

As another example, consider the policy option of increasing the term on an Eximbank credit. As discussed in more detail in Chapter 11, in 1981 and 1982 the Bank increased the term of some of its credits because other countries refused to agree to an acceptable international agreement to eliminate or at least to reduce greatly their export financing subsidization. To demonstrate its willingness to extend the term of its credits, on September 23, 1981 the Bank authorized a 20-year, $95.340 million credit at 10% to the Ivory Coast to finance a $136.2 million export for a hydroelectric project. The 5-year Eurodollar rate at that time was 16.75% and the spread on Ivory Coast borrowing in 1980 was 1.635%. Taking the market interest rate as 18.385% and the moratorium M as 0.5 years, the subsidy on this credit is $32.97 million. If the term of the credit had been 10-years, the subsidy would have been $25.34 million. Consequently, going from a 10- to a 20-year term increased the subsidy by 30% in this case. Extending the term of Eximbank credits thus can be a costly means of attempting to convince other countries to reduce their export financing subsidization.

IV. Estimation of the Subsidy

A. Measurement of the Variables for Direct Credits

To estimate the subsidy provided by Eximbank direct credits, the parameters r, i, M, and T in equation (1) must be measured. The Eximbank lending rates for each credit are reported in the Bank's annual report. The market interest rate r is measured as the Eurodollar deposit rate plus the spread reflecting the risk associated with the credit. Two Eurodollar rates reported by the Continental Illinois National Bank [1] have been used in the estimate. The first is the 5-year rate that is intended to

---

[7] Phaup estimates that the difference in the subsidy rate for FY1980 and for FY1973 as computed by Horvath [13] is primarily due to an increase in the term of the credits.

reflect the alternative of issuing Eurodollar bonds or of borrowing long-term Eurodollars from a commercial bank. The second is the 6-month Eurodollar rate which corresponds to borrowing at a floating interest rate based on the Libor rate.[8] During fiscal years 1979 and 1980 the 6-month Eurodollar rate was generally above the 5-year Eurodollar rate, as indicated in Table 6.3.

Estimates of the spread by country based on a weighted average of the international borrowings by private companies and government agencies during the first half of calendar year 1979 are reported in *Euromoney* (October 1979). For a number of countries the estimate of the spread was based on a small number of transactions, so the accuracy of these data may not be as high as would be desired. Also, since the Eximbank requires a guarantor on the loans it extends, the risk associated with its loans may be somewhat lower than the risks on the loans on which the estimates of the spread were made. Private and governmental agency borrowings, however, also often carry guarantees by the government of the importing country, so the reported spread may be appropriate for the risk on Eximbank credits. During FY1979 the Eximbank extended direct credits to 46 countries, but spread data were available for only 33 of those countries. To estimate the spread for the other 13 countries, the spread for the 33 for which data were available was regressed on the per capita GNP for those countries and then used to predict the spread for the remaining 13 countries. For FY1980, the spreads from *Euromoney* (February 1980) for 9 countries were estimated based on data for 29 other countries that received Eximbank credits.[9] For FY1981 spread data or

---

[8] The Eurodollar rate for 5-year deposits was the longest term for which data were available. The 6-month Eurodollar rate was used because the Eximbank used that rate to measure the cost of private financing for Ansett Airlines of Australia [17, p. 285].

[9] The regression equation ($R^2 = .519$) for FY1979 was

$$\text{SPREAD} = 1.531 - .619(\text{E} -3)\text{GNPPC} - .122(\text{E} -6)(\text{GPPPC})^2$$
$$\phantom{\text{SPREAD} = } (11.19) \quad (-3.71) (-2.59)$$
$$\phantom{\text{SPREAD} = } -.727(\text{E} -11)(\text{GPPPC})^3,$$
$$\phantom{\text{SPREAD} = } (-2.01)$$

where GPPPC is the GNP per capita and the *t*-statistic is reported below the estimate. The GNP for the country was also used as an independent variable but it had no explanatory power. The regression equation ($R^2 = .397$) for FY1980 was

$$\text{SPREAD} = .832 + .487(\text{E} -4)\text{GNPPC} - .372(\text{E} -7)(\text{GNPPC})^2$$
$$\phantom{\text{SPREAD} = } (8.68) \quad (.48) (-1.39)$$
$$\phantom{\text{SPREAD} = } + .323(\text{E} -11)(\text{GNPPC})^3.$$
$$\phantom{\text{SPREAD} = } (1.74)$$

TABLE 6.3

Eurodollar Interest Rates (%)[a]

		6-Month	5-Year
1978	October	10.48	9.71
	November	11.90	10.15
	December	12.06	10.15
1979	January	11.89	10.28
	February	11.13	10.21
	March	10.98	10.15
	April	10.87	10.05
	May	10.99	10.05
	June	10.60	9.83
	July	10.89	10.01
	August	11.55	10.33
	September	12.66	10.88
	October	14.41	11.44
	November	14.89	12.11
	December	14.32	11.82
1980	January	14.43	11.92
	February	15.23	13.37
	March	18.59	14.94
	April	16.96	13.74
	May	11.29	11.25
	June	9.62	10.89
	July	9.56	11.10
	August	11.10	12.18
	September	12.55	12.89
	October	13.44	12.90
	November	15.77	13.91
	December	17.81	14.47
1981	January	16.88	14.17
	February	17.03	14.86
	March	16.38	14.93
	April	16.01	15.39
	May	18.47	16.43
	June	17.11	15.61
	July	18.22	15.98
	August	18.84	16.60
	September	18.00	16.99
	October	16.67	16.82
	November	14.10	15.44
	December	13.90	15.23

[a] Source: [1].

estimates were available for 46 of the 52 countries receiving loans and the spreads for the other 6 were estimated.[10]

For aircraft credits the date on which each aircraft credit was authorized is reported in the Bank's aircraft report [7], and for those credits the private market interest rate was measured as the Eurodollar rate for the month in which the credit was authorized, plus the spread. This provides an estimate of the opportunity cost of funds at the time the financing decision was made. For the FY1979 and FY1980 nonaircraft credits the date of the credit authorization is not available, so the market interest rate was taken to be the spread plus the average Eurodollar rate for the year in which the authorization was made. For FY1981 the authorization data for all credits is given in [11].

For aircraft credits, data are available on the number of semiannual payments to the Eximbank and to a private lender in a blended credit. Since the aircraft standstill and the arrangement specify that repayment is to begin no later than 6 months after the drawdown of the credit, the moratorium M on the repayment of principal to the Eximbank has been measured as the number of years, if any, over which payments are scheduled to the private lender, plus one-half year. For nonaircraft credits the date of the first repayment to the Bank is reported in its annual report, but no information is available on the participation of private lenders. For these credits M is measured as one-half year plus the number of years between the first payment to the Bank and the year after the credit was authorized. This measure is less accurate than that for aircraft credits and may overstate the moratorium to the extent to which the drawdown of the loan does not occur during the year in which the credit was authorized.[11]

Data on the number of semiannual payments to the Bank are available for all credits, so the term T has been measured as M plus the number of years during which the payments are to be made to the Bank.

B. Loan and Subsidy Data: Long-Term Direct Credits

As indicated in Chapter 1, the Bank entered into an extraordinary arrangement with PEFCO during FY1980 to provide blended financing for

---

[10] Spread data were not available for Liechtenstein, Nauru, Zimbabwe, Cayman Islands, Netherlands Antilles, and Malta. All the credits except that to Malta were included in the Bank's FY1981 additionality study [12], and for the other five countries the average spread for the Eximbank's country risk groups was used (see Appendix 6.B). The spread for Malta was taken to be the average for the "satisfactory" group.

[11] The sensitivity of the estimates to this assumption will be discussed in the next subsection.

TABLE 6.4d

Eximbank Direct Credits by Sector, FY1981

Sector	Number of loans	Total loans ($ million)	Percentage of total	Average lending rate (%)	Average loan ($ million)	Average spread (%)	Average moratorium (years)	Average term (years)
Agriculture/construction	2	5.1	0.1	8.750	2.6	1.289	2.17	14.67
Communication	8	336.9	6.7	8.703	42.1	0.844	3.65	11.15
Manufacturing	21	428.9	8.5	8.753	20.4	0.867	4.30	10.40
Mining/refining	31	780.8	15.5	8.895	25.2	0.804	4.47	10.86
Power	20	739.1	14.7	8.807	37.0	0.784	4.56	13.23
Aircraft	30	2,550.1	50.6	8.952	85.0	0.730	4.28	10.82
Other transportation	5	60.9	1.2	9.250	12.2	0.659	4.45	10.05
Miscellaneous	10	137.3	2.7	9.000	13.7	0.779	4.68	8.93
All credits	127	5,039.1	100.0	8.879	39.7	0.796	4.34	11.04

TABLE 6.5a

Eximbank Direct Credits by Country Risk Group, FY1979–81

Country risk group	Number of loans	Total loans ($ million)	Percentage of total	Average lending rate (%)	Average loan ($ million)	Average spread (%)	Average moratorium (years)	Average term (years)
Prime	63	3,695.1	27.4	8.547	58.6	0.591	3.39	9.86
Good	143	5,108.1	39.9	8.534	35.7	0.761	3.95	10.75
Satisfactory	136	4,235.1	31.5	8.400	31.1	0.911	4.17	10.37
Poor	21	423.2	3.1	8.684	20.1	1.271	3.85	9.90
All credits	363	13,461.5	100.0	8.495	37.1	0.817	3.93	10.40

TABLE 6.5b

Eximbank Direct Credits by Country Risk Group, FY1979

Country risk group	Number of loans	Total loans ($ million)	Percentage of total	Average lending rate (%)	Average loan ($ million)	Average spread (%)	Average moratorium (years)	Average term (years)
Prime	10	463.6	12.7	8.229	46.4	0.600	4.15	9.95
Good	30	1,418.2	39.0	8.163	47.3	0.778	4.08	11.58
Satisfactory	56	1,526.3	41.9	8.196	27.3	0.926	4.12	10.03
Poor	9	231.1	6.4	8.236	25.7	1.443	5.06	10.17
All credits	105	3,639.2	100.0	8.193	34.7	0.897	4.19	10.48

TABLE 6.5c

Eximbank Direct Credits by Country Risk Group, FY1980

Country risk group	Number of loans	Total loans ($ million)	Percentage of total	Average lending rate (%)	Average loan ($ million)	Average spread (%)	Average moratorium (years)	Average term (years)
Prime	25	1,006.9	21.1	8.401	40.3	0.584	2.78	9.04
Good	50	1,765.8	36.9	8.396	35.3	0.729	3.30	9.70
Satisfactory	50	1,844.8	38.6	8.309	36.9	0.886	3.80	10.13
Poor	6	165.6	3.5	8.417	27.6	0.995	1.67	9.50
All credits	131	4,783.2	100.0	8.365	36.5	0.773	3.32	9.73

TABLE 6.5d

Eximbank Direct Credits by Country Risk Group, FY1981

Country risk group	Number of loans	Total loans ($ million)	Percentage of total	Average lending rate (%)	Average loan ($ million)	Average spread (%)	Average moratorium (years)	Average term (years)
Prime	28	2,224.5	44.1	8.790	79.4	0.597	3.66	10.55
Good	63	1,924.1	38.2	8.820	30.5	0.778	4.40	11.20
Satisfactory	30	864.0	17.1	8.938	28.8	0.923	4.86	11.40
Poor	6	26.5	0.5	9.625	4.4	1.289	4.23	9.89
All credits	127	5,039.1	100.0	8.879	39.7	0.796	4.34	11.04

TABLE 6.6a

Eximbank Direct Credits by Area, FY1979–1981

Area	Number of loans	Total loans ($ million)	Percentage of total	Average lending rate (%)	Average loan ($ million)	Average spread (%)	Average moratorium (years)	Average term (years)
Canada	14	1,602.0	11.9	8.533	114.4	0.748	3.04	10.77
Latin America	117	2,185.3	16.2	8.577	18.7	0.823	4.30	10.37
Asia	107	5,431.5	40.3	8.495	50.8	0.781	3.72	10.32
Africa	40	1,560.9	11.6	8.499	39.0	1.160	4.12	11.26
Europe	85	2,681.7	19.9	8.392	31.5	0.705	3.73	10.04
All credits	363	13,461.5	100.0	8.495	37.1	0.817	3.93	10.40

TABLE 6.6b

Eximbank Direct Credits by Area, FY1979

Area	Number of loans	Total loans ($ million)	Percentage of total	Average lending rate (%)	Average loan ($ million)	Average spread (%)	Average moratorium (years)	Average term (years)
Canada	1	9.8	0.3	8.375	9.3	0.725	7.00	11.00
Latin America	27	501.2	13.8	8.278	20.8	0.814	4.24	10.00
Asia	38	1,688.7	46.4	8.135	61.0	0.919	3.87	10.59
Africa	15	786.7	21.6	8.092	79.4	1.248	4.63	11.63
Europe	24	652.9	17.9	8.247	46.7	0.743	4.25	10.08
All credits	105	3,639.2	100.0	8.193	54.1	0.897	4.19	10.48

TABLE 6.6c

Eximbank Direct Credits by Area, FY1980

Area	Number of loans	Total loans ($ million)	Percentage of total	Average lending rate (%)	Average loan ($ million)	Average spread (%)	Average moratorium (years)	Average term (years)
Canada	6	421.8	8.8	8.523	70.3	0.750	2.17	11.00
Latin America	40	633.9	13.3	8.403	15.8	0.833	4.09	9.99
Asia	31	2,212.3	46.3	8.252	71.4	0.685	2.89	9.69
Africa	11	244.3	5.1	8.580	22.2	1.077	3.18	9.91
Europe	43	1,270.9	26.6	8.333	30.0	0.707	3.10	9.29
All credits	131	4,783.2	100.0	8.365	36.5	0.773	3.32	9.73

TABLE 6.6d

Eximbank Direct Credits by Area, FY1981

Area	Number of loans	Total loans ($ million)	Percentage of total	Average lending rate (%)	Average loan ($ million)	Average spread (%)	Average moratorium (years)	Average term (years)
Canada	7	1,170.4	23.2	8.564	392.9	0.750	3.21	10.86
Latin America	50	1,050.2	20.8	8.878	29.4	0.820	4.49	10.89
Asia	38	1,530.6	30.4	9.065	56.5	0.720	4.26	10.57
Africa	14	529.8	10.5	8.729	65.0	1.129	4.30	11.94
Europe	18	758.0	15.0	8.729	62.7	0.650	4.56	11.81
All credits	127	5,039.1	100.0	8.879	103.1	0.796	4.34	11.04

11.9%. African and Latin American countries were granted 11.6 and 16.2% of the credits, respectively. In terms of individual countries the 10 largest recipients were

Country	FY1979–1981 direct credits ($ millions)
Korea	1775.2
Canada	1404.2
Mexico	1025.4
Taiwan	659.5
United Kingdom	648.1
Israel	580.5
Brazil	439.3
Algeria	433.2
Australia	396.6
Italy	382.5

Tables 6.5 and 6.6 indicate that Eximbank credits tend to be allocated as a function of commercial demand rather than to compensate for a country's difficulty in obtaining financing in the international capital markets.

Tables 6.7a–d present data by sector on the subsidy rates and subsidies on the Eximbank direct credits for FY1979–1981, FY1979, FY1980, and FY1981, respectively. The total subsidy received by foreign importers for the 3 year period was $3.063 billion using the 5-year Eurodollar rate as a measure of the market interest rate and $3.711 billion using the 6-month Eurodollar rate. Because of increasing market interest rates, approximately half of the subsidy for the 3-year period resulted in FY1981. The subsidy rates per dollar of Eximbank credit increased from 14% in FY1979 to nearly 30% in FY1981, with power sector credits receiving a subsidy rate of 32.7%. Nearly two-thirds of the subsidy was associated with power and aircraft exports.

The principal weakness of these subsidy estimates results from the measurement of the moratorium for nonaircraft credits. To indicate the sensitivity of the estimates to this measurement, the moratorium was taken to be one-half year for all nonaircraft credits. This assumption provides the minimum possible value of both the moratorium and the term, and since the subsidy rate is an increasing function of both, a lower bound on the subsidy is obtained. The resulting estimate of the subsidy for FY1979–1981 direct credits is $2.524 billion, using the 5-year Eurodollar rate, and $3.081 billion, using the 6-month Eurodollar rate.

TABLE 6.7a

Subsidy by Sector, FY1979–1981

	5-Year Eurodollar rate			6-Month Eurodollar rate		
Sector	Average subsidy rate (%)	Total subsidy ($ million)	Average subsidy ($ million)	Average subsidy rate (%)	Total subsidy ($ million)	Average subsidy ($ million)
Agriculture/ construction	20.25	6.602	1.320	24.38	8.344	1.669
Communication	20.75	197.749	7.910	25.71	245.763	9.831
Manufacturing	20.41	294.375	4.394	24.85	345.490	5.157
Mining/refining	26.42	382.407	7.215	29.00	455.861	8.601
Power	23.08	730.737	12.820	27.82	873.510	15.325
Aircraft	20.33	1263.060	12.888	24.86	1550.283	15.819
Other trans- portation	18.36	55.388	2.408	22.69	70.312	3.057
Miscellaneous	18.27	133.146	3.084	22.37	161.828	4.624
All credits	21.03	3,063.464	8.439	25.60	3,711.381	10.224

TABLE 6.7b

Subsidy by Sector, FY1979

	5-Year Eurodollar rate			6-Month Eurodollar rate		
Sector	Average subsidy rate (%)	Total subsidy ($ million)	Average subsidy ($ million)	Average subsidy rate (%)	Total subsidy ($ million)	Average subsidy ($ million)
Agriculture/ construction	13.31	3.075	3.075	17.88	4.131	4.131
Communication	13.09	5.581	0.620	17.58	7.609	0.845
Manufacturing	13.24	67.807	3.390	17.89	88.826	4.441
Mining/refining	15.08	74.120	9.265	20.00	98.764	12.346
Power	15.10	131.432	10.110	20.52	174.790	13.445
Aircraft	13.30	172.848	5.238	18.23	233.147	7.065
Other trans- portation	13.17	20.909	2.614	17.85	28.721	3.590
Miscellaneous	14.02	77.693	5.977	18.15	96.398	7.415
All credits	13.71	553.471	5.271	18.49	732.387	6.975

TABLE 6.7c

Subsidy by Sector, FY1980

Sector	5-Year Eurodollar rate			6-Month Eurodollar rate		
	Average subsidy rate (%)	Total subsidy ($ million)	Average subsidy ($ million)	Average subsidy rate (%)	Total subsidy ($ million)	Average subsidy ($ million)
Agriculture/ construction	12.64	1.929	0.964	15.13	2.319	1.160
Communication	19.62	87.678	10.960	23.27	105.533	13.192
Manufacturing	18.94	66.877	2.572	22.82	79.919	3.074
Mining/refining	18.22	72.020	5.144	22.00	86.461	6.176
Power	19.38	342.282	14.262	23.28	407.414	16.976
Aircraft	19.06	377.803	10.794	23.02	475.831	13.595
Other trans- portation	17.87	16.522	1.652	21.61	20.030	2.003
Miscellaneous	15.59	14.037	1.170	18.69	16.827	1.402
All credits	18.53	979.148	7.474	22.31	1,194.335	9.117

TABLE 6.7d

Subsidy by Sector, FY1981

Sector	5-Year Eurodollar rate			6-Month Eurodollar rate		
	Average subsidy rate (%)	Total subsidy ($ million)	Average subsidy ($ million)	Average subsidy rate (%)	Total subsidy ($ million)	Average subsidy ($ million)
Agriculture/ construction	31.33	1.599	0.800	36.88	1.884	0.942
Communication	30.51	104.490	13.061	37.28	132.620	16.577
Manufacturing	29.05	159.692	7.604	33.98	176.745	8.416
Mining/refining	29.06	236.268	7.622	34.49	270.636	8.730
Power	32.69	257.022	12.851	38.02	291.306	14.565
Aircraft	29.56	712.408	23.747	34.32	841.305	28.043
Other trans- portation	27.65	17.956	3.591	32.57	21.561	4.312
Miscellaneous	27.01	41.411	4.141	32.26	48.603	4.860
Other credits	29.66	1,530.846	12.054	34.88	1,784.659	14.052

Tables 6.8a–d present the subsidy data by country risk groups, and Tables 6.9a–d present that data by geographic region. Since the magnitude of the subsidy equals the subsidy rate multiplied by the credit principal and the subsidy rates do not vary greatly by country group or by

TABLE 6.8a

Subsidy by Country Risk Group, FY1979–1981

Country risk group	5-Year Eurodollar rate			6-Month Eurodollar rate		
	Average subsidy rate (%)	Total subsidy ($ million)	Average subsidy ($ million)	Average subsidy rate (%)	Total subsidy ($ million)	Average subsidy ($ million)
Prime	21.05	849.242	13.480	25.26	1,011.844	16.061
Good	22.35	1,186.567	8.298	26.95	1,441.532	10.081
Satisfactory	19.89	952.330	7.002	24.60	1,164.326	8.561
Poor	19.41	75.325	3.587	23.96	93.679	4.461
All credits	21.03	3,063.464	8.439	25.60	3,711.381	10.224

TABLE 6.8b

Subsidy by Country Risk Group, FY1979

Country risk group	5-Year Eurodollar rate			6-Month Eurodollar rate		
	Average subsidy rate (%)	Total subsidy ($ million)	Average subsidy ($ million)	Average subsidy rate (%)	Total subsidy ($ million)	Average subsidy ($ million)
Prime	12.17	48.023	4.802	17.13	66.522	6.652
Good	14.01	241.210	8.040	18.78	311.582	10.386
Satisfactory	13.47	225.986	4.035	18.26	305.448	5.454
Poor	15.86	38.250	4.250	20.45	48.835	5.426
All credits	13.71	553.471	5.271	18.49	732.387	6.975

TABLE 6.8c

Subsidy by Country Risk Group, FY1980

Country risk group	5-Year Eurodollar rate			6-Month Eurodollar rate		
	Average subsidy rate (%)	Total subsidy ($ million)	Average subsidy ($ million)	Average subsidy rate (%)	Total subsidy ($ million)	Average subsidy ($ million)
Prime′	16.19	179.174	7.167	19.44	208.672	8.347
Good	17.72	331.249	6.625	21.34	418.310	8.366
Satisfactory	20.77	438.670	8.773	25.01	531.192	10.624
Poor	16.51	30.055	5.009	19.88	36.161	6.027
All credits	18.53	979.148	7.474	22.31	1,194.335	9.117

TABLE 6.8d

Subsidy by Country Risk Group, FY1981

Country risk group	5-Year Eurodollar rate			6-Month Eurodollar rate		
	Average subsidy rate (%)	Total subsidy ($ million)	Average subsidy ($ million)	Average subsidy rate (%)	Total subsidy ($ million)	Average subsidy ($ million)
Prime	28.57	622.045	22.216	33.36	736.650	26.309
Good	29.99	614.108	9.748	35.29	711.640	11.296
Satisfactory	30.37	287.673	9.589	35.76	327.686	10.923
Poor	27.65	7.020	1.170	33.30	8.683	1.447
All credits	29.66	1,530.846	12.054	34.88	1,784.659	14.052

TABLE 6.9a

Subsidy by Continent, FY1979–81

Area	5-Year Eurodollar rate			6-Month Eurodollar rate		
	Average subsidy rate (%)	Total subsidy ($ million)	Average subsidy ($ million)	Average subsidy rate (%)	Total subsidy ($ million)	Average subsidy ($ million)
Canada	23.61	420.211	30.015	27.13	494.826	35.345
Latin America	22.52	513.014	4.385	27.50	612.480	5.235
Asia	20.32	1,203.088	11.244	25.07	1,472.996	13.766
Africa	22.05	392.807	4.621	26.01	461.271	11.532
Europe	18.96	534.342	6.286	23.23	669.808	7.880
All credits	21.03	3,063.464	8.439	25.60	3,711.381	10.224

TABLE 6.9b

Subsidy by Continent, FY1979

Area	5-Year Eurodollar rate			6-Month Eurodollar rate		
	Average subsidy rate (%)	Total subsidy ($ million)	Average subsidy ($ million)	Average subsidy rate (%)	Total subsidy ($ million)	Average subsidy ($ million)
Canada	13.76	1.345	1.345	18.49	1.807	1.807
Latin America	12.82	66.375	2.458	17.54	90.298	3.344
Asia	13.74	262.042	6.896	18.42	347.170	9.136
Africa	16.75	148.821	9.921	21.50	188.585	12.572
Europe	12.74	74.887	3.120	17.76	104.527	4.355
All credits	13.71	553.471	5.271	18.49	732.387	6.975

TABLE 6.9c

Subsidy by Continent, FY1980

Area	5-Year Eurodollar rate			6-Month Eurodollor rate		
	Average subsidy rate (%)	Total subsidy ($ million)	Average subsidy ($ million)	Average subsidy rate (%)	Total subsidy ($ million)	Average subsidy ($ million)
Canada	17.43	75.696	12.616	20.07	84.668	14.111
Latin America	20.16	131.709	3.293	24.37	157.401	3.935
Asia	18.34	499.100	16.100	22.24	606.453	19.563
Africa	17.71	43.883	3.989	20.68	54.804	4.982
Europe	17.52	228.760	5.320	21.17	291.009	6.768
All credits	18.53	979.148	7.474	22.31	1,194.335	9.117

TABLE 6.9d

Subsidy by Continent, FY1981

Area	5-Year Eurodollar rate			6-Month Eurodollar rate		
	Average subsidy rate (%)	Total subsidy ($ million)	Average subsidy ($ million)	Average subsidy rate (%)	Total subsidy ($ million)	Average subsidy ($ million)
Canada	30.31	343.170	49.024	34.41	408.351	58.336
Latin America	29.65	314.930	6.299	35.37	364.781	7.296
Asia	28.51	441.945	11.630	34.01	519.373	13.668
Africa	31.14	200.104	14.293	35.04	217.883	15.563
Europe	30.70	230.696	12.816	35.45	274.271	15.237
All credits	29.66	1,530.846	12.054	34.88	1,784.659	14.052

region, the distribution of the subsidy approximates the distribution of the credits. Forty percent of the subsidy was received by Asian countries and over 30% went to Canada and Europe. Nearly two-thirds of the subsidy was associated with exports to countries in the "good" and "prime" country risk groups.

The largest individual subsidy provided was $306 million on the $1.058 billion credit to Air Canada for the purchase of Boeing 767 aircraft. The second largest subsidy was provided on the $936 million credit to Korea to finance two nuclear power plants, including fuel.[13] The $155.5

---

[13] Of the $936 million, $432 was authorized in FY1979 with the remainder authorized in FY1980. The *1979 Annual Report* [5] states that the interest rate on the credit for the Korean

TABLE 6.10

CFF and Discount Loan Programs[a]

	FY1979	FY1980	FY1981
Authorizations ($ million)			
CFF and relending	100.2	41.7	34.0
Discount loans	650.0	490.8	352.0
Weighted average interest rate on outstanding loans (%)[b]			
CFF and relending	7.57	7.74	NA
Discount loans	8.10	8.77	NA
Yield on 3-year treasury securities (%)[b]	9.29	12.84	13.65
Prime commercial paper rate— 4 to 6 months (%)[b]	10.01	13.60	14.87
Prime Rate (%)[b]	11.75	15.25–16.75	19–20

[a] Council of Economic Advisors, *Economic Report of the President*, Washington, D.C., 1982; Export–Import Bank, *1980 Annual Report*, Washington, D.C., 1981; Export–Import Bank, "Interest Rate Expenses and Receivable Rates," Washington, D.C., 1981.

[b] February.

million credit for the purchase of fuel carried a term of only 3 years and hence has not been included in Tables 6.7–6.9, which cover only long-term credits. Using the 5-year Eurodollar rate, the subsidy on the fuel credit was estimated as $4.1 million, whereas the subsidy on the $708.8 million long-term credit was $207.6 million.

C. The CFF and Discount Loan Programs

Compared to the direct credit program, the CFF and discount loan authorizations have been relatively small with a total of $750 million

---

nuclear plants was 8.0%, while the Bank's "Authorizations for Nuclear Power Plants and Training Center" report [10] gives the interest rates on the two plants as 8.25 and 8.375%, for a weighted average of 8.313%. Those credits involved $276.8 million for the plants and $155.5 million for fuel. The credit for the plant was assumed to carry an 8.0% interest rate as a result of Mr. Moore's statement during the Ansett hearings: "For example, we did two power stations in South Korea at the end of last year at 8 percent interest . . . [17, p. 53]." The interest rate on the fuel was thus assumed to be such that the weighted average interest rate on the credit equalled the 8.313% rate, which implies an interest rate of 8.87% on the fuel credit.

authorized in FY1979, $533 million in FY1980, and $386 million in FY1981. Data on the interest rates and the repayment terms on these authorizations are not available, but data on the weighted average interest rates on the outstanding loans are available and are presented in Table 6.10, along with the market interest rates. If the average term of these loans is assumed to be 3 years, with no moratorium, and the amount outstanding in FY1979 and FY1980 averaged $600 million, the subsidy estimated, using market interest rates of 10.0, 13.6, and 14.9% in FY1979, FY1980, and FY1981, respectively, would be $18, $40, and $38 million.[14] These estimates are very rough but do suggest that the subsidies provided by these two programs are small relative to the subsidies provided by the direct credit program. As indicated in Chapter 4, the Bank discontinued the CFF program at the end of FY1981.

D. Other Eximbank Credits

A portion of the Bank's lending in fiscal years 1979 and 1980 involved increases in credits authorized in previous years and have not been included here. The total amount of these increases was $20.8 million in FY1979 and $104.1 million in FY1980.[15] Using the average subsidy rates for direct credits authorized in each year, the estimated subsidy on these credits is $22.1 million, using the 5-year Eurodollar rate.

E. PEFCO

In addition to the subsidy provided by Eximbank credits, a subsidy is provided when PEFCO participates in financing an export in conjunction with the Eximbank. PEFCO lends at an interest rate based on the estimated yield on PEFCO bonds, which carry a U.S. government guarantee and are eligible for purchase by DISCs. The subsidy associated with PEFCO credits is due to both. PEFCO's 1979 lending rates ranged from 8.75 to 9.5% with an average of 9.18% but, since market interest rates were generally rising during this period, the interest rate on the PEFCO credits has been assumed to be 9.5%. The average 5-year Eurodollar rate for 1979 was 10.93%, so a significant subsidy was provided on PEFCO credits. As an example, PEFCO provided a credit of $165.2 million with a

---

[14] For FY1981 the average interest rate on outstanding CFF and discount loans was assumed to be 10%.

[15] For FY1981 the increases in previously authorized credits were included with the direct credits.

15-year term, with payments commencing October 1987, for the two Korean nuclear power plants mentioned above. The spread on Korean borrowing was 0.716%, so the market interest rate is estimated as 11.65%. The subsidy rate on this credit is 14.7%, which implies a subsidy of $24.4 million.[16]

In calendar year 1979 PEFCO extended credits of $474.3 million, of which $232.6 million was associated with aircraft exports and $177.2 million with nuclear power exports. If a subsidy rate of 10% applies to those credits, the subsidy is $47.4 million.[17] For 1980 and 1981 PEFCO credits the corresponding figures are $41.2 and $12.0 million, respectively.[18,19]

F. The Cost to U.S. Taypayers of the Eximbank's Direct Credit Program

The burden of the Bank's direct credit program on U.S. taxpayers is a function of the difference between the Bank's lending rate and its borrowing rate. As indicated in Chapter 2, the Bank's weighted average FFB borrowing rate was 9.393% in FY1979, 11.196% in FY1980, and 13.682% in FY1981. Using these interest rates as i in equation (1), the cost to U.S. taxpayers was $2.035 billion for FY1979–1981 direct credits, with approximately two-thirds of the cost associated with the power and aircraft sectors, as indicated in Table 6.11.[20]

This estimate is only a lower bound on the tax burden because the Bank's FFB borrowing rate is the relevant interest rate only if the loans made by the Bank are riskless. As indicated in Chapter 2, however, the Bank's loans are subject to significant risk due to default, delinquency, and rescheduling, and that risk cannot be ignored in assessing the cost of

---

[16] This estimate is based on $M = 7.5$ and $T = 22$. If the moratorium is given by $M = 0.5$ and $T = 15$, which would represent a drawdown of the credit in mid-1987, the subsidy would be $13.9 million.

[17] A 10% subsidy rate was used instead of 14.7% because the credit for the nuclear power plant carried a term of 15 years, which is longer than that on the typical PEFCO credit.

[18] All 1981 PEFCO credits were issued under a deferred pricing option in which the interest rate is set at a future date.

[19] The 1980 figures do not include the subsidy provided by the $1.099 billion credits authorized in conjunction with the Eximbank's FY1980 supplemental authorization discussed in Section IV,B.

[20] As previously mentioned, this measure understates the real cost to U.S. citizens because when the Bank borrows from the FFB, the Treasury must borrow in the U.S. capital markets, which crowds out some private borrowers and/or raises the cost of funds to all borrowers.

TABLE 6.11

Cost to U.S. Taxpayers of Eximbank Direct Credits, FY 1979–1981 ($ million)

Sector	Using average FFB borrowing rate	Using 5-year Eurodollar rate	Using 6-month Eurodollar rate
Agriculture/construction	4.2	6.6	8.3
Communication	146.7	197.7	245.8
Manufacturing	189.1	294.4	345.5
Mining/refining	257.3	382.4	455.9
Power	480.8	730.7	873.5
Aircraft	837.1	1,263.1	1,550.3
Other transportation	32.6	55.4	70.3
Miscellaneous	87.5	133.1	161.8
All credits	2,035.2	3,063.5	3,711.4

the Bank's programs. The cost imposed on U.S. taxpayers by the risk associated with Eximbank credits depends on how efficiently the nation can bear that risk through its risk-sharing and diversification capabilities. Private capital markets also diversify and share risks, and whether the public or the private capital markets can bear risk at lower cost has been the subject of considerable research that has reached no definitive conclusion. If the United States can bear risk only as efficiently as can the private capital markets, the cost of the risk borne by U.S. taxpayers can be approximated by the spread at which the foreign importer could have borrowed in the international capital markets. Adding the spread to the Bank's FFB borrowing rates, the tax burden is estimated as $2.470 billion for fiscal years 1979 through 1981.

G. *Fees and Administrative Costs*

In addition to the interest the Bank charges on its credits, it also imposes a 0.5% commitment fee. The Bank received $24.5 million in FY1979, $31.6 million in FY1980, and $35.4 million in FY1981 from "Commitment Fees and Other Income," which was more than enough to cover the Bank's administrative costs of $13.3 million in FY1979, $13.9 million in FY1980, and $13.8 million in FY1981.[21] The difference between

---

[21] The Bank also received $29.5 million in FY1979 and $30.0 million in FY1980 from insurance premiums and guarantee fees, and some portion of the Bank's administrative costs were associated with those programs.

the commitment fees and other income and administrative expenses represents a reduction in the cost of the Bank's programs.

V. Analysis of the Direct Credit Data

To analyze the direct credit data in more detail, the Eximbank lending and subsidy rates have been regressed on variables intended to reflect the characteristics of the credits as well as the sector receiving the support. A more detailed analysis of aircraft credits and FY1980–1981 credits is presented in Chapter 9 with the objective of evaluating the Bank's lending decisions as a function of product competition, the availability of foreign officially supported export credits, and importers' access to capital markets. Data are not available on these factors for the Bank's nonaircraft credits for FY1979, so only a descriptive analysis of FY1979–1981 credits is presented here.

During FY1979 and FY1980, 87% of the credits were authorized under a lending policy in which the Bank exercised discretion in choosing an interest rate in the range from 7.75 to 8.75%. The other 30 credits carried interest rates of 8.75% for nonaircraft credits and 9.25% for aircraft credits under the revised lending policy established in April 1980. The credits authorized in FY1981 were approved as preliminary commitments under four lending policies: (1) the pre-April 1980 policy, (2) the policy established in April 1980, (3) the policy established in July 1981 with a uniform 10.75% rate for nonaircraft credits and a reduced cover, and (4) a 12% lending rate for aircraft (only one credit authorized in FY1981 carried this interest rate).[22]

The regression equations include (1) three descriptions of the loan (the credit principal, the term, and the moratorium); (2) one variable, the spread, associated with the borrower; (3) one variable, the 5-year Eurodollar rate, reflecting the state of the capital market at the time the credit was authorized; and (4) zero–one variables for each of the export sectors except manufacturing. A variable (D1980) has also been included to represent credits that carried the interest rates governed by the April 1980 change in the Bank's direct credit policy. For FY1981 two dummy variables, D10.75 and D12, have been used to reflect credits that carried terms set under the two 1981 lending policies. The results for FY1979–1981 and for FY1981 are presented in Table 6.12.

---

[22] In FY1982 a 12% interest rate was established for all credits.

TABLE 6.12

Analysis of Eximbank Lending and Subsidy Rates, FY1979–1981[a]

	Dependent variable	
Independent variable	Eximbank lending rate (%)	Subsidy rate (%)
Constant	7.654	−30.54
Credit principal ($ million)	0.102E-3	−2.969E-3
	(0.43)	(−1.13)
Spread (percentage)	0.114	4.507
	(1.63)	(5.78)
Moratorium (years)	0.004	−0.083
	(0.56)	(−1.03)
Term (years)	−0.004	0.248
	(−0.55)	(3.11)
Market interest rate (%)	0.037	3.771
	(3.33)	(30.59)
D1980	0.535	−2.492
	(12.06)	(−5.04)
D10.75	2.440	−10.643
	(18.80)	(−7.36)
D12	3.247	−16.889
	(9.74)	(−4.55)
Agriculture/construction	−0.165	−3.440
	(−1.10)	(−2.06)
Communication	−0.148	0.260
	(−1.96)	(0.31)
Mining/refining	0.036	−0.167
	(0.60)	(−0.25)
Power	0.053	−0.315
	(0.87)	(−0.47)
Aircraft	0.305	−0.829
	(5.58)	(−1.36)
Other transportation	0.036	−0.442
	(0.47)	(−0.51)
Miscellaneous	−0.111	−0.632
	(−1.66)	(−0.85)
R^2 ($n = 362$)	.710	.786

[a] The t-statistic is reported below the estimated coefficient.

The Eximbank lending rate is not statistically significantly related to the credit term, the principal, spread, or the moratorium, indicating that the Bank followed a practice of setting its interest rate independently of these characteristics of the credit. The lending rate is positively and statistically significantly related to the market interest rate, indicating that the

Bank increased its lending rate as market rates changed when it was operating under a variable lending rate policy. The coefficients of the D1980, D10.75, and D12 variables are positive and highly significant, as expected, indicating that the changes in policies resulted in increases of 0.5, 2.4, and 3.2% in the Bank's lending rates.

Examination of the coefficients of the sector variables indicates that the Eximbank lending rates for aircraft credits were significantly greater than the interest rates for manufacturing credits. The finding of higher interest rates for aircraft credits is consistent with the Bank's pre-1981 aircraft lending policy which will be considered in more detail in Chapter 9. The estimated coefficient for communications is significantly negative, reflecting in all likelihood the low interest rate on a credit to Cyprus made to match mixed credit offers by other countries. None of the other sector coefficients was statistically significant.

The interest rate on an Eximbank credit is not a sufficient measure of the generosity of the credit because, as indicated above, the subsidy provided to the exporter also is a function of the spread, moratorium, and term. For example, the simple correlation coefficient between the Eximbank interest rate and the subsidy rate is only -0.03. As is evident from equation (1), the subsidy rate is an increasing function of the market interest rate, and the results of the estimation indicate that a 1% increase in the market rate increases the subsidy rate by nearly 4%. The coefficient of the loan principal is not statistically significant, indicating that larger credits do not receive significantly different subsidy rates than smaller credits when the term, spread, market interest rate, moratorium, and sector are controlled for.

The coefficients of the D10.75, D12, and D1980 variables are negative and statistically significant, indicating that the increases in the lending rates had the intended effect of reducing the subsidy. For example, if all the credits authorized in FY1981 had been authorized at an interest rate of 10.75% (except the one that carried a 12% rate), the average subsidy rate would have been reduced by more than one-third, resulting in a savings of $549 million. If the 12% rate had been in effect for all FY1981 credits, the subsidy would have been reduced by an estimated $872 million. The moratorium and the term are highly correlated, so although the coefficient of the term is positive and statistically significant, the coefficient of the moratorium is negative but not significant.

Only the coefficient of the agriculture/construction sector is statistically significant, and no explanation for its lower subsidy rate suggests itself. The subsidy rate for aircraft credits is estimated to be lower than that for manufacturing credits but the coefficient is significant only at the 0.09 (one-tailed) level. When the term, moratorium, spread, and credit principal are not controlled for, however, aircraft credits carry a significantly lower subsidy rate than do manufacturing credits. The analysis of the coefficients of the sector variables does not necessarily imply that the aircraft sector receives smaller subsidy rates, because there are differences in the percentage of the export financed by the Eximbank. The effective price paid, defined in Section III, is the appropriate measure of the effect of the Bank's financing relative to the value of the exports. A more detailed analysis of this issue is presented in Chapter 9.

VI. Conclusions

The direct cost to the United States of Eximbank direct credits authorized in fiscal years 1979, 1980, and 1981 is estimated at $3.063 billion using the 5-year Eurodollar rate as the opportunity cost of Eximbank funds. In addition, the subsidy provided by PEFCO credits may have approximated $100 million, and the subsidy provided by increases in the financing on previously authorized credits added another $22 million. The cost of the CFF and discount lending programs was approximately $60 million. Subtracting the contribution from commitment fees, less the Bank's administrative costs, the total direct cost of U.S. officially supported export financing was approximately $3.2 billion.

The welfare effect on the United States of Eximbank financing is not equivalent to this direct cost, however, because, except in the case of perfectly competitive export industries, Eximbank financing can be expected to result in price changes in the export industries. The total cost of the Bank's financing thus involves the direct cost plus any consumer welfare gains or losses associated with changes in domestic prices, less the increased profits received by exporters as a consequence of Eximbank financing. These effects are considered in the next chapter.

Appendix 6.A. Derivation of the Subsidy Provided
by an Eximbank Credit and
the Blended Interest Rate on
a Credit

Consider an export financed by the Eximbank and a private lender in which the private lender takes the short maturity and the Eximbank takes the long maturity. If the export has a value V, the borrower pays D in cash, and the Eximbank lends an amount L, then the private loan is

$V - D - L$. During the first M years of the loan, principal is repaid to the commercial bank in equal installments of $(V - D - L)/M$ and interest is paid on the outstanding balance. During that period no principal is repaid to the Eximbank, but interest is paid on the outstanding balance. When the private loan has been repaid, principal payments are made to the Eximbank at an annual rate of $L/(T - M)$, where T is the term of the loan. If, for example, the Eximbank and the private lender each takes one-half of the amount $(V - D)$, the borrower will repay $(V - D)/T$ per year for T years with the payments during the first M years made to the private lender and the payments during the final $T - M$ years made to the Eximbank.

To determine the subsidy on the export credit L, let r equal the interest rate on the Eximbank loan and i equal the interest rate at which the importer can borrow in the international capital markets. Also, assume that the discount rate is equal to i. With continuous interest payments and discounting, the present value PV^E of the principal and interest payments on the Eximbank credit is

$$PV^E = \int_0^M Lre^{-it}\, dt + \int_M^T \frac{L}{T - M}(1 + (T - t)r)e^{-it}\, dt$$

$$= \frac{L}{i(T - M)}\left[\left(1 - \frac{r}{i}\right)(e^{-iM} - e^{-iT}) + r(T - M)\right],$$

where

$$\frac{L}{i(T - M)}(e^{-iM} - e^{-iT})$$

is the present value of the principal payments and

$$\frac{rL}{i(T - M)}\left(T - M - \frac{1}{i}(e^{-iM} - e^{-iT})\right)$$

is the present value of the interest payments.

When the discount rate equals the interest rate on the private capital participating in Eximbank financing, borrowing L privately instead of from the Eximbank would require payment L, so the subsidy S on the Eximbank loan is $L - PV^E$ or

$$S = L - PV^E = L\left(1 - \frac{r}{i}\right)(1 - (e^{-iM} - e^{-iT})/(i(T - M))).$$

The subsidy rate s in equation (1) is obtained by dividing S by L. If PEFCO participates in the financing of an Eximbank-supported export at an interest rate less than the market rate i, the subsidy on that loan can be computed from this same formula using the moratorium and term for the PEFCO loan.

The present value cost PVC to the borrower of an export financed by the Eximbank and a private lender is the principal $(V - D)$, less the subsidy, or

$$PVC = V - D - S. \tag{2}$$

The effective proportion $1 - \rho$ of the export value paid by the importer is thus defined as $1 - \rho = (PVC + D)/V = (V - S)/V = 1 - S/V$, where ρ is the discount provided by the subsidy.

To determine the blended rate h on an export financed by Eximbank and private capital, consider a hypothetical loan of V with the same term T, equal annual principal payments, and interest paid continuously on the unpaid balance. The present value $PV^*(h)$ of such a loan with an interest rate h is

$$PV^*(h) = \frac{V}{i}\left[\left(1 - \frac{h}{i}\right)(1 - e^{-iT})/T + h\right]. \tag{3}$$

The effective cost is defined as the interest rate h that equates $PV^*(h)$ to the present value cost PVC in equation (2) of the combined Eximbank and private financing package. Equating equations (2) and (3) and solving for h yields

$$h = \left(\frac{i(V - S)}{V} - (1 - e^{-iT})\right)\Big/\left(1 - (1 - e^{-iT})/(iT)\right).$$

This measure is thus the effective interest rate on the financing of the Eximbank-supported export.

As an example, consider the loan made to Afghanistan during the fourth quarter of 1978 for the purchase of a McDonnell–Douglas DC-10. The parameters are $V = \$53.483$ million, $D = \$8.022$ million (15% of V), $L = \$24.067$ million (45% of V), $r = 0.08375$, $i = 0.1111$, $T = 10.5$, and $M = 5.0$. The subsidy rate s is 14.0%, the subsidy S is \$3.381 million, the effective cost h is 9.4%, and the effective proportion of the price paid is 0.937.

As another example consider the largest loan made by the Eximbank during FY1981 for the purchase by Air Canada of 24 Boeing 767 aircraft. The data are $V = \$1322.2$ million, $D = \$264.4$ million (20% of V), $L = \$1057.8$ million (80% of V), $r = 0.087$, $i = 0.1673$, $T = 12.5$, and $M = 0.5$. The subsidy rate s is 29.0%, the subsidy S is \$306.3 million, the effective cost h is 10.06%, and the effective proportion of the price paid is 0.768.

Appendix 6.B. Eximbank Country Risk Groups

FY1979–1980[a]

Prime	Good	Satisfactory	Poor
Australia	Algeria	Argentina	Angola
Austria	Colombia	Bahamas	Costa Rica
Belgium	Denmark	Brazil	Dominican Republic
Canada	Greece	Cameroon	Egypt
France	Guinea	Cyprus	Liberia
Hong Kong	Ireland	Gabon	Mozambique
Japan	Israel	Honduras	
New Zealand	Italy	Iceland	
Saudi Arabia	Norway	India	
Sweden	Spain	Indonesia	
United Kingdom	Taiwan	Jordan	
	Thailand	Korea	
	Trinidad and Tobago	Mexico	
	Tunisia	Morocco	
	Venezuela	Nigeria	
		Peru	
		Philippines	
		Poland	
		Romania	
		Yugoslavia	

[a] From [8].

FY1981[a]

Prime	Good	Satisfactory	Poor
Ireland	Taiwan	India	Jamaica
Japan	Mexico	Tunisia	Angola
Canada	Spain	Yugoslavia	Turkey
Australia	China	Romania	Guyana
United Kingdom	Venezuela	Peru	Tanzania
Norway	Greece	Uruguay	Zaire
France	Bahrain	Ivory Coast	Fiji Islands
Malaysia	Algeria	Philippines	
Sweden	Colombia	Zimbabwe	
Belgium	Brazil	Jordan	
Liechtenstein	South Korea	Egypt	
	Portugal	Israel	
	Trinidad and Tobago	Morocco	
	Argentina	Costa Rica	
	Nigeria	Cayman Islands	
	Nauru	Netherlands Antilles	
	Thailand		

[a] From [12].

References

1. Continental Illinois National Bank, "Euro-Dollar Interest Rates Yield Curve," Chicago, 1982.
2. Congressional Budget Office (CBO), "The Benefits and Costs of the Export–Import Bank Loan Subsidy Program," Washington, D.C., 1981.
3. Cruse, J. and Whitsitt, S., "Eximbank in the 1980's," unpublished paper, Washington, D.C., 1981.
4. Council of Economic Advisors, *Economic Report of the President,* Washington, D.C., 1982.
5. Export–Import Bank. *1979 Annual Report,* Washington, D.C., 1980.
6. Export–Import Bank. *1980 Annual Report,* Washington, D.C., 1981.
7. Export–Import Bank, "Aircraft Report," unpublished paper, Washington, D.C., 1981.
8. Export–Import Bank, Policy Analysis Staff, "Additionality of Eximbank's FY80 Credits," unpublished paper, Washington, D.C., 1981.
9. Export–Import Bank, "Interest Rate Expense and Receivable Rates," unpublished paper, Washington, D.C., 1981.
10. Export–Import Bank, "Authorizations for Nuclear Power Plants and Training Centers," unpublished paper, Washington, D.C., 1980.
11. Export–Import Bank, "Regular Loans Approved, FY1981," unpublished paper, Washington, D.C., 1981.
12. Export–Import Bank, Policy Analysis Staff, "FY81 Additionality Study: Results," unpublished paper, Washington, D.C., 1982.
13. Horvath, J., "The scope of the international grant economy: the case of the Eximbank." In *Frontiers of Social Thought* (M. Pfaff ed.). North-Holland, Amsterdam, 1976, pp. 121–142.
14. Horvath, J., "Are Eximbank Credits Subsidized: Toward an Empirical Analysis." In *U.S. Financing of East–West Trade,* (P. Marer ed.). International Development Research Center, Bloomington, Indiana, 1975.
15. Pierce, J. B. L., "Statement on Export–Import Bank Programs and Budget," in "Hearings on Export–Import Bank Programs and Budget," U.S. Senate, Subcommittee on International Finance, Committee on Banking, Housing, and Urban Affairs, Washington, D.C., 1980.
16. Phaup, D., "Export Credit Competition," (working paper), Union College, Schenectady, New York, 1981.
17. U.S. Senate, Committee on Banking, Housing, and Urban Affairs, "Hearings on Ansett Loan and Export–Import Aircraft Financing Policies," Washington, D.C., 1980.
18. U.S. Senate, Subcommittee on International Finance, Committee on Banking, Housing, and Urban Affairs, "Hearing on Competitive Export Financing," Washington, D.C., 1980.
19. U.S. Treasury. "Tables 1, 2, 3," (memorandum distributed at U.S. Trade Representative (USTR)–Treasury Meeting on Export Financing), Washington, D.C., 1980.
20. Wallen, A., "Implications for the Arrangement of Operational Alternatives to the Present Matrix," Organization for Economic Cooperation and Development, Paris, 1980; reproduced in [18, pp. 16–65].

7

The Welfare Consequences
of Concessionary
Export Financing

I. Introduction

The effects of concessionary Eximbank financing on resource allocation and U.S. welfare are complex and difficult to measure. On the one
hand, if export industries were purely competitive, foreign importers
would capture the entire subsidy, and the Eximbank would be a vehicle
for transferring wealth to foreign citizens. On the other hand, if U.S.
exporters capture the entire subsidy by raising export prices in anticipation of Eximbank concessionary financing, U.S. taxpayers would be directly subsidizing U.S. exporters. More likely than either of these two
extremes is the case in which both the exporter and the importer share the
subsidy.[1] The amount of the subsidy captured by the foreign importer
does not measure the welfare consequences to the United States, however, because the price of and profit on the goods produced by the industries supported by the Bank may be affected. The purpose of this chapter
is to identify these effects and to provide a range of measures of the

[1] It is also possible that U.S. commercial banks capture a portion of the subsidy provided by Eximbank concessionary financing. A bank's ability to capture a portion of the
subsidy is, of course, limited by the competition among banks and the level at which the fee
is set. It seems likely that the forces of competition prevent commercial banks from captur-
ing any significant portion of the subsidy.

welfare impact of the Eximbank's direct credit program for fiscal years 1979, 1980, and 1981. The measures are limited in that they are based on partial equilibrium analysis and do not take into account the effect of the concessionary financing on prices in other sectors, either due to domestic resource allocation effects or to exchange rate adjustments. The welfare analysis presented thus provides only order-of-magnitude estimates of the direct or first-order effects of Eximbank financing.

The nature of the welfare loss to a country providing concessionary export financing is considered in the next section, with the level of foreign officially supported export financing taken as given, although it is recognized that the level of that financing may in part be due to the U.S. decisions about Eximbank financing. The focus of the analysis is thus on the net cost of the U.S. response to foreign concessionary export financing. Since the most accurate estimate of the subsidy provided by the Eximbank is for the direct credit program, attention will be restricted to that program.

II. The Nature of the Welfare Effects of Concessionary Export Financing

Unless U.S. exporters capture the entire subsidy or the domestic prices of the supported goods decrease sufficiently to offset the subsidy, permanent concessionary export financing results in a welfare loss to the United States by diverting U.S. resources to selected industries and away from other industries. As Deputy Treasury Secretary R. T. McNamar stated for the current administration [9]:

> The Reagan Administration does not intend to live with U.S. or foreign export credit subsidies on a permanent basis. In economic terms, they represent a transfer of money from the average or typical U.S. or foreign taxpayer to the subsidized industry and the foreign purchasers. In our view, the average taxpayer should not have to give his government part of his income in order to increase the after-tax profits that benefit a private company's shareholders, or to create an artificially low purchase price to the benefit of the foreign customer [p. 8].

As will be indicated below, neither the tax cost nor the subsidy are equivalent in general to the welfare consequences of permanent concessionary export financing.

In recent years the Bank has attempted to restrict its direct credits to exports facing competition from foreign products backed by concessionary financing, in part because supporters of the Bank's programs argue that U.S. concessionary financing is necessary in order to neutralize the effect of the foreign financing. While neutralization can preserve the market share of U.S. exporters, it results in greater output and, hence, a greater employment of resources, in the supported industries. To determine the welfare consequences of a neutralization policy, consider an industry facing export competition supported by foreign concessionary export financing. If the private costs incurred by U.S. exporters equal the social cost to the United States of the resources employed by those exporters, the appropriate welfare standard is the willingness of the U.S. exporter to reduce its price in response to the foreign concessionary financing. The exporter will, in lieu of losing a sale, be willing to lower its price to the incremental cost of supplying the quantity represented by the sale. If the exporter is unwilling to reduce its price sufficiently to gain the sale, the resources that would be expended to satisfy that demand must be more costly than the revenue that would be obtained from the sale. Consequently, if a U.S. exporter is unwilling to bear the cost of matching the effective price discount provided by foreign concessionary export financing, no welfare loss to the United States results, even when the export is lost. Since concessionary export financing is equivalent to a price reduction by the exporter with the subsidy borne by the United States rather than by the exporter, there is no justification for governmental financing when private and social costs are identical and the exporter is unwilling to reduce its price sufficiently.

Until convincing evidence is presented that private and social costs differ, the appropriate position for U.S. policymakers should be that private decision makers are in the best position to determine if an export should be won. For example, Westinghouse supplied eight nuclear power plants to Korea, supported by nearly $2 billion of Eximbank direct loans. As mentioned in the previous chapter, the subsidy provided by the $936 million Eximbank financing for two of the Korean plants was estimated to be $212 million. In 1980 Korea requested bids for additional nuclear power plants, and the French supplier's bid was supported by French concessionary export financing estimated by Westinghouse to carry a subsidy of $235 million per $1 billion of financing (*Wall Street Journal,* July 22, 1981). No U.S. firm bid on the job, and the contract was awarded to the French company Framatome. If Westinghouse was unwilling to lower its price sufficiently to gain this export, matching concessionary financing by the Eximbank undoubtedly would have resulted in a welfare loss to the United States.

Two basic arguments have been raised against the point of view that neutralizing foreign concessionary export financing results in a loss to the United States. First, it is argued that equity considerations warrant Eximbank concessionary financing in those cases in which U.S. products compete against foreign products supported by subsidized financing. Whereas equity considerations are difficult to reconcile with the objective of economic efficiency, U.S. policies and economic principles generally do not recommend support for firms that are permanently unable to compete in international markets because of factors beyond their control. For example, the dramatic increase in the value of the dollar relative to many other currencies during 1981 weakened the ability of many U.S. firms to compete on a price basis in certain export markets. Direct support of the exports of those industries, however, would not be warranted on equity grounds however small the welfare losses resulting from that support. Although the effects on the price competitiveness of U.S. exports may be similar to that of currency appreciation, foreign concessionary export financing differs in that it is targeted rather than neutral across industries and hence results in equity claims. Responding to that financing whenever that financing is permanent, however, results in welfare losses to the United States.

A second argument is that the welfare loss from concessionary export financing is real but that a failure to provide such financing would result in even greater losses in the future. For example, the United States would be well advised not to respond to permanent export subsidies and should willingly accept such subsidies when offered. But matching a foreign credit offer could be warranted if those subsidies were only temporary, reflecting, for example, foreign attempts to export their unemployment during a recession. As the Congressional Budget Office study of the Bank stated [2]

> U.S. citizens as a group do not gain economically from matching foreign credit subsidies to a foreign industry, because the cost of shifting resources out of the activity in the United States is only incurred once, while the matching subsidy would be permanent. If it is expected that the foreign subsidy will be temporary, then U.S. matching might be justified on the grounds that it prevented an inefficient switch of resources first out of and then back into that activity [p. vii].

If the subsidies are temporary and are being used to promote new industries or to drive competitors out of the market, higher prices and reduced welfare could result in the future. However, unless there are significant costs to entry, or to reentry, in these industries, the ability of foreign exporters to raise prices will be limited by the threat of entry.

If the private costs of exporters do not represent the full social costs to the United States, however, this analysis is inappropriate, and the failure to respond to foreign concessionary financing could result in a misallocation of U.S. resources. For example, if the cost to the United States of no longer producing nuclear power plants domestically is substantial, Eximbank's matching of foreign concessionary financing offered in support of nuclear power plant exports may be warranted. Furthermore, employment will be lower, at least in the short run, if the United States does not respond to foreign concessionary export financing, and if there are social costs associated with unemployment that are not dealt with by other programs, some response by the United States could be warranted.

One indication that the Congress believed that there may be social costs associated with unemployment resulting from U.S. foreign trade policies is the trade adjustment assistance program, which provides special benefits for workers who lose their jobs as a result of foreign imports. The benefits provided by this program may reflect the social costs resulting from foreign-trade-induced unemployment, but it is also possible that the benefits were provided in order to obtain political support for trade liberalization policies. The current administration does not support the special benefits provided by this program, as President Reagan stated in his February 18, 1981 economic message to the Congress:

> The trade adjustment assistance program provides benefits for workers who are unemployed when foreign imports reduce the market for various American products causing shutdown of plants and layoff of workers. The purpose is to help these workers find jobs in growing sectors of the economy.
>
> And yet, because these benefits are paid out on top of normal unemployment benefits, we wind up paying greater benefits to those who lose their jobs because of foreign competition than we do to their friends and neighbors who are laid off due to domestic competition.
>
> Anyone must agree that this is unfair. Putting these two programs on the same footing will save $1.15 billion in just one year (*Chicago Tribune,* February 19, 1981).

The argument that unemployment resulting from foreign trade should be treated no differently from unemployment resulting from other causes is persuasive, and hence no special social cost will be ascribed here to unemployment resulting from exports lost because of the failure of the United States to meet foreign-subsidized export financing.

Although unemployment resulting from international competition should be treated no differently from unemployment resulting from domestic forces, Eximbank financing has been supported politically as a means of responding to the problem of aggregate unemployment. The Congressional Budget Office report concluded that [2]

> export subsidies could be used to support employment in chronically depressed industries or regions. The cost of the subsidy could be considered an alternative to unemployment payments if it is clear that, in the absence of the subsidy, the unemployed labor in a particular industry or region would not be employed elsewhere. But pursuing such a policy over a long period would incur increasing losses to the United States by extending the period of time during which resources were used inefficiently [p. 6].

As the CBO report indicates, the appropriate time horizon for policy decisions pertaining to official export support is the long run, so the emphasis in such situations should be on facilitating the reallocation of resources in order to promote long-run efficiency. As Deputy Treasury Secretary McNamar stated [9]

> Viewed in economic terms, export credit subsidies can never provide a permanent advantage that increases domestic employment. Given the competitive industrial countries' established export credit subsidies, today no government can gain even a temporary employment advantage—only a project-by-project advantage and an ever increasing budgetary deficit [p. 8].

Although no welfare benefits are likely to result from permanent export financing subsidization by the United States, benefits may result from matching temporary foreign export subsidization. Furthermore, as will be argued in Chapter 11, a policy of responding to foreign concessionary export financing may be warranted as a component of a strategy to convince other nations to eliminate such financing. The cost of that response should be recognized and measured, however. The remainder of this chapter is devoted to measuring that cost.

III. Estimates of the Net Cost of Eximbank Concessionary Financing

A. Export Industry Competitiveness and Price Effects

The net cost of concessionary export financing depends on the extent to which that financing affects export and domestic prices. In a competitive export industry with a perfectly elastic supply function, the importer necessarily captures the entire subsidy, and the cost to the exporting country equals that subsidy. If the supply function of a competitive industry is an increasing function of the supply price, however, the equilibrium price in the industry will be affected by the concessionary financing, and hence the welfare of producers and domestic consumers will be affected. Furthermore, if the factors of production are not perfectly elastically supplied, the prices of those factors will increase.[2]

---

[2] The Carter administration addressed this issue in the *Economic Report of the President 1981* [4]:

> subsidies often end up losing their effectiveness in promoting exports. Initially, profits and employment in a subsidized activity will increase and a competitive advantage will emerge. Gradually, however, the extra profits that are created by the subsidy may be diluted by higher wages for the workers in that activity, or if

If the export industry is not competitive because, for example, the average cost function of producers is decreasing in the quantity produced, the domestic and the export prices charged by firms will also be affected by concessionary export financing. Furthermore, a concentrated industry may be able to price discriminate between domestic and export markets, and in that case concessionary financing would have more complex effects on domestic consumers and producers.

The industries supported by Eximbank direct credits produce long-lived capital assets and, while no general statement can be made about the structure of those industries, some cannot be considered to be structurally competitive. The commercial jet aircraft industry, for example, has been composed of a dominant U.S manufacturer, two smaller U.S. producers, one of which announced in December 1981 that it would cease production, one large European manufacturer, Airbus Industrie, and a few producers of smaller commercial jet aircraft, such as Fokker and British Aerospace. Furthermore, the performance of the industry, particularly for the new generation, fuel-efficient aircraft, may not be effectively competitive, as evidenced by the expressed concern of U.S airlines about McDonnell–Douglas's unwillingness to offer a new generation aircraft to compete with Boeing's 757 and 767 (see *Business Week,* December 1, 1980).

In addition, the aircraft market might be segmented into the U.S. market and the non-U.S. market. The Airbus has been purchased by only one U.S. airline and hence cannot be considered to be an effective competitor within the United States, although its availability should limit the opportunity of U.S. manufacturers to price as they would in the absence of Airbus. Airbus, however, is a successful competitor in non-U.S. markets. From 1978 through 1981 the Airbus A-300 captured 94% of the non-U.S. medium-range market in competition against the DC-10, and L-1011-100, whereas the A-310 captured 50% of the market against the 757 and 767 [5]. U.S. commercial jet aircraft manufacturers thus might be expected to face an export demand that is more price elastic than is domestic demand, which suggests that price discrimination might be attempted.

---

the activity is a large user of scarce resources—in higher prices for those resources. A familiar example is the bidding up of the price of farm land suitable for a particular crop when the price of that crop is supported by the government at higher levels. The bidding up of costs of production in this way ultimately tends to eliminate the competitive advantages that the subsidy provides, thus increasing pressures for yet further subsidization to restore the advantage and making removal of the subsidy increasingly difficult [p. 211].

Because the export industries supported by the Bank may not be perfectly competitive, concessionary export financing can be expected to affect the price charged to foreign importers as well as the price paid by domestic consumers. The analysis of the effects of Eximbank concessionary financing developed in this section focuses on the welfare consequence of the exports supported by the Bank since the effect on the prices paid by domestic consumers is even more difficult to analyze. Since concessionary export financing for a competitive industry would be expected to increase the domestic price of the supported products unless the industry were characterized by an infinitely elastic supply function, the estimates presented here are lower bounds on the cost to the United States of the Eximbank's concessionary export financing. If production is characterized by increasing returns to scale or by learning curve effects, the increased volume due to export subsidization can result in lower domestic prices. Boeing, for example, has claimed that "The difference in cost derived from a worldwide market base compared with a U.S. market base alone could be as much as 30% to 40% [8, p. 529]." The extent of the effect on domestic prices is impossible to determine from the available data, so only the net cost of the Eximbank's direct credit program will be addressed.

B. Expressions for the Export Effect of Concessionary Financing

The export price charged to foreign importers can be represented as a function $p(\rho)$, where ρ is the discount from the stated price provided by the concessionary export financing. The export revenue $E(\rho)$ of Eximbank supported exports can then be expressed as

$$E(\rho) = p(\rho)Q((1 - \rho)p(\rho)),$$

where $Q((1 - \rho)p(\rho))$ is the export demand given the level of foreign concessionary financing provided and $(1 - \rho)p(\rho)$ is the effective price paid by the foreign importers. Net export earnings $NE(\rho)$ equals $E(p)$ less the subsidy $S(\rho)$ provided to foreign importers which is given by

$$S(\rho) = \rho p(\rho)Q((1 - \rho)p(\rho)),$$

so

$$NE(\rho) = E(\rho) - S(\rho)$$
$$= (1 - \rho)p(\rho)Q((1 - \rho)p(\rho)).$$

The effect of a change in the discount ρ on net export earnings depends on the demand elasticity and the effect of the discount on the export price. The discount elasticity η of the export price is defined as

$$\eta = \frac{\rho}{p} \frac{dp}{d\rho},$$

and as shown in Appendix 7.A, for competitive industries η is proportional to the ratio of the elasticity of demand to the sum of the elasticities of demand and supply or

$$\eta = \frac{\rho}{1 - \rho} \left(\frac{\varepsilon}{\varepsilon + \gamma} \right),$$

where

$$\varepsilon = -(1 - \rho)pQ'/Q$$

is the elasticity of demand evaluated at $(1 - \rho)p$ and

$$\gamma = pF'/F$$

is the elasticity of supply F evaluated at the price p received by exporters. If an export industry has an infinitely elastic supply function, $\eta = 0$ indicating that the export price is unaffected by the discount provided by concessionary export financing. For an industry with an increasing supply function, the increase in demand generated by the discount results in a higher export price in order to generate the output to satisfy the demand. The greater is the demand elasticity the greater is the increase in the export price.

In this relationship for η, the supply function depends only on the exports of the industry receiving financing support, but a more general expression can be given for the case in which some output does not receive that support. The exact form of this expression is not crucial because the analysis that follows will be parameterized on the discount elasticity η, so that a general expression for both competitive and imperfectly competitive industries can be used.

The marginal net export earnings relative to the discount are given by[3]

$$dNE/d\rho = pQ(\varepsilon - 1)(1 - \eta(1 - \rho)/\rho) \tag{1}$$

---

[3] The discount is assumed to be independent of the quantity, which is confirmed by the regression results presented in Table 6.12, which indicate that the effective price paid is independent of the value of the export.

where the arguments of the functions have been suppressed. If the export industry were purely competitive, η would be zero, and equation (1) would be

$$dNE/d\rho = pQ(\varepsilon - 1).$$

The total effect ΔNE of the discount on net export earnings can be approximated as

$$\Delta NE = \rho \frac{dNE}{d\rho}. \tag{2}$$

For a competitive industry, $\Delta NE = S(\varepsilon - 1)$, and if $\varepsilon > 1$, as seems reasonable, net exports increase as a result of concessionary financing. If $\eta \neq 0$, the effect on net exports is given by

$$\Delta NE = S(\varepsilon - 1) - S(\varepsilon - 1)\eta(1 - \rho)/\rho, \tag{3}$$

where the second term on the right side is the change in net exports resulting from a change in the export price. If $\eta > 0$, indicating that the export price increases as a result of concessionary export financing, the effect on net exports is reduced. If $\eta < 0$ for a noncompetitive industry with decreasing average costs, net exports increase more than for a competitive industry, other things equal.

C. Additional Exports

In order to estimate the effect of Eximbank financing on U.S. exports, the elasticity of the export demand for those exports supported by the Eximbank must be estimated. One approach to estimating that elasticity is based on the "probability of additionality" used in the Treasury studies [1, 11] of the FY1976 and FY1978 Eximbank direct credits, and in the Bank's studies [6, 7] of its FY1980 and FY1981 direct credits. The three most recent additionality studies are analyzed in the next chapter and, although they are subject to considerable criticism, they may reflect the Bank's implicit estimate of the elasticity of demand for the exports it supports. The estimated overall probabilities of additionality were .72, .78, and .88 for the Bank's FY1978, FY1980 and FY1981 direct credits programs, respectively.

The "probability of additionality" is to be interpreted as the probability that a supported export would not have been made in the absence of Eximbank financing, which implies that

$$a = \Delta Q/Q,$$

where a is the probability of additionality, ΔQ is the additional quantity of exports, and Q is the quantity of supported exports. If the probability of additionality calculated in the two studies takes the export price as given, as they seem to, then the additional exports are $\Delta E = p\Delta Q$, so[4]

$$\Delta E = apQ. \tag{4}$$

An expression for the additional exports derived in a manner analogous to that used to obtain equation (3) is[5]

$$\Delta E = pQ[\eta + \varepsilon(\rho/(1 - \rho) - \eta)]. \tag{5}$$

Equating (4) and (5) yields the following expression for the price elasticity of supported export demand as a function of a, η, and ρ

$$\varepsilon = (a - \eta)/(\rho/(1 - \rho) - \eta). \tag{6}$$

For a competitive industry $\eta = 0$, and the elasticity is given by

$$\varepsilon = a(1 - \rho)/\rho. \tag{7}$$

The average discount ρ for fiscal years 1979, 1980, and 1981 can be determined by dividing the subsidy of $3.063 billion estimated in the previous chapter by the $22.087 billion of supported exports to obtain $\rho = 0.139$.[6] Taking the probability of additionality for FY1979 to be the same as that for FY1980, the weighted average probability is .82. The price elasticity of supported demand calculated from equation (6) is 5.1, if $\eta = 0$, and is 6.9 if, for example, $\eta = 0.05$. While these estimates indicate that the exports supported by the Bank's direct credit program are highly price elastic, such estimates may not be unreasonable. If exporters bring to the Bank only those exports that face substantial product and financing competition or that would not be financed in the private capital market, the elasticity of the demand for those exports might be substantial. Furthermore, if the Bank is successful in providing only the amount of concessionary financing needed to secure the sale, the importer should only

---

[4] The first Treasury study [1, p. 160] viewed the probability of additionality as a number to be used in computing the exptected additional exports determined by multiplying the supported exports by that probability.

[5] The expression in (5) can be derived by differentiating $E(\rho)$ to obtain

$$dE(\rho)/dp = pQ\varepsilon/(1 - \rho) + \eta pQ(1 - \varepsilon)/\rho$$

and multiplying by ρ.

[6] With the 6-month Eurodollar rate, the average discount is 0.168.

marginally prefer the U.S. product, so the price elasticity at the granted level of support should be high.[7]

The net export earnings effect ΔNE of Eximbank direct credits when $\eta = 0$ can be rewritten by substituting equation (7) into equation (3) to obtain

$$\Delta NE = S(a(1 - \rho)/\rho - 1).$$

Given an average discount of $\rho = 0.139$, Table 7.1 presents the change in net exports for FY1979–1981 as a function of the probability of additionality.

The estimates presented in Table 7.1 indicate that if the additionality probability were 0.82 and export prices were not affected, U.S. net exports increased by $12.5 billion as a result of the Bank's fiscal year 1979, 1980 and 1981 direct credit programs. For the individual years the changes in net exports are

Fiscal year	S ($ billion)	E ($ billion)	ρ	a	NE ($ billion)
1981	1.531	8.152	0.188	0.88	4.425
1980	0.979	7.736	0.127	0.78	4.270
1979	0.553	6.199	0.089	0.78	3.862

These estimates depend importantly on the accuracy of the estimate of the additionality probability for the exports supported by the Bank's direct credit program, and to provide an alternative estimate of the net exports, the expression in equation (3) for the change in net export earnings has been evaluated in Table 7.2 for various values of ε and η given $\rho = 0.139$.[8] The range in these estimates is great and little can be said about which values of ε and η are appropriate. The more effective the Bank is in targeting its support to exports that otherwise would be lost in

[7] The analysis of the dispositon of preliminary commitments presented in Chapter 5, however, suggests that the Bank's direct credit program may be overly generous and hence that ε may not be as great as suggested by this analysis.

[8] To assess the accuracy of the probability of additionality, the net additional exports computed as ΔE in equation (4) minus the subsidy was regressed on the right side of equation (3) using FY1981 data. The resulting estimates of ε and η are $\varepsilon = 1.429$ and $\eta = -2.025$, and both estimated coefficients are statistically significant. While the estimate of the elasticity of demand is plausible, the estimate of η is implausibly large. This suggests that either the probabilities of additionality are inaccurate and/or the expression in equation (3) is a poor approximation. As will be indicated in the following chapter, the probabilities of additionality are likely to be inaccurate.

TABLE 7.1

Net Exports as a Function of the Probability of Additionality

a	ΔNE ($ billion)
0	−3.063
.10	−1.161
.20	0.741
.30	2.643
.40	4.545
.50	6.390
.60	8.349
.70	10.251
.80	12.154
.82	12.534
.90	14.056
1.00	15.958

TABLE 7.2

Net Exports as a Function of ε and η

ε	η	ΔNE ($ billion)
0.0	−0.05	4.014
0.0	0.00	3.063
0.0	0.05	2.112
0.0	0.10	1.161
1.0	All	0.000
2.0	−0.05	4.014
2.0	0.00	3.063
2.0	0.05	2.112
2.0	0.10	1.161
4.0	−0.05	12.040
4.0	0.00	9.189
4.0	0.05	6.336
4.0	0.10	3.482
6.0	−0.05	20.070
6.0	0.00	15.315
6.0	0.05	10.560
6.0	0.10	5.804
8.0	−0.05	28.098
8.0	0.00	21.441
8.0	0.05	14.784
8.0	0.10	8.127

the absence of the support, the greater ε and ΔNE would be. The less competitive are the industries receiving support, however, the greater η would be, which would reduce the impact of the Bank's financing on net export earnings.

D. Welfare Consequences

The welfare consequences of Eximbank financing depend importantly on the relevant value of η, but the extent to which Eximbank concessionary financing affects export prices is an empirical question about which little is known. Some who have been concerned with the Bank believe that export prices may be increased as a result of the availability of Eximbank financing. For example, during the Ansett hearings, Senator John Heinz of Pennsylvania raised this issue with Eximbank board member Donald Stingel in the context of aircraft exports [10].

Senator Heinz. Before you get into that, let me just sharpen the question slightly. What I'm concerned about is that you have on the one hand Boeing and you have on the other Airbus. And that is nominally direct competition. But in fact, it is possible for Boeing to bid a higher price and make a higher profit because they have a competitive advantage, maybe, namely, you, where you can, through the financing terms that you provide, be a powerful selling tool.

If you can get low-interest, long-term money, the price becomes a lot less relevant, particularly when the interest rate is 7.99 or 8 percent and the inflation that you're experiencing is at 12 or 15. That's a pretty darn good deal. It means you make 3 or 4 or 5 or 6 percent every year off of you.

Mr. Stingel. You have sharpened the question. What we do is keep a pretty good file on the sales of different types of aircraft. We look at the date that they're going to be delivered and we try to figure out how much escalation for inflation and so forth would be encountered, what the seat configuration is, and what extra equipment such as radio equipment and so on goes into a plane. And we've pretty well satisfied ourselves that we are getting the correct information. We're not getting inflated figures to offset lower financing by Eximbank and lower interest rates or things like that.

If you get away from aircraft for a minute, we've actually gotten to certain companies in the United States where we thought they were bidding too high and couldn't win job after job. We've actually looked at their figures and seen a breakdown of how they priced their product, and then given a financing offer that was perhaps better, for example, where they have cut their price substantially to win a case, in South America or somewhere else, against strong competition.

Senator Heinz. Were those, generally speaking, instances where there was only one American company bidding?

Mr. Stingel. Where there was usually one American company, yes. And I think in aircraft we have a pretty good file on what a 727, a 737, a 767, and so on, really should cost with basic equipment. If it's delivered this year or delivered next year or delivered the year after and so on, we have to take that into account.

I don't think we've had the wool pulled over our eyes on that, and that we have been used, in effect, as a shill for getting a better price for Boeing, McDonnell–Douglas, or Lockheed [pp. 110–111].

The Reagan administration apparently has concluded that Eximbank concessionary financing results in higher export prices and increased profits for exporters or, if it is not convinced of this, was at least willing to so state in order to garner support for its 1981 and 1982 budget cuts. In his February 18, 1981 economic message to the Congress, quoted in Chapter 1, President Reagan stated that Eximbank financing primarily benefits U.S. exporters presumably both through greater volume and higher prices.

On April 1, 1980 the Bank adopted a policy intended both to respond to a demand for direct credits that exceeded its authorization and to test the willingness of exporters to lower their effective export prices in order to increase the likelihood of winning the export. The Bank reduced its maximum cover to 65%, but announced that it stood ready to increase its cover to 75% if the exporter would finance 10% of the export at the same interest rate as carried by the Eximbank credit. Moore is quoted as stating that this program "allows us to say to Congress that the exporter did believe the case to be so competitive that he put his own funds in at some harm to it [*National Journal,* July 19, 1980, page 1184]." Although the objective of this participatory financing program was to conserve Eximbank resources, it indicates that the Bank believed that the export price was not as low as it could have been or else no exporter would elect to participate in the program. Furthermore, exporters that knew that the Bank stood ready to increase its cover under these terms could always take that into account in their initial price quotation. Consequently, while participatory financing allows the Bank to conserve its resources by having a cover lower than its customary 1980 level of 85%, this program is unlikely to have reduced the share of the subsidy captured by the exporter. In spite of the assertions of Mr. Stingel and the objectives of the participatory financing program, exporters in all likelihood do take into account the availability of Eximbank financing in their pricing decisions.

The export price in a competitive industry is an increasing function of the discount ρ, and the profit of the exporters receiving Eximbank support is increased by that support unless the industry supply function is infinitely elastic. Furthermore, the lower is the supply elasticity or the less structurally competitive is an industry, the greater the discount elasticity of the export price would be expected to be. The net of the Bank's financing, ignoring initially the effect on domestic prices, equals the subsidy less the increase in profit to exporters. The increase in profit is the change in export revenue given in equation (5), less the additional cost of the increased exports. Letting $C(Q((1 - \rho)p))$ denote the aggregate cost of producing the exports, the change $dC/d\rho$ in cost resulting from a change in the discount is given by

$$dC/d\rho = Q\varepsilon C'(1 - \eta(1 - \rho)/\rho)/(1 - \rho), \qquad (8)$$

where C' denotes marginal cost. The marginal profit π of the export industry is then

$$d\pi/d\rho = \varepsilon Q(p - C')(1 - \eta(1 - \rho)/\rho)/(1 - \rho) + pQ\eta/\rho, \qquad (9)$$

and the net cost of $NC(\rho)$ of the direct credit programs may be approximated as

$$NC(\rho) = S - \Delta\pi = S - \rho\,\frac{d\pi}{d\rho}, \qquad (10)$$

where $\Delta\pi$ is the change in profits.

If all export industries were perfectly competitive with horizontal supply functions, then $\eta = 0$ and $p = C'$, so the exporting country would be worse off by the amount of the subsidy it provides to foreign importers. Exporters in this case would capture none of the subsidy. If the supply function were upward-sloping ($\eta > 0$), but the export industries were competitive so that $p = C'$, then

$$NC(\rho) = S - \eta pQ, \qquad (11)$$

where the second term on the right side is an approximation of the increase in the profit of the export industry. If $\eta = 0.05$, the net cost of the Bank's FY1979–1981 direct credit program from equation (11) is \$1.959 billion, and if $\eta = 0.1$, the corresponding figure is \$0.854 billion.

If the exporting sector acts as a joint-profit maximizer in the export market, the export price will satisfy[9]

$$p(\varepsilon - 1) = \varepsilon C', \qquad (12)$$

Substituting equation (12) into equation (10) and evaluating yields

$$dNC(\rho)/d\rho = -\rho S/(1 - \rho),$$

which indicates that the United States gains (incurs a negative net cost) if the export sectors were to act jointly as a monopolist in the export mar-

---

[9] This expression is obtained by maximizing the profit π of the export sector which is given by

$$\pi = pQ((1 - \rho)p) - C(Q((1 - \rho)p)).$$

This analysis is based on the admittedly strong assumption that exporters collectively maximize their profits.

kets. Since $\rho = 0.139$ for FY1979–1981, the next gain is approximately 16% of the subsidy, or $493 million, which equals the increase in profits of $3.556 billion less the subsidy of $3.063 billion. An alternative approximation to the estimation of the net cost is to write the net cost as

$$NC = S - \Delta\pi = S - (\pi(p(\rho)) - \pi(p(0))),$$

where $\pi(p(\rho))$ denotes the profit at the price established when the discount is ρ and $\pi(p(0))$ denotes the profit when there is no discount. This expression may be rewritten as

$$NC = (1 - \rho)p(\rho)Q((1 - \rho)p(\rho)) - C(Q((1 - \rho)p(\rho))) + \pi(p(0)).$$

Approximating NC by $\rho\, dNC/d\rho$ and using equation (12) yields

$$NC = -\rho\Delta NE/(1 - \rho). \tag{13}$$

With this approximation, the gain to the United States, if the export sectors jointly profit maximize, is 16% of the change in net exports resulting from the direct credits. With a probability of additionality of 0.82, ΔNE is $12.534 billion from Table 7.1, so the net gain to the United States is $2.018 billion, which represents an increase in profit of $5.081 billion less the subsidy of $3.063 billion.

Expressing ΔNE as in equation (3) indicates that the net cost is lower the higher is the price elasticity of demand and the lower is the discount elasticity of price. The pricing relationship in equation (12) can be used to determine the relationship between η and ε. For example, if marginal cost is constant, $\eta = 0$ for a constant elasticity demand function, whereas if the demand function is linear,[10]

$$\eta = \frac{\rho}{1 - \rho} \frac{\varepsilon + 1}{2\varepsilon}.$$

As a function of ε the values of η for $\rho = 0.139$ are

ε	η
2.0	0.121
4.0	0.101
6.0	0.094
8.0	0.091

These two examples indicate that η can vary considerably as a function of the characteristics of demand and, hence, that the net gain to the

---

[10] For this example with joint profit maximization, η is a decreasing function of ε whereas for a competitive industry it is an increasing function of ε.

United States, if the supported export sectors jointly profit maximize, can vary considerably. For example, if $\varepsilon = 2.0$, the net gain using Table 7.2 is $493 million if the demand function has constant elasticity and $187 million if the demand function is linear. If $\varepsilon = 6$, the corresponding figures are $2.466 billion and $0.935 billion, respectively.

The significance of these estimates is diminished not only because of their sensitivity to the form of the demand function, but also because aggregate data are used. Furthermore, if an export sector were joint-profit maximizing in the export market and that pricing behavior were detected, not only would antitrust actions result, but the subsidization would be withdrawn because the industry was already restraining its exports through monopoly pricing. The significance of the analysis of the case of joint-profit maximization is thus not as much in the resulting estimates as in the reminder that it is conceivable that profits of the U.S. export industries could increase by more than the subsidy provided by Eximbank financing.

IV. Conclusions

The above analysis indicates that the net cost of the Eximbank's direct credit program for fiscal years 1979, 1980, and 1981 is the subsidy of approximately $3.1 billion, less the increase in profits earned by U.S. exporters.[11] Unless export industries are perfectly competitive, domestic consumers may pay higher or lower prices for the products of industries supported by concessionary export financing which would increase or decrease the net cost. Although reliable estimates of the welfare effects

---

[11] A quite different approach to the estimation of the welfare consequences of Eximbank export financing has been taken by Cruse and Whitsitt [3]. Contrary to the implicit assumption in this chapter, they assumed that resources are not generally allocated efficiently across industries in the United States and that Eximbank support may improve the efficiency of that allocation. They argue that the industries whose exports receive Eximbank support have higher rates of productivity gains than do nonsupported industries and that the Bank's financing is a means of directing resources away from low productivity industries and toward high productivity industries. They conclude that "the benefit [from not eliminating the Bank's financing] could range from $60 million (assuming the $6.0 billion in resources formerly supported by Eximbank moved to a sector with 1.0 percent less productivity) to $4.5 billion (assuming the entire sectors formerly receiving Eximbank support were replaced with sectors having 5.0 percent less productivity) [3, p. 13]. Even if these assumptions were valid and there were productivity gains from a nonmarket-dictated reallocation of resources, a direct production subsidy would be a more efficient means of achieving that gain than would export financing subsidization.

identified in this chapter are impossible to develop, given the available data, the information needed to make the estimates is clear. Estimates of the demand elasticities by export sectors can be obtained, but estimates of the discount elasticity of the export and the domestic prices would be much more difficult to determine. The alternative approach of relying on the probability of additionality also has difficulties because of deficiencies in the method used to calculate those probabilities. The next chapter considers the additionality measures on which the probabilities are based.

Appendix 7.A. The Discount Elasticity of the Export Price

If the demand function of foreign importers is $D((1 - \rho)p)$ and the supply function is $F(p)$, the equilibrium price p^* in a competitive market satisfies

$$D((1 - \rho)p^*) - F(p^*) = 0.$$

Total differentiation yields

$$-D'pd\rho + D'(1 - \rho)dp^* - F'dp^* = 0.$$

Multiplying by ρ, dividing by $pd\rho$, and rearranging yields

$$\eta = \frac{\rho D'}{D'(1 - \rho) - F'},$$

which may be rewritten as

$$\eta = \frac{\rho}{1 - \rho} \left(\frac{\varepsilon}{\varepsilon + \gamma} \right).$$

References

1. Bergsten, C. *The International Economic Policy of the United States: Selected Papers of C. Fred Bergsten, 1977–1979*. Lexington Books, Lexington, Massachusetts, 1980.
2. Congressional Budget Office (CBO), "The Benefits and Costs of the Export–Import Bank Loan Subsidy Program," Washington, D.C., 1981.
3. Cruse, J. and Whitsitt, S. "Eximbank in the 1980s," unpublished paper, Washington, D.C., 1981.
4. Council of Economic Advisors, *Economic Report of the President, 1981*, Washington, D.C., 1981.
5. Export–Import Bank, "Commercial Jet Aircraft: Export Markets and Eximbank Activity, 1978–1981," unpublished paper, Washington, D.C., 1982.

6. Export–Import Bank, Policy Analysis Staff. "Additionality of Eximbank's FY80 Credits," unpublished paper, Washington, D.C., 1981.
7. Export–Import Bank, Policy Analysis Staff. "FY81 Additionality Study: Results," unpublished paper, Washington, D.C., 1982.
8. U.S. Senate, Subcommittee on International Finance, Committee on Banking, Housing, and Urban Affairs. "Hearings on Export–Import Bank Authorization and Related Issues," Washington, D.C., 1978.
9. McNamar, R. T., "Free Trade or the 'New Protectionism': The Choice of the 1980s," *Department of the Treasury News,* June 12, 1981.
10. U.S. Senate, Committee on Banking, Housing, and the Urban Affairs. "Hearings on Ansett Loan and Export–Import Aircraft Financing Policies," Washington, D.C., 1980.
11. U.S. Treasury, "Report on the Additionality of U.S. Export–Import Bank Programs in Fiscal Year 1978," unpublished paper, Washington, D.C., 1980.

8

Additionality and Its Measurement

I. Introduction

The two previous chapters provided estimates of the cost of Exim-bank loan programs and identified their welfare consequences for the United States. Even though no welfare gains to the United States have been ascribed to the Bank's financing programs that could not have been achieved through insurance and guarantee programs or through direct subsidization, the Congress has mandated that the Bank support U.S. exports in part to neutralize the effects of foreign concessionary export financing. Since the Bank is allocated public resources for these purposes, the efficiency with which those resources are utilized to increase exports is an important measure of its performance. While exports may increase in the sectors receiving Bank support, with a system of freely fluctuating exchange rates an increase in exports results in appreciation in the value of the dollar, which acts to decrease exports and to increase imports. These second-order effects are even more difficult to identify and evaluate than the direct effects, so this chapter focuses only on the assessment of the additional exports resulting directly from the financing programs of the Bank.

The Export–Import Bank Act does not specify explicit standards for determining which exports should be supported nor does it indicate the extent of the support that should be extended, so the Bank has relied on the analysis and judgment of its loan officers, its engineering and eco-nomics staffs, and its board in a case-by-case approach to its financing decisions. To obtain a measure of the degree to which that financing has resulted in U.S. exports that would not have been made in the absence of that financing, the U.S. Treasury and the policy analysis staff of the Bank have used the concept of "additionality." Additionality was defined by the Treasury "as the probability that Eximbank programs have in fact fostered U.S. exports by overcoming capital market imperfections and by meeting the competition of foreign official export credit agencies [8, p. 1]." The first additionality study [2] on FY1976 credits was conducted by the Treasury and was followed by a second Treasury study [8] of FY1978 credits done in cooperation with the Bank. Two similar studies [3, 4] of FY1980 and FY1981 direct credits were conducted by the Bank. This chapter presents a review and critique of the three most recent studies.

An export could be additional in three ways. First, as a direct consequence of foreign concessionary export financing, a U.S. export could be lost to a foreign supplier if it were not backed by U.S. concessionary financing. Second, in the absence of U.S. concessionary export financing, a U.S. product that faces no effective foreign product competition might not be purchased by a foreign importer because of the unacceptable cost of private financing. Third, an export may be made that in the absence of U.S. concessionary financing would have gone to a foreign supplier not because the foreign supplier was supported by concessionary export financing but because of its advantage in terms of product quality, delivery, price, or reliability. The first case is a response to a market imperfection caused by an action of a foreign government and, given the mandate of the Bank, warrants a response. In the second case, private lenders are unwilling to finance the export at rates sufficiently attractive to warrant the purchase by the foreign importer, and if this is due to capital market deficiencies, Eximbank financing is warranted, given the Bank's mandate. In the third case, however, Bank support would increase U.S. exports but would constitute government compensation for the uncompetitiveness of the U.S. product and would not constitute an additional export according to the Treasury's definition. The degree of confidence that can be placed in the results of the additionality studies is a function of the degree to which the studies are able to distinguish between the extent of foreign officially supported export credits, capital market deficiencies, and product competitiveness in individual cases.

II. The Treasury Study of FY1978
Eximbank-Supported Exports

To measure the degree of additionality, the Treasury made "certain probability assumptions as to the likelihood that various loan characteristics are associated with additional exports [8, p. 2]." The loan characteristics are intended to reflect both of the categories specified in the definition of additionality: capital market imperfections and concessionary foreign export financing competition. One characteristic used in the study was intended to reflect a country's access to domestic and international capital markets, since that "determines whether a high probability exists that a particular direct credit supplements private capital market facilities [8, p. 5]." The Treasury assigned each country to one of the four groups listed in Table 8.1 with a "partial additionality probability" assigned to each group to reflect the likelihood that the country did not have access to financing in the private capital markets. In developing the categories [8],

> Treasury examined the country distribution and, to a lesser extent, the maturity distribution of Eximbank's commitments in FY1978 relative to private market norms. Treasury's assessment of private market norms is based on interviews with leading U.S. commercial banks, published information on the terms and conditions of credits extended in the Eurodollar market, and such basic economic data for countries as 1978 per capita income levels and international debt service burdens [p. 3].

For the major industrial countries plus 20 others that were judged to be able to raise capital in the private capital markets, a value of zero was assigned to the partial additionality probability. For country classes 2, 3, and 4, the assigned probabilities were .3, .6, and 1.0, respectively.

Even if a country is able to borrow in international capital markets, it may not be able to borrow for as long a term as that provided by the Eximbank. To reflect the significance of the term of an Eximbank credit on the export transaction, Treasury assumed that the portion of any credit with a term exceeding 10 years was entirely additional, even for a country that has access to international capital markets. For example, if the term of an Eximbank credit was 12 years, the payments in years 11 and 12 were assigned a partial probability of additionality of 1.0, while the principal repaid in earlier years was given a partial probability of additionality of zero.

To assess the extent of competition provided by foreign officially supported export credits, the Bank at the request of the Treasury reviewed each direct credit granted in FY1978 to determine if there was "evidence of significant credit competition." If such evidence was found, a partial probability of additionality of 1.0 was assigned to that transaction, while for cases "Where little evidence was found, or where U.S. product dominance was clear cut, the probability rating assigned was small or zero [8, p. 8]." This assessment of competition was independent of the country's access to capital markets, so, for example, in the case of a country such as Spain that is in the first country class, a "competition"

TABLE 8.1

Treasury Study: Obligor Country Classifications for FY1978[a]

Country Class 1 (partial additionality probability = 0.0)[b]

Australia	Bahamas	Iran
Greece	French Polynesia	Kuwait
Iceland	Gabon	Saudi Arabia
Ireland	Hong Kong	United Arab Emirates
New Zealand	Israel	Venezuela
Romania	Thailand	South Africa
Trinidad and Tobago	Spain	

Country Class 2 (partial additionality probability = .3)

Poland	Mexico
Portugal	Nigeria
Yugoslavia	Panama
Brazil	Philippines
Colombia	Surinam
Cyprus	Taiwan
Korea	

Country Class 3 (partial additionality probability = .6)

Algeria	Guyana	Mauritius
Argentina	Honduras	Nicaragua
Congo, P.R. of	India	Paraguay
Costa Rica	Indonesia	Senegal
Dominican Republic	Ivory Coast	Sudan
Ecuador	Jordan	Togo
El Salvador	Kenya	Tunisia
Guatemala	Liberia	Uruguay

Country Class 4 (partial additionality probability = 1.0)

Bolivia	Mozambique
Cayman Islands	Niger
Chile	Pakistan
Lebanon	Peru
Madagascar	Tanzania

[a] Reproduced from [8]. Only countries identified in FY1978 Eximbank commitments appear in the table.

[b] These countries are in addition to the major industrial countries.

partial additionality probability of 1.0 was assigned if competition from a foreign export credit agency was demonstrated. However, in the case of the sale of a used 727 aircraft to Togo, which is in country category 3, indicating that the country has limited access to international capital markets, there was no officially supported export financing competition, so the "competition" partial additionality probability was assessed as zero. Intermediate additionality probabilities were used in cases in which there was some indication of competition.[1]

To obtain an overall probability of additionality for a credit, the Treasury multiplied the scheduled repayments for the credit by each of the three partial additionality probabilities and equally weighted the sums obtained for each of the three factors. If a partial additionality probability of 1.0 was assigned to any one of the factors, however, the entire transaction was assumed to be additional in order to avoid "undue downward bias resulting from the stringency of the standard calculation procedure [8, p. 5]." An example of these calculations is given below in Section III,A.

The study concluded that the overall probability of additionality for the direct credits authorized in FY1978 was 0.72, which was interpreted to mean that the Bank was highly successful in generating exports that would otherwise not have made [7].[2]

> The direct credits program was estimated to be highly additional because the largest share—about 60 percent—of Eximbank direct credits in terms of export value was found to have unit probability of additionality in Treasury's analysis. The actual number of direct credits found to be wholly additional was only 19 of a possible 59 direct credits. Fifteen were found to be wholly additional because of Eximbank's assessment that there existed unquestionably significant foreign official export credit competition. Three cases were found to be fully additional because the obligor country in question fell into country category 4, and one was wholly additional because the credit term exceeded ten years.

---

[1] A country's access to capital markets and the extent of foreign officially supported export credit competition are taken into account by the Bank's loan officers in assessing whether a preliminary commitment should be extended in an individual case, but loan officers make no formal assessment of additionality probabilities prior to making recommendations regarding a credit application.

[2] The Treasury also evaluated in a less detailed manner the Bank guarantee and medium-term insurance commitments and concluded [8]

> Both these Eximbank programs were estimated to have a low probability of additionality—34 percent and 33 percent, respectively. This was because, in the majority of cases, they involved export credits to countries assumed in Treasury's analysis to have enjoyed ready access to financing from private capital markets. Had Treasury been able to assess foreign competition in the guarantee and insurance sector, the additionality probabilities would probably be higher than those found in our study [p. 11].

The probability of additionality for the remaining 40 direct credits was, on average, less than 50 percent. This reflects the fact that these credits were, in the main, to countries in categories 1 and 2, i.e., countries assumed to have the highest credit ratings. Support for these credits, therefore, rested critically on Eximbank's perception of the strength of the foreign official credit competition; in roughly half of the 40 cases Eximbank's rating of the foreign official credit competition was between 50 percent and 67 percent [pp. 10–11].

III. The Eximbank Studies

A. Methodology

The methodology used by the Bank in its study of FY1980 and FY1981 direct credits employed a country classification system similar to that employed by the Treasury, with classes based on the "results of two econometric models and the country economists' judgments [3, p. 3]." Partial additionality probabilities of zero for the first category, .33 for the second, .67 for the third, and 1.0 for the fourth were assigned according to the categories in Appendix 6.B. "In general, the country risk categories assigned in this study are slightly less favorable than those in the Treasury study (which increases the associated probability of additionality); presumably the less favorable rankings are principally a reflection of worsening global economic conditions between 1978–79 (when Treasury data was compiled) and 1980 [3, p. 2]." While the Treasury was skeptical of the need to supplement private capital markets in order to overcome "the alleged imperfection of international capital markets [8, p. 3]," the Bank viewed the country categories as reflecting "country risk" which would affect a country's ability to borrow in private capital markets.

With respect to the term of the credit the Bank took the position that "While supporting the concept of greater additionality of maturities in excess of ten years, the present approach attempts to avoid the 'black/white' distinction drawn in the Treasury study by incorporating gradations of additionality for maturities in the 5–10-year range [3, p. 2]." The partial additionality probabilities used for the term of the credit were

Payment received by the Bank in years	Partial additionality probability
0 to 5	.00
Over 5 to 7	.33
Over 7 to 10	.67
Over 10	1.00

Compared to the Treasury study, these probabilities result in a higher overall probability of additionality, other things equal.

The Bank's study was refined to take into account both product competition and officially supported export credit competition. For example, in the case of aircraft exports partial additionality probabilities were assessed depending on the type of aircraft involved. For the long-range 747, DC-10-30/40 and L-1011-500 aircraft the partial additionality probability was assessed as .25, since those aircraft do not compete directly with the shorter range Airbus. The exception is the short-range 747-SR which was assigned an additionality probability of .5. The narrow-bodied 727 and 737 aircraft are not directly competitive with the Airbus, but the 727 has a range that may make it an alternative to the Airbus despite its smaller capacity. For the 727, a partial additionality probability of .25 was assigned except when there was confirmed competition by the Airbus, in which case the additionality probability assigned was .75. Although the 737 competes less directly with the Airbus than does the 727, it was also assigned a .25 additionality probability except when there was confirmed competition from BAC, in which case the additionality probability was .75. The Airbus competes directly with the new generation 757 and 767 aircraft as well as the DC-9-80 and the relatively short-range DC-10-10 and L-1011-200.[3] For these aircraft an additionality probability of 1.0 was assigned since they were judged to face Airbus competition in every case and officially supported export credits are always provided for Airbus sales.[4]

For all other products five additionality probability categories were used depending on whether there was proven official export credit competition and whether the case involved bidding. The probabilities and categories used are [3, Appendix C][5]

1.00 = Official export credit competition proven through the OECD exchange of information.

[3] Although this statement gives an additionality probability of 1.0 to the DC-9-80, the Bank concluded that "two credits for DC-9-80's (Japan—$34.7 million and Venezuela—$18.3 million) were ranked .75 (instead of 1.0) due to the fact that Airbus competition was not as imminent as is typical on such sales [3, p. 4]."

[4] The partial additionality probabilities for competitiveness were determined through discussions between the Bank's policy analysis staff and its loan officers.

[5] The fourth category (partial additionality probability of .25) was apparently used for cases in which there is no present competition but for which it was judged that, if the Bank did not support the export, foreigners might be encouraged to enter their existing products in competition against U.S. products or to develop products that will provide future competition to U.S. products.

.75 = A *bid situation* in which export credit competition is alleged by the exporter or otherwise known to exist but no confirmation is received through the OECD exchange of information; or a *nonbid situation* in which competition is known to exist but no confirmation through the EOI is received.

.50 = *Nonbid situation* in which competition is possible but not imminent (e.g., competition only alleged by the exporter).

.25 = A *bid situation* in which no competition is alleged for this transaction but could be expected next time, or no case is made on competition; a *nonbid situation* in which no competition is alleged for this transaction but could be expected next time.

0.0 = A *nonbid situation* in which competition is not an issue.

Of the 92 nonaircraft credits authorized in FY1980, 36 were assigned a partial additionality probability of 1.0, 16 were assigned .75, 15 were assigned .50, 17 were assigned .25, and 8 were assigned 0.0. Of the 101 nonaircraft credits authorized in FY1981, the corresponding figures were 46, 30, 22, 3, and 0.

The Bank calculated the overall probability of additionality by applying a .3 weight to the term factor, a .1 weight to the access to capital markets or country risk factor, and a .6 weight to the competitiveness factor. The Bank study thus gave more importance to competition and less importance to country risk than did the Treasury study.

Table 8.2 presents an Eximbank sample calculation of an overall additionality probability for the case of a $70 million credit to Spain with a 12-year term and repayment to the Bank in 14 semiannual installments to be received after a 2-year moratorium and the repayment of a private bank loan payable in 6 semiannual installments.[6] The term of the credit is given a zero additionality probability for repayments during the first 5 years, one-third for repayments during years 6 and 7, two-thirds for re-

---

[6] The Bank's example presented in Table 8.2 overstates the term of the credit since the Bank defined the term to be the time between the final payment and the authorization date even though, according to the arrangement, the first payment is to be made within 6 months of the drawdown of the loan. In the example, the Bank has taken the term to be 12 years, although from the borrower's point of view the term is only 10 years since the drawdown does not occur until 2 years after the authorization date. Since the objective of the additionality study is to assess the effect of the Bank's financing on the borrower's purchase decision, the term should be 10 years for the example. The calculated additionality probability is then .42.

TABLE 8.2

Example of Additionality Evaluation, FY1980[a]

Year	Payment to Eximbank	× Term factor =	A	Payment to Eximbank	× competitiveness =	B	Payment to Eximbank	× risk =	C
1	0	0	0	0	.67	0	0	.33	0
2	0	0	0	0	.67	0	0	.33	0
3	0	0	0	0	.67	0	0	.33	0
4	0	0	0	0	.67	0	0	.33	0
5	0	0	0	0	.67	0	0	.33	0
6	10	.33	3.3	10	.67	6.7	10	.33	3.3
7	10	.33	3.3	10	.67	6.7	10	.33	3.3
8	10	.67	6.7	10	.67	6.7	10	.33	3.3
9	10	.67	6.7	10	.67	6.7	10	.33	3.3
10	10	.67	6.7	10	.67	6.7	10	.33	3.3
11	10	1.00	10.0	10	1.00	10.0	10	1.00	10.0
12	10	1.00	10.0	10	1.00	10.0	10	1.00	10.0
	70		46.7	70		53.5	70		36.5

[a] Transaction: $70 million credit to Spain. Financing: loan repayment—private lender 3 years; Eximbank 7 years—with a total term of 12 years. Competitive factor .67. Weighted average = .3(46.7) + .6(53.5) + .1(36.5) = 49.36. Additional probability = 49.36/70 = .71. Source: [3, Appendix D].

payments during years 8 through 10, and 1.0 for repayments after year 10. The partial additionality probability for country risk for Spain, which is in category 2 is .33 for all years, but since the term has an additionality probability of 1.0 in years 11 and 12, the country risk probability is 1.0 for the payments in the eleventh and twelfth years. The partial additionality probability for competitiveness is .67, which is the value used for the first 10 years, with 1.0 used for the final 2 years. Each of the additionality factors is applied to the amount repaid to the Bank in a year, and the weighted average is calculated using a .3 weight for the term, a .6 weight for competitiveness, and .1 weight for the country risk. The resulting weighted average of $49.76 million is then divided by the amount of the Eximbank credit which yields an additionality probability of .71.

B. A Summary of the Results of the Bank's Additionality Studies

Summaries of the Bank's additionality studies are presented in Tables 8.3 and 8.4, which, according to the Bank's policy analysis staff, should be interpreted as follows [3]:

As with any study relying on judgmental factors (e.g., how much foreign competition did a transaction face?), this study is not an absolute measure of additionality nor is it meant to be used as the sole measure of the effectiveness of the direct loan program. The additionality measures found in this type of study can, however, be useful on a year-to-year comparative basis; that is, given that the same judgmental "errors" presumably exist from year to year, do the relative additionality measures change from one year to the next? Such changes could indicate the effectiveness of policy actions and would, therefore, be valuable to policy designers and policy makers. Accordingly, while this present exercise offers relatively little "evaluative" information, it is hoped that future editions of this proposed annual review will provide significantly more information [p. 1].

The overall additionality probabilities for FY1980 and FY1981 weighted by the amounts of the direct credits were .78 and .88, which are somewhat greater than the .72 figure obtained by the Treasury for FY1978 direct credits. Since the methodology used by the Bank was significantly different from that used by the Treasury, no conclusion can be drawn from a comparison of the two studies, however. As indicated in Table 8.3, FY1980 additionality probabilities are greatest for the communications and power sectors, followed by the manufacturing and mining and refining sectors. The commercial jet aircraft and other transportation categories have lower indicated additionality primarily because exports in those sectors were judged to face less competition than exports in other sectors. The greater additionality in FY1981 is due to the increase in the addi-

TABLE 8.3

Summary of Eximbank's FY1980 Additionality Study[a]

Sector	Number of credits	Average additionality factor[b]			Overall additionality probability[d]
		Country access	Total term[c]	Competitiveness	
Agriculture/construction	2	.67	12.0	.63	.40
Communication	8	.59	18.4	.91	.97
Manufacturing	26	.46	17.9	.63	.85
Mining and refining	18	.39	16.8	.60	.85
Power	21	.48	25.3	.73	.96
Commercial jet aircraft	35	.30	22.7	.39	.59
Other transportation	9	.48	16.2	.58	.59
Miscellaneous	12	.56	16.3	.48	.51
All credits	131	.43	19.9	.58	.78

[a] Source: [3].

[b] Simple average.

[c] Number of semiannual payments.

[d] Weighted by the amounts of the credits.

TABLE 8.4

Summary of Eximbank's FY1981 Additionality Study[a]

| | | Average additionality factor[b] | | | Overall additionality probability[d] |
Sector	Number of credits	Country access	Total term[c]	Competi- tiveness	
Agriculture/construction	3	.56	33.0	.83	.40
Communication	10	.50	22.0	.78	.94
Manufacturing	20	.45	18.8	.83	.90
Mining and refining	36	.44	17.3	.76	.81
Power	17	.37	23.3	.93	.89
Commercial jet aircraft	28	.26	23.9	.63	.89
Other transportation	6	.39	25.0	.79	.81
Miscellaneous	9	.52	13.3	.58	.59
All credits	129	.40	19.7	.76	.88

[a] Source: [3].
[b] Simple average.
[c] Number of semi-annual payments.
[d] Weighted by the amounts of the credits.

tionality probability for the commercial jet aircraft sector which accounted for 50% of the credits.

C. Additionality of Aircraft Credits

The Bank's appraisal of the extent of competition in aircraft exports is reflected in the competitive rankings given to its aircraft credits.[7] In FY1980 the Bank approved five direct credits to finance the export of 727s and nine direct credits to finance the export of 737s. All were assigned a competitiveness ranking of .25, with the exception of a sale to the Bahamas which was assigned a .75, presumably because of competition from BAC. Ten FY1980 aircraft exports were assigned a competitiveness ranking greater than .25. Three credits supported DC-9-80s, one supported a 747-SR, three supported 767 exports, one supported an export involving DC-10s and 737s, one export involved one 747 and five L-1011-500s, and one was the 737-200 export to the Bahamas mentioned above. Since there were 35 aircraft credits authorized in FY1980, only a small portion of the exports were judged to face significant competition, but those cases did

---

[7] The aircraft credits include the financing provided by PEFCO in conjunction with the Bank's FY1980 supplemental authorization.

represent approximately 39% of the value of the supported aircraft exports. The overall probability of additionality for FY1980 aircraft credits was .59.

For FY1981, 11 of the 28 aircraft credits, representing 81% of the aircraft support, were considered to be fully additional because of competition, while only 11, representing 8% of the aircraft support, were assigned a competitiveness ranking of .25 or less. According to the Bank [4],

> The increase in aircraft additionality is primarily a result of the policy adjustment made in mid FY80 to focus Eximbank credit support on the more competitive new-generation aircraft transactions. (New-generation aircraft accounted for 80% of aircraft authorization values in FY81, compared to 20% in FY80 [p. 2].)

IV. A Critique of the Additionality Studies

The approach to the analysis of additionality taken by the Treasury and the Bank has deficiencies of at least two types. First, the measures used in the calculations and the weights given to the factors are subjective and generally bear little necessary relationship to exogenous measures of capital market deficiencies, product competition, or the generosity of foreign officially supported export credits. To some extent this is unavoidable, but since one of the purposes of an additionality study is to evaluate, in the aggregate, the decision making of the Bank, the potential for self-serving judgments about the extent of competition, for example, cannot be ignored. Since competition is accorded the greatest weight in the calculations, the potential is real, although it was mitigated to some extent because the 1978 study was conducted by the Treasury, with the Bank providing the competitiveness ratings, and the Bank's studies were conducted by its policy analysis staff and not by its lending officers. The lending officers, in conjunction with the policy analysis staff, did provide the competitiveness rankings, however. To the extent that the subjectiveness of the measures used and the judgments of the loan officers and those conducting the studies are questioned, confidence in the results of the studies is diminished.

Second, the decision of a foreign importer to purchase from a U.S. exporter depends on the available product and financing alternatives, and the measurement of additionality should be based as directly as possible on those factors. The studies conducted by the Treasury and the Bank, however, are based on individual factors, such as term and country risk, which are thought to affect an importer's decisions rather than an aggregate measure of the generosity of the Bank's credit relative to the cost to

TABLE 8.5

Additionality Calculation for an 85% Cover Credit[a]

Year	Payment to bank	Term × factor =	A	Payment to bank	Competi- tiveness =	B	Payment to bank	× Risk =	C
1	10	0	0	10	.50	5	10	.67	6.7
2	10	0	0	10	.50	5	10	.67	6.7
3	10	0	0	10	.50	5	10	.67	6.7
4	10	0	0	10	.50	5	10	.67	6.7
5	10	0	0	10	.50	5	10	.67	6.7
6	10	.33	3.3	10	.50	5	10	.67	6.7
7	10	.33	3.3	10	.50	5	10	.67	6.7
8	10	.67	6.7	10	.50	5	10	.67	6.7
9	10	.67	6.7	10	.50	5	10	.67	6.7
10	10	.67	6.7	10	.50	5	10	.67	6.7
	100		26.7	100		50	100		67.0

[a] Transaction: $100 million Eximbank credit for an export with value $117.6 million with a 15% cash payment. No private credit. Ten-year term. Weighed average $= .3(26.7) + .6(50.0) + .1(67.0) = \$44.71$. Additionality probability $= \$44.71/\$100 = 0.471$.

the importer of borrowing in the private capital markets or from a foreign export credit agency. For example, the probability of additionality does not depend on the interest rate charged by the Bank nor does it depend on the cover provided. The generosity of a credit should be measured by the effective price paid by the importer, as defined in Chapter 6. Further-more, since the objective of an additionality study is the assessment of the dollar volume of exports that resulted from Bank financing, that assess-ment should be a function of the export value and not only of the amount of the credit. A measure of the effect of an Eximbank credit on exports thus should be a function of the interest rate, the amount of the credit relative to the export value, the export value, the repayment schedule, and the competition faced by the product.

To illustrate the significance of the amount of Eximbank financing relative to the export value, recall that two credits of the same amount, term, interest rate, and schedule of payments would be treated in an identical manner in both the Treasury's and the Bank's additionality studies even though they finance exports of different values. In fact, if one of those credits covered 85% of the export value, while the cover for the other was 42.5%, with a private bank also taking 42.5%, the former credit would have a lower probability of additionality than would the latter

TABLE 8.6

Additionality Calculation for a 42.5% Cover Credit[a]

Year	Payment to Bank	Term × factor =	A	Payment to Bank	Competi- tiveness × =	B	Payment to Bank	× Risk =	C
1	0	0	0	0	.50	0	0	.67	0
2	0	0	0	0	.50	0	0	.67	0
3	0	0	0	0	.50	0	0	.67	0
4	0	0	0	0	.50	0	0	.67	0
5	0	0	0	0	.50	0	0	.67	0
6	20	.33	6.6	20	.50	10	20	.67	13.4
7	20	.33	6.6	20	.50	10	20	.67	13.4
8	20	.67	13.4	20	.50	10	20	.67	13.4
9	20	.67	13.4	20	.50	10	20	.67	13.4
10	20	.67	13.4	20	.50	10	20	.67	13.4
	100		53.4	100		50	100		67.0

[a] Transaction: $100 million Eximbank credit for an export with value $235.3 million with a 15% cash payment and a $100 million private credit. Ten-year term. Weighted average = .3(53.4) + .6(50.0) + .1(67.0) = $62.72. Additionality probability = $52.72/$100 = 0.5272. Note: The private credit is assumed to be repaid before the Eximbank credit.

credit since no additionality is credited to the "term" factor during the first 5 years of repayment. As an example, consider two 10-year, $100 million credits with 8.5% interest rates granted to importers in countries in the "satisfactory" category, and assume that both exports have a competitiveness ranking of .50. Credit I covers 85% of the export value of $117.6 million, while credit II covers 42.5% of the export value of $235.3 million with the other 42.5% financed by a private bank.[8] As is customary in Eximbank credits, the payments for II in the first 5 years will be assumed to be made to the private bank, with the payments in the last 5 years made to the Eximbank. The computed probability of additionality for these two credits are .447 and .527, respectively, as indicated in Tables 8.5 and 8.6. The difference between the two probabilities of additionality would be even greater if the term of the credits had been taken to be 12 years, since the payments in years 11 and 12 would be considered fully additional. If the private market interest rate is 13%, the subsidy provided by the two credits and the effective prices paid can be deter-

[8] This analysis assumes that private credit is as available to finance large exports such as II as it is to finance smaller exports such as I.

mined, as in Chapter 6. The results showing the relationship between the additionality probability and the effective price paid are summarized below.[9]

	Credit	
	I	II
Additionality probability	.447	.527
Subsidy to borrower ($ million)	15.25	21.32
Effective price paid ($ million)	.870	.909

While the additionality methodology indicates that Credit II is more likely to result in the export than is Credit I, the reduction in price to the importer as a result of the concessionary financing is greater for I and, other things equal, is more likely to secure the export for the U.S. supplier.[10]

If the probability of additionality is thought of as a probability that may be used to calculate the expected additional dollar exports resulting from Eximbank financing, the expected values are $52.57 million for I and $124.0 million for II.[11] Whether these values are a reasonable reflection of the importance of a price reduction of 9.1% for II relative to a price reduction of 13.0% for I remains an open question. One approach to investigating this issue would be to compare the additionality probabilities and the effective prices paid for those preliminary commitments issued for exports that are won by the United States with the additionality probabilities for those that are lost. Unfortunately, data for this comparison were not available for this study, although such data could presumably be obtained from the Bank's records on individual preliminary commitments.

To evaluate the Bank's method of measuring a borrower's access to capital markets, note that factors such as term or country risk are priced

[9] The subsidy is greater for II than for I because the payments to the Bank are not made until year 6 for II, while they begin in year 1 for I. The average periods over which the credits are outstanding are thus 5 years for I and 7.5 years for II.

[10] It might be argued that this example is unrealistic because such different covers would not be provided for otherwise similar exports, but the purpose of the example is to focus on the relationship between the additionality probability and the amount of support, as measured by the effective price paid, for the export.

[11] The Bank indicates that the overall additionality probability of 0.88 is to be interpreted as saying "that the chances of any $1 of Exim credit authorization in FY1981 being additional were 88 out of 100 [4, cover memorandum]."

in private capital markets by the spread above the market rate of interest. In measuring additionality, these factors should be taken into account through the spread used in the calculation of the effective price paid. For some countries, data are available on their international borrowing, so the spread relevant for the transaction financed by the Eximbank can be estimated directly. For those countries for which data are not available, econometric methods can be used to estimate the spread, or judgmental estimates of the spread could be provided by the Bank's lending officers, the Treasury, or private banks. The Bank and the Treasury used such methods but chose to group countries rather than to measure more directly the cost to the importing country of borrowing in private markets. When adjusted for the loan term, estimates of the spread and its impact on the effective price paid should be a sufficient reflection of the country risk associated with the credit.

Both the Treasury and the Bank's methods of computing additionality probabilities ascribe considerable importance to the Bank's financing in those cases in which there is no product or export financing competition but for which the importing country is assumed to have difficulty borrowing in private capital markets. For example, for a country in category 4 the overall additionality probability for any export would equal 1.0, regardless of the degree of product or financing competition. As an example of the importance of the country risk category and the term, the additionality probabilities for aircraft credits were calculated by assuming that the competitiveness rating for every FY1980 export was zero. The resulting overall additionality probability was .29, which is 51% of the additionality probabilities reported above when the Bank's competitiveness rankings were used. These methodologies seem to attach too great an importance to country risk, or similarly to term, as measures of "capital market imperfections," about which the Treasury stated in its study [8]:

> It is often asserted that funds for financing world trade are inadequate, especially by comparison with financing available within countries for domestic sales of similar products. Long-term financing is said to be less readily available for financing export sales; formal and informal borrowing limits are said to apply with particular stringency to developing countries.
>
> The rejoinder to these assertions is that private capital markets are simply allocating funds to borrowing countries according to two sorts of perceived risk, commercial and so-called "country" risk. Since information about foreign borrowers is likely to be less precise than information about domestic borrowers, the commercial risk involved in lending to foreign borrowers is naturally greater.
>
> With respect to country risk, foreign borrowing must reflect the possibility of political upheavals, or of imprudent foreign financial policies that could lead to the imposition of credit controls, defaults, or debt reschedulings. To compensate

for these added risks, lenders will normally charge foreign borrowers premium interest rates, with the result that market funds for financing exports may appear to be inadequate [pp. 2–3].

Whereas the effective price paid by an exporter receiving Eximbank financing measures the benefit to the importer relative to the alternative of borrowing in the private capital markets, it does not reflect any competing foreign concessionary export financing offers. A measure of the generosity of competing financing offers is required in order to assess the relative advantage or disadvantage of the Bank's financing. Although the arrangement provides for the exchange of information, that information is not always complete and, hence, judgment is likely to be required. Those judgments should focus on the interest rate, term, and moratorium on the repayment of the foreign offer and not on an aggregate measure of "competitiveness" such as that used by the Bank and the Treasury. Once these factors have been assessed, the generosity of the foreign offer, measured in real terms, can be determined and can be compared to the generosity of the Bank's credit offer.

The partial additionality probability used by the Treasury and the Bank for competitiveness is not an adequate measure of the extent of official export credit competition both because it does not directly measure the generosity of foreign credits and because it confounds credit competition and product competition. The aircraft ratings, for example, reflect the extent of product competition and do not directly measure the official export credits offered in support of a foreign supplier, presumably because concessionary export financing is always available in support of Airbus sales. A better approach would be to separate product competition from foreign concessionary export financing by assigning separate measures to each. Since the Bank's policy is (1) to provide less generous support for an export facing little product competition than for an export facing substantial product competition, even if in both cases the foreign exports were supported by identical financing, and (2) to provide more generous support for an export facing highly concessionary financing than for the same product facing less concessionary financing, any method of assessing the additionality of Eximbank financing should distinguish between product and financing competition.

The above recommendations would improve the measurement of the additionality of Eximbank credits, but the difficulty of taking into account the effect of Eximbank financing on the prices charged by U.S. exporters would remain. To the extent that the U.S. exporter increases its price in anticipation of Bank financing, the likelihood of winning the sale is reduced, so the additionality of the Bank's financing is reduced. Conversely, if by reducing the generosity of its financing the Bank can induce

U.S. exporters to lower their prices, the Bank might be able to generate additional exports with lower levels of support per transaction. The Bank should attempt to investigate an exporter's price responsiveness and could in individual cases ask for price comparisons with other exports made by the same exporter that are not supported by the Bank.

Perhaps the most glaring weakness of the Bank's method of assessing additionality is that it is based on the credits authorized and not on the preliminary commitments issued by the Bank. A comparison of the PCs converted into authorized credits and those cancelled should provide information about the importance of the generosity of the Bank's financing relative to foreign financing and product competition. Such an analysis should be the basis for the assignment of weights to such factors in any calculation of a probability of additionality.[12] Furthermore, any method of measuring additionality should be confirmed by the data on the disposition of PCs. For example, the preliminary commitments that are converted into loan authorizations should have a higher measured additionality than those that are cancelled due to the export being lost to a foreign supplier.

V. The Information Problem

The Bank's lending policy is to provide the minimum of (1) the financing required to secure the sale for the U.S. exporter and (2) the financing required to match a foreign officially supported export credit. Implementation of this policy, however, requires an assessment of whether the U.S. supplier has product advantages or disadvantages relative to foreign suppliers. The Bank's engineering division has some expertise in assessing the degree of product competition, but determining the extent of product competition and comparing prices is likely to be very difficult in most cases because of incomplete information. Particularly with large-scale projects or custom designed equipment, the Bank's ability to compare the performance characteristics and price of U.S. products versus foreign products is limited. One source of information, of course, is the U.S. exporter, but that information might be biased. In addition,

---

[12] The ideal approach for determining the extent of the additionality of Eximbank programs would be to conduct a controlled experiment in which support is granted for some export applications, while support is denied for other applications that are otherwise identical. An analysis of the number of those cases that were gained and lost in each group would provide a direct measure of the probability of additionality. Such a controlled experiment is, of course, not practical.

implementation of the Bank's lending policy requires that the generosity of the foreign officially supported credit offer be estimated. Since that offer is made privately to the foreign exporter or to the importer, the Bank does not generally have complete information about it in spite of the information exchange required by the arrangement. Furthermore, the foreign importer and the U.S. exporter have an opportunity to overstate the generosity of the foreign credit offer in an attempt to obtain more generous Eximbank financing.

Given this incentive for strategic behavior, the Bank must distinguish between the actual financing offered and the claimed offer and must anticipate the likely response, if any, of the foreign export financing agency to an Eximbank financing offer. During the 1973 hearings on the Eximbank, Robert L. Sammons of the Department of Commerce commented on these problems [5]:

> I suspect, although I do not know for a fact, that Eximbank is not staffed to make that kind of analysis of products and markets that would enable it to make sound judgments about the need for its financing in many individual cases. I am afraid that it may tend to rely too heavily on the information provided by the borrowers and the sellers, which information, to put it mildly, may not always be the most reliable.

> One might ask that stronger procedures be instituted to screen out unnecessary credits, such as requiring any would-be borrower to prove that he had tried and failed to obtain financing in the private market. Such a procedure could surely be applied in cases such as jet aircraft where it is generally admitted that effective competition does not exist. Other measures might include insistence that the Eximbank specifically and adequately document the need for individual credits in its submissions to the National Advisory Committee.

> However, I do not believe that it is possible to design a screening procedure that will prevent borrowers who are perfectly able to obtain private credit from trying to avail themselves of Eximbank credit as long as the interest rate offered by Eximbank is far below market rates [p. 82].

Although this statement may be overly pessimistic, it does identify the nature and complexity of the information problem. The arrangement, which was agreed to subsequent to Sammons' testimony, does require the exchange of information about credit offers, but the information provided is not always complete nor reliable. Furthermore, neither the aircraft nor the power sector is covered by the arrangement, and information can be expected to be even more incomplete for cases in these sectors. According to J. B. L. Pierce, treasurer of the Boeing Company, the aircraft standstill has been inadequate in generating accurate information on Airbus offers [6]:

> Also of concern is the inability of cognizant U.S. Government agencies, through the Standstill Agreement, to confirm that the terms of a foreign offer

have been fully disclosed. Such agreements were circumvented in a recent competition, with the resultant loss of a 767 sale to a foreign manufacturer. This was a case of British Caledonia Airways, wherein several unsuccessful attempts were made by Exim and the U.S. Treasury to determine the true terms extended by Airbus as reported verbally by the customer. The intelligence system established under the Standstill Agreement failed because the financing mechanisms used were outside the scope of the agreement [p. 175].

Even if the formal offer is known to the Bank, information on side deals may be more difficult to obtain. For example, in the Ansett Airlines case, to be considered in Chapter 10, the Airbus financing offer provided a term of 10 years, but in referring to Ansett's claim that they could get a 12 year term, John Moore stated "Yes, I think they're jockeying both sides on that and I would imagine the Airbus salesman has done the usual rigmarole saying that we won't give it to you in writing but if you buy we'll see that you get twelve years [7, p. 215]." Unfortunately, incomplete information appears to have led the Bank to assume that foreign agencies have offered the most generous credit terms consistent with the terms of the relevant international agreement.

Because information is likely to be incomplete, or at least difficult to verify, and since an importer may have an incentive to misrepresent the foreign financing offer, the Bank in its lending decisions and in its evaluation of the additionality of its financing should attempt to obtain a hard copy of the foreign offer. Because the foreign credit agency has no incentive voluntarily to provide accurate and complete information, the Bank should require the foreign importer to provide documentation of the financing offer thus placing the burden of proof on the borrower. When documentation has not been provided, the Bank should discount the claims of the importer about the financing terms needed to secure the sale for the U.S. supplier. To some extent, such an approach has been taken in the Bank's additionality study in that the additionality probabilities have been assigned as a function of whether a credit offer was confirmed through the OECD information exchange, but to improve the allocation of the Bank's resources such an approach must be used by the Bank's lending officers.

In the case of an exporter that deals frequently with the Bank, some discipline is imposed on the reporting of information because the exporter has an ongoing relationship with the Bank and may discourage its customers from exaggerating the generosity of the foreign credit offer. Similarly, the exporter might be reluctant to bring export transactions to the Bank for financing that do not face foreign officially supported export credits. The Bank should be able to strengthen this discipline by developing statistical information on the profile of loan applications and on the claimed foreign offers, even though it may not have specific information in an individual case under consideration. The statistical profile could be used to determine which applications for preliminary commitments should be investigated in more detail.

Whereas the incentive to misrepresent the foreign offer may be limited by the exporter's desire to maintain a reputation for credibility in future dealings with the Bank, importers who deal infrequently with the Bank would be expected to have an incentive to solicit a product and financing offer as an alternative to any U.S. offer. Furthermore, to demonstrate the need for the Eximbank to match the foreign concessionary financing, importers would have an incentive to assert that the foreign product is competitive with the U.S. product in terms of price and quality. If the Bank reveals a willingness to provide concessionary financing to compensate for price or performance advantages of foreign products, the Bank can expect that the need for that compensation will be confirmed by the claims of foreign importers and U.S. exporters. To avoid these self-fulfilling expectations, the Bank should follow a policy of doing no more than matching the real (and not nominal) subsidy provided by the foreign officially supported export credit.

The Bank's policy is also to provide the minimum support required to secure an export sale for a U.S. supplier but, even when accurate information is available in a particular case, the Bank may feel that it needs a margin of safety beyond matching the foreign financing offer in order to reduce the risk that the export may be lost. This appears to have been the Bank's attitude in the Ansett case in which a sweetener was offered to Ansett in the form of an increased Eximbank cover on the financing of 727 and 737 aircraft if Ansett would choose the 767 over the Airbus A-300. The Bank's incentive to err on the side of not losing an export in the face of incomplete information reduces the efficiency with which it utilizes the resources provided to it.

VI. An Alternative Approach to the Measurement of Additionality

An alternative approach to the evaluation of the Bank's financing decisions is to analyze the generosity of its financing and to determine if more generous terms are granted in those cases where there is direct product or export financing competition and where the importer's ability to raise capital in domestic and international capital markets is limited. In the next chapter, the FY1979, FY1980, and FY1981 aircraft credits are analyzed in this manner by regressing the effective price paid for the aircraft on a set of exogenous variables and on the Bank's competitiveness ranking as developed for its additionality studies. The only effective commercial jet aircraft product competition during this period came from the Airbus and, since concessionary financing is available for all Airbus exports, the objective is to determine if greater product and financing competition has resulted in more generous financing by the Eximbank and hence a lower effective price paid by the foreign importer. This approach also permits examination of other Eximbank policies, the results of which are provided in the next chapter.

References

1. Bergsten, C. Fred. *The International Economic Policy of the United States: Selected Papers of C. Fred Bergsten, 1977–1979*. Lexington Books, Lexington, Massachusetts, 1980.
2. De Rosa, Dean A. and Nye, W. W. "Appendix 16A: 'Additionality' in the Activities of the Export–Import Bank of the United States," in [1, pp. 159–167].
3. Export–Import Bank, Policy Analysis Staff, "Additionality of Eximbank's FY 80 Credits," unpublished paper, Washington, D.C., 1981.
4. Export–Import Bank, Policy Analysis Staff, "FY81 Additionality Study: Results," unpublished paper, Washington, D.C., 1982.
5. U.S. Senate, Committee on Banking, Housing and Urban Affairs, "Hearings on Export–Import Bank of the United States," Washington, D.C., 1973.
6. U.S. Senate, Subcommittee on International Finance, Committee on Banking, Housing, and Urban Affairs, "Hearings on Export–Import Bank Programs and Budget," Washington, D.C., 1980.
7. U.S. Senate, Committee on Banking, Housing, and Urban Affairs, "Hearings on Ansett Loan and Export–Import Aircraft Financing Policies," Washington, D.C., 1980.
8. U.S. Treasury, "Report on the Additionality of U.S. Export–Import Bank Programs in Fiscal Year 1978," unpublished paper, Washington, D.C., 1980.

9

A Test of Additionality

I. Introduction

This chapter provides an analysis of FY1979–1981 aircraft credits and all FY1980–1981 credits in order to determine if the Bank's export financing decisions show evidence that it responded in an effective manner to its legislative mandate. The focus is on aircraft credits because they represent well over 40% of the Bank's credits authorized during this period. The analysis of aircraft credits will be discussed in detail in the next six sections, and the results for all FY1980–1981 credits will be summarized in Section VIII.

Financial support of commercial jet aircraft exports has traditionally accounted for a high percentage of the Bank's direct credits, reaching 50% in FY1981. As airlines replace aging and fuel-efficient aircraft with new generation equipment during the 1980s, and as competition from the Airbus persists, the Bank can expect a continuing heavy demand for aircraft export financing. Aircraft financing is important not only because of the magnitude of current exports but also because the fleet characteristics of airlines are now being established which will determine demand patterns for aircraft and parts for the rest of the century. The Eximbank's financing policy for aircraft exports will be an important determinant of both the size of the aircraft market and the share that U.S. manufacturers receive. Not only will that policy affect the fate of the new generation aircraft, including the 757, 767, and the DC-9 Super-80, but it will also influence the decisions by U.S. and foreign manufacturers to develop new aircraft models.

The Bank's financing policy is to meet foreign concessionary export financing and to respond to capital market deficiencies that inhibit U.S. exports while minimizing the cost of its own concessionary financing. To implement this policy, the Bank attempts to finance an aircraft export only if the sale would not be made in the absence of that financing. Whether or not a supported export is "additional" in such a case is difficult to determine, since it depends not only on the financing offers but also on the extent to which foreign-produced aircraft are viable substitutes for U.S. aircraft. Substitutability is a function of performance characteristics, such as capacity and operating cost, as well as price, and for an individual airline also depends importantly on its route structure and demand patterns.

The Eximbank [8] has concluded that during the 1980s the United States will face competition primarily in the class of medium-capacity, medium-range aircraft, which includes the 727, L-1011-100, L-1011-200, 757, 767, 737-300, DC-9 Super-80, and the DC-10-10. The Bank also concluded that the United States will face little competition for short-range aircraft such as the 737 and the DC-9, or for the very long-range aircraft such as the 747, DC-10-30/40, and the L1011-500. This assessment was based on the judgment that the principal competition for U.S. manufacturers during the 1980s will be from Airbus Industrie's A-300 and A-310 aircraft, although it is also possible that Airbus Industries may develop either a smaller short-range version of the A-300 that would compete with the DC-9 and the 737 or a longer range aircraft to compete with the 747, DC-10, and L-1011.

In a 1977 report Boeing took exception to this competitive assessment, stating that "The major carriers can, and do, operate both long- and medium-range aircraft on many routes which could effectively be handled by medium-range aircraft. For this reason, the current A-300 is a viable competitor to the Boeing 747—and other (long-range) U.S. aircraft for that matter—in all but the very long-range portion of an airline's system [8, p. 14]." In commenting on Boeing's assessment, the Bank's policy analysis staff stated, "This statement is not necessarily contradicted by the preceding analysis. However, that analysis would suggest rewording Boeing's first sentence (above) to the effect that some airlines operate long- and medium-range aircraft on routes that *should* (rather than could) be served exclusively by medium-range aircraft [8, p. 14]."

As these comments indicate, the extent of aircraft competitiveness is subject to some disagreement. For its additionality studies [11, 14] the Bank developed a "competitiveness ranking" for each aircraft model that, since concessionary export financing has been available for all Airbus sales, primarily reflects the degree of product competition. Table 9.1

TABLE 9.1

Data on Aircraft Models[a]

	Capacity (seats)	Range (nautical miles)	Competitiveness ranking
Boeing			
737	130	1500	.25[b]
737-200	130	2050	.25[b]
727	163	1670	.25[c]
727-200	163	2500	.25[c]
747	385	4900	.25
747-SR	500	3500	.50
757	175	2300	1.00
767	210	2300	1.00
737-300	149	NA[d]	.25
McDonnell–Douglas			
DC-9	135	1300	.25
DC-9 Super-80	172	1310	1.00
DC-10-10	275	3400	1.00
DC-10-30/40	275	5470	.25
Lockheed			
L-1011-100	275	3600	1.00
L-1011-200	300	4500	1.00
L-1011-500	250	5300	.25
Airbus			
A-300-B2	265	1500	—
A-300-B4	265	2400	—
A-310	210	2100	—

[a] Sources: [8] [10] [11].
[b] .75 if there is confirmed BAC competition.
[c] .75 if there is confirmed A-300 competition.
[d] NA = Not available.

presents the competitiveness rankings as well as capacity and range data for the currently available U.S. and Airbus models. The Bank assigned a competitiveness ranking of 1.00 to the 757, 767, DC-9 Super-80, DC-10-10, L-1011-100, and L-1011-200, which compete most directly with the Airbus, and assigned a ranking of 0.25 to all other aircraft except when there was confirmed competition.

That Airbus is significant competition for U.S. aircraft in international markets is evidenced by Airbus' market share in the medium range segment of the market, as indicated in Table 9.2. The United States captured 97% of the 1978–1981 short-range aircraft sales (737, 727, and DC-9) but only 27% of the medium-range wide body aircraft sales (including the

TABLE 9.2

Market Shares of U.S. and Foreign Commercial Jet Manufacturers in the Nondomestic Markets (CY1978–1981)[a,b]

	Number of orders and market share (%)							
	1978		1979		1980		1981	
Manufacturers	Number	Share (%)	Number	Share (%)	Number	Share (%)	Number	Share (%)
Short- and medium-range narrow body								
Old generation								
U.S. (737-200, 727, DC-9-30/41)	173	100	106	99	101	98	74	88
Foreign (BAC-111, F-28)	0	0	1	1	2	2	10	12
New generation								
U.S. (737-300, DC-9-80)	8	100	16	100	0	0	1	100
Foreign (A-320, BAE-146)	0	0	0	0	0	0	0	0
Medium-range wide body								
Early versions								
U.S. (DC-10-10, L-1011-100)	3	8	6	9	1	4	0	0
Foreign (A-300)	35	92	58	91	26	96	35	100
Newest versions								
U.S. (757[c], 767)	0	0	41	53	11	41	23	49
Foreign (A-310)	0	0	36	47	16	59	24	51
Long-range								
U.S. (747, DC-10-30/40, L-1011-200/500)	81	100	113	100	71	100	31	100
Foreign (none)	0	0	0	0	0	0	0	0
Totals								
U.S.	265	88	282	75	184	81	129	65
Foreign	35	12	95	25	44	19	69	35
All planes	300	100	377	100	228	100	198	100
Value of U.S. orders ($ million)	7680		9510		5925		3735	

[a] Source [13].
[b] Excludes all sales into the United States and all sales by aircraft producers to their home markets (e.g., Airbus sales to France, Germany, and the United Kingdom).
[c] Technically a narrow body, but basic characteristics compete more with wide bodies.

757), with the rest going to the A-300 and A-310. One hundred percent of the long-range aircraft sales were accounted for by U.S. manufacturers since there are no competing aircraft. By 1980 Airbus had moved to second position in sales, surpassing McDonnell–Douglas and Lockheed combined, and in December 1981 Lockheed announced that L-1011 production would be terminated once current orders were filled.

In addition to the Airbus, two short-range commercial jet aircraft have been introduced. Fokker is producing the twin jet, 80-seat F-28, which Altair first put in service in the United States. British Aerospace has developed the four engine, 100-seat BAE-146, which has been ordered by Air Wisconsin and Pacific Express in the United States. In May 1981, McDonnell–Douglas and Fokker agreed in principle to design a 150-passenger aircraft but cancelled the agreement in February 1982, reportedly because of the financial problems of the airline industry. Boeing is reportedly studying whether to introduce a similar aircraft, possibly in conjunction with Japanese firms. Airbus intends to decide in 1982 if it will continue with its plans to produce a 150-passenger aircraft designated the A-320.

The commercial success of these aircraft will be determined in part by the availability of export financing. While the aircraft financing agreement reached in 1981 by the United States, France, Germany, and the United Kingdom has increased the interest rate on aircraft export credits to approximately 12%, the interest rates on French franc and dollar credits are still highly concessionary. The subsidy provided by the export credits will both increase the demand for the supported aircraft and affect the market share of individual aircraft models. For example, the Eximbank's 1981 decision to restrict its aircraft financing to new generation aircraft will reduce the foreign demand for older generation aircraft, while stimulating the sale of 757, 767, DC-9 Super-80, and 737-300 aircraft.

The importance of Eximbank financing for the U.S. commercial jet aircraft industry is indicated by the share of aircraft exports supported by the Bank. Data for the 1970–1974 period indicate that 79% of the aircraft exported received Eximbank support [5]. Between 1973 and 1977, Eximbank direct credits and financial guarantees are estimated to have financed 33% of the value of commercial jet aircraft exports [6]. In its testimony [17] in 1978, Boeing indicated that, during the 1970–1976 period, the percentage of commercial jet aircraft exports supported by the Bank ranged between approximately 60 and 90%. Tables 9.3a–c present 1979–1981 data on aircraft deliveries for Boeing and 1980–1981 data for McDonnell–Douglas and Lockheed, respectively. Deliveries to foreign airlines account for between 50 and 75% of total deliveries, and the Eximbank has financed between 25 and 50% of those deliveries.

TABLE 9.3a

Boeing Commercial Jet Aircraft Deliveries and Role of Eximbank Support: 1979–1981[a]

	1979			1980			1981		
	DC[b]	LDC[b]	Total	DC	LDC	Total	DC	LDC	Total
727: All deliveries			136			132			87
Foreign	28	27	55	26	24	50	15	20	35
Exim supported	7	12	19	16	5	21	15	10	25
(Exim share—%)	(25)	(44)	(35)	(62)	(21)	(42)	(100)	(50)	(71)
737: All deliveries			77			92			100
Foreign	29	12	41	58	9	67	68	16	84
Exim supported	9	5	14	30	5	35	14	8	22
(Exim share—%)	(31)	(42)	(34)	(52)	(56)	(52)	(21)	(50)	(26)
747: All deliveries			67			73			49
Foreign	24	26	50	25	37	62	33	15	48
Exim supported	1	9	10	3	7	10	12	4	16
(Exim share—%)	(4)	(35)	(20)	(12)	(19)	(16)	(36)	(27)	(33)
Total: All deliveries			286			300			236
Foreign	81	65	146	109	70	179	116	51	167
Exim supported	17	26	43	49	17	66	41	22	63
(Exim share—%)	(21)	(40)	(29)	(45)	(24)	(37)	(35)	(43)	(38)

[a] Source: [13].

[b] DC = developed country; LDC = less developed country.

II. Additionality and Aircraft Financing

The efficient use of the resources allocated to the Bank requires that credits be extended only in those cases in which in the absence of Eximbank financing the export would not be made, and in that case the financing provided should be the minimum necessary to secure the sale. The principal difficulty in implementing this policy is that the Bank has only imperfect information about the financing and product offers of foreign suppliers and about the importer's preferences regarding the nonprice characteristics of the alternative aircraft offered. Because of this incomplete information, the Bank would be expected to have difficulty determining the minimum amount of concessionary financing required to secure an export that faces foreign competition. As a result of this difficulty the Bank under the Moore administration adopted a policy of matching the officially supported export financing offered by foreign governments

TABLE 9.3b

McDonnell–Douglas Commercial Jet Aircraft Deliveries and Role of Eximbank Support: 1980–1981[a]

	1980			1981		
	DC[b]	LDC[b]	Total	DC	LDC	Total
DC-9-Other: All deliveries			18			9
Foreign	2	6	8	3	3	6
Exim supported	—	—	—	—	—	—
(Exim share—%)	(—)	(—)	(—)	(—)	(—)	(—)
DC-9-80: All deliveries			5			57
Foreign	4	—	4	24	4	28
Exim supported	1	—	1	12	3	15
(Exim share—%)	(25)	(—)	(25)	(50)	(75)	(54)
DC-10-10: All deliveries			9			8
Foreign	—	—	—	—	—	—
Exim supported	—	—	—	—	—	—
(Exim share—%)	(—)	(—)	(—)	(—)	(—)	(—)
DC-10-30/40: All deliveries			31			9
Foreign	18	7	25	6	3	9
Exim supported	10	6	16	3	2	5
(Exim share—%)	(56)	(86)	(64)	(50)	(75)	(56)
Total: All deliveries			63			83
Foreign	24	13	37	33	10	43
Exim supported	11	6	17	15	5	20
(Exim share—%)	(46)	(46)	(46)	(45)	(50)	(47)

[a] Source: [13].
[b] DC = developed country; LDC = less developed country.

when there was demonstrated product competition. However, as the Ansett case considered in the next chapter indicates, the Bank may in some cases do more than match the foreign credit offer. In other cases the Bank may not respond sufficiently to a foreign financing offer, but the analysis of the preliminary commitment disposition data in Chapter 5 suggests that the financing provided by the Bank has been more than sufficient since no aircraft sales were lost because of financing during the October 1, 1978 to March 3, 1981 period. This suggests that the Bank's financing of aircraft may have been overly generous and constituted an unnecessary burden on the U.S. economy.

Even if the Bank's financing of aircraft exports has not been overly generous, the effectiveness with which the Bank allocates its resources in attempting to achieve its mandated objectives warrants investigation. The

TABLE 9.3c

Lockheed Commercial Jet Aircraft Deliveries and Role of Eximbank Support: 1980–1981[a]

	1980			1981		
	DC[b]	LDC[b]	Total	DC	LDC	Total
L-1011-100/200: All deliveries			8			7
Foreign	4	1	5	2	—	2
Exim supported	—	1	1	—	—	—
(Exim share)	(—)	(100)	(20)	(—)	(—)	(—)
L-1011-500: All deliveries			16			21
Foreign	4	5	9	12	3	15
Exim supported	—	—	—	—	—	—
(Exim share)	(—)	(—)	(—)	(—)	(—)	(—)
Total: All deliveries			24			28
Foreign		6	14	14	3	17
Exim supported	—	1	1	—	—	—
(Exim share)	(—)	(17)	(17)	(—)	(—)	(—)

[a] Source: [13].
[b] DC = developed country; LDC = less developed country.

purposes of this chapter are to analyze the Eximbank direct credit policy for aircraft exports and to determine if the Bank provided more generous financing in those cases facing greater product or financing competition and those where a country's access to capital markets was limited. The hypotheses to be tested regarding the Bank's decision making are

1. The Bank provides more generous financing the greater is the degree of product or financing competition, as measured by the Bank's competitiveness ranking.
2. The Bank provides more generous financing the less access the importing country has to capital markets.
3. The Bank provides more generous financing the greater is the potential export value.

The first two hypotheses are directly related to the Bank's mandate, whereas the third hypothesis reflects the Bank's supposed aversion to losing large exports.

The principal weakness of the tests to be presented here is that data are available only for those cases in which the U.S. exporters were successful in winning the export, and hence cases in which a preliminary commitment was issued but the export was lost are not included. The test

TABLE 9.4

Aircraft Loan Applications Denied by Eximbank: 1970–1981[a]

Year	Number of denied applications	Number of aircraft	Export value ($ million)	Countries
1981	2	8	181	Mozambique, Turkey
1980	2	3	127	Zambia, Bolivia
1979	2	2	16	El Salvador, Cyprus
1978	—	—	—	—
1977	1	1	16	Cameroon
1976	3	6	220	Iran, Ghana, Senegal
1975	1	1	4	Peru
1974	4	8	101	Kenya Ghana, Yugoslavia, Germany
1973	2	2	40	Taiwan, Algeria
1972	7	15	212	Korea, Jordan, Romania, France, Sudan, Dominican Republic, India
1971	4	7	65	United Kingdom, Lebanon, Ghana, Ghana
1970	2	2	13	Peru, Sweden

[a] Source: [7].

thus only provides information about the cases in which the financing provided by the Bank was at least sufficient to secure the export, but since very few aircraft PCs have been cancelled, the data do represent almost all of the cases for which PCs were issued. The analysis, however, does not take into account the effect of Eximbank financing on the decisions of U.S. exporters to apply for preliminary commitments from the Bank for some, but not all, export opportunities.

The data also do not include those cases in which an application for a PC was made but was denied by the Bank. Table 9.4 presents a summary of the aircraft credits denied from 1970 through 1981 and indicates that during the FY1979–1981 period covered by this study 98 applications were approved and only 6 applications were denied, presumably because they did not meet the reasonable assurance of repayment standard. The countries involved in these 6 cases were Cyprus, El Salvador, Bolivia, Zambia, Mozambique and Turkey, each of which was experiencing significant economic difficulties. Because nearly all aircraft cases brought to the Bank are won by the U.S. exporter, the analysis of the credits actually authorized should provide an informative test of the Bank's decision making.

III. The Bank's Aircraft Financing Policy

The Bank's decision making regarding aircraft credits is subject to the conditions of the OECD aircraft standstill, which restricts financing to no more than 90% of the export value and the term to no more than 10 years [15, p. 37]. The Bank, however, has at times provided terms beyond 10 years in order to match the term provided by Airbus Industrie, but there is little evidence to suggest that the Bank used the credit term as a policy variable in aircraft financing during the period of the study.

In addition to the conditions of the aircraft standstill, the Bank's decision making is governed by its own interest rate and cover policies. Beginning in 1977 the Bank adopted a policy of lending at interest rates between 7.75 and 8.75%, and in April 1980 established a rate of 9.25% for all aircraft credits.[1] All of the aircraft credits authorized during FY1979 and FY1980 carried interest rates consistent with these policies. When the Bank changed its lending rate in April 1980, it also adopted a new policy regarding the cover provided for various aircraft types [9]. For the short-range 737 and DC-9, a 30% cover was customary, while for medium-range aircraft (757, 767, 727, DC-9 Super-80, DC-10-10, L-1011-1, L-1011-100) the cover was expected to average approximately 63.75%, with half the cases receiving 85% cover and the other half receiving 42.5%. For long-range, high-capacity aircraft (747, DC-10-30/40, L-1011-200, L-1011-500) the policy was to rely on financial guarantees, except in those cases in which viable Airbus competition was present. The Bank estimated that direct credit support would average no more than 30% for long-range aircraft. Within these limits the Bank provided cover to the extent warranted based on competitive and capital market considerations.

In 1981 three major changes in the Bank's aircraft financing policy were made. First, the Bank restricted its direct credits to new generation aircraft; 757, 767, DC-9 Super-80, and 737-300. No data are available on which, if any, credits were affected by this policy but, since this policy was adopted late in FY1981, it is unlikely that it had a significant effect on credits authorized in that year. Second, an accord was reached with France, Germany, and the United Kingdom that increased lending rates to 12%. Third, the Bank reduced the maximum percentage of the export value financed from 85 to 62.5% and imposed a 2% fee on all credits. Only

---

[1] The April 1980 change may have resulted in part from the Bank's aircraft financing activities, as indicated in the next chapter. More likely, however, the policy change appears to have been made in response to increasing market interest rates and authorization constraints, so it will be considered to be exogenous to the aircraft financing decisions.

one of the aircraft credits authorized in FY1981 carried a 12% interest rate and that credit also carried the 2% fee.

Although the Bank's congressional authorization limit had generally been sufficient to meet the demand for the Bank's financing, the Bank may have been restricted by that authorization limit during the period of the study. According to the *1979 Annual Report*, "Because of budgetary limitation, only $432.3 million of the credit amount [to the Korean Electric Company] is reported as a 1979 authorization. The remainder will be shown as a 1980 credit [3, p. 9]." Whether the authorization limit actually affected lending decisions during FY1979 is unclear. In FY1980 the Bank's authorization was delayed in Congress until August 1980 and the Bank was faced with the possibility of operating under the same authorization as in FY1979. In August the Congress provided a $251 million supplemental authority for the Bank, but that was insufficient to fund the outstanding preliminary commitments for which sales had already been won by U.S. exporters. To meet these obligations, the Bank entered into an arrangement with PEFCO to finance the bulk of these transactions, as indicated in Chapter 6. Under this arrangement, PEFCO provided $1.099 billion in financing, or 66.6% of the $1.651 billion export value associated with the credits authorized under the supplemental authority, whereas the Bank's $251 million credits provided 15.1% cover. Five aircraft credits with an export value of $764.0 million were authorized under this supplemental authority. Because the PEFCO credit is equivalent in cost to an Eximbank credit at the interest rate authorized in the preliminary commitment, and because PEFCO credits are backed by the full faith and credit of the U.S. government, those credits have been taken to be equivalent to Eximbank credits of the same amount. The aircraft lending policies instituted in FY1981 were both a response to the Bank's impending operating losses and a response to the excess demand for the Bank's financing. Because those changes were made late in FY1981, the impact on funds available for aircraft financing is likely to have been minor.

IV. The FY1979–1981 Aircraft Credits

The aircraft direct credits authorized in fiscal years 1979, 1980, and 1981 are listed in Appendix 9.A. Tables 9.5a–d present summary data on the aircraft credits authorized during FY1979, FY1980, FY1981 and FY1979–1981, respectively. During FY1979–1981, the Bank authorized 95 credits for $5.857 billion, which supported an export value of $11.374

billion.[2,3] The term of the credits averaged 10.8 years, and the moratorium on the payment of principal to the Bank was 4.3 years on average due to the repayment of private credits.[4] The average Eximbank interest rate was 8.65%, whereas the average private market rate, the 5-year Eurodollar rate [1] plus the spread as defined in Chapter 6, was 13.2%. The gap between the Eximbank lending rate and private market interest rates widened from FY1979 to FY1981 because of increasing market interest rates and a slower rate of adjustment of Eximbank lending rates.

The subsidy rate on the aircraft credits as defined in Chapter 6 averaged 20.4%, with a range between 7.8 and 40.2%. The average subsidy on the 95 transactions using the 5-year Eurodollar rate was $13.2 million, with a range between $0.5 and $306 million, with a total subsidy of ap-

[2] Three aircraft credits were authorized during FY1979–1980 but were subsequently cancelled and hence have been excluded from the analysis. These three credits were included in the study of additionality in Chapter 8 because they were included in the Bank's FY1980 additionality study.

On February 9, 1979 the Bank approved a $47.520 million direct credit to El Al Israel Airlines, Ltd. for the purchase of one 747 and also approved a financial guarantee for a $17.5 million PEFCO credit for the purchase of another 747. These two transactions have been treated as one.

On the last day of FY1980, the Bank approved a $223.550 million financial guarantee to PEFCO to finance the export of five 767s to the United Kingdom, with a value of $263.0 million. This case was not included in the Bank's additionality study presumably because an interest rate subsidy was not granted to PEFCO; hence it has not been included in this study.

In addition to the direct credits issued for the purchase of new commercial jet aircraft, the Bank financed the sale of one used aircraft, provided financial guarantees for four commercial jet aircraft exports, provided financing for the export of two Lear jet, two Piper, and three Metro II Commuter aircraft, and provided financing for one transaction involving DC-9 galley equipment. These cases are not included in the analysis.

[3] The Bank also issued $708 million of financial guarantees for six other aircraft exports with a value of $1.374 billion. In addition to the aircraft financing provided by the Eximbank, Japan, in response to criticism of its large trade surplus with the United States, operated a leasing program (the Samurai Lease Program) between April 1, 1978 and September 1979 that financed purchases of capital goods from the United States and the EEC. This program involved U.S. dollar financing at 8.25% in the form of a 10-year lease with an option to buy the good at a nominal price (e.g., $1). "The principal, if not only, use of the Samurai Lease Program in the United States was for the purchase of aircraft [4, p. 2]." This program financed the sale of 7 U.S. aircraft to Japanese airlines and 20 new and 4 used U.S. aircraft to other countries. While data are not available on the export value of these transactions, using the average export value per aircraft of Eximbank credits, the 27 aircraft would have an estimated export value of $1.04 billion.

[4] The computed term of the Eximbank credits exceeds the 10-year limit specified in the aircraft standstill primarily because of credits supporting exports delivered over several years. Since no data are available on the delivery schedule, the term computed as indicated in Chapter 6 may in some cases exceed the average term of the credit.

TABLE 9.5a

Aircraft Lending Data: FY1979[a]

Variable	Mean (standard deviation)	Minimum	Maximum
Eximbank credit ($ million)	43.448 (49.343)	3.600	222.846
Value of export ($ million)	92.466 (107.787)	12.000	524.200
Eximbank share (%)	46.580 (15.333)	27.933	90.000
Eximbank interest rate (%)	8.404 (0.119)	8.000	8.625
Market interest rate (using 5-year Eurodollar rate) (%)	11.080 (0.425)	10.210	12.361
Blended cost of financing the export (%)	9.433 (0.362)	8.422	10.310
Subsidy rate (%)	13.516 (2.496)	7.752	19.430
Subsidy ($ million)	5.394 (5.400)	0.527	19.035
Effective price paid (%)	93.902 (1.519)	89.765	96.369
Moratorium (years)	4.688 (2.166)	0.500	7.500
Term (years)	10.703 (0.717)	8.500	13.500

[a] Number of credits is 32.

proximately $1,253 billion. As defined in Chapter 6, the blended cost of the export financing, including the cash payment, averaged 10.6% with the cash payment costed at the private market interest rate. The subsidy provides the importer with a reduction in the price paid for the aircraft relative to the price that would have been paid had the importer borrowed in the private capital market at market rates. The effective price paid is defined in Chapter 6 as the net cost of the export, the export value minus the subsidy, divided by the export value. The effective price paid averaged 90.8%, with a range between 76.8 and 98.3%.

The use of the effective price paid as a measure of the effect of concessionary financing on the foreign importer's choice among various product offerings is based on the simple logic that the total cost of an import is the purchase price plus the cost of financing. Concessionary financing is equivalent to a reduction in the purchase price, and hence the

TABLE 9.5b

Aircraft Lending Data: FY1980[a]

Variable	Mean (standard deviation)	Minimum	Maximum
Eximbank credit ($ million)	58.074 (75.852)	4.350	360.000
Value of export ($ million)	116.113 (128.118)	10.900	669.735
Eximbank share (%)	46.395 (14.986)	13.467	85.000
Eximbank interest rate (%)	8.614 (0.354)	8.000	9.250
Market interest rate (using 5-year Eurodollar rate) (%)	12.75 (1.141)	11.339	15.786
Blended cost of financing the export (%)	10.300 (0.759)	9.144	12.632
Subsidy rate (%)	18.754 (4.436)	12.397	29.732
Subsidy ($ million)	11.308 (16.110)	0.684	68.260
Effective price paid (%)	91.223 (3.558)	79.358	98.331
Moratorium (years)	3.894 (2.334)	0.500	7.000
Term (years)	11.015 (1.433)	8.500	16.500

[a] Number of credits is 33.

effective price paid is the appropriate measure of the effect of the financing on the cost of the import. The viewpoint is supported by the Bank's study of buyer's decision-making [12].[5]

> Although price was mentioned most often as the critical factor in the buyer's decision, it is apparent that buyers often link price and financing together in their consideration of competing offers. This combination, call it "cost," is the value against which quality, technology, etc., are compared [p. 5].

[5] The use of the effective price paid as the measure of the impact of financing on the importer's aircraft purchase decision is based on the assumption of an efficient international capital market, but the Bank is mandated to compensate for imperfections with respect to term and country risk in that market. As discussed in Chapter 3, however, those imperfections are primarily due to political risks that should be dealt with through insurance. Because long-term insurance is not available, Eximbank credits provide a risk-bearing function for those political risks. The cost of that risk-bearing is reflected in the spread on a country's international borrowings and hence has been taken into account in the empirical study.

TABLE 9.5c

Aircraft Lending Data: FY1981[a]

Variable	Mean (standard deviation)	Minimum	Maximum
Eximbank credit ($ million)	85.002 (193.549)	2.899	1,057.773
Value of export ($ million)	152.770 (251.481)	4.800	1,322.200
Eximbank share (%)	44.88 (16.34)	24.00	85.00
Eximbank interest rate (%)	8.952 (0.733)	8.000	12.000
Market interest rate (using 5-year Eurodollar rate) (%)	16.002 (1.273)	13.665	18.348
Blended cost of financing the export (%)	12.024 (1.474)	8.887	14.933
Subsidy rate (%)	29.558 (6.439)	13.653	40.193
Subsidy ($ million)	23.747 (55.206)	0.742	306.348
Effective price paid (%)	87.045 (4.763)	76.830	93.181
Moratorium (years)	4.283 (2.664)	0.500	8.000
Term (years)	10.817 (1.095)	6.500	14.000

[a] Number of credits is 30.

Similarly, SRI International concluded from a survey of foreign airlines that "all agreed [that rate of return, operating profits, or cash flow] were the primary factors in the purchase decision [16, p. 15]."

V. The Model and Hypotheses Tested

The Bank's credit allocation problem may be thought of as maximizing the additional exports generated by its financing by choosing the interest rate and the cover for those exports that meet the reasonable assurance of repayment standard. The resulting allocations will be analyzed in terms of both the reduced form of the equations characterizing the Bank's credit allocation and an expression measuring the generosity of the Bank's financing. The two reduced form equations have the Eximbank

TABLE 9.5d

Aircraft Lending Data: FY1979–1981[a]

Variable	Mean (standard deviation)	Minimum	Maximum
Eximbank credit ($ million)	61.651 (120.872)	2.899	1057.773
Value of export ($ million)	119.724 (171.861)	4.800	1322.200
Eximbank share (%)	46.0 (15.4)	13.5	90.0
Eximbank interest rate (%)	8.650 (0.513)	8.000	12.000
Market interest rate (using 5-year Eurodollar rate) (%)	13.214 (2.260)	10.210	18.348
Blended cost of financing the export (%)	10.556 (1.429)	8.422	14.933
Subsidy rate (%)	20.401 (8.087)	7.752	40.193
Subsidy ($ million)	13.191 (33.065)	0.527	306.348
Effective price paid (%)	90.806 (4.462)	76.830	98.331
Moratorium (years)	4.284 (2.388)	0.500	8.000
Term (years)	10.847 (1.121)	6.500	16.500

[a] Number of credits is 95.

lending rate (EIRATE) and the cover (COVER) as dependent variables and independent variables reflecting the exogenous factors taken into account in the Bank's lending decisions. The generosity of the Bank's financing will be measured by the effective price paid, denoted EPP, by the importer. Before specifying these equations, the exogenous variables included in the study will be defined.

In choosing its interest rate and cover, the Bank takes into account a number of factors associated with the export itself, the competition it faces, the borrower, and financial market conditions. For example, the additionality studies conducted by the Bank in FY1980 and FY1981 direct credits considered three factors believed to affect the additionality of aircraft direct credits: (1) the TERM of the credit, (2) the country risk or access to domestic and international capital markets which will be measured by the SPREAD on that country's international borrowings, and (3) the COMPetition faced by the aircraft. These factors will be considered to be exogenous to the Bank's interest rate and cover decisions. Another exogenous variable, the VALUE of the export financed by the Bank, will be included as a measure of the importance of the case to the Bank's mandate of promoting U.S. exports. A TIME variable will also be used to reflect the tightening authorization restrictions on the Bank during the study period. Because long-term market interest rates tended to rise during this period, this variable will also reflect changing capital market conditions. As previously indicated, the Bank changed its aircraft lending policy in April 1980, and hence, a dummy variable D1980 will be included to reflect this change. A dummy variable D12 has also been included to reflect the change in the Bank's aircraft financing policy that resulted in one FY1981 credit being authorized with a 12% interest rate.[6] The exogenous variables included in the estimation are thus: TERM, SPREAD, COMPetition, VALUE, TIME, D1980, and D12.

The TERM of an aircraft credit is measured as the number of years that principal payments are made to a private lender, if any, and to the Eximbank, plus one-half year.[7] When the Bank lends at a concessionary interest rate, the generosity of the Bank's financing is increasing in the term, so the sign of the coefficient of TERM in the EPP equation should be negative.

The subsidy provided by Eximbank financing and the effective price paid also depend on the moratorium on the repayment to the Bank, which is defined as the time from the drawdown of the credit to the first payment of principal to the Eximbank. If no private lender is involved in the financing, the moratorium is customarily 0.5 years. If a private lender and the Bank each provide a 42.5% cover for a 10-year term credit, for example, the first 10 semiannual payments are made to the private lender, which implies a moratorium of 5.5 years. The moratorium is thus directly dependent on the Bank's cover decision and hence will not be included in the analysis as an independent variable.

A country's access to capital markets and its country risk are priced in private capital markets by the spread above the market rate that lenders charge for its borrowings, and that SPREAD will be measured as in Chapter 6.[8] Two hypotheses about the relationship between the spread and the

[6] The third dummy variable, D10.75, used in Chapter 6 reflected a change in nonaircraft financing and hence did not affect aircraft interest rates.

[7] This is not the same as the time interval between the date of the loan authorization and the final payment to the Bank because the borrower typically does not draw down the loan at the time of authorization.

[8] A weakness of the SPREAD as a measure of country risk is that it is determined from a weighted average of the borrowings of a country, and to the extent that the spread is a function of the term of those borrowings, there may be measurement errors present.

generosity of the Bank's financing seem plausible. First, since the effective price paid by an importer is defined relative to the cost of borrowing in private markets, the greater is the spread the lower is the effective price paid, other things equal. Thus, if the Bank followed a lending policy that did not take into account the country risk, the effective price paid should be negatively related to the spread. Second, if the Bank followed the arrangement guidelines that permit lower interest rates for lower income (and generally higher spread) countries than for higher income (generally lower spread) countries and loaned to the former countries at higher interest rates than to the latter countries, the effective price paid would be even more negatively related to the spread. The data do not permit distinguishing between these two hypotheses, so the only hypothesis that can be tested is that the spread and the effective price paid are negatively related. The alternative hypothesis, that SPREAD and EPP are positively related, may be thought of as corresponding to a policy of increasing the interest rate on the Eximbank credit to compensate at least for the risk reflected by the spread.

The extent of product competition is a function of a variety of characteristics of the foreign airline's route structure, demand patterns, competitive situation, and in many cases the importing country's political, strategic, and economic objectives. No direct information is available on these characteristics, but as indicated in the previous chapter the Bank's studies provided a "competitiveness ranking" intended to be a summary measure of competition (COMP) faced by U.S. aircraft, as indicated in Table 9.1.[9] The additionality study provided competitiveness ratings for each FY1980 and FY1981 aircraft credit but not for FY1979, so the rankings in Table 9.1 have been assigned to each FY1979 credit. Since the Bank's policy is to provide the minimum financing required to secure the sale for a U.S. exporter, the less direct is the product competition the less generous the financing should be. The hypothesized sign of the coefficient for COMP in the EPP equation thus is negative, and acceptance of this hypothesis would constitute evidence that in its efforts to increase U.S. exports the Bank provides more generous financing the greater is competition. Such a finding would support a conclusion that the Bank is allocating its resources with some degree of efficiency.

The Bank has no formal policy of varying its interest rate or cover as a function of the export value, but conversations with Bank officials sug-

---

[9] The weakness of the competitiveness ranking is that it is assessed *ex post* rather than at the time at which a preliminary commitment is issued. The rankings do, however, correspond ordinally to the aircraft categories that would be judged to compete most directly with the Airbus in terms of technical and performance features.

gest the hypothesis that the Bank provides more generous financing the larger is the export value for which financing is sought. First, the Bank's mandate to promote U.S. exports may make the Bank reluctant to lose a large export and, hence, the Bank may provide more generous financing, other things equal, the larger is the export value. Second, one claimed deficiency in international financial markets is the difficulty in raising large amounts of capital for a single project or import. The largest aircraft export supported by Eximbank financing was $1.322 billion to Canada, and international capital markets should have been able to finance this and the transactions included in this study with little difficulty. However, if this alleged deficiency is real or if the Bank believed it to be, the Bank might have provided a greater cover, and hence more generous financing, the greater was the export value. Both of these lines of reasoning suggest that the effective price paid may be negatively related to VALUE.

The TIME variable has a range of 1 to 12 for the quarter in which the credit was authorized and is intended to reflect both the Bank's tightening budget authorization during the study period and any exogenous interest rate trends that occurred. In addition to the authorization limit in FY1979, causing the Bank to defer a portion of the financing of a nuclear power plant export to Korea until FY1980, and the failure of the Congress to provide the Bank with a FY1980 authorization until August, the Bank during this period recognized that it would soon incur an operating loss due to the increasing difference between its lending rates and the rates at which it was funding its credits through FFB borrowing. As a response, the Bank may have increased its lending rates in an attempt to reduce its losses. Although the Bank's authorizations were at their peak in FY1981, the Reagan Administration had made it clear that authorizations would be reduced in the future. To the extent that the authorization limits or the impending losses caused the Bank to reduce the cover provided on the exports it financed, the effective price paid by importers would be expected to be positively related to TIME.

During the period of this study, however, market interest rates were rising, with an average interest rate of 11.08% for FY1979 and 16.0% for FY1981, as reported in Tables 9.5a–c. A higher market interest rate implies a lower effective price paid for a given Eximbank financing package. Since this effect acts in the opposite direction of the effect of the tightening authorization restrictions and the impending losses, no hypothesis about the sign of the coefficient of TIME can be made.

The D1980 variable that reflects the increase in the interest rate for aircraft credits to 9.25%, and the decrease in the cover provided should be negatively related to EPP because both changes increase the effective

TABLE 9.6

**Hypothesized Relationships: Effective
Price Paid (EPP) Equation**

Independent variable	Hypothesized sign
TERM	−
SPREAD	−
COMPETITION	−
VALUE	−
TIME	?
D1980	+
D12	+

price paid, *ceteris paribus*.[10] Consequently, the sign of the coefficient of the variable D1980 should be positive. Similarly, the sign of the coefficient of D12 should be positive. The hypotheses for the signs of the coefficients of the independent variables in the EPP equation are summarized in Table 9.6. In addition to the three regressions with EIRATE, COVER and EPP as dependent variables, the SUBSIDY provided on the credits was regressed on the same independent variables in order to provide a description of the effect of the variables on the subsidy.

VI. Results

The results of the estimation are presented in Tables 9.7–9.10 for FY1979, FY1980, FY1981 and FY1979–1981, respectively. Although the results for the individual years differ somewhat, the discussion will focus on the results for the 3 years combined as presented in Table 9.10. That discussion will be organized in terms of the relationship between the independent variables and the Eximbank financing decisions and the resulting cost of that financing. The Eximbank lending rate (EIRATE) is not significantly related to VALUE, indicating that the Bank did not set its

---

[10] The data give the date the credit was authorized, but the interest rate is determined when the preliminary commitment is issued. Because no information was available on the date of the preliminary commitment, any credit that carried an interest rate of 9.25% was assigned a value of D1980 = 1; otherwise D1980 = 0 was assigned.

TABLE 9.7

Estimated Equations: FY1979[a]

Dependent variable	Constant	VALUE	SPREAD	COMP	TERM	TIME	R^2
EIRATE (%)	7.317	−0.364	0.090	0.119	0.085	0.033	0.51
		(−2.34)	(2.15)	(1.49)	(3.52)	(1.96)	
COVER (%)	−9.782	1.962	3.505	8.076	4.129	2.197	0.06
		(0.07)	(0.47)	(0.57)	(0.97)	(0.74)	
EPP (%)	98.135	1.990	−2.129	−0.587	−0.136	−0.293	0.34
		(0.87)	(−3.36)	(−0.50)	(−0.38)	(−1.19)	
SUBSIDY ($ million)	−17.654	0.045	2.209	1.616	1.335	0.748	0.91
		(15.19)	(2.79)	(1.07)	(2.94)	(2.37)	

[a] The t-statistic is reported below the estimated coefficients. Number of cases: 32.

TABLE 9.8

Estimated Equations: FY1980[a]

Dependent variable	Constant	VALUE	SPREAD	COMP	TERM	TIME	D1980	R^2
EIRATE (%)	7.841	0.009	0.335	0.172	0.033	−0.010	0.806	0.94
		(0.05)	(3.57)	(2.50)	(2.24)	(−0.48)	(18.62)	
COVER (%)	−8.183	−0.050	21.112	28.700	2.674	0.028	13.095	0.40
		(−0.00)	(1.62)	(3.00)	(1.30)	(0.10)	(2.18)	
EPP (%)	100.469	−0.805	−6.305	−6.154	−0.408	0.184	4.594	0.51
		(−0.16)	(−2.26)	(−3.00)	(−0.93)	(0.30)	(3.56)	
SUBSIDY ($ million)	−19.152	0.101	12.793	12.371	0.730	−0.322	−5.326	0.82
		(7.58)	(1.70)	(1.70)	(0.62)	(−0.20)	(−1.54)	

[a] The t-statistic is reported below the estimated coefficients. Number of cases: 33.

interest rate as a function of the value of the export.[11] The Eximbank cover does not depend significantly on the export value in any year. The effective price paid (EPP) is negatively related to the export value, as hypothesized, but the estimated coefficient is not statistically significant. Consequently, the Bank provides essentially the same financing for large exports as for small exports.

[11] One-tailed tests are appropriate for the hypotheses summarized in Table 9.6, and in the discussion of the results an estimated coefficient will be said to be statistically significant if the absolute value of its t-statistic is at least 1.65. The t-statistics are reported in Tables 9.7–9.10 if the reader wishes to use other standards of significance.

TABLE 9.9

Estimated Equations: FY1981[a]

Dependent variable	Constant	VALUE	SPREAD	COMP	TERM	TIME	D1980	D12	R^2
EIRATE (%)	7.834	0.114	0.461	-0.060	-0.012	0.042	0.810	2.986	0.92
		(0.51)	(1.47)	(-0.36)	(-0.24)	(1.04)	(8.70)	(7.30)	
COVER (%)	54.729	19.338	0.645	12.101	-2.958	1.535	-9.914	-4.054	0.35
		(1.40)	(0.03)	(1.17)	(-0.99)	(0.37)	(-1.71)	(-0.16)	
EPP (%)	108.381	-1.393	-0.757	-3.369	-0.157	-1.815	4.491	6.878	0.51
		(-0.40)	(-0.15)	(-1.28)	(-0.21)	(-2.83)	(3.06)	(1.07)	
SUBSIDY ($ million)	-55.362	0.207	20.261	-4.364	0.550	3.255	-8.905	-25.746	0.92
		(12.93)	(0.90)	(-0.36)	(0.16)	(1.12)	(-1.33)	(-0.88)	

[a] The t-statistic is reported below the estimated coefficients. Number of cases: 30.

TABLE 9.10

Estimated Equations: FY19179–FY1981[a]

Dependent variable	Constant	VALUE	SPREAD	COMP	TERM	TIME	D1980	D12	R^2
EIRATE (%)	7.835	-0.042	0.152	0.042	0.036	0.012	0.786	3.361	0.92
		(-0.40)	(2.60)	(0.69)	(2.39)	(2.07)	(17.63)	(19.32)	
COVER (%)	27.654	0.011	3.366	16.273	0.848	0.082	-11.342	-5.156	0.20
		(1.13)	(0.62)	(2.88)	(0.60)	(0.15)	(-2.75)	(-0.32)	
EPP (%)	103.055	-1.648	-2.856	-3.423	-0.205	-1.105	4.641	7.873	0.64
		(-0.86)	(-2.71)	(-3.10)	(-0.75)	(-10.22)	(5.77)	(2.51)	
SUBSIDY ($ million)	-22.677	0.164	8.878	3.164	-0.240	1.938	-8.746	-15.504	0.81
		(16.17)	(1.59)	(0.54)	(-0.16)	(3.38)	(-2.05)	(-0.93)	

[a] The t-statistic is reported below the estimated coefficients. Number of cases: 95.

The estimated coefficient of the SPREAD in the lending rate equation is positive and statistically significant, indicating that the Bank sets higher interest rates the greater is the country risk even though it nominally has no such policy. The value of the coefficient, however, indicates that the Bank adjusted its interest rate by only 15.2% of the difference in the spread among borrowing countries. By FY1981, however, only 13 of the 30 aircraft credits authorized carried interest rates governed by a discretionary interest rate policy. The Bank also tended to provide a greater cover the greater is the SPREAD, but the estimated coefficient is not statistically significant.

The effective price paid is, however, negatively and statistically significantly related to the SPREAD, indicating that the effect of the greater cover more than offset the effect of the higher interest rate charged to more risky borrowers. This confirms the hypothesis that the Bank provided more generous financing the greater the country risk or the more limited is the country's access to private capital markets. Given the interpretation of the lending rate equation, the Bank appears to have provided more generous financing (relative to private market costs) to countries with a greater country risk, even though higher interest rates are charged to those countries.

The estimated coefficient of the COMP variable in the lending rate equation is positive but is statistically significant only for FY1980, indicating that the Bank does not charge a significantly different interest rate as a function of the competition. The estimated coefficient for COMP in the COVER equation is positive and statistically significant, indicating that the Bank tends to use the cover as a means of providing more generous financing for those exports that face greater competition. The estimated difference in cover provided for an export with a competitiveness rating of 1.00 and one with a competitiveness rating of .25 is 12.2%. The effect of the greater cover outweighs the effect of the higher interest rate, and thus the effective price paid by the exporter is negatively and statistically significantly related to COMP. These results support the hypothesis that the Bank attempts to use its resources effectively by providing more generous financing for exports facing more severe competition.

The estimated coefficient of TERM is positive and statistically significant in the lending rate equation, indicating that the Bank charges about four basis points more for each additional year of term. While the bank has no explicit policy of charging a higher interest rate the longer is the term, this result is consistent with the "normal" term structure of private market interest rates. The Bank provided a slightly greater cover for each additional year of loan term, but the estimated coefficient is not statistically significant. The estimated coefficient of TERM in the EPP equation is also not statistically significant, although the sign for every period is consistent with that hypothesized. For FY1981 the TERM did not have a statistically significant effect on any of the three dependent variables, which reflects the nondiscretionary lending policy applicable to most of the credits authorized in that year.

The coefficient of TIME in the lending rate equation is positive and statistically significant, indicating that the Bank did increase its lending rate over the period of analysis in addition to the increases in interest rates reflected in the coefficients of the dummy variables. The cover provided by the Bank was not significantly related to TIME, however. The effective price paid is negatively related to TIME indicating that more generous financing was provided over time as a result of the increase in private market interest rates during the period studied.

The coefficient of the D1980 variable in the lending rate equation is positive and highly significant, reflecting the increase in lending rates in April 1980. The coefficient in the COVER equation is negative and statistically significant, indicating that the Bank reduced its cover by approximately 11% at the same time. These two effects resulted in an increase of approximately 5% in the effective price paid by the importer.

The coefficient of the D12 variable in the lending rate equation is positive and highly significant, and the coefficient in the cover equation is negative but insignificant. These two effects increased the effective price paid by nearly 8%. This indicates that the Bank did not compensate for the higher lending rate in 1981 by financing a larger share of the export value.

The dollar SUBSIDY provided by Eximbank financing is increasing in the export value for all periods, as would be expected with a $1000 increase in the export value associated with a $164 increase in the subsidy over the FY1979 to FY1981 period with an increase from $45 in FY1979 to $194 in FY1981. The higher values over time are most likely due to the effect of the increase in market interest rates not captured by the TIME variable. The subsidy is positively related to SPREAD in all periods, as would be expected, but is statistically significant only for FY1979 and FY1980. The higher the competitiveness ranking the greater is the subsidy provided for FY1979 and FY1980 but not FY1981, and the estimated coefficient is not statistically significant for FY1979–1981. In all likelihood, the significance in FY1980 is due to the discretionary lending policy applicable to most of the credits authorized in that year and to the increased sales of new generation aircraft that compete directly with the Airbus. The subsidy is positively related to TERM in all periods but is not statistically significant in FY1980 or FY1981. The subsidy is not significantly related to TIME, and the estimated coefficients vary considerably

TABLE 9.11

Eximbank Aircraft Financing by U.S. Manufacturer, FY1979–1981

Manufacturer	Export value ($ million)	Credit ($ million)	Subsidy ($ million)
Boeing	8,705.9	4,638.5	1,019.8
McDonnell–Douglas	1,973.6	870.5	163.6
Lockheed	693.8	347.9	87.4
	11,373.3	5,856.9	1,268.1

across the individual years. The subsidy is, of course, negatively related to the dummy variables, although the coefficient of D12 is not statistically significant.

The equations were also estimated in log form for the FY1979–1980 data, and the results were quite similar to those estimated in the linear form. The signs of all the coefficients were the same, and all those coefficients that were statistically significant in the linear form were also statistically significant in the log form. The coefficient of SPREAD in the log form of the SUBSIDY equation is statistically significant, however, while it is not in the linear form.

When a foreign airline considers purchasing aircraft, potential suppliers may include Airbus and the three U.S. manufacturers. In such a situation, Eximbank policy is to remain neutral by issuing preliminary commitments with the same terms provided to each of the three U.S. aircraft manufacturers. During FY1979–1981, 70 of the 98 credits authorized supported Boeing exports, 18 supported McDonnell–Douglas exports, 4 supported Lockheed exports, 2 involved both Boeing and McDonnell–Douglas aircraft, and 1 involved Boeing and Lockheed aircraft. Table 9.11 presents data on the Bank's financing by manufacturer and, as would be expected, Boeing received approximately 80% of the Bank's aircraft support. To test if the Bank's practices are neutral with respect to individual manufacturers, the equations were reestimated for FY1979–1980 with the inclusion of dummy variables indicating the manufacturer.[12] Neither of the estimated coefficients associated with those variables was statistically significant, which supports the conclusion that Eximbank lending practices are neutral with respect to the aircraft exporter. For FY1981, however, Lockheed exports received less generous support than Boeing exports.

---

[12] The cases involving more than one U.S. supplier were not included in the estimation.

The 5-year Eurodollar rate has been used here as the measure of the market interest rate, but firms and government agencies also borrow from banks at floating interest rates based on a short-term Eurodollar rate. The 6-month Eurodollar rate thus was also used to measure the market rate of interest, and the EPP and SUBSIDY equations were reestimated using the 6-month Eurodollar rate. The signs of all except one of the estimated coefficients were the same as those in Tables 9.7–9.10, but the significance levels tended to be smaller, presumably because of the volatility of the 6-month Eurodollar rate.[13] That volatility gives less confidence to the estimation results obtained with the 6-month than with the 5-year Eurodollar rate, and thus those results are not reported here.

VII. Conclusions

In responding to foreign officially supported export credits and to perceived deficiencies in the international capital markets, the Bank's policy has been to provide no more support than is required to gain the export for the U.S. supplier or to match the foreign credit offer, whichever is less. Given the interest rate policy of the Bank during the period studied, the principal instrument of the Bank in providing this support is the cover. The analysis of FY1979–1981 aircraft credits provides support for the following conclusions:

1. More generous support was provided through a greater cover for those exports facing greater product and officially supported export financing competition than for those facing less competition.

2. More generous support was provided to importers in countries with a limited access to private capital markets than to countries with a more ready access.

3. The Bank did not provide more generous financing the greater was the export value when country risk, competition, and term are controlled for.

4. The Bank's financing of individual aircraft exports did not differ significantly among the three U.S. suppliers.

5. In its financing decisions, the Bank charged a higher interest rate the greater was the private market measure of country risk, as reflected in the spread, but the Bank also provided greater cover the greater was the spread. Similarly, the greater was the product competition the greater was the interest rate charged by the Bank, but greater cover was also pro-

---

[13] The *t*-statistics for the coefficients whose signs differed were 0.05 and −0.16.

vided. The Bank followed a policy of charging a higher interest rate the longer was the term of the credit, and the lending rate increased over the period of the study presumably because of the increase in market interest rates and the excess demand for the Bank's financing.

When it was operating under a lending policy that allowed some discretion, the Bank appears to have responded to foreign product and concessionary export financing competition and to perceived capital market deficiencies by providing more generous financing. This, of course, does not imply that this financing should have been provided, but instead indicates that the resources provided for aircraft financing were allocated with some degree of efficiency in an attempt to fulfill the Bank's mandate.

The majority of the FY1981 credits were authorized under policies that allowed less case-by-case discretion, and hence the regression results provide less information about the effectiveness of the Bank's lending activities in that year.

VIII. An Extension of the Methodology to All FY1980–1981 Credits

The same equations reported in Tables 9.7–9.10 for aircraft credits were estimated for all FY1980–1981 credits with the inclusion of a dummy variable AIR indicating if the credit financed is an aircraft export.[14] The estimation results are reported in Table 9.12, but because a much higher percentage of supported nonaircraft exports than aircraft exports were lost, the results must be interpreted with more caution than those discussed previously for aircraft credits. Because the results are generally consistent with those for aircraft credits, only the EPP equation will be discussed here. The effective price paid is not significantly related to either the VALUE of the export or the SPREAD for the borrowing country. The Bank does respond to greater COMPetition by increasing its cover and reducing its interest, resulting in a significantly lower effective price paid. This supports the conclusion that the Bank backs up its assessment of competition with more generous financing. The Bank's financing is also more generous the greater is the term of the credit, and that generosity increased over time because of the trend of higher market interest rates. The increase in the Bank's lending rates in FY1980 increased the effective price paid by 3% of the export value and the increase

---

[14] FY1979 credits could not be included because data on the export value associated with each credit were not available.

TABLE 9.12

Estimated Equations: All Credits FY1980–1981[a]

Dependent variable	Constant	VALUE	SPREAD	COMP	TERM	TIME	D1980	D10.75	D12	AIR	R^2
EIRATE (%)	7.652	0.001	0.122	-0.107	0.021	0.042	0.501	2.393	3.149	0.294	0.80
		(0.00)	(1.41)	(-1.61)	(2.92)	(4.05)	(11.34)	(20.36)	(10.57)	(5.94)	
COVER (%)	35.443	0.011	0.645	23.440	1.817	-0.740	-7.050	-14.909	4.364	-14.648	0.48
		(1.31)	(0.14)	(6.92)	(4.98)	(-1.40)	(-3.12)	(-2.48)	(0.29)	(-5.80)	
EPP (%)	109.133	0.128	-0.953	-5.035	-1.227	-1.118	2.989	9.147	4.858	4.853	0.67
		(0.53)	(-0.75)	(-5.21)	(-11.80)	(-7.44)	(4.63)	(5.33)	(1.12)	(6.73)	
SUBSIDY ($ million)	-17.884	0.192	5.497	-0.054	0.405	1.509	-5.922	-12.052	-6.180	-9.564	0.89
		(37.06)	(2.01)	(-0.03)	(1.81)	(4.66)	(-4.26)	(-3.26)	(-0.66)	(-6.15)	

[a] The t-statistic is reported below the estimated coefficient. Number of cases: 243.

in the nonaircraft interest rate to 10.75% resulted in a 9% increase in the EPP. A 5% increase resulted from the FY1981 policy of charging a 12% interest rate, but the estimated coefficient is not statistically significant.

The estimated coefficients of the variable AIR indicate that aircraft credits are less-generously financed than nonaircraft credits because of both a higher interest rate and a lower cover. The result is that aircraft importers pay an average of about 5% more of the value of the export than do nonaircraft importers. Consequently, although the commercial jet aircraft industry receives more support from the Eximbank than any other industry, that support has been less generous on average than that provided other industries.

APPENDIX 9.A

Aircraft Export Financing: FY1979[a]

Country	Export value ($ million)	Eximbank cover (%)	Eximbank interest rate (%)	Market interest rate (%)	Subsidy[b] ($ million)	Subsidy rate on Eximbank loan (%)	Effective price paid (%)
Afghanistan	53.483	45	8.375	11.110	3.381	14.0	93.7
Australia	25.964	40	8.250	10.762	1.387	13.4	94.7
Australia	30.226	40	8.375	10.942	1.640	13.6	94.6
Brazil	65.000	42.5	8.500	11.047	3.704	13.4	94.3
Brazil	262.158	37.2	8.500	11.047	17.367	14.9	93.4
Brazil	33.700	42.5	8.500	11.327	2.111	14.7	93.7
Cameroon	78.357	80	8.625	11.550	6.989	11.1	91.1
Canada	32.582	30	8.375	10.775	1.345	13.8	95.9
Denmark	33.900	40	8.375	10.876	1.796	13.2	94.7
Denmark	27.200	42.5	8.375	10.606	1.379	11.9	94.9
Denmark	41.000	30	8.500	10.606	1.495	12.2	96.4
Egypt	215.000	42.5	8.500	11.384	13.711	15.0	93.6
Ethiopia	40.100	40	8.375	12.025	3.030	18.9	92.4
Finland	34.740	50	8.250	10.775	2.522	13.4	92.7

France	62.000	42.5	8.500	11.360	3.924	14.9	93.7
India	179.000	27.9	8.375	11.715	9.398	18.8	94.7
Israel	103.310	46.0	8.250	10.753	5.101	9.8	95.1
Jordan	75.000	85	8.500	11.205	6.639	10.4	91.1
Malaysia	9.000	42.5	7.750	10.273	0.242	6.3	97.3
Morocco	16.000	42.5	8.375	11.293	1.036	15.2	93.5
Norway	12.000	30	8.375	10.943	0.592	14.6	95.1
Pakistan	61.000	42.5	8.500	12.361	5.037	19.4	91.7
Portugal	30.000	60	8.500	11.152	1.840	10.2	93.9
Singapore	524.210	29.5	8.000	10.643	19.035	12.3	96.4
Spain	43.809	42.5	8.375	11.087	2.654	14.3	93.9
Spain	77.000	42.5	8.375	10.637	3.952	12.1	94.9
Taiwan	140.450	90	8.250	11.205	14.380	11.4	89.8
Thailand	157.600	55	8.375	11.117	12.149	14.0	92.3
Trinidad and Tobago	67.000	42.5	8.500	10.826	3.513	12.3	94.8
Tunisia	27.600	42.5	8.375	11.045	1.649	14.1	94.0
United Kingdom	318.351	70	8.540	10.210	17.275	7.8	94.6
Venezuela	35.550	42.5	8.375	11.107	2.168	14.4	93.9
Yugoslavia	55.400	55	8.500	11.060	4.317	13.1	92.2

[a] Source: [2].

[b] The subsidy is computed using the 5-year Eurodollar rate.

APPENDIX 9.B

Aircraft Export Financing: FY1980[a]

Country	Export value ($ million)	Eximbank cover (%)	Eximbank interest rate (%)	Market interest rate (%)	Subsidy[b] ($ million)	Subsidy rate on Eximbank loan (%)	Effective price paid (%)
Algeria	62.771	70.0	8.50	12.57	7.841	17.8	87.5
Argentina	232.750	13.5	9.25	11.66	4.778	12.4	97.9
Austria	166.000	40.0	8.500	12.38	9.589	14.4	94.2
Bahamas	14.500	30.0	8.375	15.77	1.296	29.8	91.1
Belgium	103.812	60.0	8.375	12.36	12.141	19.1	88.3
Brazil	51.185	36.9	8.50	14.27	5.854	28.6	88.6
Canada	220.000	40.0	8.438	12.19	12.358	14.0	94.4
Canada	71.100	60.0	8.500	12.57	7.668	18.0	89.2
Canada	24.641	41.4	8.500	12.00	1.819	17.8	92.6
Canada	48.000	60.0	8.500	12.00	4.536	15.7	90.6
Canada	180.605	80.0	8.700	13.64	28.871	20.0	84.0
Canada	179.569	60.0	8.500	13.64	20.444	19.0	88.6
Denmark	16.100	30.0	9.25	11.82	0.684	14.2	95.7
France	122.800	40.0	8.00	11.34	8.335	16.5	93.2

Greece	98.686	42.5	8.50	11.78	8.084	19.3	91.8
Guinea	19.847	80.0	9.25	11.73	0.878	13.7	95.6
Iceland	17.900	42.5	8.375	12.10	1.438	18.9	92.0
India	82.353	42.5	8.438	13.94	9.367	26.8	88.6
Italy	669.735	53.8	8.563	12.56	70.004	19.0	89.5
Japan	192.000	40.0	8.250	13.83	14.898	19.4	92.2
Japan	86.824	40.0	9.250	11.71	4.399	12.7	94.9
Jordan	325.100	85.0	8.625	15.79	67.108	24.3	79.4
Mexico	102.300	40.0	8.50	12.87	8.839	21.6	91.4
New Zealand	11.600	42.5	8.375	12.30	0.976	19.8	91.6
Norway	101.880	72.5	9.250	13.46	11.534	15.6	88.7
Philippines	50.407	50.0	8.375	11.79	4.394	17.4	91.3
Thailand	10.900	42.5	8.375	12.55	0.967	20.9	91.1
Tunisia	27.016	42.5	9.25	12.08	1.651	14.4	93.9
United Kingdom	228.000	38.1	8.375	12.89	19.230	21.1	91.6
United Kingdom	192.900	40.0	8.375	11.60	13.331	16.7	93.1
Venezuela	45.673	40.0	9.25	12.01	2.659	14.6	94.2
Yugoslavia	36.000	42.5	8.500	14.27	4.064	26.6	88.7
Yugoslavia	38.776	42.5	8.500	13.79	3.120	18.9	92.0

[a] Source: [2].
[b] The subsidy is computed using the 5-year Eurodollar rate.

APPENDIX 9.C

Aircraft Export Financing: FY1981[a]

Country	Export value ($ million)	Eximbank cover (%)	Eximbank interest rate (%)	Market interest rate (%)	Subsidy[b] ($ million)	Subsidy rate on Eximbank loan (%)	Effective price paid (%)
Australia	235.1	85.0	8.00	16.00	53.914	27.0	77.1
Australia	69.6	49.6	8.375	16.00	11.316	32.8	83.7
Australia	152.2	36.1	8.40	16.00	18.959	34.5	87.5
Bahrain	44.1	50.0	9.25	14.47	3.007	13.7	93.2
Belgium	56.0	30.0	9.25	17.43	6.289	37.4	88.8
Brazil	124.7	28.0	9.25	17.89	13.704	39.3	89.0
Canada	1,332.2	80.0	8.70	16.73	306.348	29.0	76.8
Canada	15.6	60.0	8.50	14.66	2.396	25.6	84.6
Canada	4.8	60.0	8.50	14.66	0.742	25.6	84.5
Canada	62.3	42.5	8.50	15.61	6.414	24.2	89.7
Canada	12.6	42.5	8.50	15.68	1.738	32.4	86.2
Canada	66.7	60.0	8.50	17.74	14.076	35.2	78.9
Canada	95.0	30.0	8.75	17.74	11.455	40.2	87.9

Fiji Islands	17.0	30.0	9.25	15.44	1.501	29.4	91.2
France	171.6	32.3	8.00	16.91	22.064	39.8	87.1
Israel	230.1	75.0	9.25	16.17	43.330	25.1	81.2
Israel	38.0	30.0	9.25	16.76	4.050	35.5	89.3
Japan	50.6	40.0	9.25	14.93	5.319	26.3	89.5
Japan	230.0	40.0	9.25	14.93	18.138	19.7	92.1
Japan	208.1	45.0	9.25	15.85	20.930	22.4	89.9
Malta	166.6	55.8	9.93	17.56	30.918	33.2	81.4
Morocco	16.0	30.8	9.25	16.35	1.598	33.3	90.0
Nauru	15.6	30.0	8.50	13.66	1.245	26.6	92.0
Norway	92.6	55.0	9.25	17.56	17.570	34.5	81.0
Portugal	250.0	24.0	8.00	13.78	18.327	30.5	92.7
Taiwan	80.1	60.0	8.50	15.17	14.027	29.2	82.5
Trinidad and Tobago	82.6	30.0	9.25	16.36	8.252	33.3	90.0
Turkey	18.8	42.5	12.00[c]	18.35	1.947	24.3	89.6
United Kingdom	605.0	40.8	9.25	14.67	48.702	18.9	92.0
Uruguay	49.5	30.0	9.25	14.89	4.133	27.8	91.7

[a] Source: [2].
[b] The subsidy is computed using the 5-year Eurodollar rate.
[c] Plus a 2% fee.

259

References

1. Continental Illinois Bank, "Euro-Dollar Interest Rates Yield Curve," unpublished paper, Chicago, Illinois, 1981.
2. Export–Import Bank, "Aircraft Report: From Inception (1934) through September 30, 1981," unpublished paper, Washington, D.C., 1982.
3. Export–Import Bank. *1979 Annual Report*. Washington, D.C., 1980.
4. Export–Import Bank, "Memoranda from Alex McCullough to Mr. Cruse, Re: Japan's Program of Financing U.S. Imports," unpublished paper, Washington, D.C., 1980.
5. Export–Import Bank, "Commercial Jet Aircraft Deliveries—Foreign, 1970–1974" unpublished paper, Washington, D.C., 1975.
6. Export–Import Bank, "Eximbank-Supported Share of U.S. Commercial Jet Aircraft Exports (Estimate)" unpublished paper, Washington, D.C., 1978.
7. Export–Import Bank, "Denial Listing by Date-Denied as of 10/31/81," unpublished paper, Washington, D.C., 1981.
8. Export–Import Bank, Policy Analysis Staff, "Aircraft Policy Options," unpublished paper, Washington, D.C., 1979.
9. Export–Import Bank, Policy Analysis Staff, "Commercial Jet Aircraft: The Export Market and Eximbank Activity, 1978 and 1979," unpublished paper, Washington, D.C., 1980.
10. Export–Import Bank, "Commercial Jet Aircraft Update," unpublished paper, Washington, D.C., 1978.
11. Export–Import Bank, "Additionality Study," unpublished paper, Washington, D.C., 1981.
12. Export–Import Bank, Policy Analysis Staff, "Primary Factors in Buyer's Decisions; 'The Causation Study,' " unpublished paper, Washington, D.C., 1979.
13. Export–Import Bank, "Commercial Jet Aircraft Export Markets and Eximbank Activity, 1978–1981," unpublished paper, Washington, D.C., 1982.
14. Export–Import Bank, "FY81 Additionality Study: Results," Washington, D.C., 1982.
15. Glick, W. W. and Duff, J. M., Jr. "Export–Import Bank of the United States," unpublished paper, Washington, D.C., 1979.
16. SRI International, "Assessment of U.S. Government Export Financing of High-Technology Products: Phase I Research Approach," Menlo Park, California, 1981.
17. U.S. Senate, Subcommittee on International Finance, Committee on Banking, Housing, and Urban Affairs, "Hearings on Export Policy," Washington, D.C., 1978.

10

The Ansett Case

I. Introduction

The analysis in the preceding chapters has focused on the evaluation of the Bank's programs at an aggregate level, but the Bank's performance is the result of a collection of individual case-by-case decisions. This chapter is concerned with the case of an application by Ansett Airlines of Australia for a long-term credit for the purchase of 25 Boeing commercial jet aircraft, valued at $832 million, as an alternative to the purchase of aircraft from Airbus Industrie. This case is not considered because it is representative of the Bank's decision making but rather because a public record is available that provides considerable detail on the case. Although the Bank authorized only a $290 million credit to Ansett, the magnitude of the subsidy provided and a concern about possible political motivations for the credit resulted in hearings by the Senate Committee on Banking, Housing, and Urban Affairs [6] on May 12 and 13, 1980. The resulting public record is unique in that it includes a written statement of the Airbus financing offer, a record of Eximbank's analysis of that offer, and information on Ansett's and Boeing's strategic behavior pertaining to the two aircraft alternatives. The hearings also provide an indication of the standards used by the Bank in evaluating the foreign credit offer and in determining its response to Ansett's request for credit.

II. The Aircraft Offers

The Airbus offer to Ansett involved four A-300 aircraft, with an export value of approximately $150 million, with the possibility of options on additional aircraft. The Boeing proposal included twelve 767, four 727, and nine 737 aircraft, with an export value of $719 million, and spare parts, ground support equipment, and flight crew training with an export value of $113 million, for a total of $832 million. The difference in the scale of these two offers is in part a function of the official Australian domestic airline policy, which had been to maintain parallel operations between its two domestic airlines: Trans-Australian Airlines (TAA), which is 100% government-owned, and Ansett, which is 100% privately owned. According to the then Bank chairman John Moore, "TAA and Ansett from the beginning of their operations have had exactly the same equipment delivered the same days. They fly within 5 minutes of each other on every route. . . . Right now the fleets are exactly the same [6, p. 215]."[1] Until December, 1979, Ansett had been controlled by Sir Reginald Ansett, but Mr. Rupert Murdoch and Sir Peter Abeles gained control at that time. During the period of the takeover, TAA had decided to purchase four A-300s and had taken options on eight others, while Ansett had ordered no new aircraft. Ansett was thus eager to obtain new aircraft in order to remain competitive with TAA, and if Murdoch had decided to follow the tradition of parallel operations, Ansett would have taken the Airbus offer plus options on eight other A-300s.

However, Murdoch saw an opportunity to break from the traditional parallel policy. In commenting on his February 19, 1980 meeting with Bank officials, Murdoch described his strategy as follows [6]:

> I explained what the proposal [Airbus] was, what our choice was . . . and it was a very complicated choice, to remain with the old two-airline policy in Australia or buy Airbus [Murdoch apparently meant Boeing]. We were under a great deal of pressure by a lot of people, both outside and inside the company, to close with Airbus, although I preferred Boeing and made no secret of that. I said that we mapped out the strategy of fighting the other airline by retiring our DC-9's and bring in 737's and by fighting the Airbus with 727's. It will be remembered that we were going to be 18 months behind the Airbus, which was a very severe risk for us to take, quite apart from the other risk of deciding to compete with the Government. [p. 173].

J. B. L. Pierce, treasurer of Boeing, in a February 15, 1980 letter to Charles E. Houston, vice president–Asia of the Eximbank, used the same argument in supporting Ansett's request for a preliminary commitment for Eximbank financing [6].

> Under consideration by Ansett are two fleet alternatives. One provides for the acquisition of twelve (12) Airbus A300 B4 aircraft; the other a fleet of Boeing aircraft consisting of twelve (12) 767s, four (4) 727s, and nine (9) 737s. . . . Should Ansett decide on Boeing equipment, it is Ansett's plan in 1981 to add to

---

[1] The parallel policy is described by Davies [1, 2], who also compared the performance of TAA and Ansett.

their present jet fleet of (12) DC-9-30s and (12) 727-200s with (4) more of the 727-200s. This is necessary to counter the earlier deliveries available on the Airbus A-300 prior to our deliveries of the 767 in November 1982. (Airbus has offered an initial A300 delivery position of October 1981.) Ansett would use the widebody aircraft to satisfy the traffic demand and growth between its major market centers—Melbourne, Sydney, Brisbane, Adelaide and Perth. The 737 aircraft would be primarily used to satisfy the needs of their frequency-sensitive local eastern and other smaller routes. . . . Ansett has been conducting in-depth studies in their evaluation of the Airbus/Boeing fleet alternatives. The Airbus offer has made financing a critical factor in Ansett's equipment selection decision. For Boeing, this is an "all-or-nothing" proposition. If Ansett decides to purchase the Airbus, it is unlikely that Boeing will be able to sell any additional aircraft of any type to Ansett for at least the next five years. Moreover, Trans-Australia Airlines (TAA), Ansett's government-owned competitor, has already decided to purchase the A-300, again at very favorable financing terms. This has placed considerable pressure on Ansett to also purchase Airbus [pp. 325–326].

The relationship of the 727s and 737s to Ansett's choice between the 767s and the A-300s was an important factor in the Bank's consideration of the appropriate response to the Airbus financing offer. Boeing and Murdoch argued that Ansett wanted to put new aircraft on its routes at approximately the same time that TAA received its A-300s and, because the delivery date of the 767s was later than that offered by Airbus, the 727s were required. The alternative view was that Ansett needed the 727s and 737s to expand its narrow-bodied service and to replace its aging DC-9 fleet and thus had bundled these aircraft with the 767s in order to obtain Eximbank financing for the entire package. The wide bodied, 265-passenger Airbus would not be an economical alternative for Ansett's "frequency-sensitive local eastern and other smaller routes" on which the smaller 737s would be used, so Ansett's only alternatives to the use of the 737s for those routes were to continue their DC-9s in service or to use their present 727s with additional A-300s serving the routes presently served by the 727s. Eximbank Board member Thibaut de St. Phalle summarized this point of view: "They're still going to have to have short-range aircraft to replace their DC-9's [6, p. 230]." It was to Ansett's advantage to try to include the 727s and 737s with the purchase of the 767s in order to obtain the more generous Eximbank financing typically made available for new generation aircraft than for older generation aircraft. Airbus, however, also could have offered the smaller A-310 with a capacity of 210 seats that might have been a viable alternative to the 737s and 727s on some routes, although there is no mention in the record of the possible purchase of A-310s. The role the 727s and 737s played in the Eximbank's deliberation will be considered in more detail in Section IV.[2]

_____

[2] In 1981 Midway Airlines announced that it would purchase eight DC-9s and related equipment from Ansett for $46 million.

III. The Airbus Financing Offer

The Airbus financing offer was contained in a February 11, 1980 cable from Airbus Industrie to Murdoch. It provided a credit for 85% of the delivered price of four A-300s with a 10-year term, and payments to be made in 20 semiannual installments, with the first payment due 6 months following delivery of the aircraft.[3] The credit would be 40% in French francs with an interest rate of 8.75%, 40% in deutschemarks at 6.5%, and 20% in U.S. dollars at 9.25%. This was the same financing offer made to TAA.[4,5] Airbus had offered TAA an alternative financing plan of full U.S. dollar financing at 9.25% [6, p. 350], and it was believed that Airbus was prepared to offer Ansett full U.S. dollar financing at the same interest rate [6, p. 187]. Moore stated, "Informally, in the meeting they indicated that they thought they could press Airbus to an entire dollar offer at $9\frac{1}{4}$% [6, p. 210]." No confirmation of an all dollar financing offer was obtained prior to the date on which the Bank made its decision, however.[6]

Because Ansett had a bona fide financing offer from Airbus at highly concessionary interest rates, the possibility was real that Ansett would not choose Boeing unless concessionary financing were provided by the Eximbank. The initial issue before the Bank was thus to determine what interest rate was equivalent to the Airbus offer.

Ansett took the first formal step in the interest rate discussions during the February 19, 1980 meeting at the Bank attended by Murdoch, executives of related companies controlled by Murdoch, Boeing representatives, Moore, and staff members of the Bank.[7] The next day Murdoch

---

[3] In addition to these terms there were certain standard drawdown conditions and fees associated with the transaction.

[4] The dollar portion of the credit represented the British participation in Airbus.

[5] Airbus apparently had initially offered Ansett the mixed currency package with a 7% deutschemark interest rate, a 9% French franc rate, and a 9.5% dollar rate, but after negotiations reduced the interest rates to those granted to TAA.

[6] The record is unclear about when the Bank learned that there was no Airbus offer of all dollar financing. After the Bank had made its decision, Board member Donald E. Stingel visited Airbus Industrie and confirmed that there was no all dollar financing offer [6, p. 51]. Also, subsequent to the Bank's decision, it was learned that Airbus had offered an alternative financial package of 60% cash and 40% deutschemarks at 6.5%.

[7] On February 15, 1980 Heidrich of the Bank had met with Ansett personel in Melbourne and reported that "the financial people that we met with—we talked about our scales depending on the deliveries here of somewhere between $8\frac{1}{2}$ and $8\frac{3}{4}$ and they thought that was a very reasonable interest rate in U.S. dollars. In addition, the market in Australia had one of the top rated companies come to the market with a ten year bond and it went out at 12%. So that's the prevailing scene in Australia [6, p. 235]." Ansett had already received the Airbus financial offer by the time of the February 15 meeting.

wrote to Moore and stated [6]

> As you consider your offer, I would like to emphasize that we truly believe that a matching competitive interest rate would be 7.95%, as offered by Airbus even if the loan is entirely in U.S. dollars. As we explained in the meeting, we have great confidence in the strength of the Australian dollar against all hard currencies in the next decade, including the Deutsche mark and the French franc. This confidence is based on excellent prospects for energy self-sufficiency and increasingly valuable mineral exports supporting a very strong balance of payments position. I would also like to emphasize our concern that the loan term be 12 years, which we believe to be available from Airbus [pp. 303–304].

The 7.95% interest rate referred to by Murdoch is the weighted average of the French franc, deutschemark, and U.S. dollar interest rates contained in the Airbus offer. Murdoch also indicated that the Airbus offer was good only until February 29 if the promised delivery dates were to be met and, hence, a prompt response by Eximbank was required.[8]

The Ansett strategy was clear. Ansett sought to obtain a U.S. dollar loan for the entire Boeing package at an interest rate equivalent to a weighted average of the nominal interest rates in the mixed currency credit offered by Airbus. Ansett may have chosen this strategy because it knew that the Eximbank had a policy of matching the nominal interest rate of a competing financing offer, or it may have based its request on its own analysis of real interest rates. The latter seems less likely than the former, however.

One interest rate that the Bank could have chosen to match was the interest rate on the dollar portion of the Airbus financing package. As indicated in a March 18, 1980 *New York Times* article:

> Several Export–Import Bank and Administration officials argued that the financing package for the Boeing 767's was much more generous than the financing offered by Airbus.

---

[8] The record contains no information about how the February 29, 1980 deadline had been determined or why Ansett and Boeing had waited until February 19 to approach the Bank for financing. Since Airbus had an advantage over Boeing with respect to the delivery date of the new generation aircraft, Airbus may well have strategically set the deadline in an attempt to gain the sale. The timing of the Boeing and Ansett approach to the Bank may have been the result of the natural course of their negotiations, or it may have reflected a strategic decision on their part to put pressure on the Bank. The board apparently did not have full information about how the deadline had arisen. As Murdoch later explained, "Airbus was holding $500,000 of Ansett funds to secure preferential delivery position and the Airbus obligation was to become firm unless cancelled within 3 weeks—that is, on March 1 [6, p. 168]." Subsequent to the Bank's decision, the Bank learned that Ansett had obtained a 2-week extension of the deadline.

TWO FINANCING OPTIONS

According to those officials, Airbus had offered Ansett two financing options. The first included a multicurrency loan at an average interest rate of 7.95 percent. The second option included financing in United States dollars at an interest rate of 9.25 percent.

"We considered these financing options to be equivalent," one Airbus representative said in an interview. Although the mixed-currency loan would carry a lower interest rate, because of fluctuations in exchange rates, paying back the loan "would probably be more expensive in the future," he said.

Several Treasury Department officials agreed.

"We could have offered 9 percent and have still been under the Airbus offer" said one Treasury Department official.[9]

In referring to the Ansett request that the Eximbank meet the weighted-average interest rate, John Lange, director of the Office of Trade Finance, Department of the Treasury, wrote in a memorandum to Assistant Treasury Secretary Bergsten [6]:

Ansett and Boeing have asked the Bank to match the *nominal* blended rate of the Airbus offer (about 7.99%) without reference to the fact that the U.S. Eximbank portion will be entirely in dollars. This is interest rate illusion at its most galling. Clearly, the Eximbank rate should be around 9.25%, to match what Airbus is charging for the dollar portion of its loan [p. 203].[10]

At its February 26, 1980 meeting, the Eximbank board initially contemplated a 9.25% interest rate because that was the interest rate on the dollar portion of the Airbus financial package. In discussing this interest rate with the Ansett and Boeing representatives at their February 19 meeting, Moore stated that he had taken the position [6]

that Airbus was arguing that the dollar equivalent was 9¼ and I didn't depart from that in the argument with them. They rejected it on the grounds that they had studied the relationships historically and as they predict them in the next twelve or fifteen years the Australian dollar to the Deutsche mark to American dollars and they felt that we had to look at the 7.95% blended rate of the package rather than the 9¼. I can't believe in the thing even at that. I think it's political too in that they are not going to take an offer that's got a stated rate of interest that's higher than TAA had because they would be afraid they would be uncompetitive [p. 214].

To judge the appropriateness of the 7.95% U.S. dollar interest rate requested by Ansett versus the 9.25% rate, the likely future changes in exchange rates must be used to determine the real interest rate to an

---

[9] © 1980 by The New York Times Company. Reprinted by permission.

[10] The Eximbank and Airbus both included a 0.5% management fee, so the Bank calculated the effective weighted average interest rate as 7.95% ÷ .995 = 7.99%.

TABLE 10.1

**U.S. Interest Rate Equivalent to the
Airbus Financing Offer**

Discount rate (%)	U.S. dollar interest rate (%)
5	8.32
10	8.25
15	8.21

Australian buyer. Even though Mr. Murdoch called attention to the real cost of borrowing in a foreign currency by arguing that the Australian dollar would be strong against the major currencies, the Australian dollar would not be expected to be equally strong against each of the three currencies.[11] The best predictors of future changes in exchange rates are market interest rates, and to reflect those market rates, long-term, domestic, risk-free government interest rates in French francs, deutschemarks, and U.S. dollars will be used. In February 1980, those interest rates were 14.11, 8.4, and 11.55%, respectively, as reported in the OECD-sponsored Wallen report [7]. These interest rates indicate that versus the Australian dollar the French franc would be expected to depreciate more (or appreciate less) than would the U.S. dollar which would depreciate more than the deutschemark. Consequently, the subsidy provided by the Airbus offer was greatest on the French franc portion and lower on the U.S. dollar and the deutschemark portions.

Given the assumption that exchange rate changes are best predicted by the relative domestic rates of interest, the U.S. dollar interest rate that is equivalent, from the point of view of an Australian importer, to the Airbus mixed currency offer can be determined using the approach developed in Appendix 10.A. The equivalent U.S. interest rate is a function of the discount rate used by Ansett and the domestic Australian interest rate, so the data in Table 10.1 are parameterized on the discount rate with the assumption that the Australian domestic interest rate is 10%. As indicated in Appendix 10.A, the U.S. dollar equivalent interest rate depends on the difference between the discount rate used by Ansett and the Australian interest rate and not on the levels of those rates, so a discount rate of 20% and an Australian interest rate of 15% result in an equivalent U.S. dollar interest rate of 8.21%.

---

[11] As will be indicated below, Murdoch's reference to exchange rates may have been in response to Moore's assertion that the interest rate on the Eximbank credit should match the U.S. dollar interest rate included in the Airbus offer.

Although the equivalent U.S. dollar interest rate is relatively insensitive to the Australian interest and discount rates used, it is relatively sensitive to which market interest rates are used in the calculations. For example, the domestic corporate bond rates in France, Germany, and the United States were 14.57, 8.50, and 12.88%, respectively, in February 1980 [4], which imply an equivalent U.S. dollar interest rate of 9.02% for the Airbus financing offer. In general, the higher are the market rates, the higher is the equivalent U.S. dollar interest rate. Since market interest rates were generally rising in early 1980, the Airbus financing offer may have been equivalent to a U.S. interest rate of slightly more than 9%.

Based on this analysis, the blended interest rate of 7.95% obtained by a simple weighting of the nominal interest rates in the Airbus offer is significantly less than the equivalent U.S. dollar interest rate, which was in the range of 8.2 to over 9%. Ansett may have evaluated the real interest rates, and in finding that the equivalent rate was close to the simple weighted-average, made its request to the Bank in nominal terms, but there is no such indication in the record.[12] The Eximbank staff apparently recognized the significance of the difference between real and nominal interest rates, although there is no evidence in the record that an analysis of likely exchange rate changes was performed. In referring to the 7.95% weighted-average interest rate, the preliminary commitment memorandum prepared by the staff for the Eximbank board stated "A large, though intangible, element in comparability is the relative exchange rates of the various currencies over the life of the loans. We have been requested to match the Airbus financing without considering this intangible element and have therefore presented [to the Board] 8.0% as the requested Eximbank interest rate [6, p. 288]."

A February 19, 1980 Eximbank memorandum summarizing the meeting that day between Ansett, Boeing, and Eximbank officials indicated that Moore also recognized the relevance of exchange rate movements [6]:

> Mr. Moore pointed out that the Airbus offer included 40% Deutsche marks, a currency that had been rapidly appreciating against the dollar and 40% French francs, a currency that also has appreciated against the dollar. He suggested that

---

[12] In response to a question during the hearings about Lange's statement quoted above, Moore argued that the financing package actually provided by Eximbank had matched the $9\frac{1}{4}$% dollar rate contained in the Airbus offer. Moore stated "On the entire package, the blended interest rate to Ansett Airlines is 9.3 percent, Senator, and it's quite consistent with what Treasury is saying [6, p. 45]." There is no indication in the transcripts of the February 26 or 28 board meetings, however, that the Bank analyzed the blended interest rate on the entire financing offer. As indicated below in Table 10.6, the blended interest rate to Ansett was approximately 8.8%, using the methodology in Appendix 10.A.

Ansett, in evaluating financing proposals, should give weight to the currencies involved and the possibility that U.S. dollar obligations might prove to be less burdensome than those denominated in Deutsche marks and French francs.

The Australian visitors disputed the suggestion, pointing out that Australia had large energy resources and many other resources as well; that they expected Australia to have a strong balance of payments position and a strong currency in coming years so that they were not concerned by Deutsche mark and French franc obligations [p. 329].

This suggests that although the Eximbank recognized that real interest rates are relevant, it apparently accepted Ansett's statement that Ansett was evaluating the financing offers based on the weighted average of the nominal interest rates. To strengthen the credibility of its claim, Ansett attempted to put pressure on the Bank through Boeing. A February 20, 1980 Boeing memorandum written by Clarence F. Wilde stated [6]

In Tex's absence I took a call from Rupert Murdoch who wanted to convey his concern about XM being responsive to their financing requirements. He said that he had made it quite clear in his meeting with XM (attended by Pierce and Hong [Boeing executives]) that they would have to meet the Airbus offer of 7.9% (mixed currency) in 12 years.

He said he doesn't accept XM's translation of 7.9% mixed currency to 9.+% U.S. currency and our deal is dead unless it's 8% or less [p. 340].

Although Moore did not mention it at the board meetings, Boeing also put pressure on him through the U.S. ambassador to Australia, Philip H. Alston, Jr., who was a former law partner of Moore. Alston stated [6]

On February 25, 1980, I received a telephone call from Mr. Robert A. Clarke who represents Boeing in Sidney. Mr. Clarke explained that the most important fact in the Boeing–Airbus competition for the Ansett order were the respective financing arrangements available through Airbus and those available from the Export–Import Bank. He informed me that there was pending before the Eximbank a proposed sale to Boeing and that a favorable decision by the Eximbank would help to put Boeing in a competitive position. Mr. Clarke emphasized that a prompt decision was essential because the delivery schedule included in the Airbus offer was valid only until March 1. The Ansett Board of Directors needed an indication that competitive financing was available through Eximbank in order to justify a decision to defer final action beyond the March 1 deadline. Mr. Clarke asked that I contact the Export–Import Bank and urge that a prompt and favorable decision be reached on the Ansett proposal.

Among many of the responsibilities of an Ambassador, one of the most important, in my view, is that of promoting the interest of American businesses abroad. I, therefore, regarded it as my duty to do everything I legitimately could to assist Boeing. Shortly after my conversation with Mr. Clarke, I telephoned John L. Moore, Jr., President and Chairman of the Export–Import Bank. Mr. Moore and I were law partners for many years in Atlanta. In our conversation I stressed the importance of the transaction to Boeing and to the American economy. I urged that a prompt decision be reached, and expressed my hope that the decision would be favorable. Later, I believe the same day, I called Bob Clarke to let him know I had reached John Moore. It is my recollection that Mr. Clarke was not in and that I left word with his secretary to the effect that Eximbank was aware of my interest in the Boeing–Airbus competition [pp. 162–163].

IV. The Eximbank Board Meetings

A. *The Issues and Strategic Behavior*

The Ansett application was discussed at two Eximbank board meetings, the first held February 26, 1980 and the second held February 28, 1980. The discussions at these two meetings provide information on three factors: (1) the strategic behavior of Ansett and Boeing in seeking Eximbank financing, (2) Eximbank's attitude toward the export, and (3) the analysis the Bank made as a basis for determining the financing package to offer. The Bank had to decide on the following issues: (1) what interest rate and cover to offer on the 767s, (2) the number of 767s to be financed, (3) the financial package to offer for the 727s and 737s, and (4) the terms of the credits.

Both the Bank staff and the board members recognized that Boeing and Ansett may have been acting strategically in requesting Eximbank financing. With respect to the general incentives of the importer and exporter, board member Donald E. Stingel stated [6]

> Boeing, naturally anxious to sell its planes in the Australian market and cognizant of potentially later delivery schedules than could be offered by Airbus, and Mr. Murdoch went all-out to convince Eximbank that there was strong Airbus financing competition. In doing so they acted no differently than many other U.S. exporters or foreign purchasers which have approached the Bank hand-in-hand to secure the best possible Eximbank financing package. If either an exporter or a buyer can convince us to give more loan cover at a lower rate of interest it makes selling easier for the exporter and costs the buyer less in the long run [p. 21].

Mr. Peacock, the loan officer, also stated, "I would like to say that I think the negotiating tactics of Boeing and Ansett should make us very wary of this deal. First of all, it's inconceivable to me that an old customer of ours like this could have been contemplating an 800 million dollar purchase without having given the Asia division any kind of inkling about this [6, p. 209]."[13] Moore, however, pointed out that it was only in December 1979

---

[13] Ansett had borrowed from the Bank on seven occasions in the past, and one financial guarantee had been issued for a commercial bank credit to Ansett. As of December 31, 1979, the Bank's exposure on Ansett credits was $49 million.

that Murdoch and Abeles gained control of Ansett and that prior to that time the previous management was busy attempting to thwart the take-over effort and hence had not been considering aircraft purchases.

B. Financing of the 767s

The initial proposal presented by the Bank staff to the board for its February 26, 1980 meeting was the Ansett–Boeing proposal to finance all 25 aircraft at an 8% interest rate with a 15% cash payment and an 85% Eximbank cover of $657 million. The staff made no recommendation to the board regarding the Ansett–Boeing proposal but instead forwarded the proposal to the board under a "Request for Board Guidance" designation.

The 85% cover was consistent with Eximbank aircraft lending policy which had been formulated in 1979 by the Bank in conjunction with the National Advisory Council on International Monetary and Financial Policies. Bank policy for medium-range aircraft at the time of the Ansett case was [3]

> Medium range (B-757, B-767, B-727, DC-9 Super 80, DC-10-0, L-1011-1, L-1011-100)—Eximbank's policy would be to provide a minimum of 42.5 percent direct credit for *all* sales in this category. Recognizing that this area faces the most competition, allowance would be made for an actual average participation of 63.75 percent (i.e., one-half the cases at 42.5 percent credit, one-half at 85 percent credit) [p. 2].

At the February 26 board meeting, Moore expressed his judgment that it was necessary to provide the financing package that Ansett and Boeing had requested [6]

> Now, I agree that there is some jockeying going on here because they are putting it in a package, but I'm convinced that whether we like it or not it's an all or nothing situation. We cover this whole thing, 85% cover at 8%, or there's just no decision. Now we may decide not to do that because its too painful, but I don't think we should fool ourselves that there's any way to jockey this package into less than presented to the board [pp. 216–217].

However, two of the board members present, Kahliff and de Saint Phalle, objected to financing all twelve 767s, the 727s, and the 737s at 8%. Consequently, the board deferred a decision on the Ansett application until its February 28 meeting.

One source of confusion during the board deliberations centered on how many Airbuses were being considered by Ansett. Since the Eximbank policy is to match credit offerings when deemed necessary to obtain the export, the board had to decide if it should believe the Boeing claim that twelve Airbuses were involved or whether it should focus on meeting the firm offer for four aircraft. During the first of the two board meetings, the Bank considered financing all twelve 767s based on the hypothesis that otherwise orders for four A-300s would be placed immediately and options would be taken for 8 additional A-300s. In discussing the situation further and drawing an analogy with TAA, Moore asked, "What did TAA buy? Four plus options on eight more [6, p. 218]." Heidrich replied "I think that's the way I think they're going to do it. First delivery is October 1981 on the first 4 [6, p. 219]."

Since there was considerable confusion at the February 26 board meeting regarding how many aircraft were included in the Airbus offer, Mr. Peacock checked on the Airbus offer before the February 28 board meeting and found that it covered only four aircraft. He stated, however, "Mr. Murdoch, however, feels confident that they would get the same financing on future orders of A-310's [6, p. 242]."[14] Moore at the same time indicated that immediately prior to the board meeting he had received a cable from Boeing conveying the same message.

At the February 28 meeting, the board initially agreed to finance four 767s and to commit to financing eight additional 767s at interest rates that would be determined at the time the orders were placed. Heidrich, however, pointed out that in his February 15 meeting with Ansett representatives in Melbourne, Ansett had indicated that the 767s were not equivalent to the Airbuses because an A-300 has approximately 250 seats whereas the 767 has only 200 seats. The board therefore decided to finance five 767s since they would provide a seat capacity equivalent to that of four A-300s. The Bank also issued a letter of interest stating that it would finance additional 767s purchased by Ansett: "Eximbank is interested in supporting sales of U.S. built aircraft to Ansett and in this connection we would consider the financing offers which Airbus Industrie may make to Ansett or to Trans-Australian Airlines for Airbus aircraft [6, p. 305]."

At the February 28 meeting, the Bank thus decided to offer financing for five 767s, with 85% cover at 8%. The board agreed to the 8% interest rate requested by Ansett and Boeing because it was unwilling to risk losing the export, and in part because the Treasury had backed down in its opposition to the 8% rate. John Lange, the Department of the Treasury representative at the Eximbank board meetings, stated "we hear what you're saying—that the decision maker in this case is playing Mexican standoff with us and wants an 8% rate. We [Treasury] can't, obviously,

---

[14] It is not clear if Peacock misspoke in mentioning the A-310s or if Ansett had planned to purchase A-310s if it were to choose Airbus.

not being participants in those conversations, we can't and we don't feel it appropriate to even try and second guess you on this [6, p. 243].'' Consequently, even though the Treasury felt that an 8% interest rate on the financing of the 767s was too low, it was not prepared to challenge the judgment of the Bank regarding Ansett's likely basis for choosing between the aircraft offers.

In March, 1980, however, the Bank revised its aircraft policy because of an increased demand for export financing and because Congress had failed to approve the Bank's fiscal year 1980 authorization. The Bank, faced with the very real possibility of having to operate under a continuing resolution that provided only a $3.75 billion direct loan authorization, adopted a policy of providing a 30% cover for old generation aircraft and 65% cover for new generation aircraft, both at a 9.25% interest rate. This policy revision, coming shortly after the approval of the Ansett preliminary commitment, suggests that the Bank may have concluded that a 9.25% rate was competitive with the financing that Airbus was likely to offer in the future. The reduced cover, however, was more likely to have been a response to the authorization problem.

The Airbus financial package provided a 10-year term, but Ansett had indicated to the Bank that Airbus was prepared to provide a term of 12 years. The Ansett strategy was to obtain the longest maturity possible, and Ansett probably decided to request the 12-year term because that is the maximum allowed under the OECD aircraft standstill. As Mr. Moore stated, ''Yes, I think they're jockeying both sides on that and I would imagine the Airbus salesman has done the usual rigmarole saying that we won't give it to you in writing but if you buy we'll see that you get twelve years [6, p. 215].'' Apparently the Eximbank board did not view the request for a 12-year term as very important, since it decided to offer only a 10-year term.[15]

Although the Airbus financing offer stated that ''The loans will fi-

---

[15] From its preliminary survey of aircraft manufacturers and importers, SRI International concluded [5]

> Another area of uncertainty on data availability concerns *side agreements or credit memoranda*. These may include such items as extra spare parts or maintenance facilities, extra training, extra performance guarantees, and direct financing incentives. Such agreements were included in one of our Phase I cases, and data were provided. However, manufacturers advise us that these are considered more confidential than other offer features and may not be made available to SRI by carriers, even though confidentiality is assured. To the extent that side agreements substantially alter the value of the product received or price paid, such information is essential in making a comparative cost analysis of competing offers. There is a problem here also in that such side agreements may not become final until negotiations are completed with the selected manufacturer [p. 16].

nance eighty five (85) percent maximum of the delivery price of each
firmly ordered aircraft [6, p. 299]," Moore stated "Normally, they support 85 percent of the plane without the engines and leave either Rolls or
the American companies to finance the engine itself [6, p. 103]." The
Bank apparently did not believe it important to determine if the financing
covered the engines or not, although the engines constitute about 20% of
the delivered price of the Airbus. Because Eximbank policy is to finance
only the U.S. content of exports, the Bank covered 85% of the 91% U.S.
content of the 767s. If the Airbus financing covered 85% of the 80%
European content and the engine manufacturer financed the rest at market rates, the U.S. financing package had a definite advantage over the
Airbus package. If the engine manufacturers, however, had offered concessionary financing, the Airbus financing may have provided approximately the same cover as provided by the Eximbank.

C. The Financing of the 727s and 737s

The initial proposal to finance the 727s and 737s with 85% cover at an
8% interest rate drew considerable attention. de St. Phalle stated [6]

> it seems to me that this is the typical case where we should have some sort of a
> package deal where you can get a better rate if you buy the 67s which is a really
> competitive item in terms of what you would get in financing on the 727s and
> 737s. But it seems to me extraordinary that we would finance all of the 737s and
> all of the 727s at an 8% rate [p. 215].

Mr. Moore agreed in stating that "anything we do on the 737's and 727's
has to be tied to buying the 767's [6, p. 240]." The question of the interest
rate and the cover remained, however.

The Bank decided to sweeten the 767 offer by offering a higher cover
on the 727s and 737s if Ansett also purchased the 767s instead of the A-
300s. The Bank issued two preliminary commitments to Ansett, the terms
of which are presented in Table 10.2.

The interest rates for the 727s and 737s were the same in the two
preliminary commitments, and thus the sweetener was provided by the
higher Eximbank cover. In addition to the cover provided by the Bank,
financing was also to be provided by PEFCO, and since PEFCO's lending
rate at the time of the Ansett application was 14%, the substitution of
Eximbank cover for PEFCO cover resulted in a considerble benefit to
Ansett.

Whether a sweetener was needed and whether it was an all or nothing
deal depended in part, of course, on whether Ansett was predisposed
toward Boeing or Airbus. In addition to Murdoch's statement quoted in

TABLE 10.2

Preliminary Commitments Offered to Ansett

	Eximbank financing		PEFCO financing cover (%)
	Interest rate (%)	Cover (%)	
P.C. 80-0-4738			
767	8	85	0
727	8.375	50	35
737	8.4	30	20
P.C. 80-0-4745			
727	8.375	42.5	42.5
737	8.4	30	30

Section II, there was other evidence that at least some individuals at Ansett preferred to go with Boeing. Heidrich of the Eximbank, in referring to his February 15 meeting in Melbourne with Cooper and Franklin of Ansett, stated [6]

> I got the impression that they wanted an opportunity to buy the Boeing airplanes. This was Cooper and Franklin conveying this to me and they felt that it was for the first time an opportunity to sort of break away from this parallel policy they had had. They also thought that they would have an opportunity to maybe fly more frequencies because the capacity of the Airbus would be higher, therefore they could schedule a flight and later schedule a second flight [p. 222].

Moore in the Hearings, however, stated "the marketing people at Ansett were said to favor purchase of the Airbus, whereas the engineers preferred the Boeing 767 [6, p. 14]."[16]

---

[16] There were other indications that Ansett preferred Boeing. A February 15 cable from the U.S. consulate in Melbourne, which for some unexplained reason did not arrive until March 7, reported [6]

> "On confidential basis, (Ralph Cooper) revealed Ansett's plan for transition to Boeing 767's during period that TAA will have European Airbuses." Ansett will have greater frequencies by introducing 727s and 737s.

> Rupert Murdoch "had taken the matter (purchase of Boeings) into his own hands by going into Eximbank and making presentation" according to Ansett's Bill Franklin.

> "While Ansett Execs are not likely to tip us off when they reach the watershed of going all the way with Boeing, we have the feeling that they are at that point. Our Consular section has had visa applications from 3 Ansett personnel during the last half of February for trips to Boeing "to evaluate the use of Boeing 737 aircraft within Australia" and for 'new aircraft program [pp. 353–354].' "

In considering its financing offer, the Bank looked beyond the transaction under consideration and attempted to assess the impact that this transaction would have on the U.S. position in the Australian market. Houston of the Bank, in discussing whether the Bank should finance 85% of the 767s or provide a lower cover, stated [6]

> One of those airlines [Ansett and TAA] is in the market for U.S. aircraft and I would strongly suppose that TAA will not in the future buy any more U.S. aircraft. So, what we are looking at is the question of trying to retain half of the Australian domestic market. One which I would believe in the future will be a rapidly growing market, and I don't want to sound cavalier about a 100 million dollars even though we deal in large numbers here, are we not sort of losing sight of what to me is the very central issue here. Are we going to try to hold on to the half of the market that now remains available to you, and is there undue risk in trying at this time to economize on the $100 million that we have identified here as the saving by applying the strict policy rather than going to 85% [p. 231].

This view was apparently shared by the board, as Moore stated, "Yes, after all that, I think that's right [6, p. 231]."

Treasury was critical of sweetening the offer, as Lange stated [6]

> First, the Bank is proposing a package deal of three different types of aircraft, when only one—the B-767—is truly competitive with the Airbus in this situation. The Bank is offering the two types of aircraft at soft terms to sweeten the pot. This approach fritters away Bank resources [p. 203].

Although it is certainly the case that the sweetener provided on the financing of the 727s and 737s could equivalently have been provided by lowering the interest rate on the 767 credit, it is the concessionary financing, and not how it is provided, that is the appropriate test for the efficiency of the use of Bank resources. Furthermore, the financing for the 727s and 737s in the second preliminary commitment was not extraordinary in that the cover provided was consistent with Bank policy for financing short-range aircraft (737 and DC-9). "Normally, Eximbank policy would be to provide 30% direct credit support for planes in this category [3, p. 1]." While the Bank's aircraft financing policy did not specify interest rates at the time of the Ansett case, the interest rates of 8.375 and 8.4% were commensurate with the average interest rate of 8.384% on aircraft credits in fiscal year 1979 and above the median of the Bank lending rate range of 7.75 to 8.75%.

Another means of assessing whether or not the 727 and 737 financing contained in the second preliminary commitment (P.C. 80-0-4745) was consistent with Bank policy is to examine the other direct credits authorized for the same aircraft. No data on preliminary commitments are readily available, so Table 10.3 presents the direct credits authorized between February 1980 and September 1980. Since preliminary commit-

TABLE 10.3

Approved Loans for 737 and 727 Aircraft: February–September 1980

Date	Country	Aircraft	Cover (%)	PEFCO cover (%)	Interest rate (%)
2-21	India	737-200	42.5	—	8.375–8.5
2-28	Yugoslavia	727-200	45.0	—	8.5
3-20	Bahamas	737-200	30.0	—	8.375
5-1	Greece	737-200	42.5	—	8.5
5-8	Canada	737-200	42.5	—	8.5
5-22	Tunisia	737-200	42.5	—	9.25
5-27	Denmark	727-200	30.0	—	9.25
6-24	Guinea	737-200	30.0	12.6	9.25
9-17	Ecuador	727-200	—	42.5	—
9-23[a]	Canada	737	[b]	[b]	8.5
9-23[a]	Yugoslavia	727-200	9.5	33.0	8.5

[a] These credits were approved under the Bank's FY1980 supplemental budget authority of $251 million. The Bank covered 15.2% of the export value and PEFCO covered 66.6% for the credits approved under this authorization.

[b] This credit financed the export of two DC-10s and six 737s with an Eximbank cover of 13.5% and a 46.5% PEFCO cover.

ments typically are not converted into approved loans for several months after insurance, these data should only be taken as suggestive of Bank practice at the time. The cover provided in P.C. 80-0-4745 was comparable to that provided in the other transactions reported in Table 10.3, while the interest rates offered to Ansett were only slightly below those granted prior to the policy revision that established the 9.25% rate in April 1980. The PEFCO participation was greater in the Ansett case, however.

D. Price Concessions as an Alternative to Concessionary Financing

An aspect of the Boeing offer that the Bank did not investigate was Boeing's ability to reduce the price of the aircraft as a means of sweetening its offer. As indicated in Moore's responses to questioning by Senator Proxmire, chairman of the Senate Committee on Banking, Housing, and Urban Affairs, the Bank did not believe that Boeing was in a position to do so [6].

> *The Chairman.* Isn't it true that Eximbank made no effort in evaluating and deciding the Ansett loan request to look at the price Boeing was charging for its

767's, 737's and 727's to determine whether Boeing could make some price or other competitive adjustment that would give Ansett incentives to buy Boeing without requiring the Bank to increase its subsidies?

Mr. Moore. I think that's substantially correct, as in all our cases, although we have our cases reviewed by the engineers to see as best they can see that the price is within a normal range.

The Chairman. But you made no effort to determine whether or not Boeing could make a concession?

Mr. Moore. We did not in this case; that is correct.

The Chairman. Why not?

Mr. Moore. It just had not been done. Since March 7, Senator, we have begun that kind of program and Boeing has participated in at least one package since that time.

The Chairman. Now in this deal Boeing was in a position to hike its price by $2 to $5 million because of the low-interest loan offered by the Bank. Did you look at Boeing's books to see whether the 727's, 737's, or 767's could have been shaved to make the sale?

Mr. Moore. No.

The Chairman. Your answer is, no, you did not?

Mr. Moore. No. I don't believe they are in a position to raise their price, Senator, because I think they already had quoted it at the time we were considering the case [pp. 61–62].

Although Boeing had made a firm offer to Ansett, Moore's answer was not fully responsive to the issues raised by Senator Proxmire since Boeing could have based its quoted price on the anticipation of receiving Eximbank financing.

Although the Bank had not investigated Boeing's willingness to reduce its price, Boeing may not have had complete flexibility in its pricing of Eximbank-financed exports because of the Bank's monitoring of its prices in other cases and its desire to maintain the Bank's confidence. As Stingel stated in response to questioning by Senator Heinz [6]:

And I think in aircraft we have a pretty good file on what a 727, a 737, a 767, and so on, really should cost with basic equipment. If it's delivered this year or delivered next year or delivered the year after and so on, we have to take that into account. I don't think we've had the wool pulled over our eyes on that, and that we have been used, in effect, as a shill for getting a better price for Boeing, McDonnell–Douglas, or Lockheed [p. 111].

Kahliff added [6],

Senator Heinz, may I tell you something interesting? I heard Senator Proxmire one time question Mr. DuBrul—before this Board came on board—about how carefully we studied the invoices of the aircraft to know that. So I took it upon myself—and I'm sure Mr. Stingel did a much better job—to look into this. I went down to the engineering department after every sale and said, 'when do we get the bill of sale and what is the difference? If there's a $2 million difference, what is it? I'd like to see what it is.' I did that for a long time. They finally convinced me that if they weren't satisfied with it, that they would come and tell me. I really hounded them. I didn't know what I was talking about, except that I knew a bill of sale when I saw it and I knew that I could compare prices. And I never found a case where I felt that it had been padded. Because you can compare what they're selling one plane for, one set of spares and one set of engines, and we did that [p. 111].

It is, of course, possible that Boeing consistently prices higher than it otherwise would in the absence of Eximbank financing and, if so, an examination of preliminary commitment applications received by the Bank would not detect overpricing. It appears at the least that the pricing in the Ansett case was not sufficiently out of the ordinary to call attention to it.

V. Analysis of the Subsidy Provided by the Eximbank Financing

The strategy of the Bank thus was to match the Airbus offer with (1) equivalent 767 capacity, (2) an interest rate on the 767s that was approximately equal to the weighted average of the nominal interest rates in the Airbus financing package, (3) the same term and cover for the 767s as offered by Airbus, and (4) a sweetener provided by a greater cover on the 727s and 737s than would otherwise have been provided if Ansett had not purchased the 767s. The relevant measures of the generosity of the Eximbank financing are the subsidy provided by the concessionary financing and the effective price paid by the purchaser. The subsidy and the effective price paid by Ansett are measured as defined in Chapter 6. The subsidy defined in this manner measures the cost to the United States, or equivalently the benefit received by Ansett relative to borrowing in the private capital market, given the price charged by Boeing.

To determine the subsidy, the interest rate at which Ansett could have borrowed in private capital markets is required. While there is some uncertainty about that interest rate, Moore apparently believed that it would be high. In the hearings he stated [6]

I do point out that our coverage on the 727's was 50 percent and on the 737s was 40 percent, plus 20 percent guarantee support at private market rates of interest. The total cost to Ansett Airlines was 9.3 percent, if you compute the private bank financing at 17 percent and it's hard to know how people do compute that when rates were at about 20 percent at that time [p. 22].

The Bank's analysis of the interest rate on the private capital portion of the 727 and 737 financing provides another estimate of the market rate of interest for Ansett. The preliminary commitment memorandum to the

Board of Directors (2nd revision, P.C. No. 80-0-4738 [6, p. 285]) states
that the estimated rate on a private loan would be the 6-month Libor rate,
which was 17.5% at the time, plus 0.5%, for a cost of 18%.[17]

Eximbank's assessment of Ansett's financial condition indicated that
in all likelihood Ansett was not in a position to obtain private credits at
highly favorable private market rates without a guarantee by the Australian government.[18] The preliminary commitment memorandum stated
[6][19]

> Ansett appears undercapitalized and somewhat illiquid, however, its highly
> leveraged financial structure and rather tight working capital position have not
> affected the airline's continued capability of meeting its obligations to Eximbank
> under existing credits. Operations are profitable.

> The financial condition of Ansett, strengthened by the guarantee of the
> Government of Australia, provides a reasonable assurance of repayment [p.
> 290].

The market interest rate at which Ansett could have borrowed will thus be
taken to be 18%, but a lower rate of 14% will also be used in the analysis.[20]

The concessionary financing provided by the Bank resulted both because the credit extended by the Bank carried an interest rate below the
market rate and because the financing of the 727s and 737s anticipated a
PEFCO loan.[21] The preliminary commitment memorandum to the Eximbank board estimated the PEFCO interest rate at 14%. The difference
between the PEFCO interest rate and the market interest rate also provides a subsidy to Ansett and imposes a cost on the United States.

The estimates of the subsidy and the effective price paid by Ansett
are presented in Table 10.4, and Appendix 10.B details the method used
to determine the subsidy on the 727 and 737 mixed financing. With a
private market interest rate of 18%, the estimated total subsidy received
by Ansett for the five 767s is $62.7 million, and the subsidy on the financ-
ing of the four 727s and the nine 737s is $40.2 million, for a total of

---

[17] The average spread on Australian borrowing during the first half of 1979 was 0.612%,
as reported in *Euromoney*, October 1979, p. 130.

[18] The government of Australia also provided a guarantee for the Airbus financing.

[19] Ansett, however, could have been backed by the substantial resources of Murdoch
and Abeles.

[20] Ansett probably could not have obtained an interest rate lower than 18% on a commercial bank loan in February 1980 even with an Eximbank financial guarantee since the
minimum fee on the guarantee is 0.5%. Consequently, even if the guarantee eliminated the
spread of 0.5%, the rate would not be reduced below 18%.

[21] Although PEFCO financing for the 727s and 737s was anticipated by the Bank, no
PEFCO credits were actually made to Ansett. The analysis of the subsidy will be based on
the financing the Bank anticipated.

TABLE 10.4

Analysis of Eximbank's Financial Offer to Ansett Private Market Interest Rate of 18%[a]

Aircraft	Export value ($ million)[b]	Eximbank loan ($ million)	Eximbank interest rate (%)	Subsidy on Eximbank loan ($ million)	PEFCO loan ($ million)	Subsidy on PEFCO loan ($ million)	Effective price paid (%)
P.C. 80-0-4738							
767	236.021	200.628	8.0	62.667	—	—	73.5
727	69.100	34.550	8.375	13.209	24.185	1.849	78.2
737	137.220	54.588	8.4	21.840	27.444	3.324	81.7
	442.341	289.756		97.716	51.629	5.173	76.7
P.C. 80-0-4745							
727	69.100	29.3675	8.375	11.600	29.3675	2.518	79.6
737	137.220	41.166	8.4	16.974	41.166	5.352	83.7
	206.320	70.5335		28.574	70.5335	7.870	82.4

[a] Source: [6, p. 254].
[b] U.S. content only. Foreign content is estimated at 7.13% by the Eximbank.

TABLE 10.5

**Subsidy on Eximbank Financing Assuming a Market
Interest Rate of 14%**

Aircraft	Subsidy on Eximbank loan ($ million)	Effective price paid (%)
P.C. 80-0-4738		
767	41.648	82.4
727	8.689	87.4
737	14.430	89.5
	64.767	85.4
P.C. 80-0-4745		
727	7.667	88.9
737	11.283	91.8
	18.950	90.8

approximately $102.9 million. The effective price paid by Ansett is thus 76.7% of the export value. If the private market interest rate were 14%, the total subsidy would be $64.8 million, and the effective price paid would be 85.4%, as indicated in Table 10.5. Relative to the cost of financing the same aircraft in the private capital market, Ansett received a very substantial reduction in cost relative to either an 18% or 14% interest rate.[22,23]

Part of the Eximbank strategy to induce Ansett to choose the 767s instead of the A300s was to offer more generous financing on the 727s and 737s if Ansett purchased the 767s than it would have offered on those aircraft if Ansett were to choose the A300s. Assuming that PEFCO would participate in both financing packages at the same interest rates, the estimated subsidy is $36.4 million. Consequently, the Bank sweetened the 767 financing offer by $3.8 million, given an 18% interest rate, and by $4.2 million, given a 14% rate.

At the request of the senate committee on Banking, Housing, and Urban Affairs, the Congressional Research Service (CRS) estimated that

[22] The loan officer, Peacock, considered Libor rates of 14 and 17% in his analysis [6, p. 244]. It seems quite unlikely, however, that Ansett could have borrowed at 14% if the PEFCO interest rate, which is based on the long-term U.S. government borrowing rate, was also at 14%. The market rate of interest was at historically high levels at the end of February. The 6-month Libor rate dropped to 9.5% by July 1980, but then rose to 21.4% in mid-December 1980.

[23] The credit authorized for the 767s was $199.8 million rather than the $200.6 million stated in the preliminary commitment. The Bank also authorized a $4.9 million, 9.25% credit to Ansett for 737 and 767 flight simulators. The subsidy on that credit, using an 18% market rate, is $1.158 million.

TABLE 10.6

Blended Interest Rates on Eximbank Financing

	Private market interest rate (%)	
Preliminary commitment	18	14
P.C. 80-0-4738	8.82	8.78
P.C. 80-0-4745	11.03	10.72

the value of the sweetener, using a discount rate of 13%, was $3.3 million [6, pp. 54–5]. While the method used by the CRS to determine this value is not entirely clear, its estimate is not inconsistent with the estimates developed here.

As indicated in Section II, both Moore and the Treasury had argued that an interest rate of 9.25% on the 767 financing was equivalent to the Airbus financing offer. If the Bank had loaned at 9.25% instead of at 8.0%, the subsidy provided would have been $54.8 million, given a market interest rate of 18%, and $33.0 million with a 14% rate. Relative to a 9.25% rate, the 8% interest rate on the 767s thus provided a concession of $7.8 million, using an 18% market rate, and $8.7 million at 14%. Including the value of the sweetener on the 727s and 737s, the total concession relative to matching the 9.25% rate on the 767s and financing the 727s and 737s at standard rates was approximately $11.6 million, at a market rate of 18%, and $12.8 million at 14%. If the Bank had accepted the Ansett–Boeing proposal to finance the 25 aircraft at 85%, the credit of $657 million would have provided subsidies of $205 million and $136 million at 18 and 14% market rates, respectively.

The blended interest rate on the Eximbank financing package is defined as the interest rate on a loan of the same term that would provide the same present value of interest and principal payments as for the actual financing package. Blended interest rates computed using 14 and 18% private market interest rates are presented in Table 10.6 for the two preliminary commitments. For the financing of the 767s, 727s, and 737s in P.C. 80-0-4738, the blended interest rate is approximately 8.8% with either market interest rate, which was somewhat below the 9.25% on the dollar portion of the Airbus loan. The blended interest rate on P.C. 80-0-4745 for the 727s and 737s is between 10.7 and 11%, so both PCs provided very attractive interest rates to Ansett.

The estimated subsidy of $102.9 million represents the real cost to the United States, as discussed in Chapter 6, but often the direct burden of

U.S. taxpayers is used as a measure of that cost. The cost to U.S. taxpayers of the Ansett credit can be obtained by using the cost of Eximbank borrowing from the Federal Financing Bank. On March 3, 1980 the Eximbank borrowed $124 million with a 10-year term at 12.694%, and $713.6 million with a 5-year, 2-month term at 13.233%, so the FFB rate will be taken to be 13%.[24] Assuming that the 14% rate on the PEFCO loan covers its cost of borrowing plus PEFCO's administrative costs, the cost to U.S. taxpayers resulted only from the Eximbank credit. Using the 13% rate of interest, the estimate of the cost to U.S. taxpayers is $55.3 million.[25] If, however, the real cost of Treasury borrowing is given by the opportunities forgone in the private market as a result of government-supported export financing, the relevant interest rate is the market rate of interest. The cost to the United States under this assumption is then the previously reported $102.9 million.

The welfare consequences for the United States from the Ansett financing depend on whether the export was additional or not. If Ansett would have purchased the aircraft at Boeing's quoted price in the absence of Eximbank financing, then Ansett captured all of the subsidy, and the cost to the United States would be in the range from $55.3 million to $102.9 million. If Boeing captured a share of the subsidy through a higher price, the U.S. retained some portion of the subsidy. Given the generous financing offer from Airbus, it seems likely that some Eximbank concessionary financing on the 767s was necessary to secure the sale, but the extent of the concession required remains unknown.[26]

VI. Analysis of the Bank's Decision Making in the Ansett Case

According to its legislative mandate, the Bank's decision making is to be guided by the objective of responding to capital market deficiencies

[24] Although 13% was a peak borrowing rate for the Eximbank in 1980, the rate should have been the best *ex ante* estimate at the date of the Ansett loan commitment of the long-term interest rate. In referring to the Eximbank's cost of funds, Mr. Moore stated "we also consider the marginal cost of borrowing which is 13 percent based on our experience during this quarter [6, p. 53]." In referring to the time at which the Ansett transaction was made, Moore stated "We had a prediction that it would be slightly higher. We thought it would be about 13.25 percent [6, p. 53]."

[25] If the Ansett–Boeing proposal to provide a credit of $657 million for the 25 aircraft at 8% interest rate had been accepted, the estimate cost to U.S. taxpayers would be $104 million.

[26] The export to Ansett was not included in the Bank's 1980 additionality study because the authorization was not approved until FY1981.

and to concessionary export financing offered by foreign countries. The additionality standard implies that the Bank is to do no more than respond to concessionary foreign export financing and is not to compensate for product quality, reliability, delivery, or price advantages that foreign suppliers have over U.S. suppliers.

In the Ansett case, no significant capital market deficiencies were present. The Australian economy had been strong, and the domestic capital market should have been able to provide the needed financing at market rates. The spread on Australian international borrowing was quite small, reflecting low country and commercial risks, so Ansett should have had access to the international capital markets. In addition, the government of Australia stood ready to provide a guarantee for Ansett's borrowing if it purchased either Airbus or Boeing aircraft. The analysis performed by the Eximbank, therefore, was appropriately focused on the concessionary export financing offered in support of the Airbus.

With respect to the product dimension, the 767 and A-300 aircraft are technically similar and have comparable capabilities, although the passenger capacity of the Airbus is greater. The advantage of the Airbus is that it was already flying in February 1980 and was available for delivery 18 months before the 767, which would not be in service until 1982. Although Ansett was predisposed toward Boeing, according to Murdoch, Airbus must be considered to have had an advantage, at least with respect to the delivery date. It is possible that Murdoch's predisposition towards Boeing was less a result of the potential advantages of the Boeing aircraft than it was a means of breaking out of the parallel policy that Ansett had followed with TAA. However, it seems appropriate to conclude that there was some advantage to Airbus along the product dimension as a result of the earlier delivery date.

As in most borrower–banking relationships, the borrower initiates the financing negotiations. In this case, however, Ansett and Boeing went further and took the initiative in structuring the competitive response to the Airbus offer, both with respect to the requested financing and with respect to the coupling of the 727 and 737 aircraft with the 767s. Ansett and Boeing also had the opportunity to state their position regarding the choice between the two suppliers, and whereas these positions were viewed as strategic by the Bank, the Bank was apparently persuaded by the arguments that the 727s and 737 were an essential part of the competitive response to the Airbus offer.

The information available to the Bank about the Airbus financing offer was quite complete because a copy of the offer was available to the Bank. Furthermore, Ansett had already succeeded in persuading Airbus to lower the interest rates on the financing it offered to the levels granted to TAA, and it would have been highly unlikely that Airbus would have

provided further concessions in its financing offer. Some confusion remained, however, about the possibility of an all dollar offer, but that did
not play an essential role in the Bank's deliberations. The only uncertainty about the product offer pertained to how likely additional sales
were, but it seems clear that at some point in the future Ansett would be in
the market for additional aircraft if it decided to purchase the four A-300s.
In assessing the product offer made by Boeing to Ansett, the Bank had
information on previous Boeing sales that could have been used as a basis
for comparison to the price quoted to Ansett, but it would still have been
difficult for the Bank to make precise judgments about the appropriateness of the quoted prices.

The opportunities for strategic behavior on the part of Ansett and
Boeing arose because Ansett, in particular, and Boeing, in part, had information that was not available to the Bank. The most important information pertained to Ansett's evaluation of the alternative of continuing a
parallel policy with TAA versus breaking with that policy. Ansett had
undertaken serious negotiations with Boeing on an admittedly hurried
basis, and the Bank might have inferred that Ansett was interested in, and
perhaps committed to, breaking from its parallel policy with TAA. Perhaps the greatest source of uncertainty about Ansett's likely choice centered on how appropriate the aircraft were for Ansett's particular routes.
What the Bank did know was that Ansett had head-to-head competition
with TAA and that TAA had purchased the Airbus. It was therefore
reasonable to assume that Ansett had a need for new aircraft of quite
similar capabilities and performance characteristics to those that TAA
had purchased. Furthermore, it seems clear that in its competitive battle
with TAA Ansett wanted to have new aircraft available at the time at
which TAA would take delivery of their A-300s. Whether the Boeing
aircraft had an advantage on Ansett's routes was not clear, and the Bank
was unlikely to be able to assess this accurately, particularly given the
time constraint under which it was operating. Certainly, there is no record
of a discussion about the relative suitability of aircraft types for Ansett's
routes other than that conveyed to the Bank by Ansett and Boeing.

In terms of its strategy, Ansett had every incentive to obtain the most
generous financing package possible. Ansett in all likelihood foresaw little
risk in its future relationships with the Bank if it were to request as much
support as possible in this case. First, there was little risk that any analysis would reveal that Ansett was attempting to take inappropriate advantage of the Bank's financing, particularly because Ansett had already been
offered highly concessionary financing by Airbus. Second, Ansett could
be confident that the Bank's door would be open to it in the future,
particularly if Ansett anticipated that the Bank was likely to offer a letter

of interest for any aircraft for which it did not provide immediate financing. Third, given the large number of aircraft involved in the Boeing offer, Ansett may not have needed for many years any additional aircraft beyond those covered in this transaction.

The availability of concessionary export financing creates a strong incentive for an export to support the claims of an importer about the need for matching financing. The exporter's incentive results at a minimum from the gain in profit resulting from greater export volume and at a maximum from the additional profit resulting from an increase in the export price that allows the exporter to capture a share of the subsidy provided by the concessionary financing. While the exporter has an incentive to learn as much as possible about competing product and financing offers in order to determine more accurately the price to quote, the exporter has no natural incentive to convey that information to the Bank. If it were requested to convey such information to the Bank, the exporter might have an incentive to misrepresent the information, although that incentive would be moderated by a need to maintain a long-term relationship with the Bank. Boeing could always claim to be no better informed than was the Bank regarding Ansett's likely decision, although, of course, Boeing had been negotiating with Ansett and would be expected to have been better informed than was the Bank.

In assessing the Bank's decision making, three elements appear to have been important. The first was the chairman's view of the transaction as a result of his discussions with Ansett and Boeing representatives; the second was the staff's analysis of the transaction; and the third was the discussion that took place during the board meetings. The chairman was clearly not willing to lose the export, although he was concerned about the extent to which the Bank would have to go to secure it. Moore argued that the 9.25% interest rate was appropriate for the Ansett transaction, but there is no indication that he considered a reduction in the amount of cover to compensate for the increased cost of an 8% rate. During his meeting with Murdoch and Boeing, Moore apparently decided to take Murdoch at his word, or at least not to risk the possibility that by challenging his word the sale would be lost.

In terms of the analysis conducted by the Bank, no formal consideration was given to the real interest rates implied by the Airbus financing offer, although it was recognized that real rates might be relevant. The staff did provide some analysis of the blended interest rate on the financing of the 727s and the 737s, but that was not given much weight in the board's deliberations. The Bank made no analysis of the likely willingness of Boeing to lower its price as a means of securing the sale, nor did it broach this subject with Boeing. There is no indication in the record that the Bank made any analysis of the cost of this financing to the United States or of the benefit to result from this transaction. The Bank, however, undoubtedly had a general understanding of the extent of the cost as well as beliefs about the likely benefits.

During the board meeting, Kahliff and de Saint Phalle questioned the generosity of the proposed credit, focusing on the cover for the 727s and 737s. All of the board members present apparently believed that a sweetener provided through the financing of the 727s and 737s was appropriate to compensate for the earlier availability of the Airbus. The board seemed to have formed no opinion about the likelihood that Ansett would purchase the 727s and 737s as replacements for its DC-9 aircraft in the event that it chose the Airbus. The board thus decided to offer financing consistent with the Bank's standard policy. The Board also apparently did not question the deadline that Airbus had given to Ansett.

In summary, the Bank's consideration of the Ansett transaction was hurried and did not sufficiently address the cost of the subsidy or the likely decision by Ansett. The Bank recognized that it had incomplete information about the transaction and was faced with the very real possibility that the information available to it resulted from strategic behavior on the part of Boeing and Ansett. The Bank basically decided to rely on the word of the borrower. In all likelihood the Bank could have secured the export with less generous financing than that actually provided, although the extent of the possible savings is unknown.

The change in the Bank's aircraft policy shortly after the approval of the preliminary commitment to Ansett suggests that the Bank may have had second thoughts about the generosity of the financing provided to Ansett. As previously indicated, the Bank adopted an aircraft lending rate of 9.25% with a maximum cover of 65% instead of the 85% provided on the 767s. The Bank also instituted a policy of testing the pricing of U.S. exporters by agreeing to provide 75% cover if the exporter would provide 10% cover at the same interest rate as that offered by the Bank. Whether these policy changes were in part due to the criticism of the Ansett decision is unclear, but at a minimum they suggest that the Bank may have been concerned with the adequacy of its decision making in this case.

VII. Implications for the Bank's Decision-Making Process

The context in which the Bank makes its decisions is quite different from that found, for example, in independent government agencies such as public regulatory commissions, and that context enhances the opportunities for strategic behavior on the part of those who seek Bank support. Public regulation has an adversarial character that provides natural checks on the ability of a participant to take advantage of informational advantages. For example, in public utility or transportation regulation, interveners have an incentive to obtain information and to evaluate the information provided by an applicant seeking a rate revision. Furthermore, the regulatory commission usually has an obligation to represent the interests of the public, or more specifically of consumers, and hence, the commission staff has an incentive both to develop its own information and to evaluate the information presented to it by the applicant and by the interveners. In addition to the incentives to reduce informational advantages, the conflicting interests of applicants and interveners tend to result in decisions that represent compromises between the competing interests.

The decision-making process within the Eximbank is quite different. Instead of having opposing interests, the U.S. exporters and foreign importers who appear before the Bank have similar interests in obtaining generous financing from the Bank. Furthermore, the Bank is charged with supporting U.S. exporters and hence sees its interests as parallel to, but certainly not identical to, those of U.S. exporters. There is thus no natural adversarial relationship that limits the opportunities for strategic behavior on the part of applicants or provides participants with an incentive to obtain and evaluate information relevant to the case in question. In particular, the foreign importer has no incentive to provide information on either its other financing offers, the quoted prices, or its preferences regarding alternative products. Although the arrangement both restricts the terms of financing offers and provides for the exchange of information, it cannot be viewed as an effective restriction on the opportunities for strategic behavior.

Another important difference between the decision-making process of the Eximbank and a regulatory commission is that the Bank does not make its decisions in public. Hence, parties opposed to the Bank's support for an export have little opportunity to intervene in the process. The Treasury, OMB, the State Department, and the Federal Reserve do send representatives to the Bank's board meetings and oversight is provided by the Congress and the National Advisory Council on International Monetary and Financial Policies (NAC), but there is a natural reluctance to question the Bank's judgment on a case-by-case basis. Furthermore, it is difficult for interested parties to evaluate the Bank's decisions on an *ex post* basis because of the lack of information about the specifics of individual cases, particularly when proprietary information is involved. The principal disciplining force in the Bank's decision-making process, in addition to oversight activities, is the Bank's own desire to use its financing authorization as effectively as possible. The Bank's decision-making process thus is based largely on information provided by U.S. exporters and foreign importers and involves the application of its judgment regarding the need for financing.

The application by the Bank of its discretion and judgment in individual cases is likely to result in errors in favor of greater concessions than necessary for at least three reasons. First, U.S. policy has been to promote exports, and in support of this policy the Bank can be expected to attempt to support as many exports as possible, given its resources. Second, the minimum concession necessary to secure an export is difficult to determine, and taxpayers who bear the direct burden of the Bank's concessionary financing are only represented through congressional oversight and executive branch policy-making. Third, lost exports are visible, and those who would have benefited from them are vocal. Furthermore, the Congress and the executive branch in recent years, until the Reagan administration's budget reductions, have supported expansion of the Bank's programs, and hence the Bank could be expected to err on the side of avoiding lost exports. Furthermore, by issuing preliminary commitments at a rate that exceeded the Bank's authorization, the Bank was able to demonstrate the need for a greater authorization. In such a situation, the Bank can be expected to have difficulty resisting compensating for product advantages that a foreign supplier may have relative to a U.S. supplier. In the Ansett case it seems clear that the Bank, through the sweetener on the financing of the 727s and 737s, was compensating for the earlier availability of the A-300. Since importers make their decisions in such cases on the basis of both product characteristics and overall cost, the Bank can be expected to have considerable difficulty in determining the tradeoffs between these two factors. In such cases, the desire to err on the side of greater generosity seems natural.

In a case-by-case decision process in which information is incomplete, decisions cannot be easily evaluated after the fact, and an adversarial relationship is not present, the opportunities for strategic behavior necessitate responses by the governmental entity. One response is to invest in expertise by building a staff to obtain and evaluate information. To the extent that the Bank is able to become better informed about the specifics of a case, it is better able to detect and hence deter strategic behavior on the part of the exporter and/or the importer. Furthermore, the Bank is then better able to apply its decision-making standards in individual cases. The Bank has, for example, established an engineering division to assess the feasibility of projects, and an economics division to provide information relevant to its reasonable assurance of repayment standard. This expertise may have had little effect on the strategic behavior of exporters and importers, however.

If an agency decides to develop expertise and to apply its judgment in individual cases, the agency is forced to defend the application of its judgment in those cases. In contrast to public regulatory decisions that can be appealed in the judicial system, agency decisions such as those of the Eximbank are only subject to scrutiny by the Congress and by those executive branch agencies, such as Treasury and OMB, that have responsibility for the Bank's activities. To the extent that the Bank's decisions are not based on firm ground, however, the Bank faces the risk of generating political opposition to its activities. With the present concern over the federal budget, the direct cost of the Bank's programs to U.S. taxpayers will continue to draw attention, and if the Bank is not able to defend its use of the resources entrusted to it, increased criticism will result.

An alternative to a case-by-case decision-making process is the use of uniform, categorical policies that require less judgment in their application. For example, the Bank could establish policies that, while differing across export categories, would treat each case within a category in an identical manner. The Bank's judgment then applies to determining the eligibility of the export for a category rather than determining the financing that will be extended. This alternative may result in some inefficiency in the use of resources, since each case would receive the average financing for the category rather than the minimum required to gain that export or to match the foreign credit offer, but it may have economic and political advantages to the Bank. Economic gains may be achievable if, for example, the adoption of categorical policies reduces the opportunities for strategic behavior on the part of U.S. exporters and foreign importers. Political gains also may accrue to the Bank to the extent that the defense of its actions is shifted to a defense of its categorical policies rather than its judgment in individual cases. In the face of criticism of its judgment, an agency might be expected to shift to a categorical policy that would lessen the chance of similar criticism in the future.

At the time of the Ansett case, the Bank's aircraft lending policy was characterized by the application of judgment within fairly broad guidelines. For example, the interest rate range for direct credits was $7\frac{3}{4}$ to $8\frac{3}{4}\%$ and the cover was limited by an 85% maximum cover, and minimums of 42.5% for 767s and 727s, and 30% for 737s. Perhaps as a consequence of the criticism of the generosity of the Ansett credit, the Bank shortly thereafter adopted a categorical policy for aircraft financing under which the same interest rate was used for all aircraft credits and the old and new generation aircraft categories received standard covers of 30 and 65%, respectively. With the adoption of this policy, the Bank was no longer in the position of having to apply its judgment in individual cases. Whether this change in policy reduced political challenges to the Bank is unclear, but at the least it shifted the focus of any potential challenge to its policies rather than its judgment.

The Bank also attempted to deal with the incentives of the exporter to seek more generous financing than needed by standing ready to increase its cover for new generation aircraft to 75% if the exporter would provide 10% cover on the same terms as the Bank. This policy has the appearance of testing the exporter's willingness to reduce its export price, while delegating the decision about the level of cover to the exporter. Such a policy has political appeal, but may not produce a more efficient allocation of the Bank's resources if the exporter takes the policy into account when making its pricing decision. Even if the exporter does not increase its export price in response to this participatory pricing policy, the cost to the exporter of its 10% financing is less than the cost of the Eximbank's additional 10% cover. For example, Boeing provided a credit of $7.64 million at 9.25% to Norway for the purchase of two 767s, but that credit was given priority in repayment so that it would be repaid in the first year after delivery of the aircraft. The cost to the Bank was greater because its 10% credit would be outstanding for a longer period.

A categorical policy may also have advantages to the Bank if it reduces complaints from its constituents, and U.S. exporters and their employees that occasionally arise when exporters or foreign importers receive different credit terms. This is in part an explanation for the Bank's decision not to base its lending rates or its insurance or financial guarantee fees on the country risk associated with a credit.

Appendix 10.A. Calculation of U.S. Dollar Interest Rate Equivalent to the Airbus Financing Offer

In a system of freely fluctuating exchange rates, changes in exchange rates can be predicted by the relative domestic interest rates in the countries in question. For example, if x French francs are borrowed at time zero, they can be converted into $y = xp_{21}$ Australian dollars, where p_{21} is the exchange rate stated as dollars per franc. If the French interest rate is r_1, the amount to be repaid at time T is $xe^{r_1 T}$ using continuous compounding. To repay this loan, an arbitrageur in Australia can save y at the

Australian interest rate r_2 and at time T buy francs to repay the loan. At time T the exchange rate $p_{21}(T)$ must satisfy

$$ye^{r_2T} = p_{21}(T)xe^{r_1T}.$$

Substituting $y = xp_{21}$ and solving for $p_{21}(T)$ yields

$$p_{21}(T) = p_{21}e^{(r_2-r_1)T}.$$

Consequently, if the French interest rate r_1 is greater than the Australian interest rate, the dollar will rise against the franc.

A loan L with repayment over T years with interest charged on the unpaid balance at rate i involves a payment

$$\left(\frac{L}{T} + i\left(L - t\frac{L}{T}\right)\right) = \frac{L}{T}(1 + i(T - t))$$

in period t. The present value PV_2 in Australian dollars of the principal and interest payments of a French franc loan L with interest rate i_1 is

$$PV_2 = p_{21} \int_0^T \frac{L}{T}[1 + i_1(T - t)]e^{-(i_2+r_1-r_2)t}dt$$

$$= p_{21} \frac{L}{T(i_2 + r_1 - r_2)}\left[\left(1 - \frac{i_1}{i_2 + r_1 - r_2}\right)(1 - e^{-(i_2+r_1-r_2)T}) + i_1T\right],$$

where i_2 is the discount rate used by Australian importers and p_{21} is the exchange rate at time zero.

The U.S. dollar interest rate i_3 that is equivalent to the interest rate on the French franc loan satisfies

$$PV_2 = p_{21} \frac{L}{T(i_2 + r_3 - r_2)}\left[\left(1 - \frac{i_3}{i_2 + r_3 - r_2}\right)(1 - e^{-(i_2+r_3-r_2)}) + i_3T\right].$$

As an example, assume that $r_2 = i_2$. The data for the French franc portion of the Airbus financing package is $i_1 = .0875$ and $r_1 = .1411$, which, given a U.S. domestic interest rate $r_3 = .1155$, yields an equivalent U.S. dollar interest rate on the Eximbank loan of $i_3 = .0655$. For the deutschemark portion, $i_4 = .065$ and $r_4 = .084$, which yields $i_3 = .0947$. The weighted average interest rate i^* is thus

$$i^* = .4(.0655) + .4(.0947) + .2(.0925) = 0.082.$$

With the alternative assumption that $r_2 = .1$ and $i_2 = .15$, the equivalent U.S. dollar interest rate is $i_3 = .08205$. If $r_2 = .1$ and $i_2 = .05$, then $i_3 = .08324$.

**Appendix 10.B. Calculation of the Subsidy on
the 727 and 737 Financing**

The Eximbank financing offers for the 727 and 737 aircraft involved both PEFCO cover with a financial guarantee and private bank cover without a financial guarantee. The customary Bank approach for the payment of principal by the borrower in a blended credit is first to repay the private bank, then to repay PEFCO, and finally to repay the Eximbank.

For example, the 737 financing in P.C. 80-0-4738 was as follows [6, p. 281]:

15% Cash payment	$20,583,000
40% Exim loan @8.4%	54,888,000
20% Private loan (PEFCO) with a guarantee	27,444,000
25% Private loan without a guarantee	34,305,000

Repayments were to be made in 20 semiannual installments, so each principal payment is $116,637,000 ÷ 20 = $5,831,850. Using continuous time repayment, the principal repaid from time 0.5 years through 3.294 years would go to the private bank, payments from 3.294 years to 5.529 years to PEFCO, and payments from 5.529 years to 10.0 years to the Eximbank. Interest is paid currently on the outstanding balance, so during years 0 through 5.529 interest is paid on the $54,888,000 Eximbank loan at 8.4%. Similarly, interest is paid on the $27,444,000 PEFCO loan during years 0 to 3.294.

Since the interest rate on the private bank loan is assumed to be set at the market rate, that loan does not carry a subsidy. When the market interest rate is 18%, the subsidy on the PEFCO loan is $3.324 million and the subsidy on the Eximbank loan is $21.840 million. If the market interest rate is 14%, there is no subsidy on the PEFCO loan, and the subsidy on the Eximbank loan is $14.430 million.

In Table 10.4, comparing the subsidy of $21.840 million for the $54.888 million loan for the 737s with the $62.667 million subsidy on the $200.618 million for the 767s indicates that the subsidy rate is greater on the 737 loan even though the interest rate is higher (8.4 compared to 8.0%). This results because the principal on the 737 loan is outstanding for a longer average term and, even though it carries a higher interest rate, the delay in repayment results in a greater subsidy. This, of course, does not imply that the borrower prefers a loan involving both private and Eximbank participation but simply that having concessionary financing repaid later rather than earlier is preferred.

References

1. Davies, D. G. "Property rights and economic efficiency—the Australian airlines revisited," *Journal of Law and Economics,* **20** (April 1977), 223–226.
2. Davies, D. G. "The efficiency of public versus private firms, the case of Australia's two airlines," *Journal of Law and Economics,* **14** (April 1971), 149–165.
3. Export–Import Bank, "Commercial Jet Aircraft: The Export Market and Eximbank Activity, 1978 and 1979," unpublished paper, Washington, D.C., 1980.
4. Morgan Guarantee Bank, "World Financial Statistics," New York, 1980.
5. SRI International, "Assessment of U.S. Government Export Financing of High-Technology Products: Phase I Research Approach," Menlo Park, California, 1981.
6. U.S. Senate, Committee on Banking, Housing, and Urban Affairs, "Hearings on Ansett Loan and Export–Import Aircraft Financing Policies," Washington, D.C., 1980.
7. U.S. Senate, Committee on Banking, Housing, and Urban Affairs, "Hearing on Competitive Export Financing," Washington, D.C., 1980.

The Future Role of the Eximbank

I. Introduction

The Eximbank is presently in a transition period. In contrast to the expansionist policies of the Carter administration in which export promotion and meeting foreign officially supported export credit competition were emphasized, the Reagan administration's policies have included a reduction in the Bank's lending authorization, coupled with renewed attempts to reach international agreements to eliminate concessionary export financing. In contrast to Bank policy under chairman John Moore, the Bank under the chairmanship of William Draper has taken the lead in unilaterally increasing its lending rates and reducing the cover it provides in order both to encourage other countries to do likewise and to reduce the Bank's losses. This chapter deals with the future of the Eximbank and with U.S. objectives and strategy regarding officially supported export financing. The recommendations presented here are based on the following set of principles for government intervention in international economic affairs:

1. In the long run the fortunes of importing and exporting industries will be determined by productivity and comparative advantage.
2. Freely adjusting exchange rates will in the long-run work to equilibrate the balance of payments.

3. Government trade policy should focus on removing barriers to international trade and reducing the extent to which governments intervene in support of their exports or their import-competing industries.
4. Initiatives for exports and imports should rest with private firms and not with the government.
5. Foreign importers will choose among alternative suppliers based on nonprice considerations such as quality, reliability, and delivery, and on the real price, including financing, of the alternatives, taking into account possible changes in currency values.
6. International capital markets are basically efficient and hence there is a direct dollar-for-dollar tradeoff between the export price and any concession provided by export financing.
7. Both U.S. exporters and foreign importers have an incentive to capture a share of any subsidy provided by concessionary export financing.
8. Whereas the matching of foreign subsidized export financing may preserve the market share of U.S. exporters, matching generally results in a welfare loss to the United States because resources are transferred to foreign importers and are diverted to the supported export sectors and away from the other sectors.

The next section deals with the appropriate objectives for international trade, export promotion, and export financing and then addresses the steps the United States might take to achieve those objectives. The basic conclusion is that the Bank should not provide financing but that its insurance and guarantee programs may be appropriate responses to certain risks that a private capital market would not be expected to allocate efficiently. However, because significant private gains are generated by its programs both for the firms receiving support and for their employees, the political reality is that there are strong forces that support the financing and export promotion roles of the Bank. The political support for the Bank may be sufficient for its continuation as a financier and promoter of exports, so Section IV of this chapter addresses the administration of the Bank given its present mandate.

II. U.S. Objectives and the Eximbank

A. Export Financing Objectives

The U.S. objective for government-supported export financing should be the elimination of all subsidization with enforcement provided by an international agreement that includes sanctions in the event of violation of its terms. This recommendation is based on four considerations. First, international capital markets have functioned relatively efficiently in financing a rapid growth in international trade during the past decade. Even during the oil boycott, the Iranian revolution, and the Iran–Iraq war, the international capital markets were able to finance international trade without major disruptions. Second, permanent concessionary export financing distorts the allocation of international resources among industries in both exporting and importing countries and imposes a direct burden on the economy of the exporting country. Third, the benefits to an exporting country of concessionary export financing are illusory and accrue to foreign consumers and the owners of domestic resources whose supply is limited. Fourth, official export financing tends to result in rivalry among exporting countries that increases the distortion and subsidy burden.

The Carter administration's viewpoint on the rivalry and distortions resulting from official export financing competition is an appropriate characterization of the situation [3]:

> the pressure for countries to match the subsidies provided by other countries means that the opportunity to increase market shares through subsidies is far less than it appears to each country in isolation. This consideration is particularly important in the area of export-credit subsidization, which has increased sharply in recent years. Most of the major industrial countries have official export-credit agencies that provide medium- and long-term financing at fixed rates of interest for "big ticket" exports, such as power plants, aircraft, and manufacturing plants. These interest rates have not risen in step with rises in market rates, thus greatly increasing the subsidy element of such trade financing. Yet, because export agencies in all countries are under pressure to match or perhaps improve on the terms provided by others as to help secure the sale for a domestic producer, the likely result is a costly standoff, with global overcapacity in subsidized sectors persisting [p. 212].

Former Eximbank chairman John Moore stated his objectives regarding export financing as follows [12]

> The European community in the Treaty of Rome adopted a rule that's supposed to apply within the community that there will be no concessional interest rates on export credits between the members of the community. We would dearly love to join that arrangement and, of course, offered to do so, and I think the rest of the world would. The only problem is that there's one exception to that and that was aircraft. So to match the continuing competition in aircraft, we have had to do aircraft financing in the rich countries where, by and large, borrowing is done in the private markets and not through export credit agencies.
>
> In a perfect world, none of us would do anything other than support by guarantees or insurance that part of credits that are necessary where the private market wouldn't cover them. We hope very much to prevail upon our trading

partners around the world to extend what is already agreed to within the community to all sectors and to all rich countries in the world [p. 86].

The Reagan administration also supports the objective of eliminating export financing competition, as Deputy Secretary of the Treasury R. T. McNamar stated

> The Reagan Administration does not intend to live with U.S. or foreign export credit subsidies on a permanent basis. . . .
>
> Our international negotiations on export credit subsidies consequently have a very high priority, and we hope to see significant progress this year. Our objectives are twofold:
> —We wish to raise the International Arrangement on Export Credit's minimum interest rates, and provide a mechanism that will allow automatic changes in the future, reflecting market trends.
> —We wish to replace the present minimum rates applicable to all currencies with a system of rates which distinguishes among currencies, reflecting the wide differences in future market conditions from currency to currency [p. 8].

For the Eximbank, chairman Draper stated, "we will continue our efforts to bring official export credits closer to market rates and terms. There can be no winner in an export credit war. All nations will benefit if we can avert such a war and achieve, through negotiations, the elimination of subsidies [4, p. 2]."

B. The Weaknesses in the Present OECD Arrangement

The Carter and Reagan administrations and their Eximbank chairmen have agreed on the goal to eliminate concessionary financing, although they may have differed on the appropriate strategy for achieving an agreement to that effect. The present arrangement is inadequate for that purpose because it lacks the two necessary features identified by McNamar: minimum interest rates do not move with market forces and do not take into account the currency in which the credit is extended. The only way to satisfy these two conditions is to base minimum lending rates on market interest rates.

Unfortunately, the use of common nominal interest rates that change only upon agreement of all signatories has continued. A weakness of the 1981 aircraft financing agreement, for example, is that the interest rates are the same for all three currencies and hence the real cost of the official financing for the Airbus and U.S. aircraft differ. A second weakness of that agreement is that the interest rates do not move with market forces, so changes in market rates can result in increases or decreases in the real cost of financing over time. Lending at market rates would eliminate both of these problems.

Before any agreement based on market interest can be reached, a consensus must be achieved on which market interest rates to use. Two candidate definitions are (1) the interest rate at which the lending agency borrows (generally the government long-term borrowing rate) and (2) the market rate of interest that the importer would have to pay in the international capital markets. As indicated in Chapter 6, the second definition is the appropriate one, although a consensus on that definition is far less likely than a consensus on the first definition. Consequently, the focus here will be on the possibility of achieving an international agreement requiring the interest rates on the credits to be at least as high as the cost of funds borrowed by the government. Proposals intended to achieve this objective have been presented in the Wallen report as a basis for negotiations regarding the revision of the arrangement.

C. The Wallen Report

At the February 13–14, 1980 meeting of the arrangement participants, a report was requested on methods of limiting the extent of concessionary export financing. Under the direction of Mr. Axel Wallen of Sweden, two proposals were developed and presented to the participants in May 1980. The first proposal was a differentiated rate system that would set minimum interest rates equal to the domestic market rates in each country. The second proposal was a uniform moving matrix based on a weighted average of interest rates, with weights based on the countries' Special Drawing Rights. The uniform moving matrix would allow high-interest-rate countries to subsidize their exports by lending at the lower average interest rate, while forcing low-interest-rate countries to lend at rates above their domestic market rates. Because of this fundamental weakness only the differentiated rate system will be considered here.

In addition to establishing minimum interest rates, the Wallen report left open the possibility that maximum interest rates could be established in order to maintain lending rates when temporary market conditions raised the domestic interest rate in a country to an unusually high level. Because market interest rates in 1980 were much higher than the minimum interest rates stated in the arrangement matrix, the Wallen proposal specified progressive increases in the interest rate minimums until market levels were reached. Whereas the interest rate floors in the differentiated rate system would reflect real interest rates, the proposal would allow the minimum lending rates also to be based on the income level of the importing country, as in the present matrix.

The securities whose interest rates would constitute the minimums in the differentiated rate system were chosen to satisfy the following five criteria [13]:

1. Risk-free instruments
2. Similar maturities, i.e., medium-term (to the extent possible with a remaining maturity of 3 to 10 years)
3. Significant amounts in several issues, relatively large holding by private non-financial entities and appropriate secondary markets
4. Similar tax treatment, i.e. interest on the instrument should be normally taxable
5. Publicity and topicality of series and internationally agreed methodology underlying their compilation [p. 45].

The Wallen report indicates that yields on government bonds in secondary markets are regularly reported to the OECD Directorate for Financial and Fiscal Affairs and could serve as the basis for the interest rate minimums.

Although the differentiated rate system would not completely eliminate the subsidy in officially supported export financing because foreign borrowers would be able to borrow at a rate below the market interest rate for private borrowings, it would substantially reduce the concession and would allow lending rates to move with market forces. Since it appears unlikely that other nations would agree to extend all export financing only at the rates at which foreign importers could borrow in the international capital markets, agreement on the differentiated rate system may be a realistic objective.

A number of improvements could, however, be made in that system. First, lending to rich countries should be allowed only at private market rates. Second, a margin above the government borrowing rate should be required to cover administrative expenses and the risk associated with a credit. Third, while the arrangement has the OECD members as signatories, a number of major trading countries, such as Brazil, South Korea, and Taiwan, are not signatories, and any agreement regarding export financing should include those countries.[1] Fourth, the present arrangement does not cover the financing of aircraft, nuclear power plants, and ships, and any new agreement or revision in the arrangement should encompass all exports. Fifth, the arrangement should be incorporated into the GATT. One means of achieving these objectives would be to

---

[1] The inclusion of such countries in the arrangement has been proposed by Stephen Sohn of United Technologies [11].

revise the MTN agreement on subsidies and countervailing measures by eliminating the exemption given to financing covered by the arrangement. This would both prohibit export financing at concessionary interest rates and would include more countries than those covered by the arrangement.

Developing countries are likely to oppose any agreement to limit concessionary financing, however, because they are major recipients of the subsidies. Furthermore, developing countries would be expected to oppose interest rates that reflect the risk associated with the credit. In addition, those developing countries that are building capital goods industries are likely to resist including the OECD arrangement in GATT because it would limit their ability to break into established markets. For example, in order to sell a computer-controlled rolling mill in the United States, Brazil recently provided concessionary financing that would violate the terms of the arrangement. Of the $67 million export value, Banco de Brazil provided a $45 million, 12-year loan with an interest rate of 8% (*Wall Street Journal,* October 6, 1981). In order to obtain the agreement of countries such as Brazil, it may be necessary to include a provision that would allow developing countries to lend with fewer restrictions than imposed on the industrialized countries. A precedent for such a provision is the present arrangement matrix that allows more generous financing for exports to lower income countries than to higher income countries.

If an agreement on the differentiated rate system were to be achieved, the United States should go further by ceasing to make any government loans to foreign importers or to U.S. exporters and by ceasing to discount commercial bank loans. In addition, the United States should attempt to convince other nations on an individual basis to discontinue their government export financing. This policy recognizes that international capital markets are capable of providing the required credit and that the refusal of private lenders to make a loan because of the associated risk, or because of the interest rate or term requested by the borrower, does not justify requiring the U.S. public to bear the costs associated with that credit. Furthermore, it is dangerous to argue that the public can bear risk better than can private markets, since that would imply a role for government financing of most economic activity.

The principal argument against eliminating the government financing of U.S. exports is based on second-best considerations arising from the view that international markets are not competitive and hence that the theories of international trade do not apply. For example, a number of trading countries have centrally planned economies in which resources are not allocated according to the dictates of supply and demand, relative prices, and comparative advantage. Some of those countries, particularly in Eastern Europe, may have trade objectives based on earning hard currencies rather than on benefiting from comparative advantage. Furthermore, many countries that rely on market-directed allocations of resources have large subsidization programs that redirect resources for domestic economic, political, and social purposes. Although the effect of these programs on international trade is not likely to be of major consequence in the aggregate, the programs can be important for individual industries or firms. With distortions such as these, one cannot be certain that export financing programs do not generate a more efficient allocation of resources than would result from imperfections in international markets. It should be the responsibility of those who advance this line of reasoning, however, to identify the specific distortions resulting from these imperfections and to demonstrate that government financing of exports will provide gains to the United States.

D. Reality and Export Subsidization

If the United States were to be successful in reaching an international agreement to eliminate concessionary export financing, it would be unrealistic to expect foreign countries not to subsidize their industries through other means when they view it to be in their own best interests to do so. The Carter administration, while not advocating such subsidies, listed a number of objectives that countries might attempt to achieve through export subsidization [3]:

> Countries subsidize exports directly or indirectly for a variety of reasons. Faster export growth is seen as a way of overcoming the balance of payments deficits that higher oil bills have caused for many countries. Subsidies may form part of an industrial strategy to promote growth of key sectors and to exploit economies of scale when they dictate a global marketing approach. Subsidies may also be a counterpart to other policies, for instance, policies to limit excess capacity and job losses in declining sectors by selling abroad. Subsidies to exports can also arise indirectly—for instance, from domestic policies that keep the price of energy, and hence the cost of production in energy-intensive sectors, artificially low. Or they can arise when investment incentives to particular regions or industries reduce the costs of capital to certain firms that produce certain goods [p. 211].

Many of these objectives could be achieved through forms of subsidization other than concessionary export financing, and as Cuddington and McKinnon argue, these forms should not be prohibited even if export financing subsidization is eliminated [2]

> Given the judicious stance of the GATT in disallowing direct export subsidies, it is unfortunate that its rules have not been extended to cover indirect subsidies in

the form of cheap export credits. To be consistent with the current distinction between direct production and export subsidies, the GATT should prohibit governments from subsidizing solely for financing exports. No attempt should be made, however, to prevent nations from using general credit subsidies that do not discriminate between domestic and foreign transactions. National governments can scarcely be expected to approve a sweeping policy that denies them the right from time to time to provide cheap financing to ailing domestic firms, such as a Chrysler or a British Leland. The most that GATT can do is to ensure that such policies do not provide unnecessary biases either in favor of foreign trade or against it [p. 179].

Although this statement emphasizes the use of subsidies as a means of supporting declining industries, countries may also use subsidies as a way of promoting growth industries. For example, if France determines that it is in its national interest to develop strong industries in high-technology fields such as aircraft and nuclear power, it will find other means of supporting those industries if it is prevented from doing so through export financing. Tax credits, direct subsidization, government support for research and development and many other measures could be used. These measures would be preferable to export financing subsidization from an efficiency viewpoint since the allocation of resources between domestic and foreign trade would not be affected. Even if these measures were used in lieu of export financing subsidization, a country that wished to promote exports over domestic consumption could achieve the same effect by means other than concessionary export financing. For example, the domestic purchases of commercial jet aircraft and nuclear power plants for use in France are by nationalized firms, and through the control of the prices of the services produced by those firms, the subsidy associated with the production allocated for domestic purposes could be recouped. An allocation of resources identical to that which would result with concessionary export financing could be achieved, in principle. If the objective of French concessionary export financing is to obtain a scale necessary to make selected high-technology industries commercially viable, production subsidies are the most efficient means of so doing, and an agreement that prohibits the less efficient export financing subsidization should be preferred.

A policy that is successful in eliminating concessionary export financing but yet engenders a response in the form of direct subsidies may, however, have some advantages to the United States, since direct subsidies may be more obvious to foreign taxpayers than are export financing subsidies. To the extent that budgets are subject to legislative scrutiny, the subsidizing country may have more difficulty obtaining a budget allocation to cover a direct subsidy and, hence, the amount of the subsidy may be reduced. If a country does decide to provide direct subsidies, however, the political reality may be such that the subsidies could become permanent, since the recipients would be expected to act to preserve those subsidies. Direct subsidies would thus likely be more difficult to eliminate once they were in place than would export financing subsidies. Recognition of this difficulty, however, should make exporting countries less willing to adopt those subsidies in the first place.

To the extent that exporting countries make subsidies permanent, importing countries, including the United States, have the alternative of availing themselves of those subsidies. As James E. Hinish, Jr., states, "The best option would be for the U.S. to cease subsidizing foreign consumers through credits, and welcome any permanent subsidies that foreign governments are foolish enough to provide, thereby increasing the amount of imported goods that the U.S. could obtain for any given volume of exports sacrificed [6, p. 682]." The view that the United States should stand ready to accept subsidies provided by foreign countries is appropriate when the subsidy is permanent, but may not be if the subsidy is temporary. To the extent that a subsidy is offered but is later withdrawn once the exporting country has achieved its objectives, substantial long-run costs may be associated with shifting resources back to domestically produced goods.

In June 1982 a case arose that illustrates the nature of the problem. The Metropolitan Transportation Authority of the state of New York decided to purchase 825 subway cars from Bombardier, Inc. of Canada for $659 million. The choice of Bombardier over a U.S. supplier, Budd Co., was due to a subsidy estimated at $230 million on a $563 million, 9.7% loan from the Canadian Export Development Corporation. The United States claimed that the interest rate violated the arrangement minimum interest rate of 11.25% for credits extended to rich countries, but Canada argued that its credit offer was only made in response to a similar French financing offered in support of French-built subway cars. Budd claimed that its price was $28 million less than Bombardier's, but that it could not provide equivalent financing. Since highly concessionary export financing is not likely to be permanent, the U.S. faced a dilemma. On the one hand, the subway riders in New York should not be denied the opportunity to have the lowest cost subway service possible. On the other hand, the efficient allocation of resources requires that Budd rather than Bombardier be chosen, if Budd is the lowest cost supplier.

The three basic alternatives available to the United States were (1) to do nothing, (2) to impose a countervailing tariff on the Canadian (and the French) subway cars, and (3) to provide U.S. subsidized financing to neutralize the effect of the foreign financing. There is no easy solution to this problem, but if there is little or no cost to the United States of a reduced volume in the subway car manufacturing industry, the United States would benefit by accepting the subsidy. In July 1982, Treasury Secretary Regan decided not to direct the Eximbank to match the Canadian export subsidy, but Budd has also taken its case to the International Trade Commission and the Department of Commerce. Neutralizing the subsidy by imposing a tariff or by providing subsidized U.S. financing would be warranted only if it would be effective as a component of a strategy to persuade other countries to discontinue their subsidized export financing. Strategies for achieving that objective are considered next.

III. Achieving Export Financing Objectives

A. Revisions in the Arrangement and Other Accords

The Carter administration's strategy for eliminating concessionary export financing was to work within the context of the arrangement to obtain agreement on one of the systems proposed in the Wallen report. As former ambassador Askew stated: "The Administration's approach was to seek improvement of the Arrangement within the OECD rather than replacement of the Arrangement by a wholly new instrument in the GATT [12, p. 135]."

Attempts to revise the arrangement began in the fall of 1979 when a number of countries indicated their willingness to enter a new round of negotiations. The Wallen report was presented in May 1980, but the signatories failed to adopt either of the proposed systems. An interim agreement was achieved, however, to raise the minimum interest rates by $\frac{1}{4}\%$ for poor countries and $\frac{3}{4}\%$ for intermediate and rich countries. The participants also agreed to set December 1, 1980 as a deadline for reaching a more acceptable version of the arrangement. Of the 22 participants in the arrangement, 21 were reported to be willing to accept one of the two alternatives proposed in the Wallen report. Some of the high interest rate countries, such as Denmark, opposed the differentiated rate system but appeared to be willing to accept such a system if maximum interest rates were imposed. France, which provides more subsidized export financing than any other country, was unwilling to agree to any revision other than a small increase in the minimum nominal interest rates. Japan also opposed further restrictions on the extension of mixed credits. Consequently, agreement was not achieved and future meetings were scheduled for 1981.

With the change in administrations in the United States and France, the Eximbank took the initiative by reducing unilaterally its export financing subsidization in July 1981, just prior to the Ottawa economic summit meeting. The Bank announced that its lending rate for nonaircraft loans would be 10.75%, financing would generally not be provided to high-income countries, and multipurpose lines of credit would generally not be provided. The Bank also imposed a 2% fee on the value of the credit as a means of reducing its projected deficit. The Bank, however, specifically omitted any decision on aircraft financing in order to invite the countries that finance the Airbus to agree to financing limitations. In August 1981, shortly after the summit, an agreement was reached that increased interest rates to approximately 12% and limited the term to 10 years. As chairman Draper announced, "The United States, France, Germany, and the United Kingdom are each unilaterally increasing their export credit rates for competing aircraft and harmonizing their aircraft financing policies to reduce export credit subsidies. We regard the successful conclusion of our informal discussions on aircraft exports to be a major breakthrough in our continuing effort to limit export subsidization [4, p. 1]." This agreement is perhaps as important for demonstrating the potential achievements of multilateral discussions as it is for the reduction in the subsidy provided for aircraft financing.[2]

Whereas this agreement reduces the subsidy provided on aircraft financing, it does not eliminate it. For example, to finance the purchase of a new aircraft, Thai Airways borrowed $10.8 million in the Eurodollar market in August 1981 in the form of a 10-year loan with an interest rate $\frac{1}{2}$% above Libor for the first 5 years and $\frac{5}{8}$% above Libor for the second 5 years. The Libor rate was approximately 18.5% at the time, so the market rate of interest was 7% above the 12% officially supported interest rate. The subsidy provided by a 12% interest rate in August 1981 is in fact greater than the average subsidy reported in Chapter 6 for FY1980 credits. For example, the average subsidy rate for FY1980 aircraft credits was 18.8% when the average Eximbank lending rate was 8.6% and the average market rate was 12.1%. The subsidy rate on a 12% loan to Thai Airways, however, would have been 21.3%. The 2% fee would reduce the subsidy rate to 19.3%, which is slightly larger than the average for FY1980 aircraft credits.

---

[2] The agreement contains a number of provisions that apparently allow the European countries to extend more favorable financing than the Eximbank:

> the agreement will allow the bank to lend only 42% of the cost of an airplane, while foreign export lending agencies may extend as much as 62.5% of an aircraft's cost. Finally, France will be able to set an interest rate one-half percentage point below the 12% minimum for loans made in French francs. [*Wall Street Journal,* August 4, 1981. Reprinted by permission of *The Wall Street Journal,* © Dow Jones & Company, Inc. (1981). All Rights Reserved.]

TABLE 11.1

Arrangement Minimum Lending Rates, September 1981[a]

Borrowing country	Terms (%)		
	2–5 years	5–8.5 years	8.5–10 years
Relatively rich[b]	11.0 (8.5)	11.25 (8.75)	n.a.
Intermediate[c]	10.25 (8.0)	10.75 (8.5)	n.a.
Relatively poor[d]	9.5 (7.5)	9.75 (7.75)	9.75 (7.75)

[a] Source: *Financial Times,* September 18, 1981. Previous minimums in parentheses. n.a. means not applicable.
[b] Per capita income over $3000.
[c] Per capita income between $1000 and $3000.
[d] Per capita income under $1000.

In September 1981, agreement was reached to increase the arrangement minimums from 2 to 2.5%, as indicated in Table 11.1. Since the minimum interest rates continued to be stated in nominal rather than real terms, the minimum interest rates exceeded Japanese yen market rates. Japan was thus allowed to lend at a 9.25% interest rate. Since market interest rates were increasing in 1981, the subsidy from financing at the arrangement minimum interest rates remained large. For example, the Eximbank borrowed from the FFB at 15.5% in September 1981, compared to a weighted-average borrowing rate of 11.2% in FY1980.

Not satisfied with the revision in the Arrangement, the Eximbank in November 1981 increased its lending rate to 12% and reduced the cover it provides from 85 to 65% for the exports of large firms. Exports of $5 million or less by small firms were, however, to be financed at 10.75% with an 85% cover. The discount loan rate was also lowered from 14 to 12% to make medium-term U.S. financing more competitive with that of other countries.

In July 1982 the minimum interest rates in the arrangement matrix were increased to 12.4% for credits with a term of 5 years or more to relatively rich countries and 11.35% for intermediate countries. The minimum interest rate for relatively poor countries was set at 10%, and a number of countries were moved from the relatively poor to the intermediate category. The interest rate for yen loans is to float at 0.3% above the long-term Japanese prime rate. In conjunction with this agreement, the Eximbank abandoned its uniform interest rate policy and adopted lending rates of 12.4, 12, and 11% for relatively rich, intermediate, and relatively poor countries, respectively.

Except for the yen rate, the arrangement matrix continues to be based on uniform nominal interest rates and hence does not equalize the cost of financing across currencies. Furthermore, as of July 1982 the matrix minimums remained significantly below private market rates and hence continued the subsidization. That accord should thus not be viewed as the satisfactory conclusion of negotiations but only as an intermediate step on the path leading to the elimination of export financing subsidization. This latest revision in the arrangement may represent a willingness of most countries to reduce export financing subsidization or they may represent the extent of their willingness to concede their own interests to the demands of the United States. In either case, the United States must choose a strategy to achieve a comprehensive agreement to eliminate concessionary export financing. The two basic alternatives are (1) to discontinue unilaterally such financing with the hope that other nations will follow the U.S. lead and eliminate their subsidization, and (2) to retaliate directly against those countries that refuse to agree to eliminate their concessionary financing.

B. The Leader Strategy

As indicated above, the Bank under chairman Draper increased its basic lending rate several times in 1981, but this may have been more a response to the Bank's impending operating loss than part of a strategy aimed at leading other countries toward the elimination of concessionary export financing. Reducing the losses resulting from the Bank's activities is a commendable objective, but the strategy of raising interest rates to market levels with the hope that other countries will follow seems unlikely to cause countries that wish to subsidize their exports to cease to do so. A strategy of retaliating against countries that are at a minimum unwilling to agree to a proposal such as the differentiated rate system may be necessary if an agreement is to be realized.

The strategy of unilaterally increasing the Bank's lending rate, reducing its cover, and focusing its financing may, however, be effective in achieving an equilibrium level of export financing competition that involves less subsidization than at present. The Carter administration sought bilateral agreements with other countries to limit export credit subsidization. As Bergsten stated, "In more than one instance, we have already been able to achieve informal agreements to reduce export credit subsidization in key sectors including a very sizable sector of aircraft engines [13, p. 140]." The possible gains obtainable through bilateral understandings were illustrated by Moore's discussion of the aircraft engine strategy [10],

We have discovered recently, as I said yesterday, that if we are the first party offering, if only engines on aircraft are in competition and engines are only made in the United States and England, if we stay 50 basis points above the 10-year bond rate of the U.S. Government, which was 10.2 percent—the rate was 10.2 percent in January—and if we offer a package that is 10.7 percent, then the support of the Rolls–Royce engine stays at 10.7 percent. We have begun to discover that if we take a higher approach, somewhere around the range of 10 percent blended costs to the buying airline, overall, then Airbus usually does not go below it [p. 103].

The Eximbank should, as a component of an overall strategy, lead in reducing its export financing subsidization and follow that by attempting to obtain agreement from other countries to join the United States. The success of this strategy is likely to be impeded by the continued focus on nominal interest rates, since low interest rate countries will, as in the case of Japan, be unwilling to agree to interest rate minimums that exceed their real interest rates. To increase the likelihood that a leader strategy will be successful in achieving the objectives identified in Section II,A, the Eximbank should base its actions on real interest rates rather than nominal rates. For example, as an interim step, the Bank might announce that it will lend at 90% of the Treasury long-term bond rate and invite other countries to do the same.

The Bank may be able to reach additional bilateral or multilateral agreements with its counterparts to limit export financing competition for specific exports, such as nuclear power plants. Only a limited number of countries remain as exporters, so there may be an opportunity to convince those countries that an agreement such as the aircraft financing accord would be in the interest of all the exporting countries. Because of the high export value of nuclear power plants, the potential savings are large. For example, Westinghouse reports that the concessionary financing provided by France for two Korean nuclear power plants was $235 million per billion dollars of financing (*Wall Street Journal,* July 22, 1981). At year-end 1981 the competition for a nuclear power plant export to Taiwan was intensified, in part because of the Reagan administration's efforts to aid the ailing U.S. nuclear power equipment industry. In December 1981 the Eximbank was reported to have increased its financing offer from 42.5% financing for $630 million of equipment to 65% financing of $1.14 billion of equipment (*Business Week,* December 28, 1981). Even with this substantial increase in financing, the concession provided may be significantly less than that provided by other countries since the Eximbank offer presumably carries a 12% interest rate whereas other countries are unrestrained because the arrangement does not cover nuclear power plants. An agreement restricting the generosity of the nuclear power plant export credits would not only be likely to reduce the cost of the Eximbank programs but would also place U.S. exporters on a better competitive footing with foreign suppliers.

In February 1982 the United States, Canada, Sweden, France, West Germany, and Spain reached an agreement to set a 12% interest rate minimum on financing for nuclear reactor sales to Mexico.[3] While this agreement should be applauded and an extension to all nuclear power plant exporters should be sought, the 12% nominal rate neither eliminates the financing subsidization nor equalizes the credit terms across suppliers.

C. The Retaliation Strategy

Although the United States should not, at least at this point, unilaterally disarm by having the Bank cease to provide export loans, the programs of the Eximbank should not be the sole instruments in a policy of retaliation against the subsidized financing offered by other countries. A coordinated strategy involving the United States Trade Representative (USTR), the International Trade Administration (ITA), and the Treasury should instead be developed to spur negotiations on an agreement. The Eximbank could play a role in a retaliation strategy by focusing its financing on those cases facing proven foreign concessionary financing, but the Bank should not have the primary responsibility for achieving a negotiated settlement. For example, Charles H. Bradford has recommended that [1]

> The Export–Import Bank, in consultation with ITA and the USTR, should establish a system designed to identify the worst offenders in the area of export credit subsidies. An Executive Order should be issued which contains a list of offenders. Those corporations seeking contracts in competition with such offenders should be encouraged to seek credit from the Eximbank. If the contract proposal meets the normal, commercially acceptable criteria of credit worthiness, the loan should be made at such a rate as to equal or better the foreign competition [p. 47].

One operational definition of "offenders" would be those countries that refuse to agree to the Wallen proposal. However, a weakness of Bradford's proposal is that making Eximbank financing automatically available to U.S. firms competing with the firms of offending nations essentially makes that financing an entitlement to those firms. A more appropriate approach would be to restrict Eximbank credits to those cases in which foreign concessionary export financing is documented, since otherwise all U.S. exporters would have an incentive to claim that foreign concessionary financing was being provided.

---

[3] Mexico subsequently decided to defer its plans for the power plant.

If the United States is to adopt a strategy of threatening to retaliate by matching the concessionary financing provided by other countries, that threat must be credible. To this end Senator Adlai Stevenson in 1980 introduced Senate Bill 2339, entitled "To Amend the Export–Import Bank Act of 1945 to Authorize the Bank to Engage in the Use of Extraordinary Measures of Export Finance to Counter and Ultimately Discourage the Use of Such Measures by Other Trading Countries." The bill was intended to provide the United States with the resolve and the resources to make its threats credible.[4]

The focus of S.2339 was on meeting the officially supported export credit programs of other countries and does not specifically deal with the issue of eliminating the subsidies. The bill stated [13]

> The Bank shall provide programs of export finance which are comparable in structure to those extraordinary official export credit measures offered by the principal countries whose exporters compete with United States exporters. Pursuant to such programs, the Bank shall offer export credit on rates, terms, and conditions competitive with those offered by other major trading countries. The Bank, at its discretion, shall use such programs to meet foreign official export credit competition until such time as the use of extraordinary measures of official export credit financing is proscribed in international agreements to which the United States is a party. For the purpose of this subsection, the term 'extraordinary measures of official export credit financing' shall include, but not necessarily be limited to, programs of highly concessional mixed credits, local cost financing, foreign currency financing, and lines of credit arrangements [pp. 4–5].

In introducing S.2339, Senator Stevenson stated [13]

> I hope it will not prove necessary to authorize or appropriate these amounts. S.2339 will not take effect if international agreements to put the United States and foreign exporters in substantially equal positions with respect to export financing are reached within a year after its enactment. This sunrise provision assures that the United States would not escalate the export credit war. The $1 billion authorization assures that we will not be unarmed [p. 7].

Although this statement by Senator Stevenson may be subject to interpretation, the intent of S.2339 does not appear to be the elimination of concessionary export financing. Instead, the objective seems to be to eliminate the types of extraordinary export support that the Eximbank does not routinely offer. The Carter administration asked the Senate to postpone consideration of S.2339 while the arrangement negotiations were underway.

In 1981, Representative Stephen Neal introduced H.R. 3228 and Senator Heinz introduced S.868 which would create a $1 billion "Competitive

---

[4] Such a policy would result in distortions between exports and production for domestic consumption but would be neutral across export sectors.

Export Subsidy Fund" to provide interest rate subsidies to private lenders to allow them to finance U.S. exports that compete against "exports that are assisted by financing from those foreign governments, including the French government, which are most reluctant to negotiate a meaningful reform of the Arrangement on Guidelines for Officially Supported Export Credits [7, p. 5]." In order to provide an opportunity for negotiations to take place before any escalation of export credit competition would begin, the bill specifies that the Fund or "war chest," would be created only if a "meaningful reform" is not achieved by September 1, 1982. While it does not state an objective of eliminating all concessionary export financing, the war chest bills are intended to "reduce export credit subsidies as much as possible [7, p. 4]." Use of the war chest would be restricted to those cases in which there is a high probability that the export would be lost in the absence of Eximbank financing.

Such targeting applies pressure to those countries that have opposed revision of the arrangement, but implementation of this approach is complicated by cases in which an offending nation and a nonoffending nation are competing for a transaction. For example, if France is identified as an offending nation and Germany is not, concessionary U.S. export financing offered in response to a French financing offer would place the German exporter at a disadvantage and would invite a German response. In such a situation the United States might reach an agreement with nonoffending nations that would allow them to match the concessionary export financing offered, even if to do so were in violation of existing agreements.

If the United States is to follow a policy of matching the concessions provided by foreign countries in order to achieve their agreement to eliminate their subsidization, the United States will incur a substantial cost that will have to be borne directly by U.S. taxpayers. Consequently, the Bank should be required to report to the Congress the real cost of the concessionary financing it provides, and the Congress should monitor the appropriateness of the required expenditures. One means of doing this would be to provide a separate fund from which that financing would be provided, so that the subsidy burden could be directly identified.

Both the Neal and the Heinz bills received support in the House and Senate, respectively, but final action was deferred pending the outcome of the March 1982 meeting of the arrangement signatory countries. The threat from passage of a war chest bill may have been diminished by the reduced loan authorizations for the Bank, but the United States warned that the reductions should not be misinterpreted. As Deputy Treasury Secretary McNamar stated

> Our trading partners should be under no illusions that we will continue to reduce the Bank's budget regardless of their actions. Nor should they underesti-

mate our determination to resolve this problem soon. Both the domestic and international business press have been carrying stories of an imminent export credit war. They are unfortunately correct.

. . . if there is to be a credit war, we are certainly prepared to defend U.S. economic interests. And, if we do not see quick signs of progress in the Arrangement talks, our competitors will find that our pockets are deeper than theirs, our terms of credit much longer, and our resolve even stronger than is true of them. The overwhelming passage out of the House committee last week of the so-called "Neal War Chest Bill"—a $1 billion interest subsidy fund—is evidence of the kind of support that can be mustered [p. 9].

In anticipation of the convening of the arrangement signatories in Paris on March 10, 1982, chairman Draper stated, "If we fail to get an agreement, I'd just as soon go the other way and get tough on interest rates. We have $2 billion in reserves, and our statute doesn't say we have to make a profit."[5]

That meeting produced no agreement, but export financing was discussed at the Versailles economic summit in June 1982. Prior to the meeting, the Reagan administration threatened to increase Eximbank authorizations and to seek passage of a war chest bill. As previously mentioned, in July 1982 the signatories to the arrangement agreed to increase the minimum interest rates, but real lending rates were not equalized nor was the subsidization eliminated.

A war chest bill could be effective in advancing the pace of future negotiations, but it risks irritating other countries to the point that they may be less ready to reach an accord. The substantial losses that the Eximbank is incurring, the steps it has taken to reduce those losses, and the reductions in its authorization requested by the Reagan administration, however, may indicate to other countries that retaliation by the United States may not be much of a concern. Consequently, at least the threat that a war chest bill may be enacted seems necessary. Prior to the enactment of such a bill, other countries, and in particular France, should be given a final opportunity to agree to eliminate concessionary export financing.

D. Other Retaliatory Measures

In addition to congressional action, a number of other means are available to retaliate against foreign concessionary export financing. If an

---

[5] Reprinted from the February 15, 1982 issue of *Business Week* by special permission, © 1982 by McGraw-Hill, Inc., New York, N.Y. 10020. All rights reserved.

agreement was not reached by December 1, 1980, the Carter administration was prepared to take the retaliatory measures described by Bergsten [13].

> We do not intend, however, to ignore the possibility that an improved Arrangement cannot be negotiated. If there is no progress in the next six months, we must consider the following steps in addition to those already taken during the past three years to make the Eximbank more competitive:
>
> 1. In specific cases, we might have to begin extending maturities should the budgetary cost of matching subsidized foreign interest rates prove too high. We could, for example, offer terms of 15 years for aircraft, or 20 or 30 years for power plants.
>
> 2. Where countries have export subsidy programs which are particularly nettlesome for us, we would respond on a case-by-case basis in a manner designed to discomfort them to the maximum extent possible.
>
> 3. We would seek to enlarge the financial guarantee program, and make it more attractive to investors, so that it can relieve pressure on the direct loan budget. In this regard, we would seek to involve insurance companies, pension funds and other long-term investors in export finance, an investment possibility they have not developed fully.
>
> 4. We would expand our efforts to establish common lines of financing individual transactions with countries in sympathy to our point of view. The International Arrangement has a "best endeavors" clause which promotes such efforts. In more than one instance we have been able to achieve informal agreement that reduced export credit subsidization is possible [p. 155].

Because of the failure of the negotiations aimed at reaching an agreement by December 1, 1980, the United States moved to retaliate against France.[6] Bergsten announced that the Eximbank would begin offering

---

[6] Canada also took steps to retaliate against those nations that oppose an agreement to limit the extent of export subsidization:

> The Canadian government joined the international battle on export credit terms with an announcement that it will provide as much as $900 million (Canadian) over a three-year period in special low-rate export financing.
>
> Canada said its adoption of "credit mixte" financing is in retaliation for the use of such heavily subsidized loans by other exporting nations, principally France and Japan.
>
> Credit mixte is a combination of conventional government export financing and concessionary loans that are interest free or at very low rates. . . . Interest rates on credit mixte loans might run between 4% and 6%, Canadian officials said. As well, Canada's program will add some $300 million a year to the $1 billion to $1.5 billion average of new loans written yearly by the government's Export Development Corp [*Wall Street Journal,* January 6, 1981. Reprinted by permission of *The Wall Street Journal,* © Dow Jones & Company, Inc. (1981). All Rights Reserved.]

subsidized official export credits are an unfair trade practice that adversely affects us in third markets and that our government should seriously consider
bringing a case against the offending parties, particularly the French, pursuant to
Articles XXII and XXIII of the GATT and Section 301 of the Trade Act of 1974
as amended by the Trade Agreement Act of 1979 [pp. 113–114].

Whereas the filing of such a case would risk contributing to economic
warfare among nations, it should be given careful consideration not only
because it might increase the chances of an agreement on a satisfactory
revision of the arrangement but also because it would help prepare the
way for including in the subsidies code provisions such as those in the
differentiated rate system.

E. Privatizing Export Financing

The United States should take steps to privatize the financing of its
exports by encouraging the expansion of PEFCO and attempting to include other lenders in export financing. Although PEFCO anticipates reduced near-term profits due to adverse funding risk, deferred pricing of its
loans should allow it to regain its profitability. It may therefore be possible
to persuade its owners to increase the scale of its operations, although the
demand for PEFCO financing is more likely to be due to its below-market
interest rates than to its fixed rates. PEFCO can continue to offer below-
market loans as long as its notes and bonds are eligible securities for
purchase by DISCs, but since DISCs are being challenged by European
countries, PEFCO may not be able to continue in its present role.

Although DISC eligibility is the primary factor that enables PEFCO
to make below-market loans, the Eximbank guarantees of its loans also
reduce PEFCO's cost of funds. These guarantees may be needed if
PEFCO is to continue to make fixed rate loans, but they should be priced
so that the guarantee fees cover the risk that the Eximbank bears. As long
as PEFCO primarily makes loans in support of aircraft and power exports, however, the level of risk will probably be quite low. An expanded
role for PEFCO might require it to make riskier loans and, hence, pricing
of the guarantees would become more important.

The participants in PEFCO are primarily commercial banks, along
with a few exporters and one investment banking firm, but much of U.S.
long-term debt financing is provided by insurance companies and pension
funds. Lehman Brothers Kuhn Loeb Inc. has recently proposed the formation of a Cooperative Export Financing Company (CEFCO) to supplement the Eximbank and PEFCO. If institutional investors could be at-
tracted to CEFCO, it could eventually assume the Eximbank's role in
export lending. Because of the fiduciary responsibilities of institutional

investors, government guarantees of the export loans undoubtedly would be required and could be provided by the Eximbank or by the Treasury. DISC eligibility and guarantees for the investments of the institutions in CEFCO should not be given, however, because the former constitutes a Treasury subsidy and the latter should not be necessary if guarantees are given for CEFCO loans.

Another approach to privatizing U.S. export financing would be to establish cooperative export financing banks that would provide export financing for an individual industry, perhaps with an Eximbank or Treasury guarantee. Similarly, exporters could create their own export trading companies, such as General Electric intends, possibly backed by government guarantees priced according to the risks associated with the credits. Either trading company banks or export financing subsidiaries would internalize the financing decision with the exporter who is in the best position to determine the appropriate response to foreign product and financing competition.

F. Mixed Credits and Local Cost Financing

In addition to the subsidization provided by the direct financing of exports, countries engage in a variety of other export support activities that warrant consideration. Insurance and guarantee programs will be considered in the next section, and mixed credits and local cost financing will be addressed in this section.

A number of countries provide export financing combined with aid, yet there is often no necessary relationship between the two. The decision of a country to import a product is presumably made on commercial grounds, whereas aid is generally intended for infrastructure purposes. In part, the use of mixed credits can be explained by the similarity between export financing and tied aid in which aid is granted to a country with the requirement that it be used to purchase goods from the granting country. Both provide a subsidy or grant to the importing country, but countries whose objective is to promote exports would be expected to prefer mixed credits which can be used to include goods not normally provided through aid programs. The Congress has been particularly concerned by the use of mixed credits as evidenced by the bill introduced by Senator Stevenson. As part of an international agreement on export financing, the United States should seek to separate export financing from aid, since their different purposes imply that they should be administered by separate agencies. By keeping aid and export financing separate, neither agency would be required to compromise its objectives for those of the other. Furthermore, oversight of the agencies would be simplified, and subsidies granted would be more easily identified. Since Eximbank programs are not intended to provide aid, the Bank's authorization should be separated from the foreign assistance budget and considered separately on its own merits.

In order to convince other countries to separate their export financing from their aid programs, it may be necessary for the United States to respond at times to the mixed credits offered by those countries. Whereas such responses may compromise U.S. aid programs, the administration should determine on a case-by-case basis whether the use of aid funds for this purpose is warranted. To the extent that the aid budget does not allow such a response, the United States should consider providing a special appropriation for this purpose. If a war chest bill were to be enacted, the funds provided therein could also be made available for responding to mixed credits.

Export financing agencies have increasingly provided general purpose lines of credit, but such lines are unlikely to result in additional exports unless trade between the two nations is just beginning. Otherwise, the importing country is likely to use the line to finance imports that it would have purchased anyway. The United States should attempt to incorporate into any export financing agreement a provision prohibiting lines of credit extended at concessionary interest rates. If the lines are intended for aid purposes, they should be funded under the aid programs of the offering country.

Export financing agencies also provide credits for local costs incurred in conjunction with imported equipment. In the case of the construction of a manufacturing facility, for example, the local costs may be a significant part of the total project cost. Concessionary financing for local costs can thus be an important factor in an importer's choice of a supplier, and even in the case in which the supplier has been chosen, that financing can affect the sourcing of work by a multinational firm. When concessionary interest rates are provided, the unrestricted financing of local costs provides an opportunity for financing rivalry among nations. To limit this opportunity, the financing of local costs should be limited. The present limit in the arrangement to no more than the cash payment made on the imported item is not unreasonable, but further restrictions would be desirable unless concessionary interest rates are prohibited by an international agreement.

G. *Insurance and Guarantee Programs*

If the U.S. government ceases to provide export financing, government-supported insurance and guarantee programs may still be appropriate. As indicated in Chapter 3, there are international capital market imperfections that affect the financing of international trade, and those imperfections may warrant government support. Furthermore, private insurance markets might not provide coverage for political risks associated with war, nationalization, or restrictions on convertibility of currency, or for commercial risks associated with impediments to repatriation of assets in the case of default. The private provision of insurance against these risks is preferable to government provision, but whether private insurers would be willing to provide such coverage is arguable. To the extent to which such insurance would not be voluntarily provided, government support for insurance and guarantees for specific political and commercial risks may be warranted. Any such support should be priced so as to be self-supporting, however.

The export insurance and guarantee programs offered by other countries provide subsidies in support of their exports. In particular, COFACE in France and ECGD in the United Kingdom are generally believed to have incurred substantial losses in their insurance programs, as indicated in Chapter 5. In the international negotiations regarding export financing, the United States should seek to achieve an agreement requiring that those programs be self-supporting, as Cuddington and McKinnon state [2],

> To the extent that such programs are operated on a self-sustaining actuarial basis, they perform a function that could potentially be performed by private insurance firms or commercial banks. In many instances, however, the fees charged by ex–im banks to insure exporters and overseas contractors against losses due to currency inconvertibility, confiscation of assets, etc., are very low. Needless to say, government programs absolving exporters of much of the risk of international transactions can significantly increase the volume of international trade.
>
> As in the case of export subsidies, however, these programs encourage too much trade from a social welfare standpoint. Particularly at a time when governments are becoming increasingly aware of the costs of extreme interdependence of national economies, it is inadvisable for exporters to underestimate or undervalue the losses they may experience in international dealings. Well-designed government programs may be able to help exporters pool their risks, thereby providing mutual insurance. On the other hand, government *subsidization* of such programs, which amounts to a bearing of the risks of international transactions by the general public, is certainly without merit and should be discouraged [p. 181].

One possible form of government support, as Cuddington and McKinnon suggest, would be for the government to facilitate the pooling of risk and perhaps to provide reinsurance for the pooled risk. The Eximbank has done this in the case of FCIA, but FCIA bears no political risk.

FCIA is reinsured by the Eximbank for excessive commercial risk, and it should be possible to obtain the private supply of insurance against political risks as well if reinsurance and stop-loss agreements are provided.

If a government agency such as the Eximbank is to provide insurance or reinsurance against political and certain commercial risks, the insurance programs should be operated on a self-sustaining basis. Fees should be based on the risk associated with the importing country and the importer, and the insurance program should be operated with reserves corresponding to private insurance market standards. Pricing insurance in this manner would have the added advantage of providing an opportunity for private insurers to enter the market if they are able to provide coverage more efficiently.

If insurance is provided, it should be available to all U.S. exporters, but need not be available for exports to all countries. For example, exports to industrialized countries would be expected to involve few political or commercial risks that could not be insured in private markets, so exports to those countries might be excluded from the insurance or guarantee programs. Where official export insurance programs are provided, U.S. exporters should be left the responsibility to obtain coverage when it is in their interests to do so.

The Eximbank currently offers guarantees for commercial bank financing of long-term and medium-term transactions. To the extent that such guarantee programs are equivalent to insurance, they could be continued if they are priced on a self-sustaining basis and would not voluntarily be offered by private guarantors. In effect, guarantee programs are simply a means of providing insurance to financial institutions in a manner analogous to insurance provided directly to U.S. exporters. Since insurance purchased by U.S. exporters is primarily used as a means for securing financing through the private sector, these programs can be operated according to similar criteria.

An important advantage of a self-supporting insurance and guarantee program over a direct loan program is that the initiative for export financing rests with private parties and does not depend on the extent of the concession provided by government financing. The efficiency with which U.S. resources are allocated then should be improved.

Because foreign export financing agencies provide a variety of services in addition to those of the Eximbank, the United States must decide if it will respond in kind. For example, in the 1980 Airbus sale to Saudi Arabia, France is reported to have provided cost inflation insurance against increases in the delivered price of the aircraft. The United States should resist matching such a program for three reasons. First, the exporter and the importer should be able to use commercial contracts to share the inflation risk in a mutually acceptable manner. Second, a substantial moral hazard problem is associated with cost inflation insurance since the exporter would have an incentive to raise the delivered price, recognizing that no burden is being placed on the customer due to the insurance. Third, instruments such as options on interest rates are available to hedge general inflation risks over the time period between the conclusion of the contract and the delivery of the product. In most cases this delivery period is at most a few years, and the exporter and importer have sufficient financial instruments available to hedge aggregate inflation risk. Greater difficulties may be involved in arranging hedges in the cases of nuclear power plants and aircraft whose delivery is scheduled over an extended period of time, but this is not a sufficient justification for a cost inflation insurance program.

Similarly, insurance coverage for exchange rate risk should not be provided by the United States since foreign importers can to some extent hedge these risks through a variety of means ranging from the use of forward contracts and swaps to sharing the risk with the exporter.

Although the United States should seek an agreement to prohibit the government provision of inflation risk and exchange rate insurance, an acceptable alternative would be to require that all insurance and guarantee programs be operated on a self-sustaining basis with appropriate levels of reserves. Unlike direct credit programs financed by government risk-free borrowing, insurance and guarantee programs would have no opportunity for subsidization other than through a direct government appropriation. If appropriations were prohibited, countries would be free to offer whatever insurance and guarantee programs they would like as long as the programs are self-supporting.

H. Summary of Recommendations for Eliminating Concessionary Export Financing

The recommended U.S. strategy for eliminating concessionary export financing may be summarized as follows:

1. The Eximbank should go on record as standing ready to match the concessions provided by countries unwilling to agree to the differentiated rate system (or some similar system).
2. The Bank should match the financing from those countries whenever documentation of concessionary financing is obtained.
3. The Congress should defer final passage of a war chest bill pending the outcome of the next round of arrangement negotiations, and if satisfactory progress is not made, it should be enacted.
4. The United States should seek bilateral or multilateral agreements outside the arrangement regarding individual export sectors in

which only a few countries are suppliers, as in the cases of aircraft and nuclear power plants.

5. The United States should seek bilateral agreements to eliminate mixed credits and the concessionary financing of local costs.

6. The United States should support the privatization of export financing with the Eximbank or the Treasury providing guarantees if necessary.

7. Insurance and financial guarantees for specific political and commercial risks should be provided by private insurors and guarantors with Eximbank backing, if necessary, priced to be self-supporting.

8. The Eximbank should provide neither cost inflation insurance nor exchange rate risk insurance.

IV. The Operation of the Bank in Its Present Form

A. The Political Reality and the Eximbank Mandate

The Eximbank has strong supporters both among the beneficiaries of its financing and among those members of the Congress who believe that the government should take an active role in promoting exports and who see the Eximbank as an appropriate instrument for doing so. These forces may prevail so that the Bank continues with its present mandate to act as both financier and promoter of U.S. exports. Even if the differentiated rate system is agreed to and the Bank is willing to cease extending loans, political forces may be sufficiently strong that the Bank may be directed to match foreign concessionary export financing at government interest rates as well to provide financing to countries that are unable to obtain acceptable financing in the private capital markets. In these cases the Bank should consider revising certain of its administrative procedures as outlined in the following sections in order to improve the efficiency with which it allocates the resources entrusted to it.

B. Documentation of Foreign Credit Offers and the Need for Financing

The most difficult issue for the Bank is to reconcile the objective of the efficient use of its resources with the need for its financing. If the United States is to follow a policy of neutralizing the export subsidization provided by other countries and supplementing private capital markets, the authorization of the Bank should be divided into two components. One component should be reserved for use in cases in which there is documented concessionary export financing provided by a foreign country. The other component should be used for cases in which no foreign export financing competition is present but for which international capital markets are unable to provide adequate financing for the purchase of a U.S. product.

In those cases in which foreign competing goods are not supported by subsidized foreign export financing, the Bank should be a reluctant lender. The Bank's mandate to supplement and not compete with private capital in financing exports should be strengthened to require the Bank to be a lender of last resort that provides financing only when it cannot be obtained in the private market. The burden of proof thus should rest on the foreign borrower and on the U.S. exporter to demonstrate that capital cannot be raised in private markets. Credits might be restricted to those cases in which the private capital market will not extend credit at market rates to a developing country for a commercially viable project.

In most cases the Eximbank should rely on financial guarantees and insurance with direct loans provided only as a last resort. The price of insurance and financial guarantees should be graduated as a function of the commercial and political risks associated with the transaction, and the program should be operated on a self-sustaining basis. The interest rate on any direct credit should be based on the cost of an equivalent loan provided in the private capital market, taking into account both the commercial and political risks associated with the transaction. The Bank thus should be prepared to lend at fixed interest rates if its customers so desire, but the fixed interest rate should be set at market levels. The Bank should also offer floating rate credits.

In deciding on the appropriate response to a foreign concessionary financing offer, the Bank should continue to be guided by its present policy of providing the minimum of the support required to match the foreign financing subsidization and the support required to gain the export. The Bank will continue to be plagued, however, by incomplete information about product and financing competition, as discussed in Chapters 8 and 10. In responding to claimed concessionary export financing, the Bank should seek documentation of that credit offer. In particular, the Bank should be skeptical of an importer's claims since the importer may have an incentive to exaggerate the generosity of the foreign credit offer. The Bank should place the burden of proof on the foreign borrower and the U.S. exporter to document the terms of the foreign credit offer. Although pressure on U.S. exporters and foreign importers and improvements in the arrangement information exchange can help, the Bank will be forced to make its lending decisions with incomplete information.

With respect to the standards and procedures used by the Bank in its financing decisions, the principal focus should be on the price reduction provided to the importer as a result of the financing, since that reduction measures the effect on the total cost of competing goods on the importer's choice among various suppliers. Although the Bank's judgment regarding the minimum support required will be imperfect, it should attempt to exercise that judgment on a case-by-case basis. This may be facilitated by categorical policies, such as providing financing only for new generation aircraft, but within a category the Bank should exercise its judgment rather than extending all credits at the same terms.

If the Bank is confronted with an importer or a U.S. exporter that claims that a particular level of financing is required in order to meet a foreign credit offer denominated in a foreign currency, the Bank should lend at the equivalent real dollar rate of interest determined from long-term domestic interest rates for the individual currencies, as indicated in Appendix 10.A. The Bank should also stand ready to match that offer in foreign currencies as well, since the United States can efficiently bear the exchange rate risk associated with lending in foreign currencies. Since funds to match foreign concessionary financing would be provided under a separate authorization, no difficulty would arise in identifying the gain or loss on that foreign currency loan.

C. The Cost of the Bank's Financing

In determining the appropriate interest rates for its credits, the Bank should be required to use the opportunity cost of its funds. Because the Bank's borrowings crowd private borrowers out of the capital markets, the equity and reserves of the Bank as well as its FFB borrowings should be costed at the long-term private market interest rate and not the average cost of its borrowings. If the Bank does provide concessionary financing in order to meet foreign officially supported export credits, it should be required to report to the Treasury and to the Congress the subsidy associated with each transaction using the market rate of interest that would have prevailed had the transaction been financed in the private capital markets, as considered in Chapter 6.

The practice of the Bank has been to set the interest rate on its credits at the time at which a preliminary commitment is approved rather than at the time the loan is authorized or the funds disbursed. During a period of increasing market rates, this practice tends to increase the subsidy associated with Eximbank loans, and even if the Bank were to set its interest rate at market levels when the PC is granted, a subsidy would be provided when the funds were actually disbursed if in the interim market interest rates had increased. Alternatively, if market rates began to fall, the Bank's borrowers would undoubtedly demand that their loans be refinanced if the interest rate they received was above the market rate at the time the funds were drawn down. To alleviate these problems, the Bank should set the interest rate on its loans at the time the funds are disbursed. At the time a preliminary commitment is approved, the borrower could be quoted an interest rate at a fixed spread relative to the Libor or the corporate bond rate. This would both base the lending rate on current market interest rates and help the borrower estimate its real financing costs.

The appropriate level of the Bank's reserves relative to its exposure has been of continuing concern to Bank policymakers. The actual level of reserves maintained by the Bank is, however, irrelevant, since the Bank can simply borrow more or less from the FFB based on its loss experience. What is relevant is whether the revenue received by the Bank on its programs is sufficient to cover the opportunity cost of the funds it uses, its administrative costs, and the losses it incurs. To the extent that insurance and banking industry reserve standards can be useful in pricing its services, reserve levels are relevant.

Whereas reserves have relevance for pricing, the dividend policy of the Bank is irrelevant. As the Senate Subcommittee on International Finance stated in its report on "U.S. Export Policy [14],"[8]

> The Bank should end its practice of returning an annual "dividend" to the U.S. Treasury. No public purpose is served by shuffling U.S. Government funds from one account to the other. Eximbank need not perpetuate a fictional financial independence [p. 28].

A policy of the Bank that misrepresents its financial position while serving no purpose is its reluctance to write off defaulted loans. As indicated in Chapter 2, at the end of fiscal year 1981 the Bank had $887.7 million in delinquent loans and $275.6 million in purchased loans that were carried on its books as assets even though, for example, loans to China have been in default for 40 years. A more accurate picture of the Bank's financial position would be presented if the Bank established a reserve and wrote off loans against that reserve when collection appeared

---

[8] The purpose of the subcommittee, however, was to add the dividends to the Bank's reserves so that the Bank could increase its support for U.S. exports.

unlikely. This also would present more accurately the net income of the Bank, since in FY1980 the $110 million net income included $93 million of uncollected interest, and the collected interest was $89.3 million in FY1981, with profits of only $12.1 million. The Bank has been reluctant to write off defaulted loans because of a belief that collection of those loans would be less likely once they had been written off. This reasoning is unpersuasive because the loans written off could remain debts owed to the United States by transferring them to the Treasury. The purpose of the Bank's financial reporting should be to present accurately the Bank's income and financial position, using accepted accounting standards.

The Bank is currently incurring a substantial operating loss, and losses are expected to continue in the forseeable future. If an agreement is not reached to prohibit concessionary financing, the Bank's financial and operating condition will continue to deteriorate. Although from an accounting viewpoint the Bank can continue to draw down its reserves and capital stock, the drain on Treasury resources and the opportunity cost of the reserves and capital stock have become excessive. The magnitude of the problem can be indicated by computing the real cost to the Treasury of the Bank's performance. The capital stock and the reserves of the Bank are in effect a loan from the Treasury with a zero rate of interest. The opportunity cost of that loan for FY1981 was over $400 million, using the Bank's average FFB borrowing rate, so the operating loss of the Bank in FY1981 was nearly $400 million rather than the $12 million operating profit reported. If defaulted loans and delinquent interest were accounted for properly, the cost would have been far greater. The difference between this cost and the Bank's reported profits indicates that a different budgetary treatment of the Bank is required.

D. Eximbank and the Budgetary Process

In 1974 Senator Proxmire proposed that the reserves and capital stock of the Bank be treated as borrowings from the Treasury carrying current interest rates, with the Bank's losses covered by a Congressional appropriation. Senator Proxmire stated his objective as follows: "I am trying to assert fuller Congressional control over those subsidy operations, by requiring that the budget reflect the full amount of the subsidy and that Eximbank come before the Appropriations Committee of Congress every year to justify the subsidy [10, p. 145]." Although this budgetary approach could cause problems if changes in market interest rates resulted in costs greater than the appropriation, it is preferable to the current authorization approach because it forces the Congress to face the actual cost of government export financing. If the present authorization approach is to be continued, the Bank should at least be required to report the actual cost of its programs to the Congress.

While the Bank is presently an on-budget agency, its on-budget status could be changed if it continues to operate under an authorization limit. In particular, if the Bank provides concessionary financing only under a separate authorization restricted to cases in which foreign officially supported export credits are offered, the Bank could be made an off-budget agency and included in a federal credit budget. The important factor is not whether the Bank is an on- or off-budget agency but that the Bank's performance be reviewed regularly, that the Congress determine the level of its authorization, and that oversight activities be conducted. If the Bank remains on-budget, it should be separated from the foreign assistance budget and might be considered with, for example, the Commerce department budget.

E. The Additionality Standard

The additionality standard should be the basis for the allocation of the Bank's resources. Additionality studies are useful in focusing attention on the likelihood that additional exports resulted from Eximbank financing and may provide some indication of how the subsidy was shared by the exporter and the importer. The knowledge that an *ex post* assessment of additionality will be conducted should also provide some discipline to the loan officers and the board in their authorization decisions, but greater discipline would be generated if the loan officers were to assess the likely degree of additionality at the time the authorization decison is being considered. The *ex post* assessment of additionality could then focus on the difference in additionality probabilities between those cases won and those lost.

In institutionalizing the evaluation of additionality, the refinements indicated in Chapter 8 should be incorporated. In particular, the additionality methodology should take into account the lending rate, the export value, and the loan principal, as well as the term of the credit, through a measure such as the effective price paid for the export. The access to capital markets should also be incorporated through the spread on international borrowings by the importing country. Both the extent of product competition and foreign concessionary financing competition should be included with the latter evaluated in real terms. Since there is a direct trade-off between the export price and the subsidy provided by concessionary financing, the Bank should make every effort to determine if exporters raise their prices in anticipation of Eximbank financing.

As a part of the evaluation of the efficiency of Eximbank programs and the additionality of the exports it supports, the Bank should be required to reconcile the analysis of why preliminary commitments were cancelled with the results of its additionality studies. The Bank should also be required to analyze the disposition of the exports for which applications were denied or discouraged. To provide information for these purposes, the applicant for financing should be required as a condition for the application to report on the ultimate disposition of the transaction. This policy would have the added advantage of discouraging exporters from seeking support when it is not required, because if the application were denied and the export were to go forward with private financing, the exporter's credibility would be damaged.

The Bank should avoid issuing lines of credit, since it is more difficult in those cases to determine if the U.S. goods purchased are additional or would have been purchased in the absence of the line. During the Moore administration, the Bank began to extend lines of credit to foreign governments in response to lines offered by other countries. When the use of these lines is unrestricted, the likelihood that they would generate additional exports is lower than for credits authorized for specific projects. Furthermore, the goods financed by the lines are not as likely to face foreign competition as the goods supported by direct credits. Although a number of foreign countries use lines of credit as a part of their trade and foreign aid agreements, the United States should resist using the Bank and its resources for this purpose. This does not mean that lines of credit might not be appropriate for political or strategic objectives, but the Bank should not be used for these purposes, worthy as they may be. If trade is to be facilitated to achieve those objectives, the Department of Commerce in conjunction with the State Department should provide the lines of credit.

The Bank currently provides supplier credits in the form of insurance that allows exporters to finance their inventories and receivables and in the form of commercial bank guarantees for debt obligations obtained by banks from U.S. exporters. The advantage of the supplier credit programs is that the administrative burden on the Bank is reduced because covered transactions do not have to be reviewed individually. The additionality of the exports supported under these programs would, however, be expected to be lower than for buyer financing, and the measurement of that additionality would be even more difficult given the limited information available. Perhaps the best approach to dealing with the additionality measurement for these programs is to price insurance and guarantees as a function of the associated risks, using private market standards. This can best be achieved by encouraging private insurers to provide the coverage backed by Eximbank excess-risk coverage, if necessary.

F. The Eximbank and Foreign Policy Objectives

Since the Bank provides financing, insurance, and guarantees that would not be supplied by private markets, its programs are valued by the recipient countries. Consequently, the provision or denial of that financing to individual countries can be used as an instrument of U.S. foreign policy. For example, the Bank's programs have been denied by the Congress to South Africa and to communist countries, with the exceptions of Poland, Romania, and Yugoslavia. In reprisal for the imposition of martial law in Poland in December 1981, President Reagan prohibited on human rights grounds the extension of Eximbank insurance to Poland. Similarly, when Argentina seized the Falkland Islands in 1982, President Reagan cut off Eximbank financing for exports to Argentina. The Bank's programs have also been used to reward countries such as Spain and Panama at the request of the State Department. As long as the Bank's programs provide significant benefits to importing countries, the executive branch and the Congress can be expected on occasion to attempt to use the Bank's programs to further U.S. foreign policy objectives. Although this is certainly contrary to the fundamental purpose of the Bank, it is the prerogative of both the Congress and the president to do so. If concessionary export financing is eliminated, however, the incentive to use the Bank for such purposes would be diminished greatly.

G. Board Independence

One of the principal factors affecting Eximbank policy and performance has been the philosophy of the chairman, the board, and the executive branch. Presently, the chairman and the board serve at the pleasure of the president, which allows the executive branch to influence directly, if it chooses to do so, the policies and practices of the Bank. This facilitates the coordination of Eximbank policies with U.S. international trade policies, but it lessens the status of the Bank as an independent agency. If the Bank is to assume the role of an insuror, guarantor, and neutralizer of foreign concessionary export financing, the independence of the Bank should be enhanced by giving board members fixed and staggered terms, with the chairman designated by the president. If the Bank is to serve more general purposes as it now does, the present policy regarding board membership may be more appropriate.

H. Promotion of Exports

The Eximbank currently has a responsibility to promote U.S. exports, but a continued promotional role is inappropriate since it would directly conflict with the Bank's role as an insuror, guarantor, and financier of last resort. The Department of Commerce has the general responsibility for the promotion of specific economic activity and should play that role for exports as well. Similarly, the Department of Commerce and not the Eximbank should be responsible for developing trading relationships with nations and for providing programs to support small business. The government has a variety of means other than the programs of the Eximbank to assist small businesses in export markets and those measures should be given precedent. As previously discussed, the government could assist in the formation of private cooperative export financing banks that would provide financing at market rates and terms. The government could also make it possible to form trading companies that would act as agents for exporters seeking markets for their products. Export facilitating efforts, such as General Electric's trading company, can also be expected to be adopted without government support when opportunities for profit are available.

V. Conclusions

Fiscal year 1982 marked a potentially important transition for the Eximbank from the expansionary policies of the late 1970s to a period of reduced authorizations, higher interest rates, and intensified international negotiations to eliminate export financing subsidization. From FY1979 to FY1981 Eximbank programs cost the United States approximately $3.2 billion, and although the lending policies adopted in late 1981 would have reduced the FY1981 cost by 40%, export financing subsidization by the United States continues to be costly. The long-term benefits of this financing are illusory at best and, hence, the appropriate long-term objective should be the privatization of export financing with the government providing only the backing required for privately provided insurance and guarantee programs to function.

Unfortunately, the present reality is a far cry from this objective, and the question remains of how to get from here to there. Negotiations are always preferable to economic warfare, but if those negotiations are unsuccessful, the United States should adopt a retaliation strategy against the recalcitrant countries. Achieving an agreement to eliminate subsidized export financing is, however, unlikely to dissuade the recalcitrants from finding other means of subsidizing their industries, but at the least those subsidies should be more apparent and hence more likely to receive public scrutiny.

Domestically, the Eximbank will continue to be buffeted by political pressures both from those who seek its support and wish to promote U.S. exports and from those who seek to reduce its costs and the government's role in export financing. The outcome of this political contest is difficult to predict and can always be overturned by the course of events, but in the interim the Bank can continue to improve its administrative procedures to reduce its costs, increase its effectiveness in generating additional exports, and further negotiations regarding export financing. The Bank's administrative tasks are inherently difficult because of incomplete information and its conflicting mandates, but one can hope that with some additional progress in the international negotiations, those tasks can in the near future be relegated to the private sector where they belong.

References

1. Bradford, C. A., "Commerce," in [5, pp. 33–88].
2. Cuddington, J. T. and McKinnon, R. I. "The United States and the World Economy." In *The Economy in the 1980s: A Program for Growth and Stability* (M. J. Boskin, ed.). Institute for Contemporary Studies, San Francisco, California, 1980.
3. Council of Economic Advisors, *Economic Report of the President, 1981*, Washington, D.C., 1981.
4. Export–Import Bank, "Exim News," Washington, D.C., 1981.
5. Heatherly, C. L. (ed.). *Mandate for Leadership: Policy Management in a Conservative Administration*, The Heritage Foundation, Washington, D.C., 1981.
6. Hinish, James E., Jr.," "Regulatory Reform: An Overview," in [5, pp. 697–708].
7. House of Representatives, H.R. 3228, "A bill to amend the Export–Import Bank Act of 1945 to offset foreign export credit subsidies through the establishment of the Competitive Export Subsidy Fund," Washington, D.C., April 1981.
8. Marer, P. (ed.). *U.S. Financing of East–West Trade*, International Development Research Center, Bloomington, Indiana, 1975.
9. McNamar, R. T. "Free Trade or the 'New Protectionism': The Choice of the 1980's," *Department of the Treasury News*, Washington, D.C., June 12, 1981.
10. Proxmire, William, "Views on Eximbank Subsidies," in [7, pp. 143–145].
11. Sohn, S., "Proposed Position on the International Credit Arrangement," (draft), United Technologies Corporation, Hartford, Connecticut, 1980.
12. U.S. Senate, Committee on Banking, Housing, and Urban Affairs, "Hearings on Ansett Loan and Export–Import Aircraft Financing Policies," Washington, D.C., 1980.

13. U.S. Senate, Subcommittee on International Finance, Committee on Banking, Housing, and Urban Affairs, "Hearing on Competitive Export Financing," Washington, D.C., 1980.
14. U.S. Senate, Subcommittee on International Finance, Committee on Banking, Housing, and Urban Affairs, "U.S. Export Policy," Washington, D.C., 1979.
15. U.S. Senate, Subcommittee on International Finance and Monetary Policy, Committee on Banking, Housing, and Urban Affairs, "Hearings on International Affairs Functions of the Treasury and the Export Administration Act," Washington, D.C., 1981.

Index

ECONOMIC THEORY, ECONOMETRICS, AND MATHEMATICAL ECONOMICS

Consulting Editor: Karl Shell

UNIVERSITY OF PENNSYLVANIA
PHILADELPHIA, PENNSYLVANIA

Franklin M. Fisher and Karl Shell. The Economic Theory of Price Indices: *Two Essays on the Effects of Taste, Quality, and Technological Change*

Luis Eugenio Di Marco (Ed.). International Economics and Development: *Essays in Honor of Raúl Presbisch*

Erwin Klein. Mathematical Methods in Theoretical Economics: *Topological and Vector Space Foundations of Equilibrium Analysis*

Paul Zarembka (Ed.). Frontiers in Econometrics

George Horwich and Paul A. Samuelson (Eds.). Trade, Stability, and Macroeconomics: *Essays in Honor of Lloyd A. Metzler*

W. T. Ziemba and R. G. Vickson (Eds.). Stochastic Optimization Models in Finance

Steven A. Y. Lin (Ed.). Theory and Measurement of Economic Externalities

David Cass and Karl Shell (Eds.). The Hamiltonian Approach to Dynamic Economics

R. Shone. Microeconomics: *A Modern Treatment*

C. W. J. Granger and Paul Newbold. Forecasting Economic Time Series

Michael Szenberg, John W. Lombardi, and Eric Y. Lee. Welfare Effects of Trade Restrictions: *A Case Study of the U.S. Footwear Industry*

Haim Levy and Marshall Sarnat (Eds.). Financial Decision Making under Uncertainty

Yasuo Murata. Mathematics for Stability and Optimization of Economic Systems

Alan S. Blinder and Philip Friedman (Eds.). Natural Resources, Uncertainty, and General Equilibrium Systems: *Essays in Memory of Rafael Lusky*

Jerry S. Kelly. Arrow Impossibility Theorems

Peter Diamond and Michael Rothschild (Eds.). Uncertainty in Economics: *Readings and Exercises*

Fritz Machlup. Methodology of Economics and Other Social Sciences

Robert H. Frank and Richard T. Freeman. Distributional Consequences of Direct Foreign Investment

Elhanan Helpman and Assaf Razin. A Theory of International Trade under Uncertainty

Edmund S. Phelps. Studies in Macroeconomic Theory, Volume 1: *Employment and Inflation.* Volume 2: *Redistribution and Growth.*

Marc Nerlove, David M. Grether, and José L. Carvalho. Analysis of Economic Time Series: *A Synthesis*

Thomas J. Sargent. Macroeconomic Theory

Jerry Green and José Alexander Scheinkman (Eds.). General Equilibrium, Growth and Trade: *Essays in Honor of Lionel McKenzie*

Michael J. Boskin (Ed.). Economics and Human Welfare: *Essays in Honor of Tibor Scitovsky*

Carlos Daganzo. Multinomial Probit: *The Theory and Its Application to Demand Forecasting*

L. R. Klein, M. Nerlove, and S. C. Tsiang (Eds.). Quantitative Economics and Development: *Essays in Memory of Ta-Chung Liu*

Giorgio P. Szegö. Portfolio Theory: *With Application to Bank Asset Management*

M June Flanders and Assaf Razin (Eds.). Development in an Inflationary World

Thomas G. Cowing and Rodney E. Stevenson (Eds.). Productivity Measurement in Regulated Industries

Robert J. Barro (Ed.). Money, Expectations, and Business Cycles: *Essays in Macroeconomics*

Ryuzo Sato. Theory of Technical Change and Economic Invariance: *Application of Lie Groups*

Iosif A. Krass and Shawkat M. Hammoudeh. The Theory of Positional Games: *With Applications in Economics*

Giorgio Szegö (Ed.). New Quantitative Techniques for Economic Analysis

John M. Letiche (Ed.). International Economic Policies and Their Theoretical Foundations: A Source Book

Murray C. Kemp (Ed.). Production Sets

Andreu Mas-Colell (Ed.). Noncooperative Approaches to the Theory of Perfect Competition

Jean-Pascal Benassy. The Economics of Market Disequilibrium

Tatsuro Ichiishi. Game Theory for Economic Analysis

David P. Baron. The Export-Import Bank: *An Economic Analysis*

In preparation

Réal P. Lavergne. The Political Economy of U. S. Tariffs: *An Empirical Analysis*